Susan Angeline Collins:
With a Hallelujah Heart

Janis Bennington Van Buren

WESTBOW
P R E S S®
A DIVISION OF THOMAS NELSON
& ZONDERVAN

This book is a work of non-fiction. Unless otherwise noted, the author and the publisher make no explicit guarantees as to the accuracy of the information contained in this book and in some cases, names of people and places have been altered to protect their privacy.

WestBow Press books may be ordered through booksellers or by contacting:

WestBow Press
A Division of Thomas Nelson & Zondervan
1663 Liberty Drive
Bloomington, IN 47403
www.westbowpress.com
844-714-3454

Because of the dynamic nature of the Internet, any web addresses or links contained in this book may have changed since publication and may no longer be valid. The views expressed in this work are solely those of the author and do not necessarily reflect the views of the publisher, and the publisher hereby disclaims any responsibility for them.

Scripture quotations are from the ESV® Bible (The Holy Bible, English Standard Version®), copyright © 2001 by Crossway, a publishing ministry of Good News Publishers. Used by permission. All rights reserved.

ISBN: 978-1-6642-2575-6 (sc)
ISBN: 978-1-6642-2576-3 (hc)
ISBN: 978-1-6642-2574-9 (e)

Library of Congress Control Number: 2021904163

Print information available on the last page.

WestBow Press rev. date: 04/20/2021

To my husband and best friend, James R. Boyle.
And to the women throughout the ages who have risked their lives to
bring education, love, and security to children throughout the world.
And in loving memory of my parents, Glen and Mildred Bennington,
for instilling in me an inquisitive nature and the joy of learning.

Contents

Introduction

On a blustery Sunday evening in March, with the snow still piled high from a long, cold Iowa winter, I squirmed uncomfortably in the oak church pew while the minister's voice droned. I not so subtly elbowed my five-year-old sister, three years my junior, and earned a stern glare from my father. Fabricating an innocent smile, I looked upward as if in deep contemplation.

That's when my roving eyes spotted a bright, star-shaped light twinkling from the sanctuary ceiling above the lectern. Its white, translucent glass cover and satin-finished aluminum frame against the light tan ceiling seemed out of place.

Fearing more stern looks from my father, I patiently waited until bedtime to ask my mother about the star. Her reply was, "Oh, that's Susan's Star," as though she was a relative. "Susan was a missionary in Africa until 1920 when she returned to Fayette in retirement. She died in June 1940, seven months after you were born. Reverend John Clinton and Mr. Lysle Wooldridge, our local blacksmith, designed and created the star. Sunday school classes donated the money to pay for the star. It was put up in the church right before Christmas in 1937. Susan lived to see her star take its high place to watch over our congregation."

As an eight-year-old, there were still some questions leaping into my mind. Who was this Susan? What was a missionary? What did a missionary do, and why did she want to go to Africa? How could she just leave her parents behind and go to a place as far away as Africa?

Soon after that 1948 evening, I forgot about my questions and Susan. It was sixty years later during a visit to Fayette, Iowa, that my mother's friend Merle Sternberg suggested I learn more about Susan Angeline Collins. I was intrigued as I studied this single woman who decided to leave the security of home and support system and travel to a continent about which little was known. I could no longer forget about Susan. I was hooked, knowing I had to learn about her life story.

While growing up near Fayette, I didn't perceive the uniqueness of the town. As an adult, I finally realized that Susan and other African Americans worshipped freely in our predominately white congregation nestled in the heart of the Midwest and in Northeast Iowa. This was not typical in the late 1800s and into the 1900s. What had set the stage for this to occur?

Many more questions filled my mind. Why did our mostly white congregation honor this African American woman? What called her to travel to West Central Africa, a direct distance approximately 7,500 miles from Fayette? What dangers did she face? How long and exactly where was she in Africa? Why did she make this personal sacrifice? How could she do this as a single female?

I began the quest to learn about Susan on a spring afternoon in 2009. I was originally looking for a Bible that had belonged to Susan and was described in an archived document I had discovered in the Upper Iowa University Library. The smell of mold filled the air as I entered the United Methodist Women's room located in the northwest corner of the basement in the Fayette United Methodist Church. That smell became stronger when I excitedly flung open the doors of a walnut cupboard containing the organization's supplies. I was there at the suggestion of the church secretary.

Books, small boxes, office supplies, napkins, and paper cups filled the shelves. Quickly, I searched the top two shelves. No Bible there. The third shelf contained hymnals and Bibles about the size of the one I'd seen Susan holding in a 1937 picture with Bishop G. Bromley Oxnan, when he visited her at the farm where she was living with childhood friends. I skipped the hymnals and systematically opened each Bible, hoping to see Susan's name or some identifying feature, with no success, only frustration as the minutes slipped past!

On the back of the fourth shelf and nearly out of sight, I spied a smaller volume six inches long and one and a half inches thick. My breath caught as I reached slowly to touch the volume. Was I holding history?

Would the Bible tell me stories of Susan? What tangible evidence of her life would I find?

The back spine was missing except for a thin, fragile section near the bottom. There I saw Christian Herald imprinted in gold letters. Heavy black thread, doubled and stitched through the front and back covers in a crisscross pattern, held the book together.

Was this it? What an adrenaline rush! Was this it? Had this volume belonged to Susan? With care, I extracted it from among the other books. Slowly and gingerly, I opened the cover, turned a page, and saw clearly written on the white cover page: Susan Collins, Quessua, Africa, May 21, 1917. It was a match! Her handwriting matched the signature on a picture she had autographed and given childhood friends, the Graham siblings. My treasure is that I personally have this photo.

At that moment, I quivered, realizing I was holding a book Susan had held. I turned the next page and discovered it was the New Testament Susan used during her last three years in Africa while teaching the children she loved and for whom she labored.

Leafing through the testament, I discovered pencil-marked passages dated from May 4, 1920, through May 11, 1928. Perhaps those passages gave special meaning to her on those dates as she continued her daily Bible study after returning home to Fayette. I found tucked throughout the volume a Suid Afrika stamp, a dried three-leaf clover, two common mallow leaves, and a 4.5-by-3.5-inch drawing of a pink rose. I speculated whether the rose represented an expression of Susan's artistic skills or that of a student or friend. What did these items mean to Susan? Why did she keep them?

Would my search tell me why Susan wrote the names Ervin, Addie, Julia, and Harriet at the back of her New Testament? The mold had permeated my nose when I finally finished examining the volume.

The next morning, my eyes were crusty from the mold I had encountered. Just as I arrived at the church, the cupola bell topping Upper Iowa University's Alexander-Dickman Hall chimed eight times. My basement room search continued. I quickly scanned minutes of the local Woman's Foreign Missionary Society and the Woman's Home Missionary Society from October 2, 1891, to October 4, 1918. Susan's work in Africa was briefly and sporadically described. My hunt through a file cabinet in a first-floor storeroom supplied old church bulletins and membership records pinpointing dates of some of Susan's activities after her return to the States until her death.

The gathering room provided a small treasure trove of pictures Susan had shared with Reverend John Clinton from her Angolan years. Several showed Susan with the children she loved. I noticed her hair was parted in the middle and pulled conservatively back into a bun. Another picture revealed Susan sitting sidesaddle on a mule and wearing a dark skirt, a white, long-sleeved blouse, and a wide-brimmed straw hat with a dark band encircling the crown.

I continued looking for remnants of Susan's life, even returning to the dank basement room housing two large bookshelves. They provided nothing. Then I recalled an oak and glass bookcase near the elevator at the back of the sanctuary. I paged through each of the books, hoping to find more surviving traces of Susan. Upon reaching the lowest of the four shelves, I began to think my time had been wasted. How wrong I was! I found two of Susan's treasures, *The Picture Bible* and the *Kimbundu Gospels*, containing her name on a fly page, "Susan Collins, Quessua, Malange, Angola, Africa, Dec. 1915." What could I find out about Quessua and the people who spoke the Kimbundu language? Were there other artifacts of this woman's life in Northeast Iowa and Africa waiting for discovery? Where would they lead me?

My venture had begun! The questions were overwhelming. How did Susan's life mirror other African Americans of her time, and how did migration patterns and social, economic, and religious changes influence her? Why would a single black woman decide to go to Africa as a missionary, surrounded by uncertainty and danger? What were her fears as she left the predictability of life in the Midwest? Why would she leave family and friends? Did she receive a calling from God? Was she lured to Africa by a sense of adventure? Did she not know what she was getting into? Was she driven by a need to leave Iowa to find greater opportunities and a place where she could make a difference? Did she escape her employment barriers? Was she a pioneer or a follower? This search led me to discover a full-blown adventure, a tragedy, and other lost links in Susan's life. Susan's story provides the opportunity for self-reflection, awareness of what can be accomplished when one is courageous, and the value of family, church, and community support.

Others need to know about Susan's accomplishments. There was a spark in her showing the world she was exceptional and represented the best qualities in people. Reading her story will inspire those of faith. Susan and other early women missionaries lived with multiple dangers but went forward at the risk of their lives. I want her life story to be told so she will not simply vanish into the musty pages of history with no value attributed to her life as a pioneering African American educator and missionary in Africa. Susan contributed to the betterment and spiritual and intellectual life of many, especially young girls and women. She opened up the lives of people in Africa and America while demonstrating the value of faith, education, and love—but most of all love.

I could no longer forget about Susan, picturing her as a courageous woman and a brave pioneer ready to take on new challenges. Then I wondered how I would feel as I discovered more about her life. Because we both grew to womanhood on farms located within miles of each other east of Fayette, I felt some affinity for her even though we are of different generations.

Now that I have researched, studied, and contemplated Susan's life, sharing her story seems even more imperative than when I began my work in 2009. Her story offers encouragement for today. In this time of racial and ethnic strife amid rising tensions, Susan's story exemplifies what can happen when people are accepted in a community and allowed to thrive regardless of race, gender, and creed. Her life illustrates how birth into a humble family need not limit having a joyful and bountiful life. It reveals how love given and received freely multiplies. Susan's story conveys overcoming obstacles at a time when there were fewer protective laws for African Americans. She demonstrates navigating a system where white males were in charge, but she pushed forward to help those who were disenfranchised. Susan found a way to respond to her call against numerous obstacles and circumstances. With a hallelujah heart, she persisted, attained her dream of becoming a missionary and serving her people, and was lauded for her years of outstanding service. Susan is a part of the Methodist's women story of reaching girls and women throughout the world.

Susan Angeline Collins went through doors when open, often traveling to remote places. I couldn't always ascertain if she alone shoved them open or if she required assistance. Join me and discover Susan's life story for yourself.

Time Line: Life and Missionary Career of Susan Angeline Collins

1808   Father Isaac Collins born in Waik, North Carolina—March 1

1815   Susan's stepmother, Hannah, born in Kentucky

1825   Susan's mother, Sarah Ann (Sally) Joiner, born in Tennessee

1839   Sally emancipated on September 17 in Illinois

1844   Susan's parents married on January 4 in Illinois; Mary Collins, first daughter, born in Illinois

1845   Isaac emancipated on May 12 in Illinois

1847   Martha Indiana Collins, second daughter, born in Illinois

1849   Maranda Collins born on March 10 in Illinois

1850   John A. Joiner, age fifteen, born in Missouri, living with Collins family

1851   Susan Angeline Collins born July 3, Madison Co. near Edwardsville, Illinois; village of Westfield, Iowa platted

1854   North of Westfield, largest concentration of African Americans settled in Iowa; William Collins born December 3 near Edwardsville

1855   David Livingstone in Pungo Andongo, Angola; Susan there in 1890s, located approximately sixty-two miles from Malange

1857   Classes started at Fayette Seminary of Upper Iowa Conference

1858   Seminary named Upper Iowa University of Upper Iowa Conference;

Lincoln-Douglas debate;

Richard Collins born Wisconsin

1864	Isaac enlisted in army on August 6 in Friendship, Wisconsin
1865	President Lincoln assassinated on April 14
1865	Isaac mustered out of army, returned to Wisconsin in June; Lima, Iowa, cemetery laid out; Collins family moved near Fayette, Iowa, in November
1867	Albert Collins born in Iowa, Sarah age forty-two
1869	Transcontinental railroad completed at Promontory Summit, Utah, on May 10; Isaac purchased six and a half acres in Westfield Township in late fall
1870	Isaac purchased ten adjoining acres early in year; Fifteenth Amendment ratified February 3, giving freed slaves and other African American men the equal right to vote; Martha Indiana Collins married William Thompson on February 10
1873	Maranda died of consumption (TB) on February 10, buried in Lima Cemetery
1874	Susan's mother, Sarah, died of TB on January 18, age forty-nine, buried in Lima Cemetery; Martha died February 19, buried next to mother and sister; Fayette founded
1876	Jason Paine, 1862 UIU graduate appointed to board of trustees, September, served twenty-four years; Susan started classes at UIU
1877	William died on March 15, buried next to mother and two sisters
1879	Isaac's will filed on September 15; married Hannah; Susan, UIU's first African American student, purportedly completed Normal Training Program; Alexander G. Clark Jr. becomes first African American to graduate from University of Iowa Law School
1880	United States Federal Census showed Susan living at home and employed as a domestic servant

1882 Susan traveled to Dakota Territory, opened a laundry, and purportedly took a claim in Huron; claim record not found in Beadle County Recorder's Office

1884 Hannah died, Albany, Iowa, March 4;
Isaac joined Susan in May after Hannah's death;
Susan started taking correspondence courses through the Chicago Training School (CTS);
Isaac died November 3, buried in Huron's Riverside Cemetery;
Bishop William Taylor departed for Liberia, Africa, December 13, planned to expand missions in the Congo and Angola

1885 Bishop Taylor landed at Luanda, Angola, March 18; traveled to interior, established mission stations at Dondo, Nhanguepepo, Pungo Andongo, Malange, and Quessua;
Isaac's will was recorded and probated by Fayette County Circuit Court Clerk, April 23;
Susan sold laundry, traveled to Chicago, likely in November, and enrolled at Chicago Training School for City, Home, and Foreign Missions, started by Lucy Rider Meyer

1887 Susan, age thirty-five, completed her CTS requirements and was recruited by Bishop Taylor; departed from New York City April 4 for Africa;
Amanda Berry Smith, African American evangelist, met Susan at Old Calabar, West Africa, in late May; Susan was first African American to serve at a Methodist Episcopal Mission in the Belgian Congo;
Susan in Kabinda, Congo, received a letter from Bishop Taylor dated October 31;
Susan and Mary Kildare reported in Natumba near Banana and Congo River mouth, December 3

1888 Susan and Mary reported working at Chavunga near Banana

1889 Susan's brother Albert, twenty-one, petitioned to administer Isaac's estate, January 12;
Susan left Natumba, Belgian Congo, in July; went to Pungo Andongo, Angola

1890	Susan appointed teacher at Dondo Day School; Susan arrived midyear at Malange mission
1892	Susan left Malange early in year
1893	Susan established girls' school at Canandua, one mile from Pungo Andongo; Albert Collins sold sixteen and a half acres willed to him by father; Dr. Jennie Taylor sailed from New York City to Africa with Uncle Bishop Taylor, December 5
1898	Susan formally recognized as a missionary by Methodist Board of Managers; Susan's Canandua girls' school relocated to Quessua, originally known as Munhall
1900	Susan returned to US with colleagues Reverend Charles Gordon, Mary Shuett, and Hilda Larson; Susan arrived on August 1 in Fayette
1901	Susan spent much of year in California, raising money for missionary work; Susan briefly visited Fayette and left for Angola, concluding US travels November 13
1902	Susan arrived at Quessua on January 18, remained there eighteen years; supported by Pacific Branch of Woman's Foreign Missionary Society (WFMS); she was first African American missionary sponsored by the WFMS
1904	Susan managed completion of long-wished-for cistern at Quessua
1905	Susan purchased Fayette home at northeast corner of State and Alexander Streets
1906	Martha Drummer arrived in Quessua in May; assisted Susan with twenty girls and served as nurse missionary
1907	Susan superintended construction of a new house at Quessua Mission; twenty-nine girls attended school
1909	House construction completed
1910	Susan took three-week vacation in Luanda; returned with five girls
1911	Martha Drummer took a furlough

1915	Cilicia Cross arrived midyear at Quessua; assisted Susan and Martha with fifty-one girls
1916	Cilicia Cross served as principal, and Susan as housemother; seventy girls at boarding school;
	WFMS determined missionaries would enter retired status at the furlough nearest their sixty-fifth birthday; policy effective January 1, 1917
1918	Cilicia Cross and Martha Drummer took furloughs, left Susan managing Quessua and supervising sixty-five girls
1919	Cilicia Cross and Martha Drummer returned to Quessua by October
1920	August 4, Fayette newspaper stated Susan would be home soon; August 26, the Nineteenth Amendment to the Constitution ratified, giving women the right to vote and hold office
1921	On home leave, Susan was in California; by October, she was living with Mrs. Jason Paine, Fayette
1922	Susan's home leave continued until early in year; lived with Mrs. Jason Paine until her renters' lease expired; moved to her home;
	Susan is officially retired upon completion of her home-leave status
1924	Susan's cousin Iva Joiner McClain shot in Kansas City by brother-in-law, December 29
1925	Iva Joiner McClain died January 3, buried in Des Moines several days later
1935	Susan's health started to fail; moved to Graham siblings' farm northeast of Fayette
1937	Methodist Episcopal Bishop G. Bromley Oxnan visited Susan at farm;
	Susan's Star dedicated Sunday, December 19 in Fayette Methodist Episcopal Church
1940	Susan died June 7, age eighty-eight, a few weeks prior to her birthday; buried in Lima Cemetery adjacent to her mother and siblings
2002	Upper Iowa created the Susan Angeline Collins Memorial Scholarship

1

⊸⊱⊰⊶

Susan's Formative Years

Susan's Parents' Early Lives:
Indentured Servitude in Illinois

Explore with me Susan's parents' early lives and the dangers they and other African Americans experienced during the early decades of the 1800s. Imagine how their years of hard physical work influenced Susan's life.

Stories about people's lives are often deeply embedded in a community's oral history. One such story Fayette residents believed was that Susan's parents, Isaac and Sarah Joiner Collins, had been slaves. I wanted to determine if that was true and the circumstances of their early lives. Susan's obituary revealed she was born near Edwardsville, Illinois, a clue that led me to the Illinois Servitude and Emancipation Records. Those records documented Isaac had been indentured to Low Jackson as a child and had completed his term of service to Jackson on May 12, 1845, in Madison County, Illinois.[1] Edwardsville is the county seat. Her mother, who had seven older siblings, was a servant freed from indenture on September 17, 1839, at age fifteen in adjoining St. Clair County.[2] Isam Joiner and his wife likely came to Illinois from either Virginia or Tennessee. Sarah (a.k.a. Sally) and Isaac were married on January 4, 1844, in Madison County.[3]

Isaac's Civil War enlistment papers listed his birth in Waik (a.k.a. Wake), North Carolina.[4] *When and how did he get to Madison County?* I wondered. County records document he was brought there with a boy named Dick in 1816 by Low Jackson, who purchased land in the American Bottom along the Mississippi River. The May 31, 1816, Madison County, Illinois, Court and Indenture Records transcript provided the following details. "This day personally came Low Jackson of Madison County & Wood River Township and Registered agreeable the Statute in such case made and provided—Two negro boys one by the name of Isaac, seven years old the first day of March in the year of our Lord 1815, & the other by the name of Dick, six years old on the thirty first day of December in the year of our Lord 1815. Before me Josias Randle, CCC, MC."[5] I postulate Isaac and Dick were brothers or very close friends because Susan had a younger brother named Richard.

Digging deeper, I discovered this frontier county was established in 1812—eight years after Lewis and Clark's men wintered at the mouth of the Wood River along low-lying land near the Mississippi River. In this wild and undeveloped place, Native Americans roamed the land hunting deer, wild turkey, squirrels, ducks, and other game. There was still hostility even though the French and Indian War had ended in February 1763. Resenting white encroachment, the Indians defended their territory along the river. Four white women and numerous children were killed by a small band of native people in what became locally known as the Wood River Massacre. Unfortunately, this incident increased the animosity between the settlers and Native Americans, causing the territorial government to offer a fifty-dollar bounty for killing any native who came to a white settlement with the intent to murder.[6]

When considering conditions likely affecting Isaac's and Sarah's lives, I found attitudes toward slavery were becoming less stringent in Illinois than in North Carolina as more "free staters" moved into Illinois. But dangerous and potentially life-threatening situations still existed for African Americans in Wood River Township, where Isaac worked on Low Jackson's farm.

Slavery in Illinois dates back to 1720, when African slaves were brought to work in coal mines and to clear land for agricultural purposes.[7] Even though the Ordinance of 1787 prohibited slavery, many African Americans

2

like Isaac and Sarah worked as indentured servants for a stated period of time.[8] It isn't known if Susan's parents were treated any differently than the slaves living in the South. Likely, Fayette residents didn't understand the distinction, thus identifying Susan's parents as slaves.

When Isaac and other young African Americans in the heartland were growing to manhood, the slavery issue was being passionately debated in Congress. The conversations resulted from the different views Southern planters and Northern industrialists held about their labor needs. A law passed in 1805 stating the length of servitude in Indiana Territory, of which Illinois was a part, ultimately provided the reason for Isaac's emancipation. This law stated, "Slaves who were under the age of fifteen at the time of their arrival in the territory were to be indentured servants, males until they reached the age of thirty-five and females until they became thirty-two."[9] Isaac was released at age thirty-five.

Isaac, however, was positively affected when Illinois enacted a series of "black codes" after becoming a state in 1818. These codes provided legal protection to African Americans, allowing the continuation of indentured servitude but prohibiting slavery and involuntary servitude.[10] Three years prior to Susan's birth, Illinois was still experiencing issues related to slavery. When the Illinois Constitution was revised in 1848, slavery and involuntary servitude were eliminated except when a black person had been convicted of a crime. Additionally, Article XIV of the revised constitution prohibited free blacks from immigrating into the state and didn't allow slave owners to set their slaves free after bringing them to Illinois. As late as 1853, the state legislature decreed it a crime to bring African Americans into the state.[11] These laws and codes were repealed after the Union Civil War victory ending all aspects of slavery in Illinois.[12] Isaac and Sarah benefitted from these laws, but dangers were present if they traveled too far from where they were known.

African Americans freed from their servitude before the 1850 passage of the Fugitive Slave Act by the United States Congress were often at risk. They lived in fear of slave catchers who came north motivated by greed to track down, capture, and take runaway slaves south, even though no specific person was looking for them. Other times, marshals arrested free African Americans, as illustrated in the January 1853 case of an Alton, Illinois, woman. Amanda Kicherd, who the Collins family likely knew, was married only a few weeks to Alfred Chavers when she was taken into custody. After her capture, the citizens of the community raised the $1,200 and demanded her freedom, and she was returned to her husband.[13] Likely, Susan's parents and other Northern free African Americans aided fugitive slaves—with many immigrating to Canada, Africa, and Caribbean countries.

Such was the fractious political world into which Susan was born on July 3, 1851,[14] joining three older sisters: Mary, age six;[15] Martha Indiana, age four;[16] and Maranda, age two.[17] Her brother, William, was born in 1854 while the family was living near Edwardsville.[18]

Even though Isaac and Sarah were freed from their servitude, life was hard for them. Finding work was difficult in a state that had trouble accepting them as equal citizens. Presumably, Isaac continued to work for Low Jackson as a farm laborer, receiving minimal remuneration for the back-breaking toil farming entailed. Imagine him on a summer day with beads of sweat pouring off his brow, guiding a horse-drawn, one-bottom plow and feeling the newly turned, moist black earth beneath his feet. Or later in the season, think of him swinging a scythe through the tall grass, shocking oats, and husking corn. He may have dreamed of owning his own land as he trudged up and down the fields where much of his time was spent.

Susan would have learned early in life that a farm family's work is never done. She probably watched her father planting crops and cutting plentiful oak trees for fence posts and firewood to cook and heat. And if Jackson didn't provide a house, Isaac and the neighbors may have built a cabin from oak logs. Possibly Susan's older sisters trudged along with Isaac when he hunted the abundant wild turkey, squirrel, and deer that fattened themselves eating acorns.

Even with five young children, Sarah would have been expected to have a vegetable garden. Likely, one of Susan's first memories as she ran barefooted outside the cabin was her mother hoeing weeds as she pushed wisps of hair under her wide-brimmed sunbonnet. Perhaps it was these memories that created Susan's lifetime joy in gardening, a skill she shared with her students at the Angolan missions.

Envision Sarah's garden including straight rows of Irish potatoes, sweet potatoes, corn, beans, carrots, and peas with squash, pumpkin, and eading along the edge. Imagine the older girls helping

ne garden produce while Sarah picked and preserved

es, strawberries, and blackberries. Collecting black

r nuts was a fall chore involving all of the children.

winds blew and snow fell, women of this era spun, wove, and made clothing for their families. I imagine Sarah learned these skills working for either the William Bridges or the William Hart families during her indenture period.

While Isaac and Sarah were farming and providing for their growing family, changes swept the country that affected their lives and those of other African Americans. Abolitionist movements gained momentum due to efforts by leaders such as William Lloyd Garrison and Sojourner Truth. The North exploded in anger after the passage of the Kansas-Nebraska Act in 1854.[19] Shortly afterward, the Republican Party with anti-South sentiments was formed. On May 29, 1856, five years after Susan's birth, Abraham Lincoln assisted in the formation of the Republican Party of Illinois. A year later in June, he gave a speech against the *Dred Scott* decision that ruled Scott must remain a slave. The ruling created a greater division between the North and the South.[20] Small farmers in the South sold their land and migrated west and north, taking advantage of land grants. Not all whites wanted free African Americans in the North, and in some states, they were not allowed to attend public schools or vote. Some started their own schools. No records were found revealing whether or not Susan and her older siblings attended school in Illinois.

Freedom to Choose: A Move to Wisconsin

Perhaps some of these conditions contributed to the Collins family's departure from Illinois after William's birth and before Richard's 1858 birth in Wisconsin.[21] Maybe they heard of opportunities in Wisconsin from runaway slaves escaping north up the Mississippi and Illinois Rivers to African American settlements developing in the Upper Midwest. Possibly Isaac's conversations with blacks working on the steamboats traveling between St. Louis, Missouri, and St. Paul, Minnesota, revealed the availability of affordable land and educational opportunities for his children.[22] Picture Isaac walking to the river on Sunday aftern. and talking with African Americans, along with newly arrived Iri. and German immigrants who served in a variety of capacities on the steamboats. Possibly he knew some of the deck crew who operated the pumps, supplied the wood, and fired the boilers or worked as roustabouts carrying cotton, tobacco, and sugar onto and off of the steamboats.

Slaves and free African Americans were integral to the Mississippi steamboat traffic in the mid-1800s. Their work, mostly as deckhands, enabled them to serve as communication conduits between families in the North, to assist escaping slaves, and develop knowledge of the larger world. Even though African Americans rarely rose above the status of deckhands, slaves frequently associated steamboats with freedom. Some of these men later reported that riverboat work was a bright spot in their lives.[23]

Possibly Isaac and Sarah aspired to join her cousin John A. Joiner and his wife, Margaret, who had settled with several other African American families in Newark Valley, Wisconsin, located in Adams County near the Wisconsin River.[24] They may have wanted to leave the marshy Illinois wetlands that fostered malaria-carrying mosquitoes that might have caused young Mary's death. There is no Illinois or Wisconsin record of her death, and she is not listed in the 1860 Wisconsin census. It is as if she disappeared with no trace of her existence except in the 1850 Illinois census.

Leaving her siblings and the comfort of the known for the adjustment of the unknown was probably stressful for Sarah. She may have been concerned about the myriad dangers of steamboat travel and keeping her children safe. Moving preparations would have been drudgery for the family. Imagine traveling with a family of four children under eleven years of age, while having limited finances and material goods. In all probability, they went by steamboat up the Mississippi and then the Wisconsin River when they were at their highest during spring flooding. The high water allowed larger boats to go inland to the central portion of Wisconsin.

They had to be deck passengers because African Americans weren't allowed cabins. Perhaps they stayed at the back deck because it was safer than the front where the boilers frequently exploded. Deck passengers were encouraged to wear coarse clothing in which they could sleep. Boats made numerous stops along the riverbanks to obtain wood for refueling. Men could chop wood and carry it on board to lower the cost of passage.[25]

Riverboat captains raced their steamboats, often creating disastrous results. To get an edge, they occasionally ordered African American workers to sit on the boilers' safety valves to build up pressure and gain the advantage of increased speed.[26] What a sad commentary, as they jeopardized innocent lives to win a race.

Sarah cared for the children and prepared their meals after obtaining a stove from the captain. Deck passengers brought their food on board.[27] Perhaps a typical meal included grits, black-eyed peas, and cured ham hocks.

There were many ways the children could be hurt, such as a deadly fall into the river that became rough and choppy when boats passed. Other risks included fire, contracting cholera, or being pushed overboard by shifting deck cargo.

Predicting their time en route to Prairie du Chien, Wisconsin, was difficult due to various river obstructions, such as sandbars, snags, sawyers, ice in early spring, and rapids. Travel estimates varied from a few days to two weeks to cover the 455 statue miles between St. Louis and Prairie du Chien. Among the more challenging impediments were the Rock Island and the Des Moines Rapids. Passing through these rapids created a new occupation, "rapids pilot," a steamboat captain who specialized in guiding boats through the rocky passages. With the approval of the 1852 Western Rivers Improvement Act, a channel one hundred feet wide and four feet deep was cut near the Rock Island Rapids.[28] This work may have been completed by the time the Collins family traveled upriver. After the Civil War, work on the river obstructions began in earnest because good river transportation was needed for commerce, carrying mail and articles of trade, and for those migrating north with hopes for a better life.[29]

Steamboat captains ruled their domains and often did not travel or allow gambling on Sundays. When docked, passengers were encouraged to attend the church of their choice.[30]

As the Collins family took this potentially perilous journey north, they had many sights and sounds along the river upon which to feast their eyes and ears. This undoubtedly added to their joy, as most enslaved African Americans were not allowed off the property where they worked. Isaac, Sarah, and their family had the freedom to migrate northward in search of better working and living conditions.

Susan and her siblings may have been alarmed when the boat left the river's edge and smoke began belching from the stacks, later turning into feathery plumes high in the sky. Perhaps the rugged limestone bluffs along the Mississippi led their eyes skyward toward towering treetops laden with bald eagle nests. Because Native Americans still lived in the area, she may have seen teepees standing in areas where the dark earth sloped down and smaller rivers and creeks entered the mighty river, causing gentle ripples. Juniper trees with their small smoky-blue berries provided cover for wild turkeys inhabiting the area. Deer were startled when the steamboat whistle blared a warning of an approaching boat or sending out a distress signal after hitting a sandbar. Great horned owls could be heard at night as they signaled one another with their deep, soft "hoo-h-hoo-hoos." For children with active imaginations, the trees often shrouded in the morning mist may have resembled tall skeletons.

Imagine the excitement and confusion the children and their parents experienced as their boat docked at Prairie du Chien, a major steamboat hub near the confluence of the Wisconsin and Mississippi Rivers. The town's recorded history began on June 17, 1673, when Father Marquette and fur trader Louis Joliet arrived at this prairie area inhabited by Fox Indians. Fur trading between the French Canadians and the various Native Americans thrived and was conducted on a nearby island, considered neutral territory among conflicting tribes. Nearly two hundred years later, the town became a railroad hub, creating a building boom, and in 1872, it incorporated.[31] Perhaps Susan traveled through here on her way to Chicago in 1885 when she began her missionary preparation at the Chicago Training School for City, Home, and Foreign Missions.

Care was required to guide small children from the steamboat's dock to the departure point at the mouth of the Wisconsin River. Horses and bellowing oxen strained, pulling loads of lumber to building sites. No sidewalks existed, streets weren't paved, and signage was limited or nonexistent. Could Martha Indiana read enough to help her illiterate parents find a ferry traveling the Fox-Wisconsin Rivers Waterway toward the east? When they reached the Wisconsin Dells, a distance of approximately 116 statute miles at the western edge of Adams County, they may have chosen to portage and then travel north on a boat. Their other alternative was having someone meet them, likely Sarah's cousin John, and riding the remaining sixteen miles in a wagon to Newark Valley, settled in 1858 and their residence for over seven years.

Susan's roots had been pulled out of Illinois, and it was up to her to adjust to an environment filled with immigrants arriving from Germany, Ireland, and Norway via the Erie Canal and the Great Lakes. Others, second- and third-generation Americans whose ancestors had come from Holland and England, arrived in covered wagons pulled by oxen to this central Wisconsin area spared by the glaciers more than twelve thousand years ago.[32] This was the first time many of these European arrivals had seen African Americans, and they were unaware of attitudes Southerners harbored about them and their assigned place in the Antebellum South.

The trip and new location opened Susan's thoughts to a broader world that was more welcoming to African Americans than Illinois had been. Here, she and her siblings were able to pursue their education in a country school attended by both African American and white children. They experienced their father's absence due to the Civil War, allowing them to become more independent and self-sufficient. These qualities served Susan well throughout her life.

Susan did not know this boat trip would be the first of many in her life. It may have helped her mentally and emotionally prepare for her later travels to and from Africa and up and down the Congo and Cuanza Rivers. Perhaps it was during this trip that her sense of adventure began developing.

2

A Country Divided

Getting Established: Life in Wisconsin

The move to Wisconsin required Susan and her siblings to adapt to many changes. They made friends at the integrated school in their new community. Isaac and Sarah's second son, Richard, was born here. In 1860, two years after Richard's birth, Abraham Lincoln gave a speech expressing his views on slavery in New Haven, Connecticut, and indicated his belief that America "was an all-inclusive democracy" and every man should have a chance.[33] As property owners, survival depended upon cooperation within their family and with neighbors. That became even more critical after Isaac enlisted in the military in 1864 and was away for a year. Come with me as I explore the realities and possibilities of their lives during their Wisconsin years.

Three factors may have emboldened African Americans to migrate to Wisconsin, a place where they could feel safer and put down roots. First was the Northwest Ordinance, also known as the Ordinance of 1787, passed by the Confederation Conference. It outlawed slavery in the Northwest Territory of which the future state of Wisconsin was a part.[34] The state's early resistance to the Fugitive Slave Act encouraged African Americans to settle here, as attitudes appeared less threatening than in Illinois. The second factor, Article X of Wisconsin's

Constitution of 1848, provided for free common schools supported by local taxes for all children between ages four and twenty years.[35] And third, the Menominee Indians had been moved out of east central Wisconsin after signing a treaty in 1848. They had to relinquish their rights to land that included Adams County, where the Collins family settled.

The Menominee Indians exchanged their land for $350,000 cash and six hundred thousand acres in Minnesota.[36] That Native American removal provided a greater sense of security to pioneers when the land was opened for settlement to both whites and African Americans.

Even though many citizens of Wisconsin disliked slavery, they wanted to keep their distance from African Americans, whom many believed were inferior. Nevertheless, Wisconsin was one of the first states to pass a black suffrage law. The legislature authorized a referendum that was approved in 1849 by a majority of voters.[37] Only five of twenty-four Northern states allowed African American men to vote in 1865 at the conclusion of the Civil War.[38] This changed in 1870 when the Fifteen Amendment to the United States Constitution passed, forbidding denial to vote on the basis of race. No records of Isaac Collins voting in either Wisconsin or Iowa after the family moved there in 1865 were found. With the ratification of the Nineteenth Amendment in 1920, American women were guaranteed the right to vote.

These three positive Wisconsin attributes likely contributed to Isaac and Sarah settling their family in the state. They moved to the Newark Valley area, which later became part of Quincy and lived near three black pioneer families: the Valentines, the Joiners, and the Manleys. When Robert Valentine and his family came to Adams County, still frontier country in 1852, they found Newark Valley situated near an isolated expanse of land hugging the eastern shore of the Wisconsin River and along Little Roche-a-Cri Creek, where they settled.[39] The area was located roughly eighty-five miles north of Madison, the state capital. Prior to 1860, the Valentine's oldest daughter, Sarah, married Leonard Manley from North Carolina.[40] These families lived in log cabins and had children in public school, where all children were admitted regardless of race.[41] Quincy's first public school had opened in 1858, the year Susan celebrated her seventh birthday.[42]

Imagine Susan and her siblings on a brisk spring morning, trudging down a muddy trail to school, carrying their lunches in molasses pails. They likely experienced excitement and trepidation as they approached the one-room schoolhouse with frost glistening off its rooftop. This would have been Susan's first experience making new friends. Public education valued by area settlers was spotty due to time set aside for all children to assist with planting and harvesting field crops.

In 1860, the total population of the village was 118, of whom twenty were African Americans or mix-race settlers. Seven were members of the Collins family.[43]

Even in this relatively isolated and remote area, African Americans did not always feel safe, as related in a story told by an early resident and relayed orally until recorded in 1950. A few young men, not from the area, followed county survey markers placed in 1851 north to Roche-a-Cri Creek. Upon reaching Friendship, near Quincy, "they came upon a group of log cabins and people near them were running and seemed very frightened. They turned out to be African Americans who thought the boys were law officers after them."[44] Quite possibly, they were members the Valentine, Collins, Manley, and Joiner families.

Except for those in their neighborhood, Isaac, Sarah, and their children had limited opportunity to interact with other African Americans. Friendships typically were formed at church, barn and house raisings, and auctions within a day's walking distance of ten miles. There were no other African American communities that close.

The 1820 population records revealed two hundred African Americans residing in Wisconsin, compared to Illinois where 1374 African Americans resided, 917 of whom were slaves.[45] Forty years later, nearly 1,200 African Americans lived in Wisconsin and 7,628 in Illinois, putting them in a minority.[46] Besides their small enclave in Adams County, there were African American settlements in Janesville nearly one hundred miles south of Newark Valley, in the Pleasant Ridge Community 120 miles southwest, and in the Cheyenne Valley area near Hillsboro approximately forty miles west.

The African Americans in Cheyenne Valley migrated from North Carolina and Indiana to Wisconsin with the assistance of the Quaker Religious Society of Friends. It was the largest rural African American settlement in the state. Positive relationships between these pioneer African Americans and European immigrants resulted in the establishment of one of the state's first integrated schools.[47] No connection between Isaac and those from North Carolina was found.

Surviving in this environment, surrounded by the dramatic beauty of limestone rock formations along the Wisconsin River, proved challenging for Susan's father and other farmers. Near Quincy and extending eastward was a range of bluffs about three miles long, with heights reaching from fifty to two hundred feet.[48] The soil was poor quality and "attracted farmers of last resort—people of limited means who purchased inexpensive ground, no matter how infertile because that was all they could afford."[49] That description applied to the Collins family. In the late 1850s, when they reached their destination, land values were from $1.25 for swamp land to $2.50 per acre for lands granted to Wisconsin for the improvement of the Fox and Wisconsin River Valleys.

Land in Adams County had not been surveyed and made available for sale until 1852, creating opportunities for purchase attractive to people like Isaac.[50] It is unknown what quality of land he bought near Quincy, but acreages there were described as sandy, loamy, and swampy.[51] The 1860 United States Federal Census lists his real property as $300 and personal property at fifty dollars. Allowing for a log cabin and a shed for animals, he may have owned sixty acres, described as an average Wisconsin farm in 1860.[52] At that time, farmers were opening up land with an average of twenty-two acres improved and thirty-eight unimproved.

Life appeared relatively quiet and safe for Adams County residents in the late 1850s and early 1860s. That was not so in the eastern and southern portions of America as the slavery issue came to a head after years of debate and dissension. A number of people became prominent in the move to abolish slavery years before Susan was born. On January 1, 1831, William Lloyd Garrison published the first issue of the *Liberator*, an antislavery newspaper. The abolitionist movement gained momentum in 1833 when Britain freed slaves in the West Indies.[53] In 1841, Frederick Douglas gave a "stunning impromptu speech at an antislavery meeting in Massachusetts," reinforcing his belief that policies were necessary to solve the problem, and later noted a war might be "the price of emancipation."[54] Some have described him as "the greatest of black abolitionists."[55] He also supported the empowerment of all women.

In 1849, two years prior to Susan's birth, Harriet Tubman, an escaped slave, become one of the most effective leaders of the Underground Railroad. Another African American, Sojourner Truth, worked for women's rights and the emancipation of her race and is best remembered for her unplanned speech that became known as "Ain't I a Woman?" delivered in 1851 at the Women's Rights Convention in Akron, Ohio.[56] Harriet Beecher Stowe's *Uncle Tom's Cabin* captured the nation's attention in 1852 and stirred abolitionists into greater action.[57]

There were antislavery feelings in the South, but they were thwarted when the Virginia Legislature "debated and defeated emancipation proposals in 1831–1832."[58] Prior to the Civil War, the South was influenced by the wealthy planters who bought additional land to increase cotton production. The robust cotton market created the need for additional land and slaves, spawning a vicious cycle. In 1860, there were nearly four million slaves, four times the number in the early 1800s. After 1840, greater than 50 percent of America's export value was derived from cotton. Much of it was shipped to England and converted into fabric.

Periodically, Congress was forced to deal with the slave issue and ended importation in 1808 by decree. In 1820, the Missouri Compromise banned slavery in all western territories north of the southern boundary of Missouri, which was admitted as a slave state, and Maine as a free state. Continuing debate over whether territory gained from the Mexican War should be slave or free resulted in the Compromise of 1850. California was admitted as a free state. New Mexico and Utah Territories were to be decided by popular sovereignty. Slave trade in Washington, DC, was prohibited. With passage of the Kansas-Nebraska Act in 1854, tensions between anti- and proslavery factions were renewed, and there was bloodshed in Kansas, a new state.

This occurred about the time the Collins family moved to Wisconsin and the abolitionist movement had become embedded in the minds of countless Northerners. Many saw the South as a land of slavery, an odious institution, and did not want it extended to the western territories. By 1861, when Susan was ten years old, the country was in turmoil, the Confederacy was formed, and seven Southern states seceded. The Civil War had begun. Later, four other states seceded.

Civil War Rages: Isaac Enlists

When the war started, many believed it would end quickly, and it is likely that those in Wisconsin, a distance from the fighting, did not expect to be called upon to participate. As the war effort plodded along and death numbers increased, the request for more men was issued. This had an impact on the Collins family when Isaac enlisted in the army on August 6, 1864.[59] Perhaps it was at this time Susan learned about the Civil War and became increasingly aware of slavery. Or maybe it had been discussed at school when the war began.

Wisconsin Civil War records revealed Isaac enlisted in Company H, the Thirty-Eighth Wisconsin Infantry Regiment.[60] He was described as five feet six inches tall with black eyes, hair, and complexion, and born in Waik,[61] North Carolina.[62] His enlistment was the result of the Call of July 18, 1864, for five hundred thousand men, issued by President Lincoln through the Provost-Marshal-General's Office.[63] Given the rank of private, he was mustered in as a cook and mustered out as an undercook, according to his Company Muster Roll, noting he was colored.[64] General Order 323, issued on September 28, 1863, by the War Department Adjutant-General's Office, proclaimed, "That the President of the United States be, and he is hereby, authorized to cause to be enlisted for each cook (two allowed by section 9) two undercooks of African American descent, who shall receive for their full compensation $10 per month and one ration per day; $3 of said monthly pay may be in clothing."[65] This Civil War order initiated the integration of African Americans into the military, making Isaac among the first to serve his country in this way.

At the start of the Civil War, Adams County supervisors voted to pay the families of volunteers two dollars a month for every child under age twelve as long as they served.[66] William and Richard were under twelve, so Sarah was eligible to receive four dollars per month, likely a significant benefit with five children to feed and clothe while Isaac was away.

Isaac's enlistment records have a Friendship, Adams County address because it served as the post office for Newark Valley residents. Company H soldiers were recruited by Thomas Marsden and Solon Pierce of Friendship, but Isaac's enlistment was credited to the town of Trenton, Dodge County, Wisconsin.[67]

At this stage in the war, the average age of a Union soldier, who was not an officer, was twenty-five. By the war's conclusion in 1865, more than 180,000 African Americans were in the Union Army, accounting for 9 percent of its fighting strength.[68] Some of these numbers had come by freeing African American slaves with the Emancipation Proclamation in 1863. This enabled and encouraged them to fight for the North. Of those African Americans enlisted, 38,000 lost their lives. In 1860, they comprised 14.1 percent of the population, and by 1870, the percentage had fallen to 12.7 percent.[69]

Isaac's reasons to enlist at his age with young children at home may have been numerous. Possible motivations could have been loyalty to the Union, which had freed the slaves, pressure from local men Thomas Marsden and Solon Pierce, financial, or some other factor. A financial incentive may have been the $100 cash enlistment bounty, a fee granted for enlistment, paid to enrollees by the federal government for a one-year period.[70] "One-third of the bounty was paid on muster in, one-third after the expiration of one-half the term of service and the remaining one-third upon discharge or expiration of the period of enlistment."[71] Union privates had been paid thirteen dollars per month until June 20, 1864. On that date, they received a final raise to sixteen dollars per month.[72]

Whatever the reasons, Isaac apparently had a strong motivation to join the Union Army because his Declaration of Recruit Form had listed his age as forty-four.[73] Based upon census data and the Illinois Servitude and Emancipation Records, he was at least fifty-five. Men over forty-five were considered too old to serve.[74] It is baffling as to why this happened. Possibly he didn't know the requirement, no one knew his true age, or those enrolling him ignored it because they were eager to fill the federal-government-required quota for Wisconsin.

Prior to Isaac's enlistment, Companies A, B, C, and D of the Thirty-Eighth Infantry Regiment of Wisconsin were called into service at Camp Randall near Madison on April 15, 1864.[75] Sarah's cousin John A. Joiner and Isaac were mustered as privates into Company H on September 19 at Camp Randall. John was also an undercook.[76]

Curious where the Thirty-Eighth Infantry Regiment of Wisconsin traveled and fought during Isaac's enlistment period, you can imagine my excitement when five years into this research, I discovered *Battle Fields and*

Camp Fires of the Thirty-Eighth by Lieutenant S. W. Pierce, who signed Isaac into his company. Published in 1866, Solon Pierce described the company's war efforts, beginning with how it was filled.

> Men from all walks of life cast aside every consideration of home comfort, business and all ties, and unreservedly gave themselves to the army and to filling up its wasted ranks. Large local bounties were offered, and meetings were held in almost every school house, at which spirited addresses were made. The feeling of the people, while it was not wildly enthusiastic as in 1861, was equally intense and determined. By the middle of September, the Thirty-Eighth was filled. The class of men recruited for it was such as drew encomiums from all.[77]

Following is a summarization of Company H's experiences from September 1864 until the men returned home ten months later. Experience a glimpse into the life of the Thirty-Eighth Infantry Regiment of Wisconsin after Isaac became part of this detail.

The regiment broke camp and left Madison early on September 22 at eight o'clock for the South, only three days after Isaac and John arrived at Camp Randall. They traveled by train, reaching Chicago at eleven o'clock in the evening, and camped across from the Soldier's Rest, listening to the waves lapping against Lake Michigan's shores. After breakfast prepared by men at the Rest, they boarded a train bound for Pittsburgh. It chugged along in heavy rain throughout the day and into the evening. Following a supper stop in Ft. Wayne, Indiana, they continued to Pittsburgh, arriving the next evening, where they ate at a Soldier's Rest established in 1861. Then they skirted around mountains and rushed down narrow ravines, arriving in the mountain town of Altoona, Pennsylvania, and eating breakfast at another Soldier's Rest.[78]

These Rests served as way stations offering food and lodging for soldiers coming to and going from the front during the war. They were often a safe haven for the African American troops, as white people did not allow them to sleep or eat in their places of business. Volunteering at the Rests was a way for Northern women to contribute to the war effort as they provided a parlor, a dining room, reading rooms, and bathing and sleeping rooms for the weary, bedraggled soldiers. After the war ended, some of them were converted to soldiers' homes.

The company rode huddled together through the Allegheny Mountains the night of September 23 and into the next day on Pennsylvania Railroad freight cars. They saw their breath rise like mist into the air. Before dark, upon reaching the Susquehanna River Valley, the tracks turned south into Maryland. They arrived in Baltimore on September 25 and were served breakfast by the men at the Soldier's Rest. After a three-hour break, they were on their way to Washington, DC. So far, Isaac and John had not been required to cook.[79]

On September 27, the day after arriving in the Washington, DC, barracks, the men were issued Springfield rifle muskets. Many of the men knew how to use rifles from years of hunting wild game. About noon the next day, the men boarded the steamboat *John A. Warner* and departed. On September 30, eight days after leaving Wisconsin, they reported to General George Meade at the front south of Petersburg. Here the men were overworked and subjected to exposure. During October, the duties of camp guard and picket overtaxed numerous soldiers. With rest only one out of three nights, many men fell sick and were sent to the hospital.[80]

On October 27, the men were given orders to move. Isaac and John cooked for the officers and helped issue five days of rations to the other men who packed their knapsacks and moved out by 2:00 p.m. That night, the men slept in the rain, protecting themselves as much as possible. Isaac and John had boiled coffee ready for the men before dawn. Other men had begun constructing breastworks using rocks and dirt for protection from the heavy firing at the front. Losses caused the regiment to retreat and move back to camp, arriving at four in the afternoon.[81]

During the next two weeks, many men became ill, and a number of them died. When Colonel James Bintliff interceded and lighted their workload, sickness decreased at their camp near Peeble's House, Virginia, close to the James River and Petersburg. Isaac apparently remained healthy, as no record of any illnesses was recorded. During this time, the white soldiers had the opportunity to vote for the president, and Lincoln was reelected. Suffrage for African Americans had yet to occur.[82]

Back in Wisconsin, Susan, her mother, and siblings carried on without

Isaac, praying for his safe return. Preserving garden produce and picking corn, husking, and storing it for their animals were required tasks necessary to survive the bitter cold, snowy winter months. At age ten, William was old enough to chop wood used to heat their cabin, cook meals, and preserve food.

On November 29, 1864, the Thirty-Eighth Regiment was dispatched to the left of the line about three miles from Petersburg, Virginia. Marching in heavy rain and mud, Isaac, John, and the other soldiers arrived just after dark. The men set up camp and survived enemy fire. In January, they endured sleet and rain, standing for hours in knee-deep water and mud. Tents provided minimal shelter.[83]

Horses and wagons moved large equipment, including cooking gear and supplies. Cooks used cast-iron kettles suspended on tripods and heated over an open fire to do most of the cooking. When inclement weather prevented cooking, men subsisted on cracker-like biscuits called hardtack, cheese, and sweetened coffee. They often had to soak the hardtack in their coffee or water to make it edible. Some men broke their teeth trying to chew the biscuits, also called tooth dullers, sheet-iron crackers, or floor tile.[84] If lucky, they could purchase food from sutlers who traveled around following the army's regiments. When someone discovered the commissary sergeant had been stealing and selling government pork and bread, he was reduced in rank, and the men again received more rations.[85] I have wondered how this situation affected Isaac and the other cooks in the Thirty-Eighth. None of these men were apparently accused of mismanaging the food supplies.

The battles continued for six weeks as Union and Confederate soldiers fired at one another, but few injuries were sustained due to excellent breastworks. Through this dismal period of cold, rain, and mud, spirits were bright, as Savannah had fallen and Sherman's march to Atlanta was successful. Deserters came to the Union side. On March 24 and 25, 1865, General Robert E. Lee massed his forces at Cemetery Hill and hurled his men upon Fort Steadman. The cooks helped distribute five days of rations for soldiers' haversacks. Unnecessary baggage was sent to the rear. Men were to be ready to move on an hour's notice but laid in their trenches until April 1, a warm and pleasant day. Moving forward, they formed a battle line directly in front of Fort Sedgwick, and at 4:00 a.m. on April 2, they entered into a battle, capturing Fort Malone, a Rebel stronghold. The battle was fierce as "Grape and canister shriek through the air as through all demons of destruction gathered together, were holding high carnival."[86] There was danger, death, and pain as they moved victoriously toward the fort.

After this battle, the troops regrouped. About 3:00 a.m. on April 3, the line was called up and quietly advanced to Petersburg, hoping to surprise General Lee and his troops. Upon arrival, they discovered the Confederates had evacuated the city and withdrawn across the Appomattox River during the night. Two days later, they returned ravenous to camp because they had not taken their haversacks when the battle started.[87]

All remained encamped until the morning of April 14 and then left at noon. After passing through Petersburg, they camped south of town. At noon of the fifteenth, they marched up South Side Railroad, a major Confederate supply route in Southern Virginia, and set up camp fourteen miles from their starting point. They departed for Wilson's Station at 3:00 a.m. on the sixteenth and arrived near noon the following day, having marched steadily more than thirty miles to arrive at Northington Plantation. After being in trenches for five months, the exhausted men set up camp. The next day, they traversed three miles to Black and White's Station, now Blackstone, situated along the South Side Railroad, and laid out camp. They joined other troops guarding the rail lines. By this time, food supplies were very low, and the men scouted on nearby farms, depleting the owners' supplies of chicken, turkeys, and legs of mutton and keeping the cooks and themselves busy preparing hearty meat dishes.[88]

In Wisconsin, Sarah and the children had been preparing the garden and fields for spring planting, as their preserved food supply was running low. They may have searched for morel mushrooms in ash, elm, and oak forests and for watercress in the nearby creek.

War Ends: Jubilation and Celebration

While at Black and White's Station, Isaac's regiment learned of Lee's surrender at Appomattox Court House on April 10 and rejoiced as spring flowers perfumed the air. Leaves burst forth on trees that had survived the deluge of bullets during the battles, and birdsongs filled the air. The men's spirits were dashed when they learned of Lincoln's assassination on April 16, 1865. Within days after Lincoln's death, they trudged toward City Point, now Hopewell, and on to Alexandria. City Point is located in central Virginia at the confluence of the Appomattox and James Rivers. That was Grant's field headquarters during the Petersburg campaign.[89] Their final stopping place for the night was on a hill two miles above the nation's capital. Two days later, they marched to Tennally Town, north of Washington, DC. From this picturesque area covered with evergreens, the men could see the capitol dome in the distance, topped by the Statue of Freedom put in place on December 2, 1863. Here they had daily regimental drills and dress parades on Sunday afternoons.[90]

Thirteen days after Lee's surrender, the Thirty-Eighth Infantry Regiment of Wisconsin was the leading infantry regiment in the Grand Review of the Army of the Potomac and the Ninth Corps. They had bivouacked the previous night, April 22, just east of the National Capital. Hopefully Isaac and John had the opportunity to march and experience the triumphal event where "beauty smiled, and fair hands decked with the choicest flowers greeted the toil-worn victors of the nation."[91] After passing the review stand where President Andrew Johnson, General Ulysses S. Grant, department secretaries, and foreign ministers sat, the men rested and then marched back to Tennally Town.[92]

In May, Wisconsin Governor James T. Lewis visited the troops. During his address, he promised to do everything in his power to get them mustered out and sent home quickly.[93] The men of Company H rejoiced when discharged on June 2. Possibly on that day, a jumble of thoughts and plans for the future were running through Isaac's mind. Perhaps it was during the war that he had decided to move his family, including thirteen-year-old Susan, to Iowa upon his return home.

Within four days, Isaac and John marched with their company to the depot of the Baltimore and Washington Railroad. Their journey home had begun. Upon reaching Baltimore, they proceeded to the Pennsylvania Railroad depot, boarded the train, and traveled west. They were fed breakfast by men of the Pittsburgh Soldier's Rest on June 9. Arriving in Cleveland the evening of June 10, they transferred from the railroad cars to a ship.[94] Isaac and John's responsibility to feed the men of Company H had been completed.

At Detroit, they continued west by rail across Michigan to Grand Haven, where residents provided breakfast and dinner. Then they boarded a ship crossing Lake Michigan to Milwaukee. Crowded conditions and the insolent, unhelpful behavior of the crew made the journey dreary and uncomfortable. After traveling nearly one thousand miles by train and boat in six days, they reached Madison on July 11. The next morning, the men were greeted with roaring cannons and chiming bells as they marched to Camp Randall, where their war experience had begun almost ten months earlier. On June 26, these soldiers, after being paid, were discharged.[95] How Isaac and John traveled the last portion of the journey home remains unanswered.

One might wonder how Sarah and the children fared when Isaac was in the military. The children ranged from six to sixteen years when he enlisted. Susan was just two months past thirteen, and her brothers were six and ten, too young to do much farmwork except care for cows, pigs, and chickens. By this time, the boys were old enough to catch fish in the creek. Did they manage on their own, or did local community members, both African Americans and whites, help them? Given Susan's self-sufficient and can-do attitude during her missionary career, it is plausible the family relied primarily on themselves during Isaac's absence.

Knowing what happened upon Isaac's arrival in Newark Valley is speculative. Communication about the mustering out and return home of Company H men possibly came to their families by word of mouth from the families of Marsden and Piece. Upon reaching home, Lieutenant Pierce likely shared with townspeople the following description of what he saw during the Grand Review as his regiment marched in the nation's capital. "Washington was a world of flowers, and flags and streamers waved and fluttered in every breeze; and through it all, from 8 A.M. until 4 P.M., flowed a stream down Pennsylvania Avenue, of burnished steel, heaving to the measured cadence of the tread of victorious legions, and carrying upon its broad bosom, here and there, the glorious banner of the Union. Martial music lent its stirring strains."[96]

Perhaps there was a community celebration where Solon Pierce thanked the brave men in Company H and their wives and children for the privations they experienced while their husbands, fathers, and other family members were fighting this war so all citizens would be free with equal rights. He may have acknowledged other citizens for helping the soldiers' families during their absence and complimented each man in Company H for his service. After the celebration, families adjusted to the presence of the men, and old routines returned slowly to their lives.

Moving Again: Off to Iowa

At some point, Isaac and Sarah told the children they were selling their farmland and moving to Iowa after crops were harvested. It is plausible they relocated because Isaac had heard about the thriving community of African Americans living north and east of the small village of Fayette in Northeast Iowa. His information may have come either during the war or by word of mouth from their neighbor Robert Valentine, who had moved there while Isaac was away.

No record of either the preparations they made for the move or their Wisconsin departure date have been unearthed. Like others moving farther westward during this era, they likely obtained an oilcloth-covered wagon to provide protection for their belongings, shelter from the rain, cold, and perhaps snow, and a place to sleep. They may have had a cow tied to the back of the wagon and adequate food to last until spring. Typical possessions for those migrating included a heavy iron skillet, large kettle, and a meager amount of household furniture. A rough-hewn chest might have contained their valued possessions, such as a family Bible, Isaac's Civil War discharge papers, a few books, and clothing. Perhaps Isaac brought carpenter and blacksmithing tools and a plow, adding to the weight of the wagon pulled by oxen.

Their route leaving is speculative, but they had to cross the Wisconsin River either by ferry at Quincy or finding a place to ford. Then they almost certainly traveled southwest, toiling across the hilly terrain to the Mississippi River and taking a ferry across from Prairie du Chien, Wisconsin, to McGregor, Iowa.

Nine years before the Collins family made their crossing, Amorette Foote's grandmother described her arrival in Iowa by ferry as part of her journey to Fayette in 1856. The following quote provides a picture of what Isaac, Sarah, and children might have experienced. "When the ferry pulled in alongside the boat landing at McGregor, a rope would be tossed to a man at the river's edge, who would snake it around a stump. Then the planks would be let down and a crowd of men, women, and children, draft horses and wagon would stream off the boat at the foot of the town's main street, which ran up a gulch so narrow that its sides rose directly beside them and the brick buildings that lined it."[97]

After arriving in Iowa, there were more steep hills to struggle over near the west side of the river. Once out of the river valley, the hills, covered with tall, wild grasses, became gentler and more rolling as they journeyed on their southwesterly route toward Fayette. Sharp-eyed travelers could spot deer trails winding along the hillside and creeks. Ancient walnut, butternut, hickory, maple, and oak trees were shedding red, orange, and gold leaves. Occasionally, howling coyotes sent chills through travelers.

The most direct distance between McGregor and Fayette is approximately thirty-five miles. Crossing creeks, finding a shallow spot to ford the Turkey River, going through swamps, and following the numerous valleys and ridges made the journey long and rigorous. Today, the shortest driving distance, often along ridges, between the two towns is forty-nine miles.

After they had surmounted the physical obstacles of arriving in Iowa, they may have experienced reserved attitudes and behaviors from a mostly white rural population. They hoped Iowans would respect them and treat them as friends. Once again, they risked all to be another minority in a locale being settled predominately by Europeans. This was true for Sarah's cousin John A. Joiner, who after the Civil War moved his family to the Des Moines, Iowa, area. John's family and Susan remained close throughout their lives, with Susan serving as a role model for his granddaughters.

During the Wisconsin period in her life, Susan had learned to persist under difficult circumstances, developing self-sufficiency, flexibility, and adaptability. For the family to survive during Isaac's military service, she had to contribute actively to the household and farm chores, attend school, and follow her mother's requests. The work ethic she developed in Wisconsin served her well as a university student, an independent businesswoman, and a missionary.

3

~~~~~~~~

Susan's Teen Years: Experiencing Iowa

Iowa: History and Attitudes toward Minorities

African Americans begin migrating to Northeast Iowa in 1852. But York, the slave traveling with the Lewis and Clark expedition in 1803, was the first known African American to enter the territory that later became the state of Iowa in 1846. In 1839, the Supreme Court of the Iowa Territory ruled in *The Matter of Ralph* and determined because he had come into a "free state" with permission from his master, he could not be forced to return to a slave state after being in Iowa.[98] Between 1851 and 1868, African Americans were afforded more equal rights in Iowa than other states. These rights included attending integrated schools, interracial marriage, and suffrage for men.[99] That did not mean they had equal opportunity in all areas of life or that these rights were granted in all sectors of the state.

But it is important to let others know there was a neighborhood in Northeast Iowa where people of different races were living and working together at a time when our nation was fighting a civil war. Their attitude of cooperation has continued more than a century and into current time.

Perhaps acceptance of rights for African Americans led to dialogues I had with my parents and people of our generations when we grew up in Northeast Iowa. These conversations illustrated Fayette residents had an atypical and positive attitude toward people of different ethnic and racial backgrounds.

There were some students with African American heritage in our school; however, I wasn't aware of that until beginning research about Susan and discovering the race listings in the Iowa census records dating from the mid to late 1800s. And I didn't hear community members, my parents, or grandparents make derogatory comments about people who were African American or biracial. In our farming neighborhood, people helped one another in times of need, regardless of race, and all were welcome and encouraged to be active participants in Fayette churches and organizations.

These perceptions and recollections have been echoed by others who graduated from high school either with me or several years later. Correspondence from them included comments such as, "The Fayette and rural area seemed quite an accepting community," "I think we were all color neutral. I was a junior or senior before I realized two in our high school were partly black," and "Everyone was treated with neighborly respect." One classmate and her sister, whose father was listed as black in the 1940 census and whose paternal grandparents were identified as black in the 1930 United States Federal Census, wrote, "I don't remember any black families living in Fayette." Race apparently was not discussed in their family.

One classmate wrote, "When growing up in Fayette, I do not remember any overt prejudice or talk about it from the adults I knew. Only later did I learn that we were living next to a black family on an adjacent farm. They weren't black to me and did not have an ethnic label. They were a little different in appearance, darker than other people, but I never gave it a thought. If I had, I probably would have been satisfied with the thought he spent too much time in the sun while working on his farm. In later years my dad and Attie would always have the best conversations about the old times I suspect."

All those questioned mentioned they were not aware of racism or prejudice until they left Fayette for either college, the military, or government service. Another responded, "I did not recall any racial oriented or negative remarks or experiences from either my parents or grandparents, which I'm sure I would have remembered."[100]

Echoing our observations was a comment made in 1965 by Dr. Eugene Garbee, president of Upper Iowa University. "No one ever thinks about the distinction of Negroes and white in the area because the Negro farm families are so much a part of the community."[101] African American families have contributed to the fabric of the Fayette farming community since pioneer days.

It seems our normal in Fayette was different from other parts of Iowa and the nation in the 1940s and 1950s. We were raised with attitudes of respect and acceptance, just as our parents were. These communications affirmed that my truths were aligned with my peers.

But these attitudes and behaviors hadn't always been that way in the Fayette area and throughout Iowa. Iowans had been in debate about how to manage the presence of Native Americans and African Americans in the Iowa Territory formed on July 4, 1838. Removal to other locations with less productive land was the fate of most Native Americans, while African Americans struggled to obtain their civil rights in Iowa and other regions of the country.

Native Americans were the earliest inhabitants of the state. The Ioways were the first tribe to reside in Iowa and parts of surrounding states. It is from this culture that Iowa received its name. In the early 1800s, the federal government evicted the Ioways and relocated them on a reservation existing today along the Missouri River, straddling the borders of Nebraska and Kansas.[102]

The conclusion of the Black Hawk Purchase in 1832 paved the way for frontier settlement along the western side of the Mississippi River, although it is believed that Julien Dubuque was the first white man to settle within Iowa's present boundaries in 1788.[103] Several years later, land sales were held, and Europeans came to Iowa, settling along rivers that eventually flowed to the Mississippi.[104] As more settlers surged westward, 1837 and 1842 treaties with the Sac and Fox Indians were made, opening lands in central and south-central Iowa for purchase.[105] Among the settlers were men such as Barton Randle and Barton Cartwright, who came to Iowa in the early 1830s, bringing Methodism to Dubuque and the Flint Hills, now known as Burlington. Both towns are located along the bluffs of the Mississippi River. When these men arrived, people considered Iowa the far west.[106]

In 1840, a preacher was sent to the Marion Mission in east-central Iowa. Six years later, Richard Swearingen wrote, "I was received into the Iowa Conference in 1846. My first charge was Canton in Jackson County and extended up the Maquoketa and Turkey Rivers as far as civilization extended."[107] For his work, he received a yearly salary of sixty-six dollars. As pioneers moved farther west, a Marshalltown mission was established.

James F. Hestwood was assigned the Story Mission in central Iowa in 1855, and his challenges were numerous. He described his territory and housing situation thus: "This charge as I traveled it was forty-three miles north and south and over thirty miles east and west, and I cannot remember that there was a bridge over any stream, and many points to which I went I had no road but an Indian trail. There was no house for my use and I waited for the fulfillment of good promises until it got warm, then by permission went into the timber and built a log cabin sixteen-foot square."[108]

During this period, Upper Iowa Conference was considered a mission conference in a largely uninhabited territory.[109] Preachers were a cohort of organized evangelists, much like the missionaries who traveled with Susan more than three decades later.

Those missionaries coexisted with the Ioway and five other Native American tribes present in the land that became Iowa in 1846.[110] During the 1830s and 1840s, the Winnebago Indians, who were removed from Wisconsin to Northeast Iowa, lived on neutral ground near Fort Atkinson. That fort was built to protect them from Sioux, Sauk, and Fox Indians and white settlers intruding on their land.[111] The Winnebago Indians, now called the Ho-Chunk Nation, were relocated in 1848 by the United States government to a wooded region in Minnesota.[112] They received eight hundred thousand acres from the federal government along the Crow Wing River and $190,000 in exchange for their lands.[113] Seventeen years after this Indian removal, the Collins family settled in Northeast Iowa.

Two years earlier, the federal government had relocated the Sauk and Meskwaki Indians to Kansas. Unhappy in Kansas, some of the Meskwaki Indians requested to purchase Iowa land. The state's general assembly granted their request in 1856. They bought land in Tama County, situated in the central part of the state along the Iowa River, where they reside today.[114]

Slavery issues in Iowa occurred concurrently with the decisions made regarding Native Americans. The Territory of Iowa forbade slavery, but not everyone believed that African Americans were equal. In the 1840s, slaves brought to Iowa remained uninformed by their masters they were on free soil, causing many to consider Iowa a racist territory.[115] During 1839, the year after formation of the Territory of Iowa, lawmakers drafted legislation to keep free blacks out of the state.[116] The next year, they banned interracial marriage. However, in 1851, Iowa became the second state to legalize interracial marriage, more than a century before it was federally mandated. On June 12, 1967, laws prohibiting interracial marriage were declared unconstitutional by the United States Supreme Court.

By 1845, with more than seventy-five thousand residents, fifteen thousand beyond the number required, Iowa was populous enough to apply for statehood. The citizens received pressure from the federal government to be the next free state to enter the union to balance Florida, which had entered as a slave state in 1845. Adhering to the plan developed by the United States Senate to have an equal number of senators from the Northern free states and the Southern slave states, Iowa became a free state on December 28, 1846, on the signature of President James K. Polk.[117]

Four years after Iowa obtained statehood, the 1850 United States Federal Census reported slightly more than 191,000 white residents and 333 African American residents called "free colored."[118] During the decade encompassing the Civil War, Iowa's white population grew from nearly seven hundred thousand to over a million, while the African American population expanded from 1, 069 to 5,762 or from 0.15 to 0.50 percent.[119] Those numbers included Susan, her parents and siblings, as well as Alexander Clark, the son of an emancipated slave. Clark came to Muscatine in 1842 before Susan's parents were married, opened a barbershop, and lived there for forty-two years.

Susan's educational opportunities in Iowa were enhanced due to Clark's persistence. In 1868, the Iowa Supreme Court ruled there could be no segregation in schools based upon religion, race, or nationality.[120] His resolve and work paved the way for minority children to obtain an education equal to that for white children. These efforts enabled his son Alexander Jr. to become the first African American to earn a law degree from the University of Iowa in 1879,[121] the same year Susan purportedly received her Normal Training credential from Upper Iowa University. Alexander Clark moved to Chicago in 1884 and began publication of the *Conservator*, the city's first newspaper for African Americans. Three years later, he returned to Muscatine, the year Susan departed for Africa.

Clark initiated an unsuccessful campaign to obtain suffrage for Iowa African Americans prior to the Civil War. After the war, he was even more convinced African American men deserved the right to vote, based on their admirable service provided to the North as First Volunteers of African American Descent Regiment.[122]

He persisted and marshaled the 1,153 volunteers with whom he had served as their sergeant major,[123] along with the African American and white citizens of Muscatine. He took their signed petition supporting the cause to the Iowa legislature. The Republicans favored African American suffrage, and the Democrats did not.[124] Clark's efforts helped, and in 1868, when the legislature was presented with a referendum "to strike the word 'white' in the voting clause of Iowa's constitution, the amendment passed."[125] With its passage, Iowa became one of the most legally egalitarian states in the county[126] and the first state outside of New England permitting suffrage for African American males. On February 26, 1869, the United States Congress passed the Fifteenth Amendment. It was ratified on February 3, 1870, giving freed male slaves and other African American men the right to vote. No evidence of Isaac using his right to vote in Iowa has been located. In the spring, a convention was held in Mount Pleasant, Iowa, to organize the Iowa Woman Suffrage Association.[127] Amelia Bloomer spoke to the nearly 1,200 attending.

Another fourteen years elapsed, and in 1884, the Iowa legislature passed a civil rights act to eliminate discrimination in hotels, theaters, barbershops, and on public transportation. Eight years later, it became illegal to discriminate in Iowa restaurants. These laws unfortunately were often ignored.[128]

By the time the Collins family reached the Fayette area in November 1865, life there was becoming easier for African Americans. To arrive at their destination, they had to descend a steep, wooded hill as they approached the Volga River Valley. The riverbanks with jagged limestone outcroppings resembled those along the Wisconsin River. Imagine their painstaking descent along a rocky path into the valley near the villages of Albany and Lima, no longer in existence. They probably looked for the familiar faces of the Robert Valentine family and a view of the log cabin Peter Bass, Isaac's purported employer, may have provided for them. It is assumed it was during this time that Susan and the Graham children developed a friendship that became lifelong.

Iowa winters were harsh, and cold winds from the Arctic Circle frequently blew the snow into six- or seven-foot drifts. Blizzards raged across the open fields, sometimes blocking cabin and barn doors and windows, making it difficult to feed livestock and gather eggs before they froze or hungry foxes ate them.

Farmers hunted wild game such as deer, rabbits, squirrels, and turkeys to supplement their family's food supply. By the time the Collins family arrived in Iowa, elk had moved to states farther west. They joined other African American who had settled in the rural Fayette area prior to the Civil War.[129] Those coming from Illinois obtained land claims north and east of town, beginning in 1852. They were helped with the legalities by Reverend David Watrous, who settled there that spring.[130] Watrous, their Illinois minister, was a friend of the elder Sion Bass. He knew of the desire of the elder Bass to help his son Sion and others find new, inexpensive land. Watrous wrote, telling them about the availability of high-quality government land in Fayette County.

That occurred in the decade when many people were seeking land and increasing numbers were settling in Northeast Iowa.[131] Many had been squatting on the land and needed proof of their right to be there. Reverend David Watrous, who farmed in this African American settlement and served the United Brethren Church members, helped them enter their claims at the Dubuque land office located seventy miles east along the Mississippi River. His educational credentials were likely limited. But as an abolitionist, he was passionate about helping African Americans obtain land and exposing them to the doctrines of the Gospel during services at the Stone School House also serving as a church. That was a common practice in pioneer communities until a church building was constructed. The African Americans in the neighborhood eventually assimilated into local churches. Watrous assisted those living in the area until his death at age seventy-four in October 1864. He was buried in Dunham Grove Cemetery in Randalia, Iowa.[132] His son Reverend George H. Watrous, who resided to the east in neighboring Clayton County, was also credited with helping these newcomers establish their place as Fayette area farmers.[133]

The Sion Bass and the Joel Epps families migrated from their original homes in Virginia and Georgia respectively, first to Indiana and then to Kewanee, Illinois. Joel Epps, a freeman, had married Melinda Bass in Illinois.[134] These African American pioneer families eventually relocated to Northeast Iowa during the summer of 1854 after spending nearly a decade in Indiana and a similar span of time in Illinois.[135] It appears the younger Sion Bass, a blacksmith, obtained his forty acres of land from the authority of the Script Warrant Act of 1850.[136] That act, along with the acts of 1850 and 1852, granted bounty land for service in all Indian wars fought from 1790 until the beginning of the Civil War.

Several factors precipitated the younger Sion Bass's, his son Thomas Right's (T. R.), and Joel Epps's settlement in Iowa. Their Illinois community consisted of about eighty African Americans and could not easily expand, as inexpensive, good land was no longer available. They desired not to intermarry those within their enclave.[137] And attending school in Illinois was not an option for their children until the Basses had started a school associated with their United Brethren Church, the center of community life.[138]

Upon receipt of an 1852 letter from Reverend David Watrous, the younger Sion Bass, his son T. R., and a friend, Benjamin Anderson, traveled to explore the area northwest of the Volga River. Seeing timber near the river and tall grass prairie spreading beyond, they staked claims on that government land, returned to Illinois, and prepared to move.[139] After settling in Iowa, they discovered challenges breaking the prairie land. It required a team of four or five yoke of oxen and a plow that cut a furrow from twenty to thirty inches wide. Most farmers did not have eight to ten oxen, so neighbors helped one another, or they hired people to open the ground at three dollars per acre. If they could afford a twelve-inch plow costing twenty dollars, they might have broken the prairie with a single team of horses.[140]

Heartened by the positive comments of their friend Sion Bass regarding the area, Joel Epps and Seymour Wilson investigated Fayette County land in the spring of 1853. After Epps staked his claim, he wrote, encouraging other family members to come to Iowa. They did, and in three years, there were fifty-nine African Americans in the settlement, constituting less than 4 percent of Westfield Township's population.[141] By 1868, the population had grown to seventy, and in 1880, it had reached its peak of nearly 120, including members of the Collins family.

These African Americans were a small minority. However, racial prejudice surfaced even though their white neighbors purportedly didn't believe in slavery or racial differences.[142] William Loren Katz, award-winning author of African American history, explained the Bass families' reception and their adaptation to Northeast Iowa as follows:

> From Illinois, Bass sons led half of the original family, including more than a dozen school-age children, to Iowa. When they first appeared in Fayette, whites were antagonistic, and the community decided to keep to itself. With the Reverend Watrous as their minister, the settlement soon brought in successful crops, and built schools, and people made friends.[143]

> Because the Basses and other African American families proved they were as intelligent, progressive, frugal, and hard working as the European immigrants settling in the county, prejudice eventually died away and they were accepted.[144]

It is noteworthy during that time period, very few white people in the Midwest had met an African American, and their interactions with slaves were almost nonexistent.[145] "In the 19th century, the belief in black inferiority was virtually universal among whites, with the exception of abolitionists and some antislavery people."[146]

Illustrating the attitude of early prejudice is a story one of Fayette's older residents heard in her youth. She explained shortly after the first African Americans arrived in the Fayette area, they started their own Pleasant Hill Cemetery. It is located northeast of Fayette on a beautiful, wooded ridge and across the road from where the Stone School House stood. Joel

Epps donated that land after his friend Seymour Wilson died in a well cave-in north of Albany. Wilson had to be buried on his claim because the township's cemetery boards wouldn't let him or other African Americans be buried with the whites. Eventually, Wilson's remains were moved to the Pleasant Hill Cemetery.[147] "African-American communities often had to organize their own cemeteries because it was illegal to bury African Americans in some town cemeteries" in Iowa.[148] For many years, a portion of Fayette's older whites unfortunately called the cemetery Blackberry Hill. This picturesque cemetery dotted with gray granite headstones and nestled among juniper trees continues to be well maintained by descendants of the early settlers buried there.

During that period, the African Americans in Fayette fortunately did not have to live in fear of the Ku Klux Klan (KKK), founded on December 24, 1865, in Pulaski, Tennessee. The KKK formed because the Southern whites feared the freed African Americans would retaliate and attempt to take their property. Years later, in 1920, after Susan completed her missionary service in Africa, the KKK came to Iowa and had followers in various locations, including Sioux City, Des Moines, Ottumwa, and Davenport.[149] Northeast Iowa locations included Mason City, Waterloo, Vinton, Dubuque, Elkader, and Independence.[150] Oelwein was the site of Klan activities in southern Fayette County in 1923.[151] Their primary targets were Catholics, Jews, immigrants, and African Americans. Likely they were thwarted in the Fayette area because organizations opposing them, such as the Masons, Farm Bureau, and the American Legion, were strong in this farming community.

Exploring Isaac's Land: Treading Where Susan Trod

Limited information is available regarding the life of the Collins family between their arrival in Fayette County and the day four years later when Isaac purchased land in Westfield Township. It is believed he earned the payment money working as a sharecropper for Peter Bass, a relative of Sion Bass.[152] A trip to the Fayette County Recorder's Office yielded a warranty deed filed on October 19, 1869, one week after Isaac, in hand, had paid twenty-five dollars for six and a half acres.[153] Twenty-four years after his release from servitude, he became a land owner. The following February 19, he purchased ten acres adjacent to his initial acquisition and recorded that warranty deed two days later.[154] The land Isaac owned and farmed is now part of the Volga River Recreation Area. In August 2016, an acre of land located two miles east of the recreation area had an asking price of $2,357 per acre.

When Isaac, Sarah, and children moved to their property is unknown. However, the 1870 United States Federal Census data collected on August 2 listed them in Illyria Township east of Lima and approximately three miles from their newly acquired land located in Westfield Township.[155] Illyria Township is adjacent to and east of Westfield Township. The family had reported personal property valued at $225.[156]

On August 13, 2009, my husband and I began exploring Isaac's land. It was a typical Iowa summer day, hot and humid, as we stepped out of our air-conditioned car. We sprayed our clothing with bug repellent to ward off mosquitoes and ticks, a protection the Collins family did not have. Nor was it available for Susan when she lived in Africa and experienced the threat of malaria and other insect-borne diseases, such as sleeping sickness and yellow fever. Then we walked along an abandoned, tree-lined road that begins about two miles northeast of Fayette to reach Isaac's property.

Copies of the properties' legal descriptions from the deed records helped us pinpoint the location utilizing Google Earth. Photos taken in 2009 by the United States Department of Agriculture (USDA) Farm Service Agency provided a logical beginning point for our search of the land Isaac had owned nearly 150 years ago. There was an alfalfa field located at the center of the section Isaac owned. Our resources were a handheld GPS, a compass, a camera, enthusiasm, and a desire to explore Susan's father's land.

After checking coordinates, we paced off the estimated distance to the northeast corner of the Collins's property. Gnats swarmed around our heads. Exhilaration overcame us when we spotted an ancient red maple tree with two strands of barbed wire grown deeply into its bark. A tree-age estimation formula indicated that rugged tree sprang to life in 1837, fourteen years prior to Susan's birth. The coordinates verified the tree marked one corner of the property. Careful observation provided evidence of wire attached to rotting wooden posts. We followed the wire remnants, stepping over fallen trees, catching our hiking boots in twisted grape vines, descending a small vale, and ascending its western slope. Near the approximated corner location, we found another tree harboring barbed wire strands. That was the northwest corner of Isaac's ten-acre purchase. Counting our steps, we continued west the estimated distance of the north boundary line of the six-acre plot. Scouring that area did not yield any observable corner marker. Retracing our steps to the northwest boundary of the ten acres, we pointed the compass south, trying to follow its line the length of the property. Underbrush and trees impeded our vision. We were disappointed when we did not find either a third corner post or evidence of a building site. With sweat running into our eyes and dripping off our noses, we ended that portion of property exploration to escape the ninety-degree temperature and drove directly to the Fayette County courthouse.

There we visited the recorder's, accessor's and treasurer's offices. Much to our disappointment, they did not have paperwork documenting building locations or type of construction. Because the northern two-fifths of the county was hilly and was timbered land, Isaac presumably cut and hewed trees growing on his property for the buildings.[157] Given the good relationships that had developed between the African Americans and the whites in the Albany neighborhood, I can imagine neighbors helping him with his construction projects.[158]

After opening up his land, Isaac might have planted wheat and some corn, oats, or hay. Fayette County settlers discontinued planting wheat between 1870 and 1880 because grasshoppers and cinch bugs decimated the crops. That was about the time commercial flour mills became prominent. As long as county farmers raised wheat, they took some to Hiram Marvin's mill on the Volga River near Albany to have it ground into flour.[159] A portion was often ground into meal.[160]

The next morning, spurred by thoughts of Susan's determination and accomplishments, my husband and I returned to continue our search for signs of a building site and perimeter markings. Descending the road bank and walking in ever-widening circles, we spotted a post with barbed wire attached, short tails of it jutting north and east. After adjusting the compass, we walked east and found a second wire-embraced wooden post matching the coordinates of Isaac's land.

With the boundaries of the property identified, we checked our accuracy by following a line as true north as possible back to the maple tree marker at the northeast boundary. This involved climbing up a steep road bank, avoiding the sting of nettles, and walking in a shaded area adjoining an alfalfa field in the ninety-two-degree noon heat. We returned to the mighty maple still standing watch over the land where Isaac had toiled to provide a living for his family, assisted by his wife and children.

Knowing of Susan's dedication to her missionary work in Africa, I felt compelled to search for the home site, attempting to model her staunchness when faced with a challenge. Walking south, we followed the east boundary. Nearing the road, we systematically cast our eyes around, examining the landscape for clues such as foundations, bits of metal, and broken pottery or glass. At last on a slight rise near the road, now used only by hikers and trail riders, possible clues emerged. We noticed an indentation several feet deep that might have been a root cellar. That site with different plant growth and grass had browned as the summer passed. Firm and compact ground revealed no evidence of tillage at any time.

The only possible proof of a building site is an approximate location in the 1879 Plat of Westfield Township. There is a square used to indicate building sites near the south end of Isaac's property where we saw the indentation. That square suggests he constructed a house and perhaps other farm buildings. Likely, the precise location of the homestead will never be determined. Perhaps I will have to be contented with the knowledge that I have trod where Susan walked and with the feeling of her presence when I reached the probable site of the Collins's family cabin.

Education Near Fayette but Where?

Susan was fourteen years old when the family arrived in the county, and she and her brothers attended a country school close to their home.[161] Prior to that time, school attendance rates for blacks was low, especially in the South. After the Civil War, black school enrollment rates rose quickly, increasing 24 percent between 1870 and 1880, when rates reached 34 percent.[162] The identity of which school they attended is uncertain. With three country schools near where they reportedly lived, they might have gone to any one of them. School attendance records for that time are not available in Fayette County. The choices were either the Lima, Frog Hollow, or Stone School House. Built in 1850, the Lima School may have been the closest, but there is uncertainty regarding where the Collins family lived upon arriving in the county. Some local historians have suggested Susan and her siblings attended the Frog Hollow School.

That seems unlikely, as documents discussing attitudes of Iowa's European immigrants regarding school integration from the late 1830s until the time of the Collins family arrival in 1865 demonstrated racist attitudes among the majority of Iowa's founders.[163] The 1839 passage of a law to establish schools in each county related only to white students' attendance; however, African Americans were expected to pay taxes to support the schools.[164] That attitude still prevailed when a similar law passed the Iowa legislature on January 28, 1847, stating schools should be available to whites between the ages of five and twenty-one years.[165] The Mann Report published in 1856 advocated education for all youth in Iowa, regardless of race. A number of Republicans supported this concept but were voted down in 1857. A year later, a law passed allowing educational opportunities for African Americans but in separate schools.[166] During the earlier period and into the 1850s and 1860s, there were small numbers of African Americans in Iowa. Some communities ignored the laws allowing both African American and white children to attend the same school. In 1860, twenty-three of thirty African American children of school age in Fayette County were enrolled.[167] These children and later Susan and her siblings were fortunate. In 1868, three years after their arrival in the Fayette area, Iowa outlawed segregated schools, the second state to do so. That was ninety years prior to the federal mandate requiring school desegregation.

It is speculated Susan's brothers attended the Stone School House, sometimes called the Stone House School, begun by the Sion Bass family upon their arrival in the mid-1850s. The 1868 Plat of Westfield Township shows the school located on the T. R. Bass property. Attending that school enabled more interaction among African American children. Walking to the school two miles north of Albany up a valley's tree-lined wagon trail was not considered difficult.[168]

A Fayette merchant, Hiram Waterbury, interested in the education of African American children, taught them reading and writing.[169] He operated a drug and book store and was Fayette postmaster from 1861 to 1876. Local, single white women later taught there. During this era and beyond, women had to stop teaching upon marriage. It was necessary for my mother to resign from her Fayette Elementary School teaching position in 1938 when she married.

The Stone School House constructed from local fieldstone also served as a church and community center for the Spring Valley Settlement surrounding it. Events held there throughout the years were political caucus meetings,[170] dances, and Shoe Box Socials,[171] sometimes used as fundraisers for school supplies and equipment. The school was built adjacent to the wagon road between Fayette and West Union and west of the Stonehouse Cemetery, now the Pleasant Hill Cemetery.[172]

The Collins family likely participated in the church services held in that stone structure.[173] Reverend David Watrous performed ministerial duties for the congregation until one year prior to the arrival of Isaac, Sarah, and children.[174] The church continued servings African Americans in the surrounding area until the early 1900s. Unknown is which minister or what circumstances influenced Susan to accept the precepts of the United Brethren Church. When Susan filled out the "Roll Call for Missionaries" after her return to Angola in 1902, she wrote that she became a Christian in 1873 at age twenty-two years.[175] Perhaps her sister Maranda's death earlier in the year led Susan to that decision, as Maranda was a member of that denomination.

In 2010, a Fayette friend, Vera Stepp Splinter, gave me a 1910–1911 Winter Term Stone School House Souvenir booklet her father, Atrus, had saved from his student days. Both African Americans and Caucasians were among the twenty-six students attending the school that term. By then, schools were in session for seven months. One student, Harry Bob Pond, wrote a poem describing the school.[176] This is valuable because pictures of the school seem to be nonexistent. The poem illustrates the amount of effort the Bass and Epps families dedicated, constructing the school from local materials. A wooden belfry holding a large bell beckoned the children to school and the Spring Valley residents to church services. Pond described walking across the doorstep rudely cut from a boulder and then through the stout oak door into the single room where pictures of Presidents George

Washington and Abraham Lincoln hung. His initials along with those of other boys were carved into the desks. Recalling the woodshed where they had played on rainy days, he lamented its deteriorating condition. When he wrote the undated poem, the bridge across the hollow was missing, and the creek southwest of the school was dry. Marguerite daisies with large golden hearts, considered rare in the area, grew near the school.[177]

The outside privies and the school were frigid in winter. One of Pond's schoolmates, Hollis Finch, told his son Bill, a classmate of mine, stories of trudging in the dark through deep, blowing snow to start the woodfire before the teacher and other students arrived. Hollis carried in enough wood supplied by local farmers and stored in a shed to keep the fire going during the day. He described sitting near the stove placed in the center of the room, which resulted in a hot face and a cold bottom. That contrasted with hot, late summer days when the only way to cool the room was wind blowing through the open windows. Hollis played at the neighboring Stepp farm with Atrus and knew his mother, Julia Graham, one of Susan's childhood friends.

Regardless of where Susan and her siblings continued their Iowa public country school education, they had the opportunity to feast their eyes on a variety wildflowers. Woodland flowers they would have seen include May apples, trillium, bloodroot, violets, Dutchman's breeches, and perhaps a rare yellow lady's slipper. There were putrid skunk cabbage growing in the swamps.

As country youth, the Collins children would have recognized songs of robins, cardinals, bluebirds, doves, western meadowlarks, and catbirds filling the air. They watched the tangled grass and weeds for signs of quail and wild turkey and learned how to find their nests when these game birds were flushed from their cover. Most local children were aware that coyotes, wolves, bobcats, and black bears had been spotted in the woods and grasslands where they walked and played.[178]

The Collins children and their schoolmates were expected to learn the basics of reading, writing, and arithmetic. Often, the only books in those early schools were brought by pupils from home. Eventually, McGuffey's Readers were used. Writing on their own chalkboards, reading aloud, and recitation were techniques used to assess students' knowledge.

As years passed, state officials decided country schools weren't efficient, and many closed when school districts merged. In 1920, the year Susan returned from Africa, the Stone School House bell no longer rang, calling children to class. With its closure, students living in Westfield Township District Number Four began attending the Fayette Consolidated Schools. Most Iowa country schools were closed by July 1, 1967, 101 years after Susan and her siblings begin attending school in Iowa.[179]

Desperately wanting to find some physical evidence of the Stone School House and its actual location, I searched plat books for ownership history. I learned the second owners of the Bass property where the school was built were William C. and Grace Finch, Hollis's parents. Hollis told Bill that after the school closed, his father had used its flat fieldstones as a foundation for a pig barn he constructed about two hundred yards south of the school's location.[180] This information led me and my friend Vera Stepp Splinter, who knew the current owners, on a search for that foundation on a November 2010 day, ninety years after the school had closed. Our breath hung in the air, and we saw corn husks pirouetting across the harvested field. We walked creating a grid pattern near the farm buildings but failed to find any structural remnants. Again, no success, as the earth did not give up any of its secrets.

We left the site feeling disappointed. The Stone School House had vanished into history, as had many aspects of Susan's early life. I wondered what else about Susan was hidden in Fayette, challenging me to discover. That is when I realized my research was still in its infancy. I desired answers about her educational attainment and accomplishments as a missionary. And I wanted to determine whether or not her ability to adjust to new environments and her dedication to her religious beliefs were characteristics that would lead to her future success.

4

<!-- ornament -->

The 1870s: Susan's Decade of Transitions

New Responsibilities and Opportunities Moving Forward

As a member of an Iowa farm family in the 1870s, there was no way to escape the work required to survive and hopefully to thrive. In 1873, a nationwide economic depression was especially hard on Iowa farmers. Susan's father managed to keep his land. During the decade, Susan experienced loss, the demands of becoming the only woman in her father's household until his remarriage, and the challenges of attending college. These circumstances required Susan to demonstrate grace, gumption, and grit that helped prepare her for a future in Africa, as yet not revealed.

The country was rebuilding after the Civil War and laying down railroad lines, making it easier for immigrants to move west and claim newly opened lands. Attending college became an increasing possibility for blacks and women. The Panic of 1873 illustrated economic inequality and caused dire situations for many southern African Americans.

That was the future her brother Albert faced as a child. Susan, age sixteen when he was born in 1867,[181] likely was expected to assume some responsibility for his care. Their mother was forty-two and beginning to age after giving birth to seven children in twenty-three years while simultaneously tackling the heavy tasks required of a frontier wife.

A mystery arose when I reviewed the 1870 and 1880 United States Federal Census data for the Collins family in both Iowa and Wisconsin. I could not find a female child named Indiana Collins listed in either state. It was as if she had totally vanished! Finding out what had happened to her became an obsession with me during a four-year search as I tried to determine her fate.

I wondered if she had stayed in Wisconsin and either had died or married someone, changing her last name. Barry, a high school friend who has become a Fayette historian, suggested she might be buried in an unmarked grave in the Lima Cemetery established in 1865. The first clue emerged when I discovered a feature story about Susan in a yellowed, brittle copy of the *Fayette Reporter* dated June 18, 1908. The article recounted aspects of Susan's life in Fayette prior to leaving for the Dakota Territory in 1882.[182] It stated she had buried her mother, a brother, and two sisters in Iowa but didn't list burial sites. I knew her mother, brother William, and sister Maranda were buried at the Lima Cemetery. But where was Indiana, one of the two sisters not mentioned by name?

Joe, another high school friend, unknowingly provided the link I needed. In my initial meeting with Merle Sternberg, she had told me Joe lived in the house Susan purchased for her retirement home while she was in Africa. Merle thought Joe had the abstracts for the house. On a sunny July 2013 morning, after numerous attempts, I found him at his Fayette home. We exchanged a few pleasantries, and then I asked if he had the abstracts and for permission to borrow them. He thought for a moment, responding, "Yes." Then I queried, "Can I take them with me and make copies?" After a long pause, he finally said, "Yes, but if you lose them, it will cost you a bundle of money to replace them."

I took the risk and arranged a return time. My brain was in high gear when I dashed to the car and sped to the local library, where I read the two-inch stack of documents and copied pertinent pages, those detailing the sale of the house after Susan's death in 1940. The missing clue was finally discovered in a legal document stating that Susan's siblings, including Martha Indiana Collins Thompson, had left no heirs. I felt joyous when I returned the abstracts to Joe the next day.

A recheck of the 1870 United States Federal Census for Illyria Township divulged a Martha Thompson living with William Thompson near Isaac and Sarah Collins. Martha and William were married on February 11, 1870, in Taylorsville, Iowa, by Rev. O. R. Robbins.[183] The Lima Cemetery Burial List showed a grave marker for Martha I. Thompson, who died on February 19, 1874, four years after her marriage. When visiting the cemetery, I had always ignored the second tombstone west of Susan's even though it was adjacent to the one marking the burial site of Sarah, Maranda, and William. Its aging condition had made it seem out of place, but finally I understood why it was in this grouping. Using my fingernails, I scraped off the tenaciously attached yellow lichen until I could clearly identify Martha's name. I felt as if I had found a long-lost relative.

My heart went out to Susan, her father, and two younger brothers because that meant they had lost four, not three, family members in four years. Maranda died February 10, 1873, Sarah died January 18, 1874, and Martha Indiana died one month after her mother at her parents' home in rural Fayette County. Three years later, William died on March 15.[184] Their deaths were caused by consumption,[185] now called tuberculosis. Considered a disease of poverty, it often resulted from living in close, unventilated quarters such as log cabins. People of that era, unaware of how germs spread, contaminated others when sharing a common drinking cup or dipper hanging on a nail by a water pail.

Sarah Collins was forty-nine when she died. An illegible and partially hidden inscription on her granite gravestone required an hour pulling weeds and scraping off lichen to see carved there, "She has done what she could." Probably this tribute was Susan's idea as she recognized the sacrifices her mother had made for the family, just as Jesus recognized the woman who poured expensive perfume on his head at Bethany. He replied to those criticizing the woman, "She has done what she could; she has anointed my body beforehand for burial."[186]

The death of her mother and older sisters left Susan, age twenty-two, as the only female in the Collins household. What was she to do? How could she best help her father and brothers, William, Richard, and Albert, only seven years old?

Likely she stayed with them and did not immediately return to the family of Reverend Jason Paine and his wife, Margaret, for whom she had worked in Monticello, Iowa, after Maranda died.[187] Susan had cared for the Paine's son Charles and newborn Amy until her mother became ill and she went home to nurse her.[188] Later, she returned to the Paine household to assist at various times and locations when two more daughters, Louie Belle and Margaret, were born. She became very attached to the children. When Susan began working for the Paine family, no one knew it was the start of a lifelong friendship. That association changed Susan's life and led her to places and experiences she could not have imagined as a young girl.

Doors Open: Experiencing University Life

Living with the Jason Paine family may have provided the inspiration for Susan's nascent Christian work and desire to further her education. The Paines resided in Fayette in 1876, and that September, Jason became a member of Upper Iowa University's (UIU) Board of Trustees,[189] serving in this capacity for twenty-four years. In 1860, the Methodist Episcopal Church had decided to send preachers to the Dakota Territory.[190] Jason graduated from UIU in 1862, and in September, he and Margaret, his wife of one year, departed for the area that later became South Dakota. That was his first appointment by the church's Upper Iowa Conference, virtually a mission conference,[191] organized in 1856. He was assigned to visit the white settlements on a 150-mile circuit up and down the Missouri River.[192] Reverend Jason Paine and Margaret made their home at Fort Brule built in 1862 to protect pioneers against hostile Sioux Indians. The fort was dismantled in 1868. All that remains is a historical monument marking its location near Richland, South Dakota, which is about twenty-five miles northwest of Sioux City, Iowa.

During that time, Methodist Episcopal preachers were primarily evangelists calling people to salvation. "They were concerned about the many special problems which confronted the frontiersman. Methodists tend to become social activists, working to remake society, both by persuasion and by political activity."[193] One of the settlers' concerns was fear of attack by the Native Americans who were losing their land to them. Another concern was slavery and, "The circuit riders preached sermons against slavery and voted, at sessions of the annual conference, for resolutions condemning it as opposed to the spirit of Christianity."[194]

After one year of traveling across the frontier on horseback through swollen creeks and rivers, blinding snowstorms, and parching heat, Reverend Paine's body was weakened. The conference had him return to Iowa, where he was assigned to the Lowden Circuit, which required less time away from home.[195] Perhaps the stories of his Christian work opened Susan's mind and heart to the possibilities of a missionary career.

Jason's father, Cortez Paine, was an abolitionist and abhorred slavery, devoting his life to the betterment of all people. He instilled that attitude in his son, who saw potential in Susan and made it possible for her to become the first African American to enroll at Upper Iowa University in 1876.[196] At that time, she was among the 20–30 percent of African Americans in the country reported as literate, 20 percent in the 1870 United States Federal Census and 30 percent in the 1880 United States Federal Census. The university graduated its first women students in 1865 at a time when the proportion of women students in colleges was growing significantly.[197] Only 21 percent of college students were women in 1870. By 1880, that percent had increase to 36.[198] In 1855, an African American woman, Susan Mosely Grandison, became the first to earn a bachelor's degree from Iowa Wesleyan University.[199] The Civil War had provided impetus for inclusion of African Americans' enrollment at colleges and universities throughout the United States. But progress was slow and met resistance in small Iowa liberal arts colleges between the 1860s and 1880s, even though white female student numbers grew after the Civil War.

It is difficult to ascertain the number of African American students who attended Iowa's private white institutions between 1870 and 1881, which include the years Susan was at Upper Iowa University.[200] Very few African American students, usually only one or two, attended these colleges if accepted.[201] Grinnell College admitted its first African American student, a female in 1863, but no enrollment record exists. In 1879, Hannibal Kershaw become Grinnell's first African American graduate.[202] Cornell College's first African American student enrolled in 1870, but none graduated until 1900.[203]

George Washington Carver, born into slavery in Missouri, studied at Simpson College, Indianola, Iowa, in 1890–1891 before enrolling at

Iowa State College. Even though Carver was accepted at Iowa State, he was not allowed to live in the dormitory. Faculty recognized his talent and found an office in a classroom building where he stayed. While there, he worked as a janitor and participated in the WMCA and the National Guard. He earned a bachelor's degree in botany in 1894 and a master's of science in 1896. Soon after, he became Iowa State's first African American faculty member.[204] During that period, Iowa's predominately white institutions made exceptional contributions to educating African Americans.[205] However, Susan and other blacks were a small minority in higher education institutions.

Those students knew that a college education would help them move their race forward. The African Americans, especially women, who attended college at that time tended to live in an area with higher concentrations of their people. Families and friends lent social support and protection from gender and racial discrimination. Often, the students stayed with their families because campus housing was not available to them.[206] Others, as Susan did, lived with a white family and earned room and board.

The path Iowa African American women followed by first seeking admission to smaller private institutions of higher learning and later pursing admission to public institutions was replicated throughout the country.[207] This pattern started to change in 1908 in Iowa as African American women began to enroll in predominately white public colleges. Susan's cousin, Iva Joiner McClain, who received her bachelor's degree from the University of Iowa in 1917, was one of these women. Two years later, Iva became the first woman of her race to earn a master's of arts degree in Iowa.[208] Quite possibly, family stories of Susan's accomplishments were an impetus for Iva's academic attainments. About that time, social and racial climates on those campuses degenerated.[209] Between 1913 and 1946, African American women were not allowed to live in campus residence halls at the University of Iowa. To meet the female students' needs, the Iowa Federation of Colored Women's Clubs purchased a house at 942 Iowa Avenue in 1919 and maintained it until 1950.[210] Later, I discovered how Iva was involved in that process.

Key Events in Black Higher Education highlights a small number of African Americans breaking educational barriers even before Susan's birth. In 1799, John Chavis, a Presbyterian minister, was the first African

American on record to attend an American college or university, at what is now Washington and Lee University. In 1823, Alexander Lucius Twilight, attending Middlebury College in Vermont, became the first known African American to receive a bachelor's degree. Twenty-six years later, Charles L. Reason broke a barrier as the first African American professor at a United States integrated institution of higher education in Central College, McGrawville, New York.[211]

The first African American woman completing any college work was Lucy Ann Stanton, who one year before Susan's birth in 1851, received a certificate in literature from Oberlin College. She is considered a graduate of the college but did not receive a bachelor's degree. Twelve years later, Mary Jane Patterson, listed as the first African American woman to earn a bachelor's degree, graduated from Oberlin and entered the teaching profession. Other notable educational accomplishments for African American women during the nineteenth century include Charlotte E. Ray earning a law degree from Howard University in 1872, Lutie L. Lytle becoming a Central Tennessee College law professor in 1897, and Mary Annette Anderson being elected to Phi Beta Kappa in 1899 at Middlebury College. Three African American women, Eva B. Dykes, Radcliffe College; Sadie T. Mossell Alexander, University of Pennsylvania; and Georgiana R. Simpson, University of Chicago, earned their doctoral degrees in 1921, the year after Susan's retirement.[212]

Susan set an example for African American women who followed in her footsteps at Upper Iowa University, in the state, and in Angola, Africa. In 2018, Upper Iowa's African American student population was 18.9 percent, and the female population was 61.9 percent. Susan demonstrated that an African American student from humble beginnings could succeed in a university program. She took risks, completing her normal Training Certification just as her father had done, moving his family to Wisconsin, enlisting in the Thirty-Eighth Infantry Regiment of Wisconsin during the Civil War, and then seeking a better life in Iowa.

When Susan began her classes at Upper Iowa University (UIU), it had operated for twenty-one years under the auspices of the Methodist Episcopal Church, having begun as the Fayette Seminary of the Upper Iowa Conference. It opened on January 7, 1857, and by year's end, the board of trustees had changed the name to UIU.[213] Because Fayette did not have a high school until 1882, the university preparatory school helped equip local students for college. In 1876, Susan began a one-year course in the English Department to prepare for admission to the Normal Training Program and for a possible career as a teacher.[214] University catalogs show Susan's enrollment from 1876 to 1879, listing her as Susie A. Collins, Fayette. Beginning in 1877, she is listed in the Normal Course of Study.[215]

During the years Susan traversed the campus as a student, Clark, Union, Madison, and Washington Streets provided the perimeter for the two-block square campus. It was still that size in the 1950s and dotted with buildings. When Susan attended classes, the only edifice on campus was "Old Sem," later identified as College Hall and currently known as Alexander-Dickman Hall. Its construction began in 1855, four years after Susan's birth.[216] The completed building housed classrooms, administrative offices, the president's quarters, and student rooms.[217] The bell ensconced in the cupola rang across campus, "to call classes to order, signal chapel, and to provide the time of day."[218] College Hall served as a church for the Methodist Episcopal townspeople and those in the nearby countryside.

The beautiful, white, native limestone, three-story, rectangular-shaped building gracing the campus is a Northeast Iowa landmark. It is situated high on a hill above the Volga River that loops lazily around Fayette, making its way to the northeast near the former villages of Albany and Lima, both of which were important to Susan in her formative years. People living in the Albany area, several miles northeast of Fayette, had to ford the river at the east end of Water Street to reach Fayette when they came for supplies.

The west side of the campus, one block east of Main Street, was a dirt road in 1857. Few trees adorned the campus. Soon after UIU's founding, enrollment grew to several hundred, complementing Fayette's small population of nearly seven hundred. Canvas-topped stagecoaches daily traversed routes across the area from McGregor situated along the Mississippi, from Postville, and also from Independence to Fayette. The drivers brought people, mail, and supplies over the rough terrain covered with tall prairie grass.

When fall turned into winter, Susan dashed from the Paine home in Fayette, where she was working, to attend classes in College Hall. Some days, she had to force her small frame through snowdrifts when winds howled across College Hill. Imagine her preparing each day for the coursework required for the two-year, six-term curriculum, designed to equip students for teaching. The thorough and practical two-year course of study required one-term courses in Analysis, Parsing (grammar), Criticism; Physiology; Comparative Physiology; Physical Geography; Constitution of the United States; and School Economy. Two-term courses were English Grammar; Orthography, where students learned the rules of spelling, writing, and reading; History; Political Geography; Penmanship; Science; and the Art of Teaching Arithmetic. Then as now, the importance of math was recognized, and students took three terms of arithmetic. Frequent oral exercises and written examinations served to evaluate a student's knowledge.[219] Given the possibility students could not afford or obtain textbooks, professors often wrote information on a chalkboard, a teaching tool introduced in the early 1800s.

Catalogs revealed tuition for the Normal Training Course was six dollars per term, one-third of the school year.[220] Board with private families ranged from $2.50 to $3.00 per week or in clubs at $2.00 to $2.50 per week.[221] Completing the course of study yielded students a certificate and recommendations for available teaching positions.

The belief is that Susan completed the program in 1879 at the age of twenty-eight. Most university academic records for the period, including Susan's, were destroyed by a fire in the library. Therefore, her actual graduation date and course grades are not available.[222]

Susan and her classmates had to abide by rigorous university rules. Influence of the church contributed to the disciplined atmosphere. Some of the rules included remaining on campus during all class times; taking exams at the conclusion of the academic year; attending chapel each day; no drinking, dancing, or betting; behaving in a cultured manner; and only mingling with the opposite sex in the parlor. Failure to follow these rules could have resulted in explosion from the university.[223] Imagine students of today adhering to those rules!

Early campus publications and local newspapers during the timeframe of Susan's university enrollment failed to provide clues regarding Susan's extracurricular life. Given her housekeeping responsibilities to Fayette families, including the Paines and to her father and brothers, she had little time for club and social activities. During the period when Susan and other first-generation African American females were on private Iowa campuses, there was less resistance to their participation in academic endeavors and social activities than for later generations of African American students.[224] It would be interesting to know how well Susan was accepted as the first and only African American student during the time she was enrolled at UIU. What were her thoughts and feelings about the experience? As she stepped onto the campus for the first time, she was making the way and setting an example for other African American students to follow. She exhibited strength and determination at a time when there were many challenges in her life, but she didn't allow them to hold her back.

The barrenness of the Upper Iowa University campus Susan knew is now a mecca with stately white pines shadowing wide, hosta-lined sidewalks in the summer. These sidewalks connect the new buildings needed to meet the demands of increased student enrollment. In the fall, bright orange and red maple leaves float gently through the air, landing on neatly manicured campus grounds that have doubled in size since Susan's college days. A large metal peacock, the university mascot, with widely spread tail feathers welcomes those who approach campus from the northwest.

After her university experience, Susan lived in Monticello, Iowa, with the Paine family and helped Margaret with the children and household work during portions of 1879 and 1880, while Reverend Jason Paine was assigned to the local Methodist Episcopal Church.[225] At the time the 1880 United States Federal Census was taken in June, she was living with her father and stepmother, Hannah, at their home in Westfield Township.[226] Hannah, born in Kentucky in 1815, and Isaac were married in 1879. That September, he prepared a will, leaving the farm to Albert Collins, who was twelve. Other assets were left to Hannah, with the expectation she would remain at the farm until her death if she outlived Isaac. Neither Susan nor Richard were mentioned in his will. By today's standards, that may seem harsh. Perhaps Isaac recognized Susan's self-sufficiency and knew she was capable of surviving on her own. It is probable that Richard, twenty-one years old, was working on the F. P. Gaynor farm in Smithfield Township, where he was listed as a laborer in the 1880 United States Federal Census.[227] Because he was earning his own livelihood, Isaac likely felt no need to provide for him.

During the 1870s when Susan experienced many transitions, so did Fayette, Iowa, and the nation. Fayette was incorporated as a town in 1874, and the first mayor was Charles Hoyt. That year, the *Fayette News* issued its first eight-column sheet on August 5. It was enlarged on September 23 to a nine-column journal, had a circulation of five hundred copies, and was Republican (Lincoln's party) in politics. Two years earlier, a private bank had been established.[228]

The first transcontinental railroad was completed in 1869, and other tracks continued to be laid into the 1870s. Fayette County residents begin asking for railroads in the 1850s, but no progress was made until after 1870 when various lines were laid.[229] Railroad development in Iowa provided employment for African Americans who worked on construction projects and in the rail yards. Others were either waiters on the trains or porters and were found in cities like Waterloo, Cedar Rapids, and Des Moines.[230]

In 1873, Jay Cooke and Company, a major railroad financier, realized it had overextended and declared bankruptcy. That precipitated the national Panic of 1873, which affected nearly everyone and exposed the effects of economic inequality. The wages of workers decreased by as much as 25 percent. For many, it meant unemployment, loss of a home, and food scarcity causing malnutrition.[231] Every region of the country suffered, including Iowa farmers, as crop and livestock prices fell. In addition to falling grain prices, farmers such as Isaac had their wheat crops wiped out due to insect infestations. Then they began growing oats and corn.

African Americans, especially in the South, were hit hard both financially and socially. The Freedman's Savings and Trust Company went bankrupt, and more than $7 million in savings was lost.[232] Northerners focusing on their new, harsh economic realities lost concern for Southern racism, and white supremacist groups resumed harassing African Americans. The Compromise of 1877 pulled federal troops out of Southern states' politics and ended the Reconstruction era. Freed African Americans in the South had to fend for themselves. With Southern whites asserting their power, many African Americans became sharecroppers and were not much better off than when they were slaves. These events led to Jim Crow laws, passed primarily in the South. These laws legalized segregation and were enforced until the Civil Rights Act of 1964 was passed. Even though segregation was not legal in Iowa, some communities separated African Americans from white people.[233] The Act (Pub. L. 88-352, 78 Stat. 241, enacted July 2, 1964) was a landmark civil rights and US labor law that outlawed discrimination based on race, color, sex, or national origin.

During that depression, people in the east became more desperate for economic security and began migrating to the Great Plains and the far west. They were joined by Europeans who felt the effect of the financial panic in their home countries.

It appears those changes had little effect on Susan and the residents of Northeast Iowa. They carried on with their work, raised their own food, and were able to maintain ownership of their property. Susan had tended her mother and three siblings as they faced death. The skills she acquired at that time later guided her when nursing her ailing missionary colleagues and children in Angola. She had experienced the never-ending labor of rural life and worked as a domestic servant caring for the Paine children. Later, Paine daughters Margaret and Amy Leigh became her lifeline in Fayette. With her strong desire to further her education, Susan didn't realize she was a role model for young black women. Susan was loved and protected by her family and the local community. That changed in 1882 when she decided to leave her safe environment and move to the Dakota Territory.

5

An Independent Woman: Leaving Iowa

Away from Family: Off to Dakota Territory

Susan's reasons for moving from Iowa to the Dakota Territory, which opened on March 2, 1861, remain obscure. Perhaps stories of her father's Civil War experience and Captain Kingman's sailing adventures enticed her to explore the western frontier. When she arrived in Huron in 1882, she found a rough frontier town.[234] The Sioux and other Native Americans had recently been moved farther west, but there were still occasional incidents between them and the settlers in the eastern portion of the territory.

At the beginning of the 1880s, Susan was working in the Fayette House Hotel for owner Hiram S. Canfield. Her supervisor was Captain "Cap" Warner E. Kingman, clerk and assistant manager. He had assumed those roles late in the 1870s. That large, bewhiskered man with a foghorn voice had traveled the world on many ships and experienced varied cultures. In the evenings, he regaled guests and staff with tales of his seafaring experiences, including sailing to India.[235] Perchance it was those stories that awakened Susan's desire to see more of the country.

The hotel, situated at the corner of Main and State Streets, was an area hub for travelers, who in the early days arrived by stagecoach, buggies, and wagons. The drivers would swing up to the hotel platform, reining in the horses with a flourish, eager to share news from Independence, a small community along the Wapsipinicon River. The thirty-one-mile journey from the south sometimes entailed crossing creeks at flood stage and breaking through drifts while fierce winds blew across the barren land. After traveling salesmen and political and social dignitaries disembarked to enter the lobby, they relaxed on a horsehair upholstered davenport brought from Dubuque via a freight wagon in 1856 four years after the hotel opened. Trains did not begin traveling through Fayette until 1873. That is when Mr. Canfield began driving his horse-drawn bus four blocks south to the depot to pick up the passengers.[236]

One of Susan's duties might have been polishing the brass candlesticks Captain Kingman set with military precision on the reception counter. When guests were ready to retire for the night, he led them to their rooms, holding the lit candles to guide them. They were allowed to keep them for illumination at night. Eventually, kerosene lamps replaced the candles. Susan helped clean the hotel's twenty first- and second-floor rooms and the third-floor ballroom used for social and political events.

Susan may have tired of the work and left Iowa because no other type of employment was available to her. That could explain why she didn't extend her university education beyond her Normal Training Certification. More likely, according to Amy Leigh Paine's recollection, Susan did not have funds to take more training.[237] No record of Susan teaching in Iowa public schools has been discovered, likely because opportunities for African American women teachers were limited to three counties and did not include Fayette County.[238] Thus her struggle for employment opportunities commensurate with her education were limited. It was frequently the case for African Americans in Iowa and the nation who struggled to attain an education and the economic success they desired. That is likely why in the summer of 1881, Booker T. Washington opened the Tuskegee Institute for African American students, where he served as an instructor at the Alabama-based academic institution.

Even with these limitations, it seems surprising Susan wasn't sought to teach at the Stone School House, attended by both African American and white children, especially since the school was founded by black leaders living in the Spring Valley Neighborhood. Possibly county politics shut that door on her. Or it may have been when she completed her higher education, certain occupations in Iowa, such as teaching and nursing, were basically closed to African American women of all generations.[239] That prohibition remained in effect for fifty years.[240]

Maybe she felt her father and fifteen-year-old brother, Albert, were being well cared for by her stepmother, Hannah, and she was no longer needed. Possibly, Susan and Hannah did not relate well. Or perhaps by 1882, Albert had moved to Black Hawk County, Iowa, to live with Indiana's husband, William. Perchance Susan wanted a life independent of family, and she thought the expanding frontier had more possibilities for an African American woman, such as a teaching position or serving as a missionary for Native Americans. Maybe she followed a man, hoping to marry, but that didn't happen, creating the reason she remained single. Or she may have traveled with another single female who wanted to establish a claim. Whatever factors precipitated her move to Huron, the decision began opening doors for her to explore an even larger world, one away from the safety and security that Fayette and surrounding communities provided. Regardless of her reasons, Susan traveled to frontier country and faced the awaiting challenges.

The Dakota Territory, like Wisconsin and Iowa, had been inhabited by Native Americans for centuries. In 1743, the first white men arrived there from France. By the 1700s, the Sioux Nation was a dominant force in the northern plains. When Lewis and Clark traveled up and down the Missouri River Valley, going to and from the west coast between 1804 and 1806, the Sioux Indians allowed their passage. Between 1855 and 1857, Lt. G. K. Warren, a civil engineer, had explored and surveyed parts of the Dakota Territory and Nebraska as the first step for settlement.[241] Violent clashes developed as more land-hungry settlers moved into Sioux Territory when it was opened for settlement in 1854.[242] But that was hampered by economic depressions and panics in 1857 and 1873.[243]

Between 1862 and 1865, there was a Santee Sioux uprising, originating in Minnesota and spreading to Dakota Territory. To ease tensions, a treaty was signed in 1868 with the Sioux at Ft. Laramie, preserving the Great Sioux Reservation.[244] However, when gold was later discovered in the Black Hills, miners and prospectors went into Red Cloud's territory. Those

Native Americans fought to protect their lands from gold seekers flocking to the area.[245] With encroachment upon their reservation, they fought back, and war began in 1876, the year Susan had entered preparatory school at Upper Iowa University. A year later, the United States government took away part of the reservation given to the Sioux Nation so Americans could more safely search for gold in the Black Hills.[246] Thus, in 1882, when Susan moved to Huron, she once again arrived at a location where Native Americans had recently been removed for the benefit of settlers and, in this case, also for miners.

The Dakota Territory, encompassing present-day North and South Dakota and much of Montana and Wyoming, was called the Great American Desert. It is questionable why anyone would have elected to leave the fertile farm land in Indiana, Illinois, and Iowa to live in this semiarid land west of the Big Sioux and Missouri Rivers, where rain was often scarce and irrigation was required. People first settled along rivers and streams near readily available wood and water.

Along with settlers came Methodist Episcopal Church (ME) missionary circuit riders. At the August 1860 session of the church's Upper Iowa Conference sessions, the decision was made to appoint a preacher to the area between the Big Sioux and Missouri Rivers.[247] The first appointee was Reverend S. W. Ingham. His circuit included Elk Point, Vermillion, Yankton, and Bon Homme. Brule was added later. During the two years Ingham was in the territory, he traveled along the Missouri River to Richland and Fort Randall and then north to Sioux Falls and Canton. Reverend Jason Paine, Susan's mentor, was his successor.[248]

By 1871, the number of charges and members had increased, and a Yankton District was organized. Shortly afterward, due to rapid population growth, a Huron District was formed. In 1880, a Black Hills Mission was created to serve the western part of the territory. On October 9, 1885, the Dakota Conference of the Methodist Episcopal Church became official. In years following, the church growth kept pace with population increases.[249]

That expansion was largely due to railroad construction after the Native American removal from the eastern Dakota Territory, as defined by the Fort Laramie Treaty of 1868.[250] The Chicago, Milwaukee & St. Paul and the Chicago & Northwestern lines had the most impact.[251] These two companies were strong social and economic forces by the time Susan traveled to Huron. Railroads came slowly to what became South Dakota because the larger land grants to rail companies were in the northern portion of Dakota Territory.[252]

Lack of transportation for people and products was not the only factor impeding settlement. Droughts and locust infestation in the 1860s and 1870s and the Panics of 1857 and 1863 caused low farm commodity prices. With few trees in this desertlike territory, building materials were limited. Other impediments included lack of fencing supplies, such as barbed wire and farming equipment, suited to the flatter terrain of the Great Plains.[253]

A New Frontier: Railroad Expansion and Settlement

By 1878, farming conditions had begun to improve, and the Chicago, Milwaukee & St. Paul Railway and the Chicago & Northwestern Railway Companies realized it was time to expand from Iowa into the southern part of the territory. With amazing speed, between 1878 and 1887, workers laid 2,179 miles of track.[254] The Chicago & Northwestern Railway crossed the country from east to west. Built farther west and going north and south was the Chicago, Milwaukee & St. Paul Railway.[255] Their completion spurred the Great Dakota Boom from 1878 to 1887.[256]

Partially stimulating that boom in which Susan and those who, according to local lore, traveled with her from Fayette participated[257] were the publicity efforts of the railroads. In an attempt to substantiate claims that Susan had traveling companions, the author compared names in the 1880 United States Federal Census for Westfield and Illyria Townships and later census and Bureau of Land Management (BLM) records for Beadle Country, where Susan lived. No name matches were found. Oh, to know what Susan read, studied, or thought that motivated her move to that undeveloped Dakota Territory, a portion of which became South Dakota in 1889, four years after she left Huron.

Railroad company posters displayed in the east and in Europe touted cheap and reliable transportation and inexpensive land that would yield bountiful harvests. Examples of the farm products grown in the territory were exhibited in railroad cars traveling in the east and Midwest. Another marketing technique was publishing letters of praise written by farmers in the territory and distributing them to potential settlers in booklet form.[258] Those efforts attracted large numbers of immigrants who wanted to farm. They were from Canada, the eastern United States, and many European countries, including Austria, Czechoslovakia, Denmark, Germany, Finland, Holland, Norway, Sweden, and Russia. The first Chinese and Irish immigrants to arrive in the Dakota Territory worked primarily for the railroad companies.[259]

There is no known existing correspondence from Susan to describe the 443-mile train ride she likely experienced between Fayette and Huron. She was able to enjoy the same travel privileges as white people due to an Iowa Supreme Court ruling in 1873. In *Conger v. The North Western Union Packet Company*, the court determined there should be no separate facilities for people based upon race.[260]

Susan probably boarded a Chicago, Milwaukee, & St. Paul train that went through Fayette and then northwest to Donnan, Hawkeye, and Waucoma to Jackson Junction. From there, the route went to Beloit, Iowa, and across the Missouri River to Canton, Nebraska; to Sioux Falls, Dakota Territory; north to Brookings; and west to Huron, named after a tribe of Sioux Indians.[261] She would have seen the terrain change from prairie to rolling hills, to cliffs along the Missouri River, and then more rolling hills and ponds created from buffalo wallows scattered throughout a nearly treeless landscape.

While Susan journeyed, she benefitted from comforts such as stream heat, plumbing, and electricity. Often, seats were upholstered rather than wooden benches pushed against the walls, like those in the earlier emigrant trains.[262] A clerestory roof allowed sunlight and fresh air to enter. Because food was expensive and not available on all trains, Hannah may have packed a basket of sandwiches and dried fruit. When Susan's train pulled into Huron's depot in Beadle County, Dakota Territory, she saw a frontier town less developed than Fayette had been upon her arrival seventeen years earlier. The county was organized in 1879, and Huron selected as its county seat.

Curious to discover if the area we know as South Dakota had been hospitable to African Americans prior to Susan's residence led to further exploration. The first African American in South Dakota was York, who traveled with the Lewis and Clark Expedition between 1804 and 1806.

He was Clark's servant and the first black man to cross the United States. The Indians were fascinated by his ebony skin.[263] Nearly fifty years later, in 1861, William Jayne, the first Dakota Territory governor appointed by Lincoln, brought forward a bill asking the legislature to prohibit slavery. Defeated in 1862, African Americans suffered from legal discrimination until 1868, when laws were passed allowing the men voting rights and their children access to education.[264]

However, when Susan arrived in Huron, African Americans were still prohibited from interracial marriage. South Dakota did not legalize it until 1957, just ten years before the US Supreme Court ruled the state bans on interracial marriage violated the Fourteenth Amendment of the United States Constitution. But even with certain legal rights, the acceptance of African Americans varied throughout the territory. People in the eastern portion rather than the western portion were more willing to give them an opportunity to succeed based upon merit rather than race.[265]

Suffrage for African American males and school access for their children may have encouraged their entry into the Dakota Territory. Even so, their numbers were small, reaching only ninety-four by 1870, less than 1 percent of the thirteen thousand population.[266] Some worked on Missouri River steamboats, and others were in the military or mined for gold in the Black Hills.[267] Nat Love, a cowboy in the Deadwood area until 1889, later became a Pullman porter and traveled on trains across the west.[268] Between 1880 and 1900, the number of blacks in the Dakota Territory nearly doubled.[269] Approximately one in ten homesteaders were women. Researchers, including Lindgren writing about ethnic women homesteading, did not include data on African American women in the Dakotas.[270] There were likely very few, based upon only 401 blacks in the Dakotas in 1880.[271]

In the mid-1880s, troubles began in western Dakota when some of the townspeople of Sturgis inflamed sentiment against African American troops.[272] These attitudes likely caused some African Americans to settle in rural isolated areas such as Sully County, about one hundred miles northwest of Huron. In 1883, one year after Susan's arrival in Huron, Norvel Blair's sons Benjamin and Patrick scouted land in the county and settled near Fairbank.[273] The elder Blair, his wife, and other children soon followed, and the colony that once numbered as many as two hundred had begun to thrive.[274] In 1908, Susan's cousin John A. Joiner[275] and his wife, Margaret, had become part of the Sully County African American Community.[276] Their granddaughters Iva Joiner McClain and her sister Marjorie moved to Fairbank with them. They had started living with their grandparents after their mother, Mary Joiner McClain, a graduate of Highland Park College in Des Moines, died in August 1897.[277] The girls attended elementary school in South Dakota, and Iva completed two years of high school before returning to Des Moines in 1908.[278]

However, "Huron was born to the accompaniment of squeaking wagon wheels"[279] as settlers journeyed west. The first platting by the Chicago & Northwestern Railway Company occurred on May 10, 1880. That process continued until August 1882 when the last railway addition was finished and the town totaled seventy blocks. Private citizens platted other areas. Many Civil War veterans arrived and were employed to build a railroad roundhouse, depots, shops, and offices designed to help settlers seeking land. A dry summer and hard winter slowed growth in late 1880 and 1881.[280] By 1882, homesteaders were again seeking cheap Dakota Territory land. Some days, eighteen trains chugged up to the depots. Sometimes more than one thousand people arrived in a week. It was a rough western town struggling with growing pains when Susan arrived in 1882. Susan was shocked when she saw saloons and drunken men. Some of the men made passes at her. With few women in the territory men attempted to seduce them. Some of the men promised marriage and then refused to marry the women. Men frequently drew their guns and shot them into the air for shock effect. A couple, who had arrived in Huron a few years prior to Susan, was appalled by the sewage and waste in the streets and all of the gambling and prostitution that was openly carried on in front of others.[281]

Imagine Susan's shock seeing these conditions. She had left a settled, small community where these types of behaviors were looked upon with distain. Now it was up to her to carve out a new life for herself away from long-established friendships and family security.

An Expanding Life and Town: Fresh Dreams

Some say Susan went to Huron to stake a claim.[282] Fayette residents reported she started a laundry[283] as did her African colleagues.[284] When my husband and I reviewed land records on July 9, 2009, in the Beadle County Recorder's Office, we did not find proof of a claim or Susan's ownership of any property. Perhaps the land agent failed to process the claim, or Susan might have chosen not to "prove it up" during the three years she lived in the Dakota Territory. One requirement for the Homestead Act for proving up was to build a residence at least eight by ten feet.[285] The first settlers resided in sod houses because wood was limited.[286] Some lived in dugouts until other building materials were available. Susan might have constructed a house by herself, or she might have had resources to hire someone.

Daily existence was grueling, but Susan was accustomed to a hard life. Settling in the eastern prairie area of Dakota Territory required a strong spirit, mind, and body. Antelope herds still roamed through Huron and the surrounding countryside when Susan arrived. Part of the design on the Corporate Seal of Huron is two antelope watching as surveyors drive the first survey stake.[287] Wolves were plentiful, roaming the outskirts of town, often howling and yelping at night for their packmates. Hail sometimes decimated gardens and crops if drought or bugs hadn't destroyed them. In order to feed herself, Susan likely gardened and dried and canned the produce.

Life in that frontier town presented challenges to Susan, a courageous entrepreneur. Based upon Fayette hearsay, she earned her living doing laundry for the harried railroad and businessmen of the town who didn't have the skills for this time-consuming chore.

Imagine this slightly built, muscular woman hauling water from the James River, heating it in large, galvanized metal washtubs, and then soaping and soaking the clothes. After applying the homemade lye soap to remove oil, grease, and dirt stains, it was necessary to rhythmically move the clothes up and down a washboard until the stains disappeared. Bluing was measured into the rinse tub to make the shirts and bedding whiter. Either clotheslines or bushes were used to let the sun and wind dry the laundry.[288] Finally, Susan would build a fire in the cookstove to heat the flat irons,[289] which she possibly brought from Iowa. She alternated irons, pressing with one while the other one heated.

Her work wasn't always routine. My cousin Audrey Hurmence, who remembered Susan from her teenage years in the Fayette Methodist

Episcopal Church, shared a story Susan told friends revealing her plucky behavior. One day when doing laundry, a man approached her while she was scrubbing clothes in a washtub full of water. When the man tried to harm her, Susan picked up the tub and threw soapy water at him. He fled quickly and never returned to bother her, nor did anyone else. She was not easily intimidated.[290]

Susan watched buildings rising rapidly after imported materials arrived and heard sounds of hammering and sawing wafting through the air. With the influx of more families, construction of a brick school building began in the summer of 1882. Three teachers started holding classes in November for 140 students. By 1883, there were three hundred students of school age, most of whom were American along with those recently emigrated from northern European countries.[291] Did Susan have thoughts of applying for one of those teaching positions even though she knew there was almost no chance of being hired? Even today, African American teachers are not hired in proportion to the number of African American students in most schools throughout the country.

Churches had sprung up before Susan arrived in Huron: Baptist, Presbyterian, Methodist Episcopal, Catholic, German Lutheran, and Episcopal. Susan attended the Methodist Episcopal church built in 1883.[292] Its cross-shaped edifice featured a brick façade over a wooden structure. The church could seat six hundred.[293] Compared to the Stone School House that served as a church, this elegant structure probably seemed palatial to her. Imagine Susan walking to church services along the boardwalks completed soon after her arrival in Huron. Visualize her holding her hat against the wind, marveling at the two towers, one over one hundred feet tall, and absorbing the beauty of the stained glass windows reflecting the sun, causing the light to dance like jewels on the ground. That is also the year the United States Supreme Court ruled part of the Civil Rights Act of 1875 was unconstitutional, thus allowing individuals and corporations to discriminate based upon race.[294]

I've wondered how Susan's life would have evolved if she hadn't read newspapers wrapped around bundles of clothing brought to her laundry. One day, she discovered an article that piqued her awakened interest in God, resulting in an epiphany that quite likely changed the course of her life. She read that Lucy Rider Meyer was considering the development of a school in Chicago to educate women for work in the mission field.[295] Susan's inquisitive mind began imagining possibilities for her future, but it required furthering her religious education. Several months later, when reading another newspaper salvaged from a laundry delivery, Susan learned that Lucy Rider Meyer was offering correspondence courses. "She immediately wrote Rider Meyer and very soon her studies commenced."[296] These courses stimulated her ten-year interest in becoming a missionary.[297] The Huron free Reading Room that opened in June 1883 and was controlled by the Women's Christian Temperance Union (WCTU) and the Young Men's Christian Association would have been a perfect place for her to study.[298] She later became a member of the WCTU. The library housed five hundred bound volumes and displayed on tables forty newspapers from various locations in the country.[299]

Susan desired to go to Chicago, but circumstances prevented it. When Hannah, her father's second wife, died on March 4, 1884, she traveled to and from Iowa by train and brought her father back to live with her.[300] He died six months later on November 3, 1884,[301] at Susan's residence "from the effects of a stroke of paralysis."[302] It is puzzling why she had her father buried in the Riverside Cemetery located along the banks of the James River in Huron rather than beside his first wife and three children in Lima, Iowa. Perhaps it was because she didn't have the time or the money to return his body to Iowa.[303]

After my husband and I had spent hours searching for proof of Susan's land ownership, we drove to the cemetery, hoping to locate her father's gravesite. We assumed since Isaac was a Civil War veteran, it would be well marked. That was a mistake! We did find markers for other Civil War veterans in the older potion of the cemetery. That required walking up and down each row of gravestones on a sweltering July 2009 day. Finally, in frustration after receiving no answers from written correspondence to cemetery officers, three years later I contacted a Beadle County historian. She confirmed Isaac's recorded burial location. However, without a cemetery map, which I have attempted to obtain through queries to the cemetery's director and area funeral directors, I cannot pinpoint the exact location of Isaac's gravesite in the tree-dotted cemetery adjacent to a bend in the James River in the southeastern quadrant of Huron.

I discovered that on September 28, 1886, a headstone was contracted to be made for Isaac by W. H. and I. S. Cross of Lee, Massachusetts, to honor his service in the Union Army during the Civil War.[304] The contract provided for sending the headstone to the city of Huron, Beadle County, South Dakota, but the line on the Card Records for "Headstone Supplied" was left blank. That may explain why we couldn't find a headstone at the Riverside Cemetery. I surmise that Susan could not afford one at the time her father died, or there may have been a simple wood marker that has decayed over the years.

Isaac's death meant Susan no longer had an aging parent requiring her physical and emotional care. Soon after he died, she joined the Methodist Episcopal Church in Huron.[305] These two events propelled her along her career path.[306] Approximately a year after her father's death, and with no reason to remain in Huron, Susan, at age thirty-four, sold her laundry, briefly visited friends in Fayette, and went to Chicago to pursue her desire to become a missionary. Oh, to know what unfilled hopes and dreams Susan left in Huron.

While in Dakota Territory, she had faced trials and challenges living in a raw, untamed portion of the Great American Desert. Her self-sufficiency and risk-taking attitude had emboldened her to become an entrepreneur. That was a courageous venture for a single African American woman, as was her decision to relocate in Chicago to further her education and pursue her dreams.

6

Living in Chicago: Preparing for the Future

Leaving the Great American Desert: Hello, Windy City

Much changed in Susan's life during the months after her father's death. The call to become a missionary pulled her eastward. She arrived in Chicago at a time when European immigrants were surging there, seeking a safe, more economically stable life. Susan did not yet know that within eighteen months she would be sailing toward the mouth of the Congo River and her first missionary assignment.

But now on a fall day in 1885, Susan watched the landscape rushing past cut wheat stubble, dry prairie grasses, and blackbirds gathering for their annual southerly migration. It had been about a year since her father's death, and she sensed she would never again visit his gravesite along the James River. The sky was beginning to glow, and soon she saw a bright orange orb rise above the horizon, welcoming her back to Iowa. She had traveled slightly less than 75 percent of her seven-hundred-mile journey from Huron to Chicago.

Susan's mind danced with many thoughts as the train slowed on the curve just before pulling through the forty-foot-high limestone cut west of the Fayette Depot. Was she hoping her brothers Richard and Albert would meet her? I perceive that was unlikely because there is no record of Richard in the county after 1880, and Albert was living fifty miles away in the Waterloo area with her deceased sister's husband, William Thompson.

Instead I envision the following scenario. Reverend and Mrs. Jason Paine greet her as she alights and breaks into a wide smile. She glances eastward, catching a glimpse of the College Hall (Old Sem.) dome. Reverend Paine drives the buggy to their home one block north of the campus, where Susan is their guest for several days.

I imagine the next morning Mrs. Paine hitches the horse to the buggy. She and Susan cross the rattling and creaking Volga River bridge, then drive northeast to the Lima Cemetery. There Susan prays and lays a bundle of goldenrod tied with bittersweet vine she has cut at the base of her mother's and siblings' gravestones. On the drive home, they visit the Graham family, and peals of laughter echo across the hillsides as childhood friends reunite and share stories of their youth.

Later that evening, I visualize the Paine children inundating Susan with questions about the Dakota Territory. They attend church on Sunday, where Susan is greeted by members of the Woman's Foreign Missionary Society who wish her well in her studies. Several days later, she boards a train to Chicago and rides across the wide Mississippi River she traversed by ferry more than twenty years ago. Soon she arrives at her destination, eager to begin another chapter in her life and yet another career.

Susan couldn't believe the hissing and braking sounds when her train and others pulled into the Union Station Deport completed in 1882. She lived long enough to see the current Union Station built in 1925 on essentially the same site. The old station was enlarged to accommodate increasing numbers of trains and passengers flocking to the country's railroad hub. As meatpacking plants expanded, trains brought cattle to the stockyards for slaughter and then took the processed meat and packaged products east for distribution either throughout the United States or Europe. Travelers reported Chicago as America's filthiest city in the 1880s.[307] Bloated cattle and waste from the Chicago Union Stock Yards were seen floating down the Chicago River.

During the decade Susan moved to Chicago, its population doubled from five hundred thousand in 1880 to more than one million in 1890.[308] In the same timeframe, the entire population of South Dakota grew from nearly one hundred thousand to almost 350,000. What an experience living in a bustling city, traveling by noisy, clanging streetcars, and residing in a four-story building must have been for Susan. Even seeing the ten-story, steel frame Home Insurance Company Building, the world's first skyscraper completed in 1885,[309] was a sharp contrast to the sod houses, open prairie, and wide skies of the Dakota Territory she had recently left.

Chicago's first permanent settler, Jean Baptiste Point du Sable, was a black man born in Haiti about 1745 to an African slave and French mariner father.[310] Jean Baptiste and his wife established a trading post and a farm along the north bank of the Chicago River sometime around 1779, approximately eighty years before settlement began in Dakota Territory. The name Chicago is derived from a Native American word translated into French, *shikaakwa*, which means stinky onion, a plant that grew in profusion along the Chicago River.[311] Much of what we know as Chicago was swampland and a breeding place for mosquitoes, some of which carried malaria. Malaria began to decline in central and northern Illinois in the 1870s, but cases were reported in the city when Susan resided there. This mosquito borne disease was prevalent when Chicago was recognized as a municipality on August 4, 1830, with the filing of the plat. Seven years later, Illinois granted Chicago a city charter. In the next decade, the city began rapid expansion. A plank road was built crossing the "dismal Nine-mile Swamp" and beyond, enabling the transport of farm produce though the Great Lakes to the East Coast.[312] In 1855, the level of the city was raised between four to seven feet above the swamps. Buildings were jacked up, and fill was brought in and distributed in the low-lying areas.

Much of the growth during the 1880s can be attributed to expanded manufacturing, which fueled urban development. The McCormick Reaper Company was a major employer. When the city was rebuilt after the 1871 Chicago fire, it employed increasing numbers of people to install water, sewer, and gas lines throughout the 1880s. These utilities were enjoyed by Susan as she settled into the hustle and bustle of life in Chicago with throngs of people crowding Michigan Avenue.

Susan may have been mesmerized by the lofty fifteen- to twenty-foot waves of Lake Michigan pounding the shoreline the autumn of her arrival.

Winter arrived quickly to the third largest Great Lake and fifth the world. Strong, bitter winds blew across the wide expanse of wat pedestrians bundled in long winter coats darted along the frequently sno covered streets. Their homemade wool scarves flew behind them as they dug their mittened hands deep into their coat pockets. In the spring, Susan might have walked on the sand dunes that protected portions of the city and watched the gulls diving for a meal. Debris from the Chicago fire had been used to expand Lake Park since renamed Grant Park. Lake Michigan, large in comparison to lakes in Iowa and Dakota Territory, likely seemed small to Susan after she had crossed the Atlantic Ocean in April 1887.

Only a few hundred African Americans lived in Chicago when Susan arrived. These free African Americans had come from either the upper areas of the South or from the eastern states. Some were of mixed African American and white heritage and were highly respected due to their ambitious work ethic evidenced as skilled workers or business owners.[313] Perhaps Susan had the opportunity to interact with some of them as she adjusted to city life.

Formal Religious Education for Women: A Pioneering Endeavor

Susan was among the first students to enroll at the Chicago Training School for City, Home, and Foreign Missionaries (CTS). That happened when her religious evolution intersected with the development of religious training opportunities for women. Lucy Rider Meyer, a medical doctor, initially proposed such a school on June 18, 1885, at a meeting of the Chicago Methodist Episcopal Church ministers. She had observed many women were either devoting or planning to devote their lives to Christian work. But they lacked experience and knowledge in effective techniques to minister to children and families, and no program existed to prepare them as missionaries or deaconesses to address systems of injustice.[314]

Several notable historical factors within society and the church contributed to the emergence of missionary training schools such as the one Rider Meyer launched. In July 1819, the Methodist Episcopal Church women met in New York City to create an Auxiliary Society to assist the

:iety. Its purpose was to aid missionaries in their
idigenous people.[315] Soon the Auxiliary Society
ms and provided an array of services, including
omen, Sunday school classes, public baths, reading
pensaries.[316]

rams were replicated by churches as the population
moved west. They were especially useful to more than fourteen million
immigrants who flooded American shores between 1860 and 1900. Susan
had empathy for these newcomers facing adjustments in a strange, new
environment because she had faced similar experiences in previous moves.
Conditions for those remaining in cities such as New York and Chicago
were wretched. During this period, Chicago was the fastest growing city
on the planet. Immigrants representing many ethnic groups, including
Irish, German, Italian, Polish, Mexican, Arab, English, Bulgarian, Czech,
Greek, Chinese, Slovak, Ukrainian, and Puerto Rican, spurred the city's
growth.[317] Crowded into inner-city tenement housing, many worked in
packing plants where runoff contaminated the water supply and foul odors
permeated the air, creating an unsanitary environment. Infant mortality
rates were high. Conditions were ripe for the spread of tuberculous in
the crowded, poorly ventilated tenements, just as they were in the cabins
where Susan had grown to adulthood. These circumstances and poverty
contributed to the rising crime rate. Susan and her cohorts were exposed
to these dangers during their evangelistic visits.

Workers were paid inadequately, and eventually there was a clash
known as the Haymarket Affair between the working poor and the city's
wealthy businessmen. Of the several versions of the riot, Adelman's account
seems most accurately researched. To briefly summarize, workers went
on strike, lobbied for an eight-hour day, and held a peaceful march down
Michigan Avenue on Saturday, May 1, 1886. Union banners were carried,
representing the eighty thousand marchers, many of whom were in the
building trades. The next day, Lucy Hayes, a former slave from Texas
with Native American, Mexican, and African American heritage, and
others staged another peaceful march of thirty-five thousand workers. On
Monday, May 3, picketing workers at the McCormick Reaper Company
were attacked by Chicago police, resulting in some deaths. The next
evening, at a gathering approved by pro-labor mayor Carter Harrison,

the situation again got out of hand, and what we know as the Haymarket Affair or Riot occurred.[318]

The gathering was small, with only 2,500 participants. When featured speakers did not appear, two substitutes, Lucy's husband, Albert Parsons, and Samuel Fielden, a Methodist Episcopal Church lay leader from England, spoke. It began raining while Fielden spoke, and many left. With only two hundred people remaining, 176 policemen attacked after an unknown person threw a dynamite bomb. In the ensuring frenzy, four workers and several police officers were killed.[319]

There was panic, and martial law was declared in the city and nation. Eight men, representing various aspects of the labor movement, were tried, including some not at the site of the shooting. All were found guilty on August 20, 1886, and sentenced to hanging. With outside pressure, several were given life in prison, and one appears to have committed suicide. Four were hanged on November 10, including Albert Parsons, who had left the May 4 rally before the police arrived. In June 1893, the three remaining in prison were pardoned by Illinois governor John P. Altgeled, at which time he condemned the judicial system for allowing the hangings.[320] Adelman summarized the core of the problem thus: "The real issues of the Haymarket Affair were freedom of speech, freedom of the press, the right to assembly, the right to a fair trial by jury of peers, and the right of workers to organize and fight for things like an eight-hour day."[321]

Because that series of events occurred while Susan was studying in Chicago, one wonders if the labor situation was discussed at the Chicago Training School (CTS). If so, how deeply did they delve into its effect on the workers and their families whom Susan and her classmates visited, prayed with, and assisted? Assuredly, the CTS faculty and students were dismayed at the inhumane treatment the strikers received and the death sentences given and those carried out. I ponder whether or not those women realized the far-reaching effect that history-making incident would have on laborers worldwide.

Those missionaries were educated to combat depressing circumstances faced by the poor and to take the place of denominations that were ignoring them. In 1869, seventeen years prior to the Haymarket Affair, the Woman's Foreign Missionary Society (WFMS) was formed. This society created a notable forward movement in the ME Church Missionary Programs.

Eleven years later, the Woman's Home Missionary Society (WHMS) was founded in the northern Methodist Episcopal Church with the vision of supporting mission work in the United States. That same year, southern women established the Home Mission Society with the purpose of helping slaves adjust to freedom.[322] Women from these organizations volunteered time, energy, and money to the missions and settlement houses. However, as the services they provided expanded, better education and training in religion, nursing, childcare, and household management were required. That need recognized by Rider Meyer, Jane Bancroft Robinson, and Belle Harris Bennett provided the impetus for training schools in America. Rider Meyer discovered the same type of deficits in the early 1880s among Sunday school teachers during her service as field secretary of the Illinois State Sunday School Association (ISSSA).[323] The training school also prepared Sunday school teachers and those working with children and young people.[324]

Volunteers in these two groups lacked skill and knowledge, spurring Rider Meyer to present a paper describing her vision at the June 1882 ISSSA Convention. She articulated the need, described a proposed curriculum, identified qualities desired in students, and provided fundraising strategies. A committee of four men met one week later, affirmed the value of such a school, and gave Josiah and Lucy Rider Meyer permission to proceed.[325] It should be noted that the CTS was never under the organizational structure of either the WFMS or the WHMS. Rider Meyer began advertising in church publications and newspapers, where Susan read about the school while she was in Huron.

There were several possible reasons Susan pursued her educational endeavor. First, the nineteenth and early twentieth centuries were a time when nearly 60 percent of missionaries were women.[326] Second, there were more satisfying and challenging opportunities for women as missionaries abroad than in the United States. Third, Susan's race prevented her from teaching in many states.[327]

Fourth may have been the religious precepts she internalized while a student at Upper Iowa University, which had begun as a Methodist Episcopal Seminary. The establishment of the Methodist Episcopal Church (ME) occurred in 1784 at a Christmas Conference in Baltimore.[328] Sixty years later in 1884, Southern congregations formed the Methodist

Episcopal Church South due to the church's stance against the practice of slavery.[329] The ME Church remained firm in its belief of equality and fostered concepts such as "education for all regardless of social standing, ethnic identity or gender; education that appropriately related faith and reason; education that helped individuals make full use of their capabilities; education aimed at high standards of achievement."[330] These beliefs may have been what attracted Susan to the church.

The Chicago Training School formally opened on the evening of October 20, 1885, with a lecture by Dr. Ph. H. McGrew, a missionary from India.[331] The school's four students were present along with three guests. The small attendance was a big disappointment to the Meyers, who had expected a large number. They kept their spirit and remained hopeful. By November 28, there were eight enrolled students, and likely one was Susan, who had entered the school about that time.[332]

Mission training provided by CTS faculty, mostly volunteers, prepared employable women. Susan and her classmates were taught skills to help the needy and to explain the relevancy of scriptures to their lives.[333] Financial support for the school came from leading clergy and lay people through fundraising efforts of Lucy's husband, an astute executive.[334] Some of the funding arrived as nickels from the women of the ME Church. In a June 1885 speech, Rider Meyer noted if each of the one million ME women gave five cents, that would raise $50,000, double what she proposed for providing a school building.[335] To keep operating expenses at a minimum, the Meyers did not accept a salary during the early years of the school.[336]

Students helped with housekeeping chores such as cleaning and meal preparation.[337] There was no charge for tuition because teachers freely shared their knowledge with the students.[338] In the early years, some of the board members contributed to the support of students who did not have the resources needed to attend the CTS.[339] In later years, the students paid a five-dollar entrance fee, a five-dollar book fee, and one hundred dollars per year for food, fuel, and electricity.[340] Students could do their laundry at no additional cost.[341]

Depending upon their resources, once approved for admission, students had three options to finance their education. They could either pay board and expenses, pay expenses only, or pay neither board nor expenses.[342] Those unable to pay anything were provided with comfortable maintenance and clothing during their time at the CTS.[343] No record of how Susan paid her expenses is available. That probably depended upon the sale and profitability of her laundry business and her savings, if any.

Lucy Rider Meyer was acutely aware of the need to select qualified women, recognizing the cost of every failure and the discouragement and discord it could cause in the missions and societies. Physical stamina, strong purpose, and adaptability were critical criteria, as were thorough prior liberal and practical education. Personal depth was expected. Wanting to do and feel good about the work was not enough to be admitted.[344] Susan's dedication, drive, and history of overcoming personal challenges made her a strong candidate for the school, as did her Normal Training certification.

No specific curriculum information was found for Susan's terms at the Chicago Training School. However, by 1898–1899, the ten departments were The English Bible, "Book by Book;" Church History and Christian Missions; Sunday School Work; Deaconess Work; Epworth League Work; Evangelistic Work; Voice, Culture and Instrumental Music; Industrial Work; Nursing and Elementary Medicine; and Elocution and Physical Culture.[345] During the 1898–1899 academic year, there were ten resident teachers and thirty special lecturers.[346]

Rider Meyer "endorsed a combination of missionary work and high academic achievement," for her female students[347] and emphasized "biblical, theological, and historical studies five times weekly."[348] The curriculum included economics, courses identifying the accomplishments of women, and basic medical training.[349] An important part of their training included study in citizenship, sociology, and social and family relations that prepared students for evangelistic visitation. Students were expected to spend time in genuine study, application of the principles learned, and nurturing their inner lives. Rider Meyer envisioned students, upon graduation, providing English training, employment counseling, and health care demonstrations.[350] She knew the importance of missionaries and deaconesses speaking the immigrants' language and for those preparing to work abroad to learn the languages spoken in those countries.[351] Deaconesses were educated to be active in social reform that included changing the prison system and promoting temperance work.[352]

Susan remained at the Chicago Training School long enough to complete the curriculum and requirements for graduation. The commencement of the first graduating class was June 2, 1887, with twelve of fifteen graduates present.[353] Two had left to serve as missionaries in Africa,[354] and Susan, listed as an 1887 graduate, was one of them.[355]

The year Susan completed her missionary education, the Meyers prepared the deaconesses to work across economic barriers and minister in a loving manner to the disenfranchised.[356] The deaconesses' training began in the summer of 1887 so the CTS facilities would not remain vacant after those prepared to serve as missionaries had graduated. Nursing was added to the curriculum, creating two tracks, one for nurse deaconesses and the other for missionary deaconesses.[357] The training provided at CTS gave women a place in the church and an opportunity to use their gifts of ministry and service.[358] The role of deaconess was accepted and recognized as an official order by the Methodist Episcopal Church General Conference in 1888.[359] The duties of the ME deaconesses outlined in the consecration service were: "You are to minister to the poor, visit the sick, pray with the dying, care for the orphan, seek the wandering, comfort the sorrowing, save the sinning, and relinquishing wholly all other pursuits, devote yourself to such forms of Christian labor as may be suited to your abilities."[360]

Because Susan's father was an orphan, this message may have resonated with her more deeply than with other students. And she had experience caring for the sick when her mother and siblings were dying.

Throughout its history, the CTS had three locations. The inaugural location, a building given to the school, was at 19 West Park Avenue, approximately ten miles west of downtown Chicago and several blocks north of Madison Avenue. When the second location was procured, the Park Avenue property was rented to provide an income source. In 1886, during the time Susan attended, the "institution was incorporated and moved to a new building at 114 Dearborn Avenue."[361] The school was in the heart of the city and only a few blocks from the Chicago Academy of Fine Arts, now the Art Institute, founded in 1879. Imagine Susan walking on Sunday afternoons to enjoy the art housed in that building on the southwest corner of Michigan Avenue and Monroe Street. The school was located near a Methodist Episcopal church and close to streetcar connections reaching throughout the city. That proximity enabled students to worship and travel more easily to serve new immigrants living in untenable conditions and in need of help adjusting to a new language and an alien environment.[362]

The following description of the Dearborn Avenue building provides insight into Susan's living and studying environment during her final months at the Chicago Training School. "The new building was four stories high and twenty feet wide. The entrance, framed by a stone arch, led into the first floor, where the reception room, the office, the library and the recitation rooms were located. Sleeping rooms for the students and resident faculty occupied the other three floors. On one of those upper floors Mr. and Mrs. Meyer had their apartment."[363]

The location of the building inside the Chicago Loop allowed the rapid expansion and the purchase of adjacent property in 1887 for $12,000.[364] Enrollment steadily increased, and in 1895, the school moved to a location at the corner of Indiana and Fiftieth Streets.[365] In the Hyde Park area, the school was about six miles south of downtown and easily available to immigrants flooding the city and badly in need of assistance.[366]

Several years after Lucy Rider Meyer opened her school, Jane Addams founded Hull House in 1889 to help struggling Chicago families. Addams and Rider Meyer were friends throughout their careers and respected each other's work.[367] "Addams compared the CTS favorably to the activities of the social settlements. Rider Meyer frequently spoke of Addams' work in the *Deaconess Advocate,* the journal of the CTS."[368] Both of these women were at the forefront in providing educational and employment opportunities for women and improving the quality of life for Chicago families.

In Massachusetts, Ellen Swallow Richards, a scientist and educator, developed correspondence courses for women with the desire to teach science. She promoted nutrition education for all people and attended the 1893 World's Fair in Chicago to demonstrate the Rumford Kitchen. In 1909, she founded the home economics profession and spoke throughout the country, including at the University of Chicago, advocating family life concepts similar to those championed by Rider Meyer and Addams. They were all, "concerned with bettering conditions affecting the health and happiness of people in the home, in the school, and in the community."[369] Those three prominent women leaders most assuredly met in Chicago to discuss the philosophies and methods they used to improve the quality of life for people in an era when the country and its population were expanding and industrialists were exploiting workers and the environment. They each recognized education as the key to a fulfilled and productive life.

Lucy Rider Meyer was not the only Methodist Episcopal Church woman who had ideas about preparing women for missionary work. Jane Bancroft Robinson, who had earned her PhD in 1884, studied the history of the deaconess movement in Europe that was begun by Theodor Fliedner. In May 1936, he and several other friends drew up and signed the statutes of the Rhenish-Westphalian Deaconess Society.[370] Fliedner began by preparing teacher deaconesses, then nurse, and finally parish deaconesses. While studying in Europe, Bancroft interacted with ME deaconesses in Zurich, Switzerland, and other countries, including France and England. She saw the possibility of a similar movement in America.[371] Upon her return to America in 1888 and after completing a comprehensive study that resulted in a book, *Deaconesses in Europe and Their Lessons for America*, she was given the newly created position of general secretary in the WHMS. Her book seems to have provided the impetus for the denomination's establishment of a deaconess program for lay women in 1888. Completion of the program allowed those women to serve the church in any capacity not requiring full clergy rights.[372] The deaconesses worked tirelessly to decrease barriers of race, class, and gender.[373]

A conflict arose between Lucy Rider Meyer and Jane Bancroft Robinson in 1888 regarding placement of deaconess work within the hierarchy of the ME Church General Conference. Rider Meyer interpreted the conference guidelines "as placing the work under the authority of the general church."[374] Bancroft Robinson, who had worked for the WHMS's Deaconess Bureau for twenty years, believed the work should be under its auspicious. She credited the inception of the movement in the United States to the WHMS. The Bureau operated on an independent financial basis from the church, which at the time was governed by men. Rider Meyer sought to seek power and opportunity in the men's sphere. Bancroft Robinson wanted autonomy from the church and believed the separation strategy helped women gain political leverage and mobilize in the larger society. She supported female institution building. Perhaps noting the control male pastors had in Europe inspired Bancroft Robinson to challenge their control in America. Both Rider Meyer and Bancroft Robinson created employment opportunities for women educated at the Deaconess Schools. Their training allowed them to help individuals and families at home and abroad. Rider Meyer's curriculum had a strong focus on evangelism and service, whereas Bancroft Robinson felt service was a deaconess labor. Both of these women were strong advocates for women's rights. Regardless, "The mission strategy of the Societies involved a language based on the extension of the private sphere, *women's work for women*."[375] When this authority debate came to a head, Susan was unlikely unaware of their differing philosophies because she was in the Congo, helping women and girls create Christian homes.

In reality, the question of women's roles in American churches had been inflaming debate among and within denominations since the late 1700s. After the American Revolution, churches gained members through persuasion and not force. In some denominations, such as Northern Methodists, African Methodists, and Freewill Baptists, women were allowed to preach because there weren't enough men to meet their evangelistic needs.[376] Besides this practical reason, many thought "religious authority came from heartfelt religious experience, not from formal education."[377] "They argued that it was possible for God to inspire women as well as men to proclaim the gospel. Education, wealth, social position, gender—all of these were meaningless to God."[378]

Female preachers served as itinerants, similar to circuit riders, and traveled to small and remote villages across the countryside. They did not receive a salary and had to depend upon the goodness of those to whom they preached. Some had to do the work of domestic servants to survive.

As Methodist and Baptist denominations prospered, they discontinued earlier support of women and opened seminaries for men. By the 1840s, female preachers were being forced out of the pulpit and not allowed to preach the Gospel. That remained so for more than one hundred years. Finally in 1956, the Methodist Episcopal Church granted full clergy rights to women.[379] Two years later, Sallie A. Crenshaw and Nora E. Young became the first African American women to receive full clergy rights.

Women did not want to be left out of church leadership roles. In order to follow God's calling, they turned to mission work, even though male leaders offered opposition. In 1869, eight women formed the Woman's

Foreign Missionary Society while meeting at the Tremont Methodist Episcopal Church in Boston. The men predicted they would fail; they did not.[380] That organization provided Susan and hundreds of other women an avenue to serve God in many countries and encouraged others to lead a Christian life.

That same year, Susan B. Anthony and Elizabeth Cady Stanton formed the National Woman Suffrage Association. Women had begun to mobilize over twenty years earlier in 1848 at the first women's rights convention in Seneca Falls, New York. Here sixty-eight women and thirty-two men, including Frederick Douglass, signed a Declaration of Sentiments outlining grievances. That document guided the agenda for the women's rights movement.[381] The faculty at the CTS integrated some of these concepts into their teaching strategies and curriculum materials for student use to decrease race, class, and gender barriers. Those concepts were aligned with the thinking of the women and men who met at Seneca Falls.

Several years later the women's club movement was initiated. Their aim was to enable women to become better educated and active in community service while developing leadership skills. Middle-class African American women began a similar movement with an additional focus on issues of race. They ultimately formed the National Association of Colored Women (NACW).[382] Their level of activism increased in the 1890s as Reconstruction faltered, incidence of lynching heightened, and the number of Jim Crow Laws increased, especially in the South. Those laws were enacted to keep African Americans and white people separated in schools, recreation areas, and other social settings.[383] Susan did not become involved in women's clubs until she settled in Fayette upon her retirement, when she had more time to commit.

Encountering Bishop William Taylor: A Life-Changing Experience

When Susan met Bishop William Taylor in early 1887, the role of women in the church was limited and prescribed by men. The church hierarchy did not want women in the mission field. Taylor disregarded the practice of established mission boards and "recruited women (including single women) without prejudice and appointed them to positions in which they were able to design, found, and direct their own mission programs."[384] Taylor, with his long, bushy, graying beard and flowing hair, visited the Chicago Training School to recruit missionaries to serve in Africa in early 1887.[385] Oh, to know how Susan felt when she met this brash, determined man who burst into places as if he owned them. Did Bishop Taylor ask her to join him in Africa due to her race and her perceived ability to relate to the native people? Apparently is wasn't her grades that attracted him because Lucy Rider Meyer wrote, "Miss Collins has not an extensive education but she is a good Bible student."[386] Records verifying Susan's Chicago Training School grades are not available. While at the school, Susan "dedicated herself to helping 'those less fortunate.' No sacrifice was too great, no challenge too difficult."[387] Presumably it was her inquisitive nature, determination, deep religious belief, compassion, and consecration to God that outweighed what may have been the lack of opportunity for stronger academic preparation. Bishop William Taylor could understand that, as he had received his sporadic formal education at a one-room school in Virginia and then risen to the position of missionary bishop to Africa of the ME Church by 1884.[388] He retired in 1896.

Bishop Taylor had high expectations and requirements for those he selected to join him in Africa. He was supremely focused on his goal of evangelizing the people of Africa. As a strong, healthy man, he sometimes overlooked the physical condition of the people he recruited. In his determination to succeed, he wrote, "Unless you can face difficulties, trials, privations, hardship, and suffering at home, and have a patient, plodding, preserving, undaunted spirit, do not apply."[389] As one of the Taylor missionaries, it was expected that Susan be fearless, rugged, robust, and self-reliant and have a consuming drive.[390]

Sometime in his conversations with Susan, Bishop Taylor determined those qualities were her greatest assets. Before Taylor accepted her or other missionary candidates, he required completion of a two-step application process. The first necessitated verification of personal information, and the second involved in-depth personal responses to a series of questions. Candidates had to obtain testimonials of religious character and general fitness for missionary work from their pastor or a presiding elder.[391] A health certificate from a reliable physician and a statement explaining intellectual capacity from a principal, professor, or a person of intellect were mandatory.[392] Either Rider Meyer, CTS faculty, or Reverend Jason Paine would have willingly verified Susan's qualifications. These included "good health, sound mind, holiness of heart and life, entire consecration to the self-supporting work, willingness to live among the people, fare as they fare, and if need be to die among them."[393]

Susan's testimonials met Bishop Taylor's expectations because he invited her to join him in Africa if she responded satisfactorily in writing to the seventeen questions that were the final part of the application process.[394] Susan apparently desired to go to Africa prior to meeting Bishop Taylor because she satisfactorily completed the application, answered the questions, and accepted his offer to become part of his second African mission team.

Bishop Taylor had developed a series of seventeen questions to assess the missionary applicants to determine if they could survive the demanding challenges of missionary work in distant lands. The first five dealt with commitment to Christ and to belief in the Methodist Episcopal Church doctrines. They were as follows: "Do you trust you are moved by the Holy Ghost to take upon the work of the foreign missionary? Do you desire and intend to make this your life work, and are you willing to work in any field? Are you conscious of being entirely consecrated to God and cleansed from sin? Are you pressed with an earnest desire to win souls to Christ, and have you any experience and success in revival work? Do you believe the doctrines of the Methodist Episcopal Church, as embodied in its Discipline and teachings, and are you a member of that Church in good standing?"

The next three questions focused on education: "Have you a thorough English or Classical Education? In what schools have you taught, and with what success? Have you any knowledge of Music, either vocal or instrumental?"

His next questions related to their health, age, debts, marital status both current and past, and if they were dependent on tobacco, liquor, narcotic, or intoxicating stimulants. He wanted to know if they had any commitments that would interfere with their work and what vocational or business skills they possessed. His last questions were these: "Have you any means or friends to assist you in defraying your expenses in the field? In the industrial schools to be established in Africa, what can you do, or what trade have you by which you can teach the natives the arts and business of civilized life? Will you do any work of which you are judged capable, and go to any field to which you may be assigned and to not leave it without the consent of the Society or its authorized representatives?"[395]

Clearly, Bishop Taylor wanted those who joined him to be aware of his expectation for total commitment and belief in the need to spread the love of Christ and salvation to the world. He believed the African cause presented more formidable difficulties than any other missionary field on the globe. I wonder if he told Susan that before she accepted his offer, an offer not made to every applicant. Only the best of those considered suitable were asked to serve.[396]

Susan would have answered the bishop's questions in the only manner she could, with complete honesty. She was not averse to hardships and sacrifices and was willing to face difficulties, both known and unknown. A Fayette resident who had known Susan summarized her character saying, "Doubt was never in her vocabulary."[397]

Susan expressed joy when Bishop Taylor selected her to join his group of missionaries.[398] Abbie Mills, a member of the Pacific Branch of the Woman's Foreign Missionary Society, met Susan at the Chicago Training School in 1887 and initially expressed surprise "to see a colored woman leading devotions."[399] In conversation with Susan, Mills concluded, "Her heart was then in Africa, and it was my privilege to bid her Godspeed, as she left there on her way to the Congo as a faith missionary."[400] Little did these two women know they would see each other fourteen years later in California. Apparently, they had not met between 1876 and 1878 when Mills was teaching at Upper Iowa University and Susan was a student.[401]

When Susan accepted Bishop Taylor's offer, she was the first African American graduate of the Chicago Training School and the first to serve the Methodist Episcopal Church mission stations in the Belgian Congo.[402] Two years later, she became the first female ME African American missionary in Angola.[403] In 1902, Susan returned to Angola, where she was the "first colored-woman representative to the W.F.M.S."[404]

Susan was a groundbreaker in the Congo when she began her missionary work, just as her father was when he had become one of the first African Americans in an all-white military unit during the Civil

War. She and her father both faced danger in new environments. Perhaps he was her role model. With her decision to commit to African missions, Susan once again was exploring a new frontier and leaving behind the security of the known as she placed her faith in God. She would be caring for children, including orphans, just as the European deaconesses had ministered to peasant women and their children, who were often destitute, ill, or homeless. The deaconesses took care of the mind and body, which then allowed one's spirit to flourish. Now Susan would be providing those services in Africa.

How fortunate that Susan was allowed to lead through her service in Africa rather than stay in the uncertain environment African Americans were experiencing throughout sections of the United States. She was ready to leave the familiar and to be a strong force in the development of Methodist Episcopal Church mission schools in Africa, specifically in Angola. As a missionary deaconess, Susan and other women were able to serve the church in ways men had historically prevented them from contributing. They had been valued as workers but not given true leadership roles at the time Susan ventured to Africa in 1887. Susan wanted to see, do, and know more. Perhaps her father had shared stories of his African ancestors. Agreeing to venture to the unknowns of Africa changed Susan's life forever.

7

⚬⚬⚬

Unchartered Territory:
Keeping the Commitment

Bishop Taylor's Philosophy: Self-Sufficiency

Africa was a target of European colonization before the Methodist Episcopal Church sent Bishop Taylor to establish missions. Interest in the continent increased after David Livingstone and Henry Morton Stanley reported untapped resources available for taking. European countries fought to obtain prime land areas rich in minerals but cared little about the indigenous people. When Bishop Taylor arrived, he negotiated with those in power for land where he could establish his mission stations. He envisioned planting industrial missions and child nurseries that would become self-sustaining entities with evangelism as a goal. Not everyone agreed with the objectives of the missionaries to convert the Africans to Christianity. That expectation along with political unrest and greed added to the stress of serving at those stations and presented many challenges to Susan and her missionary cohorts. What were the human costs they experienced beyond the lives that were lost in the zeal to obtain converts?

Similar to most people embarking on a new endeavor, Susan experienced concerns and fears when preparing for her departure to Africa.

She may have asked herself, "What have I done?" Did she wonder why she let charismatic Bishop Taylor convince her that going to Africa was a good thing, even though she wanted to help her people? She may have been concerned with Taylor's self-sufficiency model even though she knew the women of the Fayette Methodist Episcopal Church would help her. And there was a chance the women in Huron might assist. Even though she had that support, she couldn't know if it would be enough. Nor did she know who would care for her if she became ill.

She might have calmed herself by thinking, *I survived life in Wisconsin when my father was away for nearly a year. I made friends in Iowa and got through Upper Iowa as the only student of my race. My life on the Dakota frontier was rugged and frightful with those crazy men wanting a woman. How could this be any harder? I'll be with other missionaries and making a difference in the lives of children. Plus, I know God will take care of me.*

Even with positive self-talk, concerns entered missionaries' minds because Bishop Taylor expected those he recruited to follow his self-sufficiency model. That meant they all had to support themselves, build and maintain a mission, and conduct evangelical work.[405] They were not to ask the church hierarchy for funds but do as the apostle Paul had done, earn their own bread.[406] Bishop Taylor's plan was for children at the mission stations to be educated in manual skills so they could create a self-sustaining environment.[407] Engaging in commerce, raising cattle, working at a trade, and farming were moneymaking strategies attempted by the missionaries with varying degrees of success.[408] These expectations often put heavy stress on them, sometimes causing their deaths.

Bishop William Taylor, an experienced missionary, served the Methodist Episcopal Church of the United States on six continents. He spent time establishing or assisting churches in numerous places, including Chile, India, Burma, Brazil, Austria, New Zealand, Australia, Palestine, and Ceylon.[409] It was during these experiences that he developed his philosophy of self-sustaining missions. He applied his theories, creating churches in Angola, along the Congo River, southern Liberia, Mozambique, and Sierra Leone. He began his missionary career in California in 1849 and concluded it in Africa in 1896.[410]

For the duration of that time, he resisted the church mission board's structured approach to expansion, where "they insisted that the mission agencies receive and channel all funds, maintain instructional control over converts, and directly supervise the missionaries."[411] Taylor developed his missionary theory based upon the apostle Paul's mission efforts. He recognized the need for independence in the mission process, just as the apostles did when they developed self-supporting churches, not requiring costly buildings to bring the Gospel to people with whom they were living. Taylor respected cultures in Africa, Asia, Australia, and South America and wanted his missionaries "to adapt to and adopt the host culture."[412] He believed the lives of missionaries were easier if they adapted, thus eliminating the need for furloughs. Bishop Taylor had a survival-at-all-costs philosophy with an either-or ultimatum, either adapt or be sent home. That seems harsh by any measure and especially by today's standards of support. He knew he could not babysit his missionaries.

Christian missionaries began arriving in Africa many centuries before the ME Church sent Bishop Taylor, thus he and Susan joined a long-standing outreach to Africa. The first one appears to have been Mark, who traveled to Alexandria, Egypt, about AD 48, again in AD 58, and finally in AD 68, where he came across a church growing both in numbers and spirit.[413] By AD 100, Christians were reported in Algeria and a missionary had gone to Arbela, Assyria.[414] More than one thousand years later in 1276, Ramon Llull, a Spaniard, opened a training center on Majorca to prepare Christian missionaries for service in North Africa and Tunisia. Pope Pius II assigned evangelization duties to the Franciscans in 1462 along the Portuguese Guinea Coast of Africa.[415] Twenty-four years later, the Dominicans became active in West Africa. The first group of missionaries visited the Congo in 1490 at the request of King Nzinga a Nkuwu and baptized him.[416] Later, he sent his son Afonso, (sic) known as "The Apostle of Kongo," to study in Portugal. Eventually, Afonso's son Dom Henrique became the first black African bishop in the Catholic Church.[417]

In 1492, the first representatives of the Catholic Church arrived in Angola along with Portuguese explorers. The priests investigated along the coast and the Cuanza River,[418] working to obtain converts. Their attempts met with limited success, but in the mid-1600s, Queen Nzinga of the Mbundu people in northern Angola converted to Christianity along with her subjects.[419] She fought against the slave trade and European infiltration until her death in 1663. More than one hundred years later, five

United Brethren missionaries from Germany arrived in Ghana, formerly the Gold Coast, and taught in the Cape Coast Castle Schools.[420] In 1799, John Theodosius van der Kemp from the Netherlands traveled to South Africa as a missionary among the Xhosa. A few years later, two Christian missionaries arrived in Namibia.[421]

Well-known doctor, missionary, and explorer David Livingstone sailed for South Africa for his first assignment in December 1840. He was briefly in Angola when following the Zambezi River upstream and then going overland to Luanda, Angola, in May 1854. After obtaining provisions, he continued exploring and became the first European to see the cataract he named Victoria Falls.[422] He was amazed at its power and beauty as the mist created dancing rainbows from the sun's rays. Livingstone continued exploring Africa and died from a combination of dysentery and malaria in what is now Zambia on May 1, 1873.[423] It was twelve years later that Bishop Taylor began mission development in Angola.

Several factors increased missionary efforts across the globe in the nineteenth century. Travel became easier. Colonial rulers knew missionaries could provide education and health services to the indigenous people. Organizations such as the Wesleyan Methodist Missionary Society were formed in the early 1800s. In the mid-1800s, a number of mission societies began allowing single women to serve; previously, only couples were selected. Sparked by a series of revivals, Protestants began to show interest in the work due to a foreign mission movement with a goal to bring Protestant Christianity to the entire world.[424]

Each of these factors contributed to William Taylor's appointment as bishop to Africa in 1884. And by the middle of the nineteenth century, there was limited evidence of the Catholic Church in Angola.[425] Taylor was given a twofold assignment: to revive missions in Africa, specifically Liberia,[426] and to expand his work to other locations, including Angola and the Congo.[427] To expedite his work, Taylor adopted three operational principles. The first was not to interfere with the work of other churches or establish competing missions. He wrote, "Second, my plan of missionary training should embrace the industries necessary to the self-support of civilized life for all those whom we got saved and civilized. A development of that plan will in due time create self-support for the mission itself and its missionaries."[428] Finally he placed a well-qualified missionary matron at every station to establish a nursery mission, bringing the children to Christianity before they acquired the ways of their people. When he met Susan at the CTS, he saw a woman he could trust to fulfill that role.

After his appointment, William Taylor outfitted and prepared himself for travel to Africa. Preparation included obtaining money from the Transit Fund he had set up to cover missionaries' supply and transportation costs. He provided a list of supplies he anticipated needing to his friends supporting African evangelization. On the list was a variety of goods, including the following:

> Middlesex or Washington Mills indigo bloc flannel, waterproof cloth for ladies, gossamer underwear, cheap unbleached cotton cloth in large quantities, Turkey red,[429] blue cotton drill,[430] cotton hose, hammocks, handkerchiefs, etc. Sundries: Pins, needles, thread, buttons, buckles, etc. Notepaper, envelopes, slates, five by seven inches, in large quantity; lead and slate pencils; matches in tin boxes, pocket-knives, hoes, spades, etc. A hand printing press, suitable for octavo sheets,[431] with paper to suit. Groceries: Liebig's extract of meat, corned beef in cans, and a variety of preserved meals, fruit, vegetables, milk, etc.[432]

Taylor had those donated supplies marked "For William Taylor's African Expedition" and sent to the Messrs. Baker, Pratt & Co. in New York City.

He departed from New York City bound for England on December 13, 1884, and then traveled from Liverpool to Liberia with high hopes for implementing his assignment.[433] While waiting for his first group of missionaries to arrive, he visited the Liberian Conference and used his intense energy and zeal to preach in Monrovia and other locations in Liberia.[434] The first Methodist Episcopal missionary had been sent there in 1832. European missionaries had arrived earlier, traveling throughout Africa trying to instill Western culture and convert the native people to Christianity.

A strip of land on the west coast of Africa was officially called Liberia in 1824, and its capital, Monrovia, was named after President James Monroe.

The colony was initiated in the early 1800s by a group of Americans in an effort to resettle the growing number of free slaves. Many Americans did not support the idea. Liberia declared its independence from the American Colonization Society in 1847. A sovereign state was established, and laws were created to govern its commerce.[435] Fifteen years later, the United States began diplomatic relations with Liberia, easing the way for missionaries such a Taylor.

African Colonization: Impact on Indigenous People

When Bishop Taylor arrived along Africa's west coast in early 1885, colonialism was reaching its peak. European countries recognizing Africa's potential wealth had begun exploiting its natural resources as they raced to gain control of the land. Representatives from some of the European nations realized they needed to avoid conflict while completing for territory.[436] Those powers, including Belgium, France, Great Britain, and Portugal, were at the Berlin West African Conference in 1884–1885 and agreed to a set of guidelines for dividing and annexing territory. Portugal was able to keep Angola and the small state of Cabinda north of the Congo River.

Several themes emerged during the colonization process. Participating countries ignored the rights of the Africans when dividing the continent into colonies, with no thought to tribal boundaries or ethnic groups. Local kings and chiefs became figureheads in the colonial governments and lost control of their trade and natural resources. Europeans exploited the indigenous people, taking the most productive land, forcing the farmers to try to make a living on poor land, and then taking that land when they couldn't pay the high taxes imposed. Eventually, the Africans were forced to work either on the farms they once owned or in the mines. [437] Perhaps one positive aspect of colonization was the health care assistance and education the Portuguese, and later Belgium, allowed the missionaries to provide to the indigenous people.

It was necessary for Bishop Taylor to understand and negotiate with the colonial powers in Angola and the Congo Free State, bordering much of Northern Angola. Each country had different early histories that affected the work of missions. Records of the Angolan people go back to 6000 BC.[438] Centuries later in the early 1400s, the main influx of Bantu from the north entered in what became known as Angola prior to the arrival of the Portuguese in 1483. Earlier, about AD 500, the Bantu in smaller numbers had brought farming along with pottery and ironwork technology to the area. They established their own kingdoms and grew to nearly four million strong by the fifteenth century. When the Portuguese began trading on the west coast of Africa, relations between the two groups were positive, as they had similar social structures ranging from nobility to slaves. The Portuguese had expected to find gold quickly but discovered the slave trade was more lucrative. Captured Africans were taken to Brazil and the Americas for nearly three hundred years. By the 1800s, Angola was believed to be their largest source of slaves. In 1836, due to the western embargo, the slave trade was halted. Products including cocoa, coffee, cotton, ivory, and palm oil became exports during the middle of the nineteenth century.[439]

As whites encroached inland from the Atlantic coastal town of Luanda, warfare erupted with local rulers. There were battles with Brazilian-based Portuguese in the mid-1600s. Relations between the Portuguese and the indigenous people were unsettled when Bishop William Taylor was striving to establish a chain of missions in north-central Angola. After the Berlin West Africa Conference, Portugal's claim to the region was recognized by other European powers. In 1891, while Susan was doing mission work in Angola, the boundaries of the country were agreed upon through negotiations in Europe. It was not until the early 1900s when Susan was serving in Quessua, Angola, that the Portuguese had full administrative control of the country.[440]

When Bishop Taylor arrived in Angola, he found a strong presence of the Catholic Church. The Portuguese introduced Christianity in the fifteenth century, and many native people intermingled it with their traditional beliefs of honoring ancestors and a creator high god. After the Berlin West African Conference, Portugal was forced to grant religious freedom to its territories. The ruling Portuguese grudgingly tolerated non-Catholic missions from other Western nations, partially due to their teaching methods.[441]

To control the Protestant denominations, each one was assigned a certain segment of Angola where they could establish missions through Comity Agreements.[442] These agreements meant geographical separation and were devised to avoid duplication among Christian churches as they tried to evangelize unreached areas in the world.[443] During the late nineteenth century, Bishop Taylor was told to focus development of the Methodist Episcopal Church missions in the north-central high plateau region where Kimbundu was spoken. Fortunately, that was fertile agricultural land. Based upon their agreements for mission development, Baptists carved out areas in the north, and Congregationalists in the east. Consequently, Angola's Christian beliefs and creeds were formed based upon the denomination assigned to their location. The Portuguese colonial government made it difficult for the Protestants by reinforcing and subsidizing the Catholic missionary endeavors.[444] That support along with the continuation of slavery in Angola's interior until the twentieth century caused Bishop Taylor, Susan, and other missionaries great consternation.

Establishing missions in Angola, a country many considered heathen, was costly, and the estimated expenses for buildings, tools, and machinery needed at each station averaged 250 pounds or $1,215.[445] That was equivalent to the amount paid to a missionary and his wife for one year by the denomination's mission society.[446]

Bishop Taylor's first group of missionaries consisting of twenty-nine men and women with sixteen children left New York City on January 22, 1885. Liverpool was their first[447] destination, where they stayed at Hurst's Temperance Hotel, described as "accessible and commodious." It was selected because another hotel owner was emphatic about not allowing people of African origin to stay there.[448] After several days in Liverpool, they sailed to Angola on the steamer *Biafra*, owned by the West African Company. Bishop Taylor met them at Cape Palmas, and together they traveled to the Angolan seashore town of St. Paul de Loanda, now called Luanda. Dr. William R. Summers and Heli Chatelain, a talented Swiss linguist, had left Cape Palmas ahead of Bishop Taylor to procure a house for the missionaries away from the water at a high, healthy site. Unfortunately, after landing on March 18, 1885, many of the group became ill. It took them four months to recover, and then they either established a Luanda mission or moved to the interior.[449] One of the party died, and others who were ill and discouraged returned home.[450]

It seemed these missionaries went without much preparation and awareness of the challenges they would face. They committed themselves solely on faith to bring religion to the people many called heathens. While waiting for Bishop Taylor to get permission from the king of Angola to establish self-supporting missions, the recovering missionaries learned skills necessary to survive in the interior. In addition to obtaining approval, there were two other reasons for waiting: acclimating to the tropical environment and to learn the rudiments of Kimbundu, the language of the indigenous population in the region.[451]

Staying Healthy: Instructions to Follow

To help the missionaries succeed and survive, they were given a detailed set of guidelines to follow when establishing and working at new mission stations. Instructions included building on higher ground and not in gorges, valleys, ravines, or any deep depressions. The maximum air movement benefited them, alleviating the threat of mosquito bites.[452] Houses built on the grassy plains and without a cement or asphalt lower floor were to be at least twelve feet above the ground.[453] That was to eliminate the possibility of white ant invasions We know them as termites.

Missionaries were directed to avoid sun exposure, guard against dew, and the effects of chilly evenings and nights. They were to sleep with blankets covering them to their waists. Bedtime was scheduled for nine with no bathing in the evening. Bath time, using tepid water, was to occur in the morning or prior to dinner.[454] These directives, if followed, helped the missionaries avoid morning and evening contact with mosquitoes and other insects. Their suspicions that mosquitoes carried malaria were proven in 1897–1898 by Sir Ronald Ross, a British military officer. He identified female Anopheles mosquitoes as the transmitters.

To ward off malaria, each missionary was encouraged to take two grains of quinine daily, a treatment Peruvians had discovered several centuries earlier. Dr. David Livingstone recommended quinine because he believed it would help combat the disease.

There have been discussions throughout the years that African Americans are immune to malaria. Some writers have argued that West

African slaves working in the fields along the Atlantic Coastal Plains were immune due to their origins in the rice-growing regions of West Africa.[455] A Center for Disease Control and Prevention report suggested that those having the sickle cell trait have some protective advantage against malaria. Blacks with this trait have one sickle gene and one normal hemoglobin gene. Researchers have found that sickle-carriers seem to be more common where malaria is prevalent.[456] They believe the highest protection occurs early in life, prior to 18 months of age.[457] The American Society of Hematology reported that only 8 to 10 percent of African Americans have the sickle cell trait; therefore, very few would be immune to malaria. There is no record of Susan contracting malaria, but she described symptoms suggesting she might have.

Reverend Edward Davies, who helped prepare the missionaries for African life, thought the most prevalent illnesses were fevers and dysentery. To help ensure good health, he issued a prohibition against tobacco and alcohol use. He prescribed avoidance of butter, cheese, meat fat, and roasted groundnuts, what we know as peanuts, to prevent bile, rancidity, and nausea while living in the tropics.[458] A scientific basis to support Davies's dietary guidelines and the suggestion that not eating those items would prevent illness seems to be lacking. Considering the self-sufficiency model promoted by Bishop Taylor, groundnuts, which grow in western Africa, would have been a valuable protein source. When dried and roasted, the nuts are rich in protein and calories, and when ground, they provide flour that can be used as a basis for porridge and soup. Those nuts are well adapted to the hot, dry soils and resist pests and disease. The missionaries often lacked protein and calories, causing some of them serious health issues that could have been prevented if nuts had been part of their diets.

Foods for each meal and times to eat were stipulated by Davies. Dinner at eleven o'clock in the morning was to consist of "meats, fish, vegetables, dry bread, and weak black tea with condensed milk."[459] After a two-and-a-half-hour break, missionaries could resume work. For their 6:30 supper, "fish, fowl, or meats with vegetables, dry bread, rice, tapioca, sago and macaroni pudding, were acceptable."[460] Sago, a thickening agent, is a starchy product from the pith of a sago palm stem.

Reverend Edward Davies believed eating fruit in the morning was safer than eating it at dinner, as did others who lived in the tropics in the 1880s.

Available and recommended fruits were ripe bananas, mangos, guavas, pawpaws, and pineapple served as juice.

In addition to food guidelines, Reverend Davies developed detailed criteria for clothing to be worn on marches between mission stations. He specified cork helmets, sometimes called topees, and basketwork Congo caps to provide shade for the head and face. A double umbrella was deemed suitable for protection during sunny days. Men's clothing for marches of twelve or more miles, often considered a day's walk, included light russet shoes, knickerbockers of light flannel, a loose, light flannel shirt, and a Congo hat. Davies suggested placing a roll of flannel around the waist but did not provide an explanation; perhaps it was to absorb perspiration.

When working at the mission, clothing was to be light, but it was unclear if Reverend Davies meant lightweight, light colors, or both. Perhaps he was aware that tsetse flies are attracted to dark clothing. Interestingly, missionaries were frequently pictured wearing dark-colored clothing. Those ensembles featured long-sleeved garments and a floor-length skirt or trousers, probably for added protection from mosquitoes and sun.

Based upon his experience, Reverend Davies developed additional requirements for travel days. For 5:30 morning departures, the missionaries were to arise at 5:00 and cease their march by 11:30 to eat the lunch prepared prior to travel. Walking six hours under the protection of an umbrella was often considered enough exertion for one day. Two methods thought to prevent illness were seeking shelter under a shade tree and donning a lightweight flannel garment for a slow cooldown.[461] Following these guidelines, based primarily on Davies's observations, did not guarantee protection from illness and death.

Susan and her cohorts are to be admired for managing the seemingly insurmountable trials they faced. At times, their survival was in question due to lack of safe food and water. Adjusting to a different climate, lack of adequate housing and medical care, and dangers from disease and wild animals created additional stress as they faced the daily obstacles of learning new languages and developing an understanding of the people with whom they were working and serving.

Bishop Taylor: Creating a Chain of Angolan Missions

After founding the Luanda Mission, Bishop William Taylor established four inland stations. One was at Dondo, head of steamboat navigation on the Cuanza River and involving about 150 miles of boat travel from Luanda. Here, Bishop Taylor assigned one woman and two men. To reach Dondo from Luanda today entails a car ride of 105 miles on roads of varying quality. In 1885 Dondo, with about six thousand native inhabitants and a small number of traders, was a gathering placed for caravans traveling to and from the Angolan interior.[462] Traveling inland on the Cuanza River frustrated Bishop Taylor and his missionaries due to the unpredictable schedules of the slow, small steamboats.[463] He was a man in a hurry, and he wanted to save as many souls as possible.

Taylor and other missionaries forged eastward fifty-one miles from Dondo, where they developed the Nhanguepepo Mission. When the Cuanza River became too shallow to navigate, they had to walk along caravan routes paralleling the river.[464] The narrow paths only fifteen inches wide were dangerous for those who weren't surefooted.[465] Sometimes carriers transported the missionaries and their cargo to the assigned locations.[466] Two men and their wives and two single men stayed and established a school at Nhanguepepo. The men found water at the depth of six feet when digging their well.[467] They started a farming operation on 2,500 acres and planted two hundred banana trees and four hundred pineapples.[468] The goats, sheep, and chickens they raised provided food and a source of income.[469]

Reverend Joseph Wilkes, his wife, daughter, and Bishop Taylor continued twenty-seven miles along the narrow footpath toward the rising sun and Pungo Andongo.[470] Wilkes managed that mission station and operated a store to sustain his family. The village was surrounded by giant black pillars of hard sedimentary conglomerate rock, some rising majestically over six hundred feet toward the sky.[471] They saw the rock colors change during the seasons due to the growth of moss and algae. One wonders what these missionaries thought as they crossed the flat African savannah toward the field of rocks covering a rectangular area of about two thousand by four thousand feet. Susan arrived there four years after the Wilkes family. She might have seen leopard tracks and black mambas, cobras, and pythons living in the surrounding grasses, just as people do today when they climb the rocks. In earlier times, the rocks were used as fortifications during military battles.

At Pungo Andongo and other mission stations, the missionaries cultivated corn, cassava, yams, sugar, coffee, ginger, arrowroot, and eidos for their subsistence and for trade.[472] The arrowroot rhizomes are a source of starch used for thickening sauces, jellies, and glazes and provide some energy. Some believed arrowroot combated digestive disorders. Eidos, a small root vegetable, provided an alternative to white potatoes and yams in the missionaries' diets.

The last interior mission site was established at Malanje, sometimes spelled Malange, about sixty-two miles east of Pungo Andongo in the north-central fertile highlands region of Angola.[473] Taylor and the four men and two women assigned here traversed wooded country and valleys to reach Malanje, pronounced Mah-lah'-ngay, about 250 miles from Luanda.[474] Samuel Mead, his wife, Ardella, and their niece Bertha were in charge of that station. Travel on rugged but not mountainous terrain made the final portion of their journey less arduous.[475] The highest peak near Malanje is approximately four thousand feet but much lower than the mountains Taylor had climbed in Asia and South America.[476] Five years later, Susan would follow that route between Pungo Andongo and Malanje and serve there more than two years under Bishop Taylor's appointment.

Congo Mission Stations: Pleasing King Leopold

After establishing the Angolan missions, Taylor was ready to create a line of stations in the Congo Free State along the Congo River. Conditions were especially difficult for Africans living in the area that eventually became the Belgian Congo. The situation was different from Angola's as the territory along the Congo River basin was granted to King Leopold II of Belgium. That resulted after much political maneuvering, influence from missionaries who were established along the river, and the support of other European nations and the United States. The area remained the personal possession of the king after the Berlin West Africa Conference

Agreements until 1908. His rule of the Congolese people was brutal, and he used its resources, including rubber trees, to enhance his wealth. The people were basically slaves forced to work as rubber tappers, miners, ivory harvesters, woodcutters, and railway builders for other European interests.

Knowing King Leopold II had control of the river basin and had allowed the presence of other religious denominations there, Bishop Taylor sensed the time was right to meet him and request permission to establish a chain of Methodist Episcopal Church missions. Thus he traveled to meet the king after being in Angola. On December 11, 1885, he wrote to his colleague Reverend Davies, explaining what he had done.[477] "I have just returned from a trip to Brussels. I went to see King Leopold II in regard to my contemplated expedition up the Congo and Kasai, into Tushilange country. It is my custom in going into a new country to plant missions, to make myself known at headquarters."[478]

He noted, "By official routine it would have taken ten days for the U. S. Minister to secure the Bishop an audience with the King."[479] Taylor went into the king's palace, and in thirty minutes, he had an interview scheduled for the next day. When he saw King Leopold II, there was no one to present him.[480] Recalling the interview, Bishop Taylor wrote, "The king was greatly pleased with the prospect of a mission in the Congo State and would gladly cooperate with all the means of his power."[481] His willingness was likely enhanced by Taylor's confidence and passionate belief in his purpose as a missionary to the people of Africa. Taylor expected all missionaries, including Susan, to hold and act on his vision.

Bishop Taylor outlined to the king a number of guidelines he expected the native chiefs to follow if they wanted to have a mission established in their territory. Those included giving one thousand acres for immediate clearing and planting to establish a school and farm. Each chief was to build houses for the missionary preachers and teachers and plant sufficient food to provide for them, while paying a small tuition or exchanging work for day students.[482] Students taking a full course could live at the mission for up to five years.[483]

Bishop Taylor agreed to provide reliable preachers and teachers from the United States and to outfit the industrial school with tools and machinery.[484] That fulfilled a part of his responsibility when he recruited Susan from the Chicago Training School. He recognized she had the requisite skills to support the fourfold thrust of his mission program: education, industrial work, evangelism, and health care.[485]

But he was not the first person desiring to establish missions in the Congo. In 1482, the Portuguese entered the Congo River in order to develop trade and to bring Christianity to the region. Slavery was prevalent in the Congo culture. Some slaves were criminals, debtors, or war captives and could often earn their freedom. However, in the upper Congo River area, the clan chiefs sold their slaves to the Portuguese and some Europeans. The slaves were taken on crowded ships with inhumane conditions to America.[486] When in 1841, nearly 350 years later, David Livingstone arrived in Africa as the first Protestant missionary and doctor to explore the upper Congo region, slaves were still being sold. Sometimes entire villages were captured and shipped away. When Livingstone began traversing central Africa in 1883, he recognized the river would be a key factor in bringing missionaries there and hoped they would have an effect on ending slavery. Later, Henry Morton Stanley descended the Congo, reaching its mouth in 1874. Explorations of the river led England, France, Portugal, and Belgium to begin vying for jurisdiction over it as a means of claiming central Africa for their countries. Those rulers saw missions as a method to gain sovereignty.

The work of Livingstone and Stanley provided an incentive for churches to hasten their missionary presence along the Congo River. Three years after Stanley reached the Congo mouth, in May 1877, the Baptist Missionary Society was offered one thousand pounds by Robert Arthington, an Englishman, to begin the process.[487] Representatives from their society as well as other missionaries sailed up the Congo past Banana in the delta, where Susan was eventually stationed, to Musuku eighty-five miles inland. By that time, Stanley was working on the infrastructure and building a road past an area known as Stanley's Pool, and on to the falls of the Upper Congo River, named after him. Representatives of the Livingstone Inland Mission established in England in 1877 entered the Congo the next year. They worked throughout 1881 to create a mission at Stanley Pool.[488] The French sent Catholic missionaries to establish their national interest on the right shore of Stanley Pool in 1880.[489] During that time frame, Portugal sent a missionary expedition to San Salvador with the hope of strengthening its position on the Congo.[490] Several years later in 1886, African American Baptist missionaries arrived to establish their own missions. The next year, Dr. Lulu Fleming became the first African American woman commissioned by the Baptists as a missionary to Africa.[491]

Upon Susan's arrival along the Congo River in the spring of 1887, the same year as Fleming, she faced a new world with disparate needs. Various denominations were competing to convert the native people to their religion. The people of the region, although not technically slaves, had become forced laborers under King Leopold II, and many had died from harsh treatment. Earlier missionaries had experienced hostility from slave traders who vigorously disliked them. Illnesses such as sleeping sickness and malaria took the lives of indigenous people and missionaries. Health care was virtually nonexistent. It would have been difficult for anyone to be prepared for the experiences and sacrifices that followed. Susan could not know what she would face when she boarded the ship for Africa, then known as the "Dark Continent." She would have to summon all of her faith, indefatigable energy, and practical good sense to survive in this environment.

While Susan experienced many trials in Africa, African Americans faced numerous challenges during the 1880s. Railroad passenger cars were segregated in Florida, Mississippi, and Tennessee, reflecting Jim Crow Laws and attitudes in those states. Efforts were made to keep African American men from voting through intimidation and assessment of a poll tax initiated in Florida. African American men were prohibited from joining Major League Baseball teams in 1887, resulting in the establishment of the National Colored Baseball League. With the increase in the number of lynchings, Ida B. Wells, often upon threat of death, wrote a series of newspaper editorials exposing those acts.

As African American disenfranchisement increased, educational institutions were established, and some were recognized for their accomplishments. Sophia B. Packard and Harriet E. Giles founded Spelman College in Atlanta, Georgia, for African American women. That same year, 1881, Booker T. Washington opened Tuskegee Institute in Tuskegee, Alabama. In 1890, Alexander Clark, who had been a force in desegregating Iowa's public schools, was appointed as US minister to Liberia by President Benjamin Harrison. The Texas Republican Party appointed Norris Wright Cuney as chair of the party in 1886, making him the first African American to lead a major party at the state level. The previous fall, Susan had entered the Chicago Training School.

Would Susan find what she was looking for while in Africa? Was she searching for meaning and mattering that she wasn't finding in America? Or was she escaping from something? What had enticed her to travel across an ocean to a continent still largely unfamiliar to Americans? Perhaps she was going to that new environment for the opportunity to use her talents more fully and to avoid stagnation in her life.

8

Susan Sails to Africa: New Stars to Follow

Saying Goodbye: Experiencing Ocean Travel

Susan's life was a whirlwind after her recruitment by Bishop Taylor. She had to obtain the clothing, supplies, and other resources needed to survive in Africa for an unknown number of years. Thoughts of her brothers, Richard and Albert, and her deceased family members probably flashed through her mind. The support and encouragement the Paines had given her for nearly twenty years provided reassurance. She contemplated what she would experience sailing to Africa and living in an unfamiliar land among people with different languages and cultural patterns. Her strong faith in God and desire to share that faith propelled her forward. She felt she was answering her calling and was not fearful.

Susan departed for Africa in the spring of 1887 after completing a one-year course of study at the Chicago Training School. Her steamer trunk, in addition to her clothing, was filled with Bibles, religious teaching materials, and basic medical supplies. Imagine her standing on the deck of her steamship, looking at the recently completed Statue of Liberty fading away as the ship followed the earth's curvature on its eastward journey.

The statue had been dedicated by President Grover Cleveland the previous fall, with thousands of spectators watching.

Susan was one of eleven missionaries sailing from New York to the Congo on April 6 via Liverpool.[492] With newer technology, such as iron hulls, screw propulsion, and compound steam engines, crossing time to Liverpool averaged eight to nine days.

The previous year, Bishop Taylor had begun working to establish a string of missions along the Congo River, but he was challenged in getting beyond the cataracts separating the Upper Congo from the Lower Congo. Susan did not know where along the river she would be assigned. She arrived May 28, 1887, at Cabinda, an Angolan Province, and spent six months there.[493] Bishop Taylor reported King Leopold II "had been long wishing to know how to introduce American industry and energy into the Congo State, and proffered to render us every facility possible in planting missions in that country; we have ever felt the benefit of that interview in our effort to plant missions there."[494]

Bishop Taylor wanted to go to the interior and Bashinlange country to avoid interfering with established missions on the south side of the Lower Congo, such as those of the Missionary Society of English Baptists and the American Baptists' Missionary Union. He led a pioneer party of missionaries through the mountains to Stanley Pool and then went twenty miles upriver to Kimpopo. There he started a mission and used the location as headquarters for moves farther into Kassai country. On that foray, he discovered it was difficult to obtain transportation by government or other missioned-owned steamers. He decided to have one built but ran into difficulty getting materials transported to Stanley Pool by carriers who could manage a load of about sixty-five pounds. Other delays greatly complicated the process, but the steamer was finally constructed with the planned dimensions of eighty feet long by sixteen feet wide. He named it the *Anne Taylor* in honor of his wife.[495]

At the time the steamer was completed, there were no missions on the north bank of the Congo.[496] Taylor decided to open a line of stations along the river below Stanley Falls and another chain in Liberia along the Cavalla River. He later acknowledged that the Congo missions were not as successful as those in Angola.[497]

In March 1887, before Susan arrived, Bishop Taylor, Amanda Berry

Smith, an African American evangelist from Maryland, her companion, Sister Fletcher, and J. S. Pratt set sail up the Cavalla River to preach and meet some of the kings, chiefs, and others in their villages. Many requested a mission palaver to discuss the purpose of the group's visit before they let them pass upstream. At the village of Eubloky, the missionaries were treated to an evening meal of venison, fish, boiled rice, and palm butter. The next morning, agreements were reached to establish a mission station, and farmland was selected to be cleared and planted. Bishop Taylor required the mission house be built six feet off the ground and the villagers to cut and carry the pillars to the site. That process was repeated in other villages as they traveled upstream and preached usually from the Gospel of John.[498] Village drummers communicated their approach. By the time Susan and her companions arrived, Taylor and his party had returned to the coast.

Those leaving Liverpool with Susan on April 20 included seven men, one of whom was traveling with his wife and two children. A family group from Denison, Iowa, consisted of a husband and wife missionary team and his brother and nephew. Susan, who had listed Huron, Dakota Territory, as home, was the only person whose race, "colored," was identified.[499] Plans were to meet Bishop Taylor at either Cape Palmas, Liberia, or Mayumba, Gabon, on the Atlantic coast of Africa.[500]

Before leaving New York City, the missionaries conducted farewell meetings every afternoon and evening for a week at the Washington Square Methodist Episcopal Church. Held in the city of their embarkation, the purpose was to attract and win attention to their cause of spreading the Gospel in foreign lands.[501] Resembling revival meetings and drawing great crowds, the meetings helped raise funds to transport them to Africa.[502] The last two meetings for Susan and her fellow believers were held at 10:30 a.m. and 2:30 p.m. on the day they sailed.[503] Upon arrival in Africa, they would join some of the other fifty-six missionaries Bishop Taylor had previously recruited.[504]

I have wondered who was at the dock in New York to bid Susan farewell. The ship signaled its departure with a sharp, earsplitting whistle blast, indicating the beginning of the first of four ocean voyages Susan took during her career. There are no extant journals of hers describing these voyages. However, fortune smiled when I contacted the archivist at Taylor

University in Upland, Indiana, and was given access to a treasure trove of letters written by Dr. Jennie Taylor, the bishop's niece. He recruited her because she had degrees in dentistry and medicine.[505] She sailed to the west coast of Africa from New York City to serve as a medical missionary nearly seven years after Susan made her voyage. Her letters provide insights into the challenges and experiences of ocean voyages during the latter part of the nineteenth century.

Dr. Taylor reported to her friend Lizzie Akers, to whom all the letters were written, that she and her uncle boarded the steamer RMS *Majestic* on December 6, 1893. The ship's speed was sixteen to twenty miles per hour.[506] She noted the *Majestic* had a promenade deck with a smoke room and library, an upper main deck, and a salon deck with a dining room. Jennie expressed excitement over the nine hundred books in the library that included novels, works of science, and literature. She portrayed the vessel as "simply magnificent, elegant cushioned chairs in the library and salon (dining room), and Axminister carpet on the floor."[507] Handmade in England beginning in 1755, these bright-colored wool carpets were popular among the wealthy.

Assuming Susan traveled on a ship such as the *Majestic*, I have speculated how her reactions would have compared to Dr. Jennie's given their vastly different backgrounds. Dr. Jennie was appreciative of the beauty, but I imagine Susan might have been overwhelmed by the opulence, having grown up in the frontier areas where people struggled to make a living. Susan's origins were with uneducated, rural Midwestern parents, and Jennie's were educated, East Coast city parents. Their desire to help others ultimately brought Susan and Jennie together in Angola.

Dr. Jennie's early December letter to Lizzie, a former Dickinson College classmate at Carlisle, Pennsylvania, is one of five detailing the Atlantic crossing. She experienced bouts of seasickness en route to Liverpool, explaining, "I have only vomited half a dozen times altogether since we started."[508] When the crew called Dr. Jennie a "good sailor," she wrote they wouldn't have if they knew how often her stomach was uneasy. She reported that typically rough seas off the Great Banks of Newfoundland did not help her stomach, but she was delighted to later experience fair weather with no storms as they steamed toward Liverpool.[509]

Participating in the number of entertainment choices with the more than nine hundred passengers was a joy for Dr. Jennie. She noted that dancing to accordion music, card playing on the deck, rope jumping and active games, and piano and organ music in the dining room all sounded appealing. Sometimes the passengers organized evening entertainment, and one day they asked Jennie to participate. She agreed but would sing only sacred music accompanied with the autoharp. Another day, watching porpoises and a spouting whale helped pass the hours on the one-week voyage to Liverpool.[510] Likely, Susan reveled in similar experiences.

The ship's cabins were small, and Dr. Jennie shared her six-by-eight-foot space with two English women. The cabin did have the luxury of electric lighting and contained a set of bunk beds and a single berth. Writing on December 8, she expressed homesickness to Lizzie, especially as she watched her cabin mates wrap Christmas gifts and prepare their cards.[511]

Two weeks later, Dr. Jennie complained to Lizzie about being "lionized" because she was the bishop's niece. The increased pressure caused her to feel she needed to be entertaining and on her best behavior at all times. She groused, "How I dislike being on my dignity all the time … I have to be as neat as it was possible for my careless self to be. And to think I must continue to do so for the next 2 yrs! By that time will the habit of neatness be so established it will no longer be a task to keep so (will such a time ever come?)"[512]

From Liverpool, they departed for Monrovia, Liberia, on the SS *Mandingo*, owned by the African Steamship Co., expecting to arrive there on January 12, 1894.[513] The ship was named *Mandingo* after a tribe in West Africa, one of the largest ethnic groups on the continent. The steamship line had a contract to carry mail from London via Plymouth, England; to Madeira, an autonomous region of Portugal; Tenerife, a Spanish island; and on to the west coast of Africa. I am surmising that Susan and her companions traveled on a ship of similar type during the second leg of their journey to the Congo.

While writing an early January 1894 letter, Dr. Jennie described the seasickness she had experienced once again due to the rolling and pitching of the ship. She expressed relief when the water turned to a "sea of glass so they hardly knew they were moving."[514] If Susan experienced similar roiling seas, her correspondence to Iowa friends did not reveal it. She remained strong and left her fate to the Lord.

Dr. Jennie continued, "The newer vessels have electric lights, the Mandingo is an older vessel, but so far we have good accommodations."[515] When comparing the two vessels, Jennie concluded, "I much prefer this to the Majestic—the engines made the boat tremble and that motion makes me almost as sick as the rocking and pitching. On this little steamer we hardly know we have an engine. We make only about eight miles an hour."[516] They had "waves that are waves" after steaming through the Bay of Biscay and then being forced to put down anchor some distance off Las Palmas, Canary Islands, so more coal could be transported out in smaller boats. Dr. Jennie lamented, "We had to take on so much coal they couldn't store it all away and were obligated to pile it up on the lower deck, even to my 'windows' which haven't been opened since we left Canary."[517]

My mind wandered as I contemplated how those conditions might have affected Susan and whether the lack of ventilation in her boat compared to the houses where she lived as a young woman. Would she have noticed or complained?

Dr. Jennie and her uncle safely reached Monrovia on January 17, 1894. The only major challenge she described on the three-thousand-mile voyage was a twenty-four-hour rain when they were opposite the Sahara Desert and the trade winds were blowing atypically against them.[518] Hopefully Susan's travels were no worse than the Taylors'. After sailing up the St. Paul's River, Bishop Taylor presided from January 17 to 22 over the Liberia Annual Conference of the Methodist Episcopal Church at Caldwell, near Monrovia.[519] While the Taylors were in Liberia, Susan was teaching at the mission station in Canandua, Angola.[520]

On March 18, 1894, Dr. Jennie and Bishop William Taylor passed the equator while they were in the Gulf of Guinea on their way to the Congo. They were traveling on the SS *Akassa I*, completed in 1881, and operated by the Elder Dempster Co.[521] Besides the Taylors, it carried fifty-three cabin passengers and 153 deck passengers scheduled to join the Belgium army in the Congo.[522]

She lamented her mildewed kid gloves and leather shoes and rusted pins, needles, and scissors caused by high humidity.[523] This illustrates the likely disparity between Jennie's and Susan's wardrobes. Susan's clothing was probably what she had worn at the Chicago Training School, consisting of long, homemade dresses of dark-colored fabrics and sturdy, serviceable shoes.

As Dr. Jennie penned her next letter, she and her uncle were steaming up the Congo River on the *Moriaan*.[524] This Dutch Trading Company ship did not have sleeping accommodations, requiring passengers to find shore lodging. The Taylors stayed at the Natomba Mission[525] under the charge of Miss Mary Kildare.[526] Susan had briefly worked there with Mary in late 1887.[527] Jennie described the model farm at Natomba to Lizzie as a place where they "raised watermelon, squash, tomatoes, beans, eggplants, pineapple, coconuts and numerous fruits and vegetables with which you are not familiar."[528]

When beginning her missionary work, Susan had traversed up and down the Congo River.[529] Dr. Jennie described river travel conditions thus: "It is impossible to run steamers at night—too dangerous. Even by day 'it isn't any too safe:' the sandbars are always shifting & boats are in danger of running aground."[530]

Dr. Jennie and her uncle traveled ninety-three miles from the mouth of the Congo River up to Vivi and inspected mission stations along the way up and back.[531] With those visits concluded, they voyaged nearly 150 miles south from the river's month along the Atlantic coast to Luanda, Angola, where she again wrote to Lizzie on May 2. None of Bishop Taylor's missionaries were in town, so they stayed at English House, a lodge for English speakers. Luanda, through which Susan had traveled nearly five years earlier, was "situated partly on a hill and partly on the low land & near beach."[532] After a brief stay, they took the train to Pungo Andongo, which Jennie described "speeding along at the rate of twelve miles per hour. At one incline the engine made three attempts to get up but faltered each time; at last we ran about half a mile and got momentum enough to take us to the top."[533] Dr. Jennie was frustrated by the government speed regulations, the train's lack of power, baggage handling, and unpredictable arrival and departure times.[534] She was fortunate to be riding a train part of the distance because railroad construction from Luanda to Malanje, a nearly 250-mile distance, did not begin until 1885 and was not completed until the early 1900s. There was no train available to Susan for her first trip into the interior. Portugal eventually built the railway to enhance its ability to access Angola's inner regions, a country they claimed until 1975.

Another traveler Susan eventually met was Amanda Berry Smith, born into slavery in Maryland on January 23, 1837. Her father worked at night and eventually was able to buy freedom for himself and his family. Smith, a missionary evangelist, had journeyed from Liverpool to Monrovia between December 31, 1881, and January 18, 1882. Her trip took one week less than Jennie's, even with a stop at Grand Canary Port where the crew had obtained fresh vegetables to serve the passengers.[535] During one of their stops, people came on board and stole items from travelers' trunks. Mrs. Smith lost a number of possessions, and only a few were recovered, much to her dismay. Upon arrival in the Monrovia Harbor, tall, swaying palm trees dazzled Amanda Berry Smith as her eyes swept across the coastal plains. While she traversed Liberia, at times with Bishop Taylor, she commented on the absence of good books, recognizing education as the country's greatest need.[536]Mrs. Smith felt sadness when told there was not one high school for girls in the entire republic.

One can only speculate how Susan's travels compared to Dr. Jennie's and Amanda Berry Smith's. However, similar or dissimilar, these journeys required everyone upon arrival to adjust to the African climate, traditions, taboos, and beliefs. They shared a code: one must adapt.

Western Africa's Climate and Culture: Guidelines for Staying Alive

One of the adjustments Susan, Dr. Jennie, and other missionaries had to make was living in a tropical climate. It differed from most of the United States, as it was considered the Great Land of Perpetual Summer with only two seasons in most regions, rainy and dry.[537] Because Africa extends 37 degrees N to 34.5 degrees S, there is some variation in climate and temperature from the lowlands to the mountains and plateaus.

Those missionaries discovered plants grew abundantly in the rainy season, typically lasting from October to April in western Africa. Most locations received more than 75 percent of their annual rainfall during that period, reaching maximum strength between November and March. Because the air was damp with the heavy rainfall, many considered it the sickly time with the air full of malaria.[538] People believed stagnant water caused miasma, described as a noxious atmosphere by Reverend Edward Davies. "An excessive body of vegetation is continually growing and decaying, filling the air with poisonous miasma, which all must breathe, producing fever, boils, ulcers, etc. All who go to reside there, must expect to suffer this to some extent And some will die, but one cannot tell who will die and who will live."[539] It was believed overwork or exposure to rain and dews would bring on fever prematurely and with greater severity than when one practiced moderate behaviors.[540]

During the 1870s and 1880s, doctors had begun searching for the source of malaria that caused deaths in Africa, Asia, Europe, and the Americas. Alphonse Laveran and Ronald Ross were among the first to demonstrate malaria parasites could be transmitted between humans and mosquitoes. In 1902, Ross was awarded the Nobel Prize for his demonstration of the transmission mechanism of those parasites.[541] With that discovery, effective preventive treatments were developed, resulting in fewer deaths and decreasing the fear of missionaries and residents living in areas with stagnant water.

Those residing in the mountain highlands and plateaus where air and water were of greater purity than the lowlands were at an advantage prior to that discovery. Frost and ice in the elevated interior areas, found along the equator at six thousand feet, helped prevent malaria by killing the mosquitoes.[542]

Before the mosquito and malaria link was discovered, five updated guidelines were provided in 1899 to Susan and her missionary colleagues in an effort to prevent their sickness while in Africa. Some of them were similar to those outlined by Reverend Davies in 1885. They are as follows:

1. On arriving in Africa there will be *enough to do*. The constant danger is from *overdoing*. One must, therefore, at first put on the *holdbacks* till *acclimated*. Then work can be done frequently.

2. There are heavy dews, and one should be in the house by sun-down, and not go out much until after sunset. And care should be had not to get wet in the rains.

3. Eat sparingly, at first, of native fruits.

4. By some arrangement have a *fire* for fifteen or twenty minutes in every room, where one sleeps, to dry off the dampness. This will do more to save from sickness than all medicines. Too much stress cannot be laid on this.

5. Maintain a *cheerful* spirit by exercising a strong faith in God. Rest sweetly in His will and look for all needed grace at all times.[543]

I wonder if the missionaries knew or suspected the problem with mosquitoes at dusk and dawn and in moist areas, avoiding these conditions, much as we do today. Perhaps they actually thought it was something in the air or vapors causing the illnesses and death.

That continent where death was likely and cultural differences abounded is where Susan set foot in the spring of 1887 to begin her first missionary work. In the Congo, Susan's home for two years, human sacrifices were still offered, especially if a chief or leader died, and polygamy was common.[544] Slaves outnumbered free people in most towns, and they were often marched along the trails in chains and with heavy yokes. Cannibalism occurred in some areas.[545]

When Susan arrived in Angola, she lived among the Mbundu people, who spoke Kimbundu and were a predominately matrilineal society. It is believed they migrated to the area sometime in the Middle Ages. Susan learned about arranged marriages in which young girls were forced to marry older men. Girls were sold by their parents for payment of the bride price, often cattle, from the groom's family. Possibly she heard about the *mukanda* ceremony, a rite of passage into manhood, typically occurring during the May through October dry season. The twelve- to fourteen-year-old boys would go to Mukanda Camp for three to five months, where they would learn survival skills, discipline, and restraint.[546] When females reached puberty, they experienced an initiation ceremony, details of which are elusive.

There was a religious belief that ancestors play a part in the lives of the living and are still part of the community. The Mbundu believed the dead could bring disease, famine, and other loss to those who did not appease them.[547] Some followed animism, the belief that natural objects and phenomena and the universe possess souls and a spirit. Another traditional cultural religion was deism, meaning people believed in the existence of God on the evidence of only reason and nature and rejected supernatural revelation. Oh, to know how Susan reacted to these practices and thoughts, so different from the religion she practiced.

Knowledge of the Christian religions was lacking in Angola.[548] However, based upon his observations, Dr. David Livingstone thought the attitude toward Christianity was favorable in some locales. He believed fever and the slave trade were the reasons no priests lived in the African interior at the time of his travels from 1854 to 1873.[549]

When Susan reached the mouth of the Congo River, she did not know where she would be assigned. Bishop William Taylor was upriver, still searching for mission station locations. Regardless, Susan had to adapt to living in a tropical climate and learn about the dangerous insects, snakes, and wild animals. Survival included recognizing poisonous plants and dangerous animals as well as acceptance by the local communities. Those were the realities Susan, full of zeal and determination, faced upon her arrival. She was ready to help the people of Western Africa and bring Christianity to them.

9

⊱⊰⊱

Africa at Last: New Sights, Sounds, and Experiences

Congo Missions: Adjusting to Life along the River

How effective would Susan be? Did she have any brushes with death? Was she accepted by those with whom she worked and those she served? What were her reactions to her new environment? Partial answers to these questions revealed themselves as I studied self-reports of her missionary work, letters she wrote, and comments about her by bishops, colleagues, friends, and students. One of my biggest challenges was piecing together many disparate and sometimes conflicting "facts" and tidbits in order to describe her life and missionary service in Africa.

After experiencing some tumultuous times on the ocean voyage, a relieved Susan and her missionary companions arrived along the West African Guinea Coast on May 28, 1887. They stopped at Old Calabar, West Africa, which had been the center of the British slave trade. Here Evangelist Amanda Berry Smith had a chance encounter with Susan. Smith's description of their meeting suggested why traveling may not have been a major concern for Susan. "I perceived in Susie Collins, timber that meant something. She was a woman who had been well raised and well trained; she had good, broad common sense, and knew how to do a little of about everything; she was patient and of a happy, genial disposition; of high moral character and sturdy piety."[550]

After that stop, Susan and her party of at least sixteen people steamed south along the coast past the Cameroons and the Belgian Congo to the Congo River's mouth, where it drained into the Atlantic Ocean. She saw the Congo River Delta filled with lush green islands and reed marshes stretching for miles as they traveled upriver approaching Banana. As the deepest river in the world and the ninth longest, it made the Volga River Susan crossed when she worked in Fayette, Iowa, seem like a tiny stream. The river was named after the ancient Kongo Kingdom that had occupied the region near its mouth in the area where Susan lived for about a year.

Details of Susan's life along the river are sketchy. The missionaries expected transportation on the steamer *Anne Taylor*, built to travel up and down the massive river dotted with more than four thousand islands. However, there was a delay in constructing the $20,000 ship,[551] and other transportation had to be secured. Part of the slowdown was the need to raise $10,000 to pay native carriers who would transport the segmented boat parts to the Upper Congo.[552]

When Susan arrived, she apparently disembarked at Kabinda (now Cabinda), a city in Cabinda Province, a Portuguese protectorate. Its damp, tropical climate likely remined her of Iowa's hot, humid days. At one time, that area was joined to Angola, but separation occurred in 1885 when the Belgian Congo was granted a corridor to the Atlantic Ocean along the lower Congo River. While Susan was at that location, Bishop William Taylor wrote her on October 31, 1887, from Vivi, situated across the Congo River from present-day Matadi. He informed her that the Banana Creek Mission would not open until they had received authorization from the governor general at Boma, located downstream from Vivi about forty-five miles and nearly sixty-six miles from the Atlantic, whose tides reached the town.[553] That major port on the north side of the river was established as a slaving station in the 1500s by merchants from several European countries.

Bishop William Taylor, who had been waiting two months for approval after personally contacting the governor, wrote, "if you decidedly prefer to remain in Kabinda, you may by the earliest opportunity come to Vivi and remain here with our party till the field at Banana Creek can be opened and occupied."[554] Taylor sent letters of introduction to help ease her travels if she should decide to join the missionaries at Vivi who were living in a stone mission house. He asked Susan to leave one-fourth of the schoolbooks for Brother J. L. Judson, if that satisfied him, and to bring the remaining books with her to share with six unidentified Congo mission schools.[555]

What did Susan do from May through October as she waited for a mission station assignment? Perhaps she was learning the language of the Kongo people who had lived there for centuries. Undoubtedly, she was studying her Bible and mentally preparing herself for the work she would soon begin at one of the ten mission stations that were either operational or being planned in 1887. Most were to be situated along the north side of the river. Stations from the mouth of the river were Namby, Natomba, Banana, Matadi, Vivi, Brooks, Mamyanga, which was 230 miles inland, Kimpoka, located in the Stanley Pool area, and Lulaburg (now Luluabourg).[556] The most beautiful station along the river was Vivi,[557] the greatest distance inland Susan possibly traveled.

I don't know Susan's response or if she went to Vivi, which was now easier to reach than when Bishop Taylor first went upriver. By 1886, the distance from Banana to Vivi was navigable for ocean steamers. If Susan did go to Vivi, she would have seen swamp forests where tall evergreen trees such as bubinga and ovangkol thrive. Today, this expensive wood is used to make violins and luxury furniture. The thick tree canopy created a shaded, humid environment. Dozens of frog species inhabited the muddy swamp floors. Colobus and mangabey monkeys lived and thrived on tropical fruit. What did Susan think of them as well as forest elephants, buffalo, and lowland gorillas? I wonder if she wrote about the life along the river filled with crocodiles and other wildlife.

Dr. Jennie described large snakes slithering inside and outside the stone mission house of missionaries Brother and Sister Jensen when she visited them in Vivi in 1894. Brother J. L. Jensen shot a python that was nine feet and three inches long and had a sixteen-inch circumference at the largest part.[558] The snake Jensen shot was likely an African rock python, Africa's largest snake. Their bodies are patterned with triangular colored blotches varying from buff yellow, olive, chestnut, and brown. Heat-sensitive pits near their lips help them sense warm-blooded prey in the dark. Perhaps Dr. Jennie saw the crocodiles and water moccasins living in the area. Garter, bull, and timber rattlesnakes found in Iowa would not have prepared Susan for a confrontation with those snakes and crocodiles when she lived beside the Congo River.

Eventually, Susan went to Banana, sometimes called Banana Point, on the north bank of the river, where the brackish waters of Banana Creek flowed into the Congo.[559] Banana, a port by the midnineteenth century, was developed largely due to the slave trade. Here in 1879, Henry Morgan Stanley began his expedition of the Congo River. Six years later, after the European powers acknowledged King Leopold II's claim to the Congo River Basin, he announced the establishment of the Congo Free State at Banana.

Susan doubtless observed, as did Dr. Jennie, that Banana was on a narrow peninsula, with the ocean beach as its only street. When the tide was in, the beach street almost disappeared, and "The only way to get from one end of town to the other was by boat--it sounds almost Venetian doesn't it?"[560] Dr. Jennie compared the Kroosmen, who rowed the boats, to Venetian gondoliers as they sang in a "weird monotonous tone," with others responding in a "strain equally monotonous. They can get about three notes into one."[561]

Rather than going to Banana permanently, Susan was stationed at Natomba near Banana beginning December 3, 1887.[562] Remaining patient and waiting for an assignment for more than five months must have been difficult for Susan, given her eagerness to help children and spread the Gospels. Even though her journey was a short distance up the Congo, I have wondered what type of assistance this petite woman received as she managed the challenge of transporting her steamer trunk and boxes of books to her next destination twelve miles north of Banana. Here she worked with Miss Mary Kildare, described as having a spirit of indomitable zeal. Mary had paid her own way from Ireland to become a Taylor missionary. Her home stood on an acre of ground and was surrounded by a strong fence and many kinds of fruit trees. Bishop Taylor opened the Natomba Mission School in 1887 because he believed the native children were eager to learn. Susan taught them Christian songs, the Ten Commandments, and the Lord's Prayer.[563] I have wondered why in annual reports it seemed necessary to describe her as "colored" while she served in the Congo, since neither Kildare's race nor that of the other missionaries was mentioned.[564] Perhaps Bishop Taylor considered her a token, or possibly he was trying to encourage other African Americans to join his missionaries in Africa.

In early 1888, Susan sent a letter postmarked Banana, Southwest Coast of Africa, to a friend in Huron, Dakota Territory. Sharing some of her impressions of life along the Congo River Valley, she explained that she had settled into life at a beautiful station near a nice, large native village.[565] Susan wrote:

The natives seem glad to have us here, and they are very pleasant and ready to learn. What a need we have for missionaries here! Men, women, and children go around almost naked: some of them wear nothing but a "loin cloth." They know very little about good morals. The men have as many wives as they can afford to buy, and they are perfects slaves to their husbands. They will walk long distances with a child tied to their backs, going to the field to work, while the man lies around at home. Such is a heathen life here. The greatest drawback is we can do so little the first-year because we must learn the language. There are only a few here who can understand English. I think I am getting along quite well toward learning the language. My health has been good ever since I left home.

Nearly every one of the company that came out when I did have been sick of African fever, but I have not been sick a day yet, and I am very grateful for good health.

Africa is a very beautiful country, we never have cold weather. The dry season—the hot season in the United States—is the coldest season here. But now it is midsummer. Gardens are beautiful and green corn is almost ready for the table. The wood [sic] is alive with music of birds, and some of them are very pretty. I can hardly believe that it is January.[566]

It is likely the language spoken was Kishi-Congo, prevalent on the west coast of the Belgian Congo at that time.[567]

Seeking Understanding: Using Susan's Letter as a Guide

Capuchin, French, and Portuguese priests and missionaries learned various lessons when working with the Kongo people as they tried to Christianize them during the seventeenth and eighteenth centuries. The French who mastered the local language were more readily accepted than the Capuchins, who had acquired only enough of their language to teach the essentials of Christianity. The Capuchins looked down upon the Kongo people, treating them roughly and forcing them to attend church. Most Portuguese priests did not speak their language and did not interact with the people in a way that would create trust. They failed to establish a cadre of native clergy to help sustain their efforts. Jesuits in 1624 took the education of the native youth seriously and produced a Catechism in their language of Kikongo. All failed to adapt Christianity in a way the local people could understand and apply it to their lives.[568] Bishop Taylor appeared to have learned from the mistakes of those predecessor missionaries.

Clearly, one lesson assimilated was the need to speak the local language, and Susan did. Later, she learned Kimbundu when assigned to Angola. Bishop Taylor recognized the need to educate the children and selected Susan because she had the requisite credentials. In Susan's letter to her friend, it appears she had not accepted the Congolese values and was judging the people by American standards and the religion with which she was familiar. One sight that bothered American missionaries was the nearly naked African people. Their attempt to change them and instill American values was not uncommon during that period in missionary history.

Susan's values and standards seemed to reflect the comments and writings about native Africans shared by Americans and Europeans who had traveled and worked in Africa. Those travelers felt the Africans needed help in governing themselves and used that as a rationale for gaining control of much of Africa during the last quarter of the nineteenth century. European rulers reached a series of agreements at the Berlin West African Conference that aided their success as they saw opportunities to use Africa's resources to enhance their own wealth. No Africans participated in the conference. Susan arrived in Africa as those agreements were being operationalized, and changes were taking place to the dismay of those whose tribal and kinship units had been in the region for centuries.[569]

Susan expressed her distain for polygamy and the behavior of the men she described as lazy toward their wives. It is unlikely she was aware that at one time, the people of the Kongo Kingdom thought the missionaries encouraged monogamy as a means of depopulation so Europeans could more easily conquer them.[570] And she did not know the long-established gender roles in Africa, where women did the work in and around the house. That work included childrearing, house maintenance, getting water sometimes from long distances, planting, harvesting, and food preparation. The men's role was that of hunter, but between times, they didn't appear to contribute much to the family. Susan was used to rural Midwestern men whose farming included raising crops and livestock. I do not know if her thinking about those values and roles evolved, but a review of her later correspondence suggested she did not accept polygamy but eventually realized she could not change the long-practiced gender role patterns.

Susan's frustration with gender roles was likely lessened through her joy in nature, revealed when she described some of the birds she saw as "very pretty." Possibly she observed the colorful birds called turacos, especially the yellow-billed that has a tall, olive-green crest and upper body and slate-blue lower body and wings. They live in forests and have a piercing scream similar to jungle monkeys. The Guinea or green turaco has a fluffy-looking crest, a long tail, and red eyes and beak. At nineteen to twenty inches long, they are about two inches longer than their yellow-billed relatives. The great blue, at twenty-eight to thirty inches, would have been the largest turaco Susan might have seen. They have a bluish-black crest, and their wings, tail, neck, and upper breast are turquoise blue. They also sport a bright yellow, red-tipped bill and a greenish-yellow low breast and belly. Birds with those color combinations and size are not seen in the Midwest. Other birds she feasted her eyes upon may have included the greater flamingo with long, pink, stilt-like legs; square-tailed nightjar; and the white-spotted flufftail with its bronze head and white spots on its black wings and lower breast. The loud caw-caw call of the Guinea turaco may have become familiar as she learned a new language. At dawn and dusk, she might have listened to the deep, guttural sound of the great blue alternated with a softer trill as she read her Bible, prayed, and prepared the children's lessons.

Writing about the status of her health and that of her missionary colleagues became a recurring theme during Susan's thirty-three years in Africa. She assumed the role of nurse with many of them—some of whom lived, and others died. "Being better able to withstand the climate, it was she who cared for the missionaries who became sick and died, prepared them for burial, and conduced their services."[571]

Susan's first nursing experiences occurred when her mother, sisters Martha Indiana and Maranda, and brother William were suffering with tuberculosis, sometimes called the white plague. Her knowledge and confidence in nursing skills may have deepened with the medical courses she took at the Chicago Training School.

While at Natomba, then at Chavunga near Banana, and later back at Natomba, Susan had time to adjust to life along the Congo River. There she taught the local children and kept house. Whether or not Susan and Mary Kildare had the opportunity to live in the house Bishop Taylor ordered built at Natomba is undetermined because the finish date has not been found.[572] That house shipped from Liverpool was described as small, with dimensions of twenty-two by twenty-four feet. Upon completion, it sat on pillars six feet above the ground to keep the inhabitants dry and healthy.[573]

When Dr. Jennie was in the area near the mouth of the Congo River, she described staying in a corrugated iron house, the one where Susan may have resided with Mary Kildare.[574] She compared being in that house to living under a tin cup, where lizards walking on the roof sounded like troops and gentle raindrops like a torrential downpour.[575]

After serving twenty-five months in the Belgian Congo, Bishop Taylor assigned Susan to the Pungo Andongo Mission in Angola, which she reached in September 1889.[576] Angola is located along the west coast of Africa, south of the equator and 249 nautical miles or 286 miles from the Port of Banana, Congo. A current boat journey is estimated at one day. Travel time in 1889 would have taken several days longer. Angola, where Susan completed her missionary career in 1920, is slightly smaller than Texas.

I have wondered if she felt sad to leave the Congo Delta and how she embraced her new experiences in a region much different than the humid, mosquito-infested Banana Point area. Her new assignment meant learning at least one other language and developing awareness of the political situation in Angola, which in the seventeen and eighteenth centuries had been a Portuguese trading area for slaves. In 1836, the Portuguese government had officially ended the slave trade. Beginning in 1885, four years before Susan arrived, the government consolidated its power over Angola. Thus, Susan had to adjust to working with Portuguese officials and other missionaries with different expectations. Susan's two years along the Congo River were a dress rehearsal for her thirty-one years in Angola.

Alexander-Dickman Hall was originally called Main or College Hall. Construction began in 1855. It was the only building on campus during the time Susan Angeline Collins attended Upper Iowa University in Fayette, Iowa from 1876 to 1879. Courtesy watercolorist Emmett Van Buskirk.

Luanda, Angola: Harbor and lower city view. Methodist Mission is in upper right. This and other Paul Blake photos may be found at https://paulblake.smugmug.com/

Luanda: Methodist Episcopal Church Mission main residence building. Florinda Barbosa Bessa, one of Susan's students, is visible in upstairs window. Estimate photo taken in early 1890's. Courtesy Paul Blake.

Pungo Andongo Methodist Mission viewed from top of Black Rocks. White buildings at lower left and center are mission buildings. Courtesy Paul Blake.

Trail Susan walked from Pungo Andongo east to Malanje and Quessua in early 1890's. Courtesy Paul Blake.

Quessua Mission House on Quessua Mountain in early 1900's. Courtesy Paul Blake.

Susan holding a baby at the Quessua Mission, 1905. Note grass roof. Mission Biographical Reference File, General Commission Archives & History, United Methodist Church.

Susan surrounded by children at Quessua Mission, 1905. Portrait File, State Historical Society of Iowa, Des Moines.

Workers constructing an adobe building likely at Quessua Mission early 1900's. Courtesy Paul Blake.

Susan, dressed in white, and Martha Drummer, dressed in black, hosted missionaries and local workers at West Central Africa Mission Conference in Quessua sometime after 1908. Martha arrived there in May 1906. Author's collection.

Susan, at right and wearing a black dress, was responsible for construction of girls home and classroom building at Quessua Mission prior to 1910. Author's collection.

Susan, right, is with her colleague Martha Drummer and the children they cared for and educated about 1914. They worked together at the Woman's Foreign Missionary Society (WFMS) Quessua Girls School until Susan retired in 1920. Author's collection.

The mission babies and toddlers were a joy to Susan. She taught the older girls to sew and make clothes for themselves and the younger children. Author's collection.

Reverend Joseph Hartzell became Missionary Bishop to Africa in 1896 and served until 1916. He is sitting near the original buildings of the Taylor Mission first called Munhall Mission and later Quessua Mission. Courtesy of Paul Blake.

Florinda Bessa (third from right), Martha Drummer, and Susan Collins (far right) at Quessua WFMS Girls School about 1915. This boarding school was begun about 1898 and staffed by Susan and Hilda Larson, RN. Courtesy of Paul Blake.

Quarterly Mission Conference, Quessua, which Susan and Martha helped host. Susan is standing in front of central church window. Bishop Hartzell is third from right and Missionary William Dodson is on far right. Courtesy of Paul Blake.

This is the original Methodist mission station in Malange, Angola, and the furthest inland at 250 miles east of Luanda. It is one of five stations initially opened in 1885 by Bishop William Taylor. Courtesy of Paul Blake.

Journeying missionaries and carriers taking a break from the hot sun under a baobab tree. Courtesy of Paul Blake.

Missionaries encouraged villagers to burn fetishes. The round woven baskets on poles at the center back and left are used to store and protect food from animals. Courtesy of Paul Blake.

Man is playing Thumb Piano, an instrument unique to Africa. Susan played one and sang to the children. During retirement she played hers at church and community gatherings. This one is similar to the one she gave Reverend Clinton. Courtesy of Paul Blake.

Fayette was established in 1874 nine years after the Collins family moved to the area. During that decade Susan worked at the Fayette House, the three-story building in the right foreground. Guests were still staying there when she returned home in 1920. Author's collection.

Susan, in late 1920's, is displaying rugs and baskets created by her Quessua students. She is standing in the yard of her Fayette, Iowa home located at the corner of Alexander and State Streets. Courtesy of Barry Zbornik.

Susan was an active participant in the Methodist Episcopal Church in Fayette from her retirement until her death in June 1940. The STAR honoring her was in the sanctuary to the left of the bell tower. Author's collection.

Bishop G. Bromley Oxnan, Omaha, Nebraska visited Susan in April 1937. She was living with the Graham siblings, her childhood friends, on their farm northeast of Fayette. Author's collection.

Susan was buried in the Lima Cemetery located six miles northeast of Fayette. Her gravestone is adjacent to the one shared by her mother Sarah, sister Maranda, and brother William. Sister Martha Indiana Collins Thompson is buried next to them. Author's collection.

Thank Offering Program Spring 1951 at the Fayette Methodist Episcopal Church honoring work of earlier and current missionaries from the church. The author is in front row, left holding woven baskets and a farm worker's hat. Author's collection.

10

⟨∞∞∞⟩

Life in Angola: What's Next?

Traveling to the Interior: Meeting New Challenges

Susan knew she had much to learn and many adjustments to make as the steamer moved south along the flat, arid Angolan coastline in July 1889. Once again, she was facing the unknown, just as the first African slaves from Angola had upon their August 1619 arrival in Jamestown, Virginia. Those twenty-plus Africans were stolen from a Portuguese slave ship and brought to America by an English warship flying a Dutch flag. Did her father share stories about his ancestral heritage, and were her people from Angola? Going into the heart of Angola might have daunted a lesser being, but Susan's deep reserve of confidence and faith led her forward. Some believe the school Susan started in Angola in 1893 may have been the model Mary McLeod Bethune used in 1904 when she founded the Daytona Normal and Industrial Institute for Negro Girls in Daytona, Florida.

Susan viewed the occasional cliffs and bluffs of red sandstone, likely wondering what lay beyond and what had transpired over two centuries earlier that might have sealed her fate, bringing her to this moment. White, fleecy clouds moved across the bright blue sky. Susan waited for the steamer bringing her from the Belgian Congo to anchor near the Luanda harbor so she could descend a wobbly ladder on the side of the swaying

135

ship. She held the rungs tightly. Perhaps some of the local missionaries rowed a small boat out to meet her and helped her climb gingerly aboard to be taken to land.[577]

As Susan came ashore, imagine other Luanda-based missionaries extending greetings, perhaps offering a prayer of thanks for her safe arrival, and then walking her to their mission home situated on one of the highest bluffs in the city. Under Bishop Taylor's direction, it was constructed after he bought land and began mission work in Angola in 1885.[578] Later, that building became a stop and a stepping-stone for missionaries to prepare prior to going to the interior. Living higher up meant the smoke from the lower portion of the city was blown away, and the chances of contracting malaria were limited, creating healthier living conditions.

Dr. Jennie recounted the building's appearance, typical of most Luanda structures, to her friend Lizzie while she stayed there in May 1894. "The walls of stone are covered with a beautiful colored cement. There is far more variety here than in Las Palmas and other tropical cities I have seen since we have purple, green, yellow, red, etc. instead of the 'everlasting' white which though beautiful becomes monotonous. The house is built in sections or wings; my room being in the third story of the central; the other wings have each two stories. The house has six roofs each having four sides."[579]

She described bricks made of hard, fine material and looking like pipes arranged in vertical rows to form the exterior. They were covered with a cement made of plaster and supported on a bamboo-pole roof. Just as Susan had done earlier, Dr. Jennie frequently went to the roof to write letters and stay cool, catching the breezes from the Atlantic Ocean.[580]

Luanda was established in the mid-1500s, and its cathedral was completed in 1853. Ten years later, a Jesuit church was built, and in 1604, the Monastery of Sao Jose could be seen in the city. Finally, after another 150 years, the sandy, muddy streets were replaced with cobblestones, and attractive public buildings were erected.[581] By the time Susan arrived, Luanda was considered "the greatest and most developed of Portuguese cities outside mainland Portugal."[582]

Telephones were introduced in 1884, and one year later, construction started on the first section of the railroad between Luanda and the fertile Malanje highlands, Susan's eventual destination. Its completion in 1909 made it easier for Susan, her missionary colleagues, and their supplies to reach the Angolan interior. Obtaining fresh water had been a problem for the city since its inception and hindered growth.[583] About the time Susan reached the city, an aqueduct was being built to bring fresh water from the Bengo River, located approximately ten miles north.[584] Prior to that, river water had been transported to Luanda in barrels. Though not as bustling as Chicago, it was undoubtedly a change for Susan after living in the Congo River Delta region for two years.

Susan was expected to begin learning Portuguese and Kimbundu upon her arrival and to gather needed supplies for her travels to Pungo Andongo. Soon she would go east through a region of varied terrain from the coastline to the inland plains of dry savanna, called the Malanje Plateau, with a high point of approximately 3,200 feet. Carriers would transport her supplies, and she would probably ride in a hammock when walking became difficult. Susan would hear early-morning sounds of lions and hyenas permeating the air. Their grunts, growls, and snarls often unnerved first-time missionaries, as those sounds were unlike the night calls of the owls and coyotes often heard in the Midwestern United States. Likely, Susan would have expressed amazement when seeing impalas, cheetahs, African wild hogs, and elephants cross her path during her trek inland.

Bishop Taylor's first missionaries, their wives, and children, all Caucasians except Charles L. Miller, arrived in Luanda in March 1885. Charles, an African American and son of freed slaves, died three weeks after his arrival and was buried in Luanda.[585] The others stayed until about the middle of May. The Portuguese governor was surprised and dismayed to see families accompanying the men, who didn't realize the dangers of the heat, humidity, and tropical diseases. Those missionaries became the founding members of the first Methodist Episcopal church in Angola. Soon after their arrival, some of the men ventured inland and established centers, where Susan would soon serve.[586] The thrust of their programs was fourfold: education, evangelism, industrial work, and health care.[587]

Missionaries typically used four methods for crossing the African terrain: by foot, wagon, donkey or mule back, and hammock.[588] Occasionally, they traveled in dugout canoes or rode oxen. The Portuguese name for hammock is *machilla*. People using them rode in a reclining position. Sometimes they were carried in a tipoa that allowed them to sit up rather than recline. Ease of riding in a hammock depended upon the quality of the trails and the skill of the carriers. A team was considered sixteen men, and they alternated using two carriers at a time, trotting along the trail. Often the rider was jolted about as the hammock thumped on stumps or termite mounds or banged against trees. One might swelter under the canvas top if the sun was out or shiver if cold winds were blowing.[589]

Because I have found no record of Susan's travels to the interior, I used accounts by Bishop Taylor and Dr. Jennie describing their inland routes to reconstruct Susan's possible experiences. The Taylors and other missionaries began their journey to the interior by boat.[590]

To arrive at Dondo, the first inland station, Susan likely went thirty miles south from Luanda by steamer and into the mouth of the Cuanza River, located midway along the Angolan shoreline and described by Bishop Taylor "as large as the Hudson."[591] Crocodiles infested the river lined with grotesquely shaped baobab trees. One has been known to shelter up to forty people in its huge trunk. When leafless, their spreading branches look like roots sticking up into the air. They have long brown seed pods extending from long stems. One missionary thought the pods looked like monkeys hanging from their tails.[592]

The Cuanza River had cut its path through red clay soil and evolved into a major trade route. After traveling southeast 180 miles on a steamer, Susan would have reached Dondo. That interior port at the head of the Cuanza River was one of the few navigable waterways in Angola, accommodating boats of a significant size. Bishop Taylor observed, "Dondo is a noted trading centre, and has a population of about five thousand, mostly negroes."[593] He reported watching carriers passing through the town at all hours, bringing their cargoes and singing loudly. "Those who stayed danced, sang, and clapped their hands until the morning hours."[594] Dondo was laid out with long streets bordered by sidewalks and streetlamps. It was here Susan met Reverend Amos Withey, presiding elder at the Dondo Mission; his wife, Irene; son, Bertie; and two young daughters, Lottie and Florence.[595] Withey was highly regarded by Bishop Taylor and when absent appointed him to act as superintendent of Angola missions.

After getting acquainted with the Witheys and resting, Susan departed for Pungo Andongo, eighty-nine miles east. Susan's physical and mental fortitude were tested as she traversed the first fifty-one miles on a narrow fifteen-inch-wide path with increasing elevation. That ancient caravan trail went through a region of craggy, rugged mountains and precipitous cliffs to the Nhanguepepo Mission Station. Exhaustion set in at the conclusion of each day. The station consisted of 2,500 acres used as an industrial farm and school. It served as a location for missionaries to stay, learn the local language, and then move farther into the interior.[596] Taylor valued the property at $6,000. He reported an organized Methodist Episcopal church composed of thirteen native men and boys.

The path used by merchants and oxen helped to make possible missionary penetration to the Angolan interior, as did the bush stores along the trails.[597] In 1894, it took Dr. Taylor three days to traverse that portion of the trail with a guide and hammock bearers.[598] She rode in the hammock only when crossing streams; otherwise she walked. A cook prepared breakfast of baked bananas and cocoa over a small fire. Lodging for the travelers was at government shelters called *quartels*, where those who carried their own bed and provisions could stay.[599]

The next mission, Pungo Andongo, was Susan's destination. Thirty-eight miles east, it was reached by struggling across a series of ridges and valleys. Merchants had used this rugged pathway for years, often marching captured slaves to the coast. Due to poor soil, the timber was stunted and sparse.[600] The grass was not heavy, helping to prevent forest fires. Pungo Andongo was a trading center with between 1,200 and 1,500 residents in 1889.[601] Bishop Taylor graphically described the town as "wedged in between stupendous mountains, in solid blocks of conglomerate of small stones of basalt and flint, perpendicular for a thousand feet on all sides."[602] In early times, it was the capital of the Ndongo Kingdom.

Imagine Susan thinking as she trudged along, *I prefer the hills, prairies, and rolling countryside of my Iowa to these steep, rocky paths! But I will continue onward! I do miss all of the wildflowers I grew accustomed to as a teenager. Then I didn't appreciate the bright yellows of goldenrod and black-eyed Susan and the striking orange of the butterfly milkweed. Even the Queen Anne's lace was a lovely contrast against the rich purple of the chicory. I wonder if my parents ever used the roots for coffee.*

Perhaps Susan was shocked out of her day dreaming when she saw the rocks looming ahead, some more than 650 feet high jutting from the floor of the flat savanna. New technology shows that Bishop Taylor's estimate of over one thousand feet was an exaggeration. Moss and lichen grew on the rocks, but colors varied depending upon the season and the angle of the sunlight. In 1671, the Portuguese established a military fort among these rocks that covered about 7.5 by 3.7 miles. It was rumored that parents in the area told the children they would be put in the fort if they were naughty. Would Susan have used that threat when children she was teaching misbehaved? About the time Susan retired, political prisoners were held there, and later during Angola's civil war, the rock fortress was an important battleground.[603]

Dr. Jennie thought the region was wonderful and wished her friend Lizzie could see the rocks. She described them in a fall 1894 letter to Lizzie. "Imagine if you can, 'conglomerates' five hundred feet high! Some of them have a slope that permits us to climb to the top and then the view we get is magnificent Some start up perpendicularly or at an acute angle, then we can only stand at the base and wish ourselves to the top. On one of the lowest rocks we saw several footprints—perhaps cut by some convict or possibly it was imprinted there while the water still 'covered the earth' or this part of it at least."[604]

The legend of the African tribes who live among the rocks is that footprints were left by Queen Nzinga Mbande of Ndongo, also called queen of Angola. They believed she was taking a bath at the base of the rocks and was seen by soldiers. She ran to hide, leaving her footprints. The queen was known for a successful struggle against the Portuguese in the seventeenth century when she established the African state of Matambu.[605]

Susan had the opportunity to live near the majestic Black Rocks of Pungo Andongo from August 1889 until June 1890. Here she shivered in the mornings and evenings and sweltered under the fiery sun during the day. Many who came there suffered from recurring illnesses. When Dr. Jennie arrived four years later, sign language and using Portuguese remained the best ways to communicate, as most residents did not know English.[606] While Susan resided at Pungo Andongo, North and South Dakota were formed from the Dakota Territory in November 1889. That year, Benjamin Harrison, a Civil War veteran, became the twenty-third president of the United States, Thomas Edison showed his first motion picture, and King Ferdinand II of Portugal died at age seventy-three.

The Pungo Andongo Station contained "a large adobe house, including a chapel and store-room, and nearly an acre of ground with fruit-bearing trees in the town, and a good farm of about 300 acres a mile out, worth probably altogether about $4,000."[607] When the Reverend Amos Withey family was away, Reverend Charles Gordon was in charge and acted as one of the principal missionary merchants. He would eventually marry Bishop Taylor's niece, Dr. Jennie. The bishop was pleased that he and Reverend Amos Withey were bringing the Gospel into the lives of many traders who came from the "far interior and could not be reached by ordinary means."[608] The mission had grown beyond self-support and was making enough money to open new stations farther into the interior by the time Susan arrived. Bishop Taylor lamented the two missionary deaths that occurred at Pungo Andongo, "one was Henry Kelley, a noble missionary apprentice from the Vey tribe of Liberia, and the other of dear Sister Dodson (formerly Miss Brannen from Boston)."[609]

In early 1890, Bishop Taylor appointed Susan to the Dondo mission to replace workers who had suddenly left and gone back to the General Conference in the United States. She was sent to teach at the once self-supporting day school and where Reverend Charles Gordon was selected to preach. Taylor wrote, "It is an essential strategic point in our work, and must be sustained."[610] Susan was the only teacher at the station. That gave her ample opportunity to utilize the knowledge she had acquired eleven years earlier while earning her Normal Training Certificate. The assignment may have been especially meaningful because due to her race, she couldn't have a teaching position in either Iowa or South Dakota.

Later in 1890, Susan was residing at the Malanje Mission, assisting missionaries Samuel Mead, his wife, Ardella, and their niece Bertha. Bishop Taylor had initiated her move because he felt the station was shorthanded, and he recognized Susan's indefatigable energy. And he knew the growing church required more help to meet the needs of the local population.[611] Developed in the mid-nineteenth century, Malanje is located on the country's principal plateau between Luanda and the Cunago Valley. The area has a high-altitude climate.

After Susan had retraced her steps between Dondo and Pungo

Andongo, she faced an unfamiliar, rough, narrow, rocky path leading sixty-two miles to Malanje. When the bishop had walked the route one year earlier in mid-June, he covered twenty-five miles the first day and slept in the Kalunda Quartel, which he considered a crudely constructed barracks.[612]

While going twenty miles from Pungo Andongo, just as Bishop Taylor did, Susan crossed a series of ridges that had more sand and thinner grass and scrub timber than the first part of her trek.[613] As Susan continued inland, the ridges she faced became grassy, with little streams near the surface. Closer to Malanje, the ridges became less fertile and much higher, with ascents of two to four miles.[614]

When walking during the rainy season, she heard the drops land with a plop and saw little swirls of dust stirred up. After the rain ceased, droplets formed and sparkled like diamonds as the sun shone, bringing a freshness to the earth and her spirits.

I've wondered how Susan's stamina compared to Bishop Taylor's as she made this rigorous trip. He traversed nineteen miles on the second day and described his lodging that evening as a "rude construction of poles, with a roof, but sides not covered with mortar or grass. It gave shelter from dew and afforded fresh outside air."[615] Native carriers accompanied him when he made his journey across northern Angola in an easterly direction though an abundant amount of hardwood timber.[616] Those traveling that uneven path, with reported elevations of over four thousand feet, needed to be in good physical condition and have sturdy shoes to complete the arduous journey on foot. As Susan, approaching forty, reached her destination, she would have seen an old caravan trail opening out into long, wide grass plains.[617] Malanje is at latitude 9 degrees 31' 41 S and at longitude 16 degrees 20' 43 E.[618]

The trail Bishop Taylor, Susan, and Dr. Jennie traveled meant pain and suffering to many Africans. Bishop Taylor lamented "the hundreds of thousands of slaves sold in Loanda for two hundred years who trod this weary way 'mid tears and blood—poor captives who fathers had been slain because they dared to defend their homes. On each side of the path is a continuous grave one hundred-fifty miles long."[619] Evidence of the dead was visible at the side of the trail.[620]

African slave trade began in the early 1600s. In the 1650s, the Belgian

Congo started sending slaves to the Americas, and soon the trade moved to northern Angola. The practice continued until the nineteenth century when demand for slaves decreased as the decade of the 1860s ended. Later in 1897, more than four thousand slaves were shipped out of Angola when the slave trade had a recovery.[621] Transporting coffee, wax, sugar, ivory, copal often misrepresented as amber, palm oil, and natural rubber along those caravan trails increased as the slave trade diminished.[622]

Living in the Mountains: Dangers and Difficulties

It may have been difficult for Susan to fully comprehend what life on the mountain plateau of Angola meant. I've often questioned how well prepared she was to survive as she made her way to the interior. Her faith and pioneer spirit would have carried her forward, heightened by her desire to be a leader as the first African American female missionary representing the Methodist Episcopal Church in Angola. Helping her people receive and understand the Word of God was a driving commitment in Susan's life.

Bishop Taylor eventually recognized the dangers and challenges to survival his missionaries encountered while living among people who practiced rituals and ceremonies often involving animal sacrifices. At a conference, he explained his concerns to the Methodist Episcopal Church hierarchy. "Africa cannot be brought to God without an amount of holy living, and triumphant dying at the front, far exceeding all standards of computation. Our people will have to get over their mortal dread of dying in Africa, for those who God shall honor with a call, so live and labor in Africa, will it the best place in the world to die, and thus add vital force to 'their works which follow them.'"[623]

An array of varied problems caused Bishop Taylor to acknowledge the self-support attempt was a greater challenge for the missionaries than he had expected. That realization occurred five years after his 1884 appointment as bishop to Africa, when he wrote, "Two years were required for apprenticeship, experimenting in many things, with everything to learn essential to self-support."[624] At the onset, he was full of fervor and had high and perhaps unrealistic expectations for his missionaries. He believed they, in order to serve effectively, "should conform to the culture of their new home."[625] As they lived among the local people, the missionaries were to learn their language and eat their foods. Not all officials in the church agreed with Bishop Taylor and believed the missionaries were living in pitiful situations, making it difficult for them to fulfill their roles.[626] In fact, "Living conditions were rugged on those initial mission stations."[627]

Hopefully, Bishop Taylor warned the people he recruited about the dangers of disease, lack of food and potable water, and an unsafe living environment. Susan, knowing some of the potential dangers, believed she would survive due to her faith and return safely to her homeland—or she wouldn't have made the commitment to travel to Africa. Perhaps she thought dying on the continent of her ancestors would put her spiritually closer to them.

When Susan traveled through Dondo, she may have been aware that three female missionaries had perished there. During his 1889 visit, Bishop Taylor and Stella Withey, born in 1875, had walked a mile from Dondo to the mission cemetery protected with a high stone wall. They visited the graves of Sister Cooper and the woman Taylor described as "our grandest Dondo worker, Mrs. Mary Myers Davenport, M.D."[628] Inscribed on Davenport's tombstone were her last words addressed to Jesus, "I die for Thee, here in Africa."[629] About one month later, Stella was buried near her. Bishop Taylor wrote, "So that three of our missionary heroines sleep in Jesus at Dondo. Their ashes are among the guarantees of our ultimate success in giving life to millions in Africa who are, 'dead in trespasses and sins.'"[630] When she was shown these three graves, Susan might have experienced many emotions, including sadness, fear, and peacefulness that she was in the place where God wanted her to be.

Upon Susan's arrival at the Malanje Station in 1890, she would have seen the visible graves of the twelve-year-old daughter of a missionary couple and a third missionary.[631] Even with those deaths, Bishop Taylor held to his self-sufficiency ideal. Though gardening provided some food, "These evangelists were not robust, their diet was seriously inadequate, their health was often poor, several of them died or saw their children die."[632] I have contemplated how, when viewing those graves, Bishop Taylor could justify his steadfastness to the self-sufficiency model. Perhaps he simply thought there was an endless supply of Americans who wanted to be missionaries in Africa.

Missionaries often survived because the native tribes thought they had a fetish superior to their own.[633] Perhaps they thought it was the cross. While we don't know the indigenous adults' reaction to Susan and the fetishes they imagined she had, we know the children loved her dearly, as reflected in letters written to her upon her retirement.[634] Possibly Susan was able to respond to their needs with more understanding than the white missionaries. Imagine the countless adjustments the children had to make as they moved from the bush to living in a house and attending a mission school.

Often, housing for the missionaries was inadequate, compromising their health and safety. However, the Dondo house was constructed to resist the encroachment of white ants (termites), temperature fluctuation, and the effect of wet and dry seasons.[635] That one-story house made of solid masonry was 114 feet long and 26 feet wide. Divided by a central hall, it had two large rooms at each end, allowing for ventilation.[636] It would be interesting to know how much assistance and construction advice Taylor's missionaries were willing to accept from the Africans, who made their much smaller homes of mud wattle and thatched dried grass roofs.

While Bishop Taylor seemed to expect death as an outcome for many of his missionaries, how did he react when his niece, Dr. Jennie Taylor Gordon, died at the age of thirty on December 29, 1897, after a nine-day illness? She had been in Africa less than five years and was survived by her husband, Reverend Charles Gordon, and daughter, Florence Taylor Gordon, just past one year old. Some say Susan and Ardella Mead acted as midwives at Florence's birth.[637] Cause of Dr. Jennie's death was hematuric fever, a type of urinary tract infection. Her burial was at the mission graveyard in Malanje, with hundreds of Africans attending her funeral. Do you wonder how Bishop Taylor's zeal for self-sufficiency was affected when Dr. Jennie died? Her father, Andrew, the bishop's brother, had opposed her traveling to Africa. But she was headstrong and wanted adventure and to help people, so she defied her father's wishes. She had planned to remain two and a half years,[638] but after meeting and marrying Reverend Gordon, Dr. Jennie had extended her stay.

Likely, improper diet, inadequate shelter, or an insect-borne disease weakened Dr. Taylor, causing her death. Missionary William Dobson visited the Quessua home where she died and described it thus: "'a noble structure so far as the walls are concerned, but not a window in it of any description—having simply a door at each end.'" He cited lack of light and ventilation, "'with draft on opening both doors and the rotten condition of the roof'" as a fair example of the old-style mission buildings, contributing to the physical breakdown of the missionaries he knew.[639]

Bishop Taylor, until his forced retirement in 1896, continued to expect the missionary candidates he recruited to survive in varied environments. He emphasized the need for his missionaries to be self-supporting and open-minded and for all the missions to be independent."[640] The bishop was adept at adapting to new countries and their culture and lifestyles. I believe Susan's adaptability to the people and their conditions allowed her to thrive and provide an example to newly arriving missionaries. Susan demonstrated self-sacrifice and a life filled with love for all humans. She and the other missionaries had bonded based upon passion for their work and the need to survive. Continue with me and learn more about Susan's life in Angola.

11

⊶⊷⊶

Angolan Experiences: Teaching the Children

Malanje: June 1890–February 1892

Working with children to give them a better life seemed to be Susan's passion. While at Malanje, she demonstrated her initiative and leadership skills. When the time was right, she requested a transfer to Canandua, an 1890 offshoot of the Malanje mission. Her goal was starting a home and school for children, either orphaned or in difficult family situations. After nearly two years at Malanje, her request was granted. Susan was a champion for the education of girls and women in Angola.

Her transfer from Pungo Andongo to Malanje was being discussed in late 1889, the year her brother Albert petitioned to become administrator of their father's estate.[641] That was five years after Isaac's death, and Albert was twenty-two. What were Albert's motives for waiting to petition? Maybe he delayed until Susan was in Africa so she couldn't contest the will, but more likely, he needed to be of legal age. Being thousands of miles away, it is probable she didn't know about the petition and eventual sale of the land for $250 in 1894.

At the time of the sale, Albert lived in Black Hawk County, Iowa.[642]

He was still there in 1895, residing in La Porte City with his deceased sister Indiana's husband, William Thompson.[643] That is the last record I found for Albert. It is unknown if he was alive in 1900 when Susan was in the United States for a year or whether she saw him if he was living.

Susan was probably more concerned about getting safely to Malanje in 1890 than being the administer of her father's estate. Maybe she thought Richard, if he was still alive or in the area, should serve that role because he was older than Albert.

Upon her arrival in Malanje, noted for its merchandise in the open-air market, Susan would have discovered a town with two thousand inhabitants.[644] Items transported to and from this center of commerce often included rubber, coffee, and Angolan-grown bananas as well as liquor, mostly rum, and textiles. During the colonial period, Malanje Province was an important hub for Angola's coffee and cotton industries. Heli Chatelain, a Swiss missionary trained in America, traveled that area buying beans and corn during harvest time and selling buttons, bracelets, belts, clothing items, medicine, flint, lead, and gunpowder to locals.[645] He was a talented linguist recruited by Bishop Taylor to go to Angola in 1885 and prepare for the arrival of the first group of missionaries and arrange for their accommodations. William Summers, a medical doctor, eventually went to the Angolan interior with Taylor, accompanied by Chatelain.[646]

Susan lived in a serviceable home at the Malanje Mission. Organized in 1885, five years prior to her arrival, it had a combined school, farm, and mechanical work area.[647] The timbers and girders in the house were nearly all white ant–proof just as the Dondo house. It is possible the missionaries used Sneezewood, readily available at the time, for the timbers in their houses because it is extremely durable wood and resistant to termites.[648] After setting the timbers, a heavy layer of adobe clay cement was applied to keep out rats, rain, and fire. A short while later, the existing rooms were whitewashed, and a new room was finished and fitted for use as a classroom and chapel.[649] Susan and her housemates benefitted from a chimney and fireplace during the cold July weather on the mountain plateau.[650]

In the process of starting the Malanje mission farm, several of the male missionaries built a thousand-foot-long fence using trees growing on the property.[651] The fence surrounded the house and protected the residents and their garden from wild animals. Excess lumber was sold for self-support.[652]

The cleared land revealed fertile, virgin soil, allowing crops to thrive. Prior to Susan's arrival, corn, beans, sugarcane, and yams were doing well until the missionaries became ill. Unable to tend the land and protect the fencing, local people stole it for firewood, allowing hogs and cattle to devour the unprotected garden and all other green things on the farm.[653]

When an agriculture program for the boys was established, the farming operation became more successful. Keeping crops alive during drought periods was a challenge. If it had not been for a nearby river that occasionally spread out onto the plains to form a small lake and give moisture to the soil, farming that land would have been discouraging and unproductive.[654]

Bishop Taylor visited Malanje in June 1889. Prior to the visit, Samuel Mead, the missionary in charge of that station, proudly wrote about the abundant corn harvest with a total yield of 150 bushels.[655] There the "Sugar cane grew so densely on the land that nothing less than an elephant could wade through it."[656] Cane grown by the students and missionaries was juiced to create a delicious beverage. Making the beverage required a number of steps. After cutting the cane with a long-bladed, sharp knife and stripping off the leaves, the cane stalks were sent at least twice through a crushing mill to extract the juice. Either students or oxen powered the mill. The juice was finally boiled down in a huge cast-iron kettle sent by the bishop. Eighty gallons of reddish juice boiled approximately five hours would yield nearly eight gallons of cane sugar syrup. Each day during harvest, the missionaries and the male students were able to convert about fifty pounds of cane into juice to boil down. The processed cane provided all of the molasses they needed and was relished as a substitute for maple sugar,[657] commonly boiled in the Northeast Iowa location where Susan grew to womanhood. It is probable her father grew sugarcane on his land, and her mother made molasses to use as a sugar substitute in baking or served it with corn bread and griddle cakes. I remember going to the field with my grandfather and helping cut our cane to deliver to a nearby village for processing.

While visiting Malanje, Bishop Taylor determined the property to be worth $6,000, including the value of the recently completed two-story mission house.[658] Using 2015 figures, the real value of that property would be $157,849.[659] After his visit, the bishop ordered a grinding mill to make cornmeal for better utilization of the crop. Later, Susan and the other missionaries maintained a small store for the local sale of excess farm-grown produce. Some of the money was used to purchase school supplies for Susan's use.[660]

The boys learned to care for an array of farm animals, including twenty head of cattle, three yoke of oxen, eleven breeding sows and a boar, and a number of chickens that supplied eggs and meat. Value of the animals was estimated at $1,000.[661] The year after Taylor's visit, Samuel Mead and the other male missionaries constructed a milking shed with fourteen stanchions and a building for carts. Fences and the shed protected the farm animals from wild hogs, lions, cheetahs, and other predators.[662]

Bishop Taylor continued his travels on the Cuanza River after he concluded his June visit. On July 16, 1889, he described two Sunday church services he had attended a month earlier at the Malanje chapel. He was thrilled that nearly one hundred natives had joined the missionaries and mission students in singing. They were accompanied by an organ, a big bass viol, and a coronet. Hymns were sung in English, Portuguese, and Kimbundu, enabling all attendees to participate.[663]

The bishop enjoyed the children's involvement in the morning service as they recited scripture, the Ten Commandments, and the Apostle's Creed in their various languages. One of the missionaries read the lesson from a Portuguese testament. Another one translated Bishop Taylor's sermon into Portuguese. The baptism of a missionary couple's young son and several native adults and children concluded that mid-June service.[664]

Bishop Taylor was delighted two native kings had attended the afternoon service, which began with hymn singing and instrumental accompaniment. He was overjoyed as music filled the air and the kings clapped in time with the music. The American and native children were asked a series of forty-one questions, first in English and then in Kimbundu, to ascertain their religious knowledge. Next, one of the missionaries read the Gospel of John, chapter 5, translated into Kimbundu by missionary Heli Chatelain. The reading described Jesus healing a man who could not walk, telling him to pick up his mat and depart. Jesus's witnessing to God angered the Jewish authorities because he did this on the Sabbath.[665]

Then Bishop Taylor told the story of how God had appeared to Samuel as a boy, and later he became a prophet of the Lord. He was trying to help those in attendance realize that faithfulness to God brings success, while disobedience brings disaster. That service concluded with a time of testimony and the sacrament of the Lord's Supper. Of the thirty people who received the sacrament, two-thirds were native people.[666]

Continuing his July 1889 travels, Bishop Taylor reflected upon the reasons he considered the mission self-supporting. He expressed pride in a new three-hundred-acre farm site of rich black clay and loam. Numerous valuable fruit trees, protected by a growing hedge, were thriving. Domestic animals contributed to the farm's sustainability. Those enterprises supported the missionaries and their students and provided produce to sell.[667]

Worship and religious education did not end with the Sunday services at Malanje. Two or three weekly night meetings provided singing in the three languages with organ accompaniment. Those sessions allowed time for prayer and teaching, testimony for Jesus, and object lessons from scriptural history. With the chapel doors open to the street, music wafted outside, attracting caravan carries and travelers from the Angolan interior, delighting Bishop Taylor.[668]

Susan, her missionary colleagues, and students followed a strict schedule during the school week. Each morning at 8:30, the children had drill on Bible lessons, followed by singing and prayer. "At one o'clock they go into chapel to be instructed by Sister Collins who is a good instructor."[669] A generous supply of school books enabled Susan to provide enhanced educational opportunities.[670]

The children had assigned daily duties. During two of those days, the girls sewed under Susan's supervision, making clothing for themselves and the younger children. Other days, they did laundry and helped with food preparation, sometimes making corn bread and griddle cakes, a skill Susan had learned from her mother. Everyone dined about six in the evening, and from then until bedtime, they studied the Bible and read. Susan participated in two prayer meetings each week after the younger children were in bed. One was on Tuesdays in the home of a native Christian, and the other was on Thursdays at the mission.[671]

Missionaries celebrated birthdays and were thankful for each one as they recognized the daily multiple dangers and challenges in their lives. Samuel Mead explained, "A birthday in this place has more meaning than in Old Vermont. We have more thanks, praise, and prayers in our hearts."[672] Susan celebrated her fortieth and forty-first birthdays in Malanje.

Much was happening in the United States that interested Susan during 1890, her first year at that mission. In January, the National Afro-American League (NAAL) formally organized in Chicago, where its first convention was held. Had Susan still been residing in the city, she likely would have become involved, as the organization's focus was obtaining full citizenship and equality for all African Americans. The NAAL was the precursor of the National Association for the Advancement of Colored People.

In June, George Dixon became the first black to win a world boxing championship in the bantamweight category. His name attracted my attention, as several Dixon families were prominent farmers in Fayette County during my father's life, and they were Susan's friends. Many of the Dixon family members are buried in Pleasant Hill Cemetery along with the Graham siblings.

On August 16, 1890, President Benjamin Harrison named Alexander Clark as United States minister to Liberia. It was through Clark's efforts that African American children living in Iowa could attend a common school. That occurred when he won his lawsuit filed against the Muscatine, Iowa, public schools because his daughter wasn't allowed to attend.[673] Perhaps Susan was aware of the connection, as there were Methodist Episcopal Church missionaries in Liberia at that time under Bishop Taylor's purview.

Her friends in Huron, South Dakota, might have drawn one other event that occurred late in December 1890 to her attention. It was the Battle at Wounded Knee where more than two hundred Sioux Indians were killed. The US Army's Seventh Calvary surrounded a band of Ghost Dancers demanding their surrender. A fight broke out, and many women and children were killed. Susan would have grieved that senseless act if she had learned about it while at the Malanje mission. On a positive note, Bishop Taylor reported that his missionaries in Angola were well, happy, and hopeful as 1890 ended.[674]

In 1891, nearly one year after Susan arrived at Malanje, Bishop Taylor expounded, "Malange is a noble, self-supporting station with a church of 23 saved natives."[675] The villagers' response was positive, making Sunday a busy time for Susan and the other missionaries during the two church services and Sunday school. The African women wore their best, brightly patterned clothing as they followed the men along various trails leading to the worship site.

The young children held their mothers' hands and talked excitedly about seeing Miss Collins. They were eager to be among the approximately one hundred children to receive the religious picture cards she distributed each Sunday at the various classes. Each child sat with open hearts, quietly listening to Susan while she shared stories of Jesus inviting the little children to come to him. Many stayed for the afternoon services along with thirty-five adults.[676]

Back in Fayette, the women of the Methodist Episcopal church had formed their chapter of the WFMS. They reported reading a letter from Susan at their October 1891 meeting and several from her in 1892.[677] She knew it was important for those women to develop an awareness of the children's needs and the challenges she was facing. The letters were a factor in their willingness to aid her when she sent requests for supplies.

In 1891, the Portuguese agreed upon boundaries for Angola through negotiations in Europe. Their claim to the region had been recognized by some European powers during the decade of the 1880s.

Susan continued to serve at the Malanje Mission until 1892 when Luzia Gossalvish, a Bishop Taylor appointee, arrived. With Luzia's presence, the mission was adequately staffed. Noting this, Susan asked Reverend Amos Withey to place her alone at Canandua because she wanted to start a home and school for local children. Withey granted her request, and she left Malanje in February 1892.[678] When Susan departed, she along with Luzia and Ardella Mead were listed as missionaries but not members of the conference. Men had the designation, but women did not receive it until 1893.[679]

Canandua: March 1893–1898

Susan's relocation to Canandua, a substation one mile from Pungo Andongo, meant traveling sixty-two miles west and retracing the same rugged path she had taken east to Malanje in 1890. Susan was the driving force in starting and taking charge of a children's home and training school. In March, soon after Susan opened the home, two small boys were given to her, likely because their mother had died. She lived alone with them until the following September when financial help came from an American friend who sent her sixty dollars. [680] Those funds enabled Susan to take two young girls who Robert Shields, another Canandua missionary, wanted under Susan's protective nurturing. The number of children, mostly girls, trusted to her care increased slowly. By April 1893, two more children experiencing difficult family situations were under her care. Sometimes families took their children back when their difficulties eased. Other times, girls, upon reaching marriageable age, were taken from school often against their will.[681]

On June 9, 1897, five years after beginning her school at Canandua, Susan described the curriculum and reported student accomplishments to Congo Conference attendees.

> We have school usually four hours in the forenoon for four days each week. In the afternoon I teach them various things, such as sewing, cooking, washing. I teach the boys to work in the garden, cut wood, and bring water. In each case I teach them to read in their own language first, and then in English. Four of the five of them read in the English Bible as well as in the Kimbundu, so we read English or Kimbundu each morning before prayers. In the evening I teach them Bible verses and catechism, etc. Thursday evening we have our prayer and class meeting. I have regretted that I hadn't as many as I could take care of. They give me but very little trouble, and I believe that they have the fear of God before their eyes to some extent. And my greatest desire for them is that they may all be soundly converted to God.[682]

Newspaper and several missionaries' reports have described Susan's work with these children. When medical missionary Dr. Taylor reached Canandua in late August 1894, she wrote glowing comments on how well Susan had trained her students. Dr. Taylor watched with appreciation and amusement as the children struggled to learn English under Susan's tutelage.[683] Throughout her two months at Canandua and Pungo Andongo, she spent many hours with Susan. Dr. Taylor described Susan as "a colored woman 43 years old, she is a charming little body who doesn't seem to be thirty & hasn't the least streak of old maidism about her."[684]

When she visited, Susan had eight little children for whom she was acting as mother and teacher. The garden produce they raised provided some of their support. Other assistance came from the profits of the store Brother Shields and his wife operated in the village.[685]

All mission stations in Angola were reported as self-supporting on August 20, 1893, with properties valued at $30,000.[686] The value of the two trade buildings, the farmland, and the house where Susan lived was estimated at $2,700. The house had a stone floor, mud walls, and a grass roof that was typical construction for Portuguese-style homes.[687]

By 1896, the cash value of real property in Angola, including eight mission stations, capital, cattle, commercial, and cash, was $41,622.[688] Reverend Amos Withey reviewed the ten years since the first group of Bishop Taylor's missionaries had arrived and noted the challenges. Other than much illness and several deaths, another challenge was learning the key to opening the language of the people. He declared that English was not available and "the Kimbundu had not been reduced to manuscript, much less to print, and we had no interpreters, so we had to sit down and patiently pick out the words from between the teeth of the Ambunda, and write them down according to sounds. But within five years the Kimbundu Grammar was printed, also the Gospel by John. Our pioneer people learned to preach, in Kimbundu, also."[689]

That effort resulted in an increase of full church members to fifty-seven. The number of native nursery children had reached fifty-six, average attendance at day schools was 165, and average attendance at Sabbath services was 170. Withey believed these statistics revealed "fair results for ten years' labor in a new field."[690] The Gospel of John was likely selected first because it illustrates the power of belief, trust, and faith.

Dr. Jennie, whose early life experiences and environment were starkly different from Susan's, was drawn to Susan and the faith she lived while nurturing the children. She wrote, "Sister Collins herself was the chief attraction-so congenial & such a help to me spiritually. Our religious experiences were so much alike she understood me better than the majority of people do."[691]

In 1897, Susan, age forty-six, was continuing as matron, teacher, and head of the Canandua children's home she had initiated. That fall, she wrote to her cousin John A. Joiner and his wife, Margaret, who were living in Des Moines, Iowa. They sent her news to the *Iowa State Bystander,* an African American paper that published the following account. "Miss Susan Collins, a colored woman, a native of Illinois, who was educated in Fayette, Iowa, and afterward in the Chicago training school, is holding property about one mile from Pungo Andongo, Africa, as a native nursery. At present she has ten native children, boys and girls, who are being educated and trained in manual labor."[692]

Susan and Dr. Jennie were thrilled to be united at the annual conference in Quihongoa in June 1897. Here, Bishop Hartzell, during his main address, expressed admiration for Susan's skill and the rare tact she exhibited when guiding the children in their daily lives.[693] The bishop noted, "Nearly all of the adults have mastered both the Portuguese and Kimbundu languages. They have nearly fifty hymns translated into these languages."[694] He expressed his belief that Kimbundu was one of the best of the "Bantu" family of languages.

During that conference, Bishop Hartzell commemorated fourteen missionaries who had died while serving in Angola, along with nine of their children. He acknowledged African missionary service involved great sacrifice with potential for declining health and even death. Some missionaries who returned to the United States were no longer able to work.[695] He closed the Dondo Station due to lack of a missionary and the Nhanque-ia-Pepe Station for environmental reasons that compromised the missionaries' health.

Susan had succeeded in her quest to start the Canandua children's home and school, and five years later, Bishop Hartzell reappointed her for the 1897–1898 term. She was given a household budget of $250 for her expenses and those of the ten children living with her.[696]

In 1908, the Fayette, Iowa, newspaper described her work with the children at Canandua, noting that she had taught them from books and to labor with their hands. Additionally, "she guided their moral and Christian welfare as closely as if they were her own offspring. Each Sabbath morning, walking single file along a winding mountain path, they arrived at Sunday school and church with Susan in the rear cradling a baby in her arms."[697]

Amanda Berry Smith, who called herself a colored evangelist, commended Susan's dedication to the children under her tutelage at Canandua. Susan's reverence for the way Jesus had lived and her faithful and practical approach to mission work elicited Smith's glowing comments. Smith had observed earlier when visiting Pungo Andongo that Susan was the only black student who had attended the Chicago Training School. She described Susan as "one of the noblest ladies that has left that institution for a foreign field" and felt God had "made a great woman of her" while preserving her health and strength.[698]

At Canandua, Susan struggled under Bishop Taylor's self-sufficiency guidelines for several years. One challenge was to supply food for her students and herself during the hectic time she was developing the home and school. A tilled plot provided Susan the opportunity to use gardening expertise acquired while growing up in rural Wisconsin and Iowa. She taught the children how to raise vegetables such as corn, cassava, ground nuts we know as peanuts, and sweet potatoes, called yams in Africa. Dr. Jennie explained that the large yard surrounding the Canandua house contained fruit trees yielding some of their food. She affirmed, "As for fruits I just revel in pineapple, oranges, bananas, paw paws, and limes. Oranges and limes are beginning to get scarce. The season for pineapples is just beginning.[699]

Beans were a common breakfast food. Dr. Jennie reported that their largest meal was dinner, served at noon, and consisted of soup, bread made using cassava flour, rice, squash, and greens. A frequent common Western African meal was cornmeal mush and milk. Eggs were readily available when desired. Cassava, also known as manioc, was an important component of their diet.[700]

David Livingstone, doctor, missionary and explorer, recognized the food value of manioc while traveling in Angola. He found the local people's chief subsistence food was the manioc tuber, which can either be roasted, boiled, or dried and made into a fine meal similar to farina. The leaves were boiled and eaten as a vegetable.[701]

Whether obtaining food sources through gardening or from native plants, there was a schedule observed at the mission stations. Following that schedule while at Quihongoa, Dr. Jennie experienced getting up at 4:00 almost with the rising sun. Then the station's residents had prayers for about two hours, beginning at 4:30, followed by breakfast, called café, at 6:30. Next, work and school time began and continued until 11:00 when dinner, known as *almoce*, was eaten. At 1:30, prayer time commenced, after which tasks around the station continued. Supper hour, or *jantor*, began at 4:00, and evening prayers followed at 6:30 until bedtime at 8:00.[702] Dr. Taylor compared this schedule to that of the Portuguese with whom she had worked, noting they arose and retired later than the missionaries.

Even though observers, such as Amanda Berry Smith and Dr. Jennie, lauded Susan's accomplishments with the children, Susan still had travails obtaining basic needs for herself and her charges. Adherence to Bishop Taylor's self-sufficiency model had caused his early missionaries varied hardships. "An abundance of anopheles mosquitoes, lack of medicine and food, and primitive living conditions resulted in many deaths among that pioneer group."[703] Contributions from the local people, farming, and gardening aided the missionaries in following Bishop Taylor's model, but they still had unmet needs.

Another source of support was often the missionaries' home churches and friends. The Fayette chapter of the Methodist Episcopal Church Woman's Foreign Missionary Society (WFMS) assisted Susan. The WFMS established in Boston in 1869 soon had branches and chapters throughout the United States.[704] Minutes of the Fayette chapter between 1890 and 1900 revealed receipt of Susan's letters detailing her experiences and mission work. Some of her letters contained requests for supplies. The secretaries' minutes unfortunately described those letters read by various members, including Mrs. Jason Paine and Miss Davis, as interesting but with no further details provided.[705]

Susan had made many friends while working in private homes and the hotel in Fayette.[706] These friends helped supply some of her basic needs, especially during her first thirteen years in Africa, making her life more endurable.[707] Mrs. Jason Paine, Reverend Paine's wife, learned through correspondence that Susan needed dresses and shoes. Driving a horse and buggy in Fayette and neighboring areas, she canvassed the residents, including Susan's friends, and wrote, "I got goods for a dress, or a price of it here, and a pair of shoes there and finally obtained enough to fill a box."[708]

Susan once asked for some dried apples and cinnamon but was concerned Mrs. Jason Paine would think that request was too extravagant. Those items were sent along with two more boxes of supplies Susan needed. A year or so later in 1895, Fayette WFMS members "raised money for Miss Collins' outfit."[709] Susan explained that without gifts from the native people and those from Fayette, she would have experienced much suffering.[710] It was during Susan's time at Canandua in 1894 when Iowa gave women the right to vote, becoming the third state to do so.

While serving her last year there, Bishop Hartzell changed the policy of missionaries funding themselves through self-support to appropriations and gifts from the Missionary Society. Each year, the appropriations were increased. It was expected those monies would cover missionaries' salaries and personal expenses, station operating costs, and facilities management.

Quessua Mission: 1898–1900

Soon after Joseph Hartzell became bishop of Africa, he spearheaded a resolution in 1897 allowing the Congo Mission Conference members more involvement and recognition. Anyone over sixteen years old had the privilege of taking a seat and participating in the discussions regarding items on the June Conference agenda. For the first time, Susan and eight other women were seated along with the men.[711] Bishop Hartzell reported the mission stations bordering the Congo River were either in decline or closed. These closures necessitated the decision to sell the *Anne Taylor*, which for nearly ten years had traveled the river, transporting missionaries and supplies to stations along its shores. Perhaps Susan's mind danced with thoughts recalling the years she had served the Congo stations at the beginning of her missionary career.

In 1898, Bishop Hartzell went further and designated those who had been appointed by Bishop Taylor and had done faithful service in his missions, most for twelve years, as "regular missionaries."[712] They were formally recognized on April 19, 1898, by the Methodist Board of Managers.[713] Susan was among the women designated and then certified as members of the conference. Bishop Hartzell recognized Africa as the world's most difficult mission field. One wonders why it took the board over a decade to acknowledge the work of those dedicated women who risked their lives, devoting themselves to the care, vocational preparation, and religious education of the children just as the men had.

After her certification, the superintendent of missions late in 1898 moved Susan and the girls' school at Canandua to Quessua. She was matron and teacher-in-charge of that school and head of the orphanage.[714] With her guidance, the orphanage prospered, housing about twenty students. The boys who had been under Susan's care were sent to an industrial school.[715]

Originally called Munhall, Quessua was a substation six miles from Malange and part of Bishop Taylor's system of African Industrial Nursery Stations. The station was named for Dr. L. W. Munhall, who, along with his friends, raised funds to start the mission.[716] By 1892, the Quessua mission, situated on a wooded mountain site and overlooking a fertile plain, had a house, a farm for industrial training, and a girls' school.[717] Irrigation water for its fifteen tillable acres came from mountain streams. The missionaries raised cane, producing their own sugar, and found some portions of the rich soil appropriate for growing grapes. By 1900, there were sixteen buildings on the site, six used for joint purposes of residences, schools, and church services. Those facilities made it possible for the children to live at the mission and receive instruction in religion, music, and basic academic skills. The children's industry and order, along with their bright and willing faces, provided a source of pleasure and encouragement to visitors.[718]

Three buildings housed supplies and business offices, one was an industrial workshop, and seven served as missionaries' residences. There were sheds for storage of farm tools and supplies.[719] Not counted among the sixteen buildings were small adobe houses with thatched roofs where native apprentices lived.

When William Dodson became district superintendent in 1897, he acknowledged the need to create mission homes that were healthy places to live. His description of the ones in use illustrated the following obvious problems: "most of the mission property was in Portuguese trading-house style, with few windows, no glass, common closed-board shutters, and grass roofs."[720] He felt those houses had been adequate when missionaries first came to Angola, but after heavy rains, they were no longer suitable.

Part of his concern was due to what happened to his grass-roofed home in Pungo Andongo. He stated, "The rotten grass receiving the rain formed in many places large filters for letting through a liquid resembling coffee, and when these places dried up they would tumble down in the shape of a black substance resembling soot."[721] Bishop Hartzell recognized the deplorable living conditions and began developing plans for new construction. Much of that came later, after Susan had been at Quessua for nearly a decade.

During the 1899 Conference, Susan and Hilda Larson were lauded for their faithful and effective work with the children. Their efforts had contributed to Bishop Hartzell's feelings of encouragement that he shared with the attendees at the 1900 Congo Conference. He had numerous reasons for his joy about the progress in Angola. First, he thought the missionaries' lives had become more harmonious with mission best practices. Second, the sources of support from the church had more permanence than they had fifteen years earlier. That funding enabled him to purchase a good press to print Christian materials in Kimbundu, advancing publication of scriptures and educational materials. Some of these materials were used for the four Sunday schools attended by ninety pupils.[722] Third, the funding stability enabled him to recommend that Susan and other missionaries receive a yearly $300 allowance and a $200 salary.

In 1899, missionary Withey reported thirty students daily attending the Quessua mission schools and eight self-supporting apprentices receiving guidance from the missionaries. One of the challenges teachers faced was working through the superstitions the children had accepted from their elders. Teaching them took three years longer than American children because there were inadequate numbers of books in the Kimbundu language, thus the necessity for the printing press. With supervision, employed native helpers managed outstations. They assisted in teaching Sabbath services, farming, building, and publishing projects.[723]

Bishop Hartzell initiated furlough opportunities for missionaries, some of whom had been in Africa fourteen years. He recognized their need for rest and renewal after long years of heavy labors. Their work included teaching and caring for the children, managing farms, consoling and treating the sick, operationalizing moneymaking enterprises, visiting the villages for evangelistic preaching and teaching, and translating information to print in the Kimbundu or Portuguese languages. These rigors had weakened many of the missionaries. Some of them had experienced personal losses and additional responsibilities when new missionaries left early, often due to ill health.

Susan had been in Africa thirteen years without leave when, in 1900, she began her first and only break, arriving in New York City on August 1. Traveling with her were Mary Shuett and Reverend Charles Gordon, the surviving spouse of Dr. Jennie Taylor, and the Gordons' young daughter, Florence.[724] In 1910, the Board of Foreign Mission determined they would continue Florence's annual support of $150 until she reached the age of twenty-one.[725] They arrived in the United States aboard the steamer *Oceanic* just weeks before a category 4 hurricane ravaged Galveston, Texas, on September 8. An estimated 6,000–12,000 lives were lost.

Susan's African experiences had provided moments of exhilaration and sadness, and perhaps uncertainty, during her early years regarding her decision to become a foreign missionary. She adjusted to living in climates and landscapes starkly different from those in the Midwest. Some of her colleagues were weakened and died in these environments. She mourned her friend Dr. Jennie's death.

Her missionary assignments allowed Susan to employ her university education in classroom teaching, yielding great satisfaction and happiness. She quickly learned Portuguese and Kimbundu, making her teaching easier. Her leadership skills flourished when she initiated a children's school and home in Canandua. Susan experienced continued support from Bishops Taylor and Hartzell, her missionary colleagues, the Paines, and other Fayette friends. Perhaps it was Bishop Taylor who encouraged her to travel to California upon her return to the States. That trip opened new friendships and opportunities for Susan.

12

⌗

Traveling Home and Back:
A Time of Stress and Change

Challenges Ahead: Seeing Familiar and New Faces

When Susan left Angola in 1900, she had no assurance of either returning or having any visible means of support in America. That period of uncertainty required marshaling all of her faith as she wondered who among her friends would assist her in the next chapter of her life. But as in the past, her faith, fortitude, and grit led her forward to new possibilities.

Susan returned to Fayette a short time after landing in New York City and stayed with the Reverend Jason Paine family. Within weeks, she attended a church service in Randalia, Iowa, listening to missionary Miss Mabel Allen describe her experiences in China.[726] On October 3, Susan spoke at the meeting of the local chapter of the Woman's Foreign Missionary Society (WFMS). The members voted to help Reverend Blake with her expenses and collected money for that purpose. Minutes from the event revealed, "Miss Collins took charge of the meeting and gave a very interesting account of her work in Africa: also told us many things concerning their customs, work and products."[727] At the conclusion of her talk, the forty-five members agreed the presentation was profitable as they clustered around Susan, asking questions.

Susan's next speaking engagements about her Africa experiences were near Lima at the Illyria Church on Saturday and Sunday evenings, October 13 and 14. It was requested that "Everyone come with a full purse to help the lady with her good work she is now accomplishing in that far off land."[728] Her talks were well received.[729]

While in Fayette, Susan visited former neighbors, the Foxwells, still living in the rural area where she had spent her teenage years. Their four-year-old granddaughter, Bertha Medberry, was there when Susan arrived. Bertha later described Susan's visit, saying, "She 'made over' my sisters and me. I sat on her lap for a long time. I loved that and told my father about it."[730] When she described her experience, he said, "Bertha, if you grow up to be as fine a lady as Susan Collins, you will do all right."[731] Bertha later wrote that she believed the Collins family had settled north and east of Lima near her great-grandparents. She recalled that Susan and her aunt Mary Ann Foxwell were good friends.[732]

After her Fayette visits, Susan traveled to Evanston, Illinois, the week of November 4, and from there she boarded a transcontinental steam passenger train to California.[733] She experienced crossing the vast Great Plains and the Rocky Mountains, high by comparison to the mountains she had trekked across in Angola. Possibly Bishop Taylor's encouragement and the hope of finding sponsorship to return to Quessua were the reasons Susan traveled to California.

Did she relish the trip, or did she feel frustration caused by the Methodist Episcopal Church hierarchy's guidelines that missionaries over fifty were too old to serve in a foreign field? The average life expectancy in 1851, the year of Susan's birth, was about thirty-nine, and she had surpassed that by eleven years. The Mission Board was concerned the older missionaries did not have enough stamina and might die abroad. Also, they deemed Susan unsuitable because she did not meet their educational requirement of having a bachelor's degree.

Undaunted, Susan moved forward to attain her goal of returning to Angola. While in California, she spoke to members of the Pacific Branch of the WFMS. Her earnest Christian spirit, energy, knowledge of the African people, modesty, and work ethic impressed these women, and they expressed an interest in sponsoring her.[734] The branch members contacted Bishop Hartzell, and he gave consent for Susan to return to Africa, but she would need a sponsor.[735]

Eager to move forward and obtain an appointment by the WFMS, she had to complete an application different from the one she had done in 1887 for Bishop Taylor. Susan easily met the twenty-five years of age requirement. The WMFS application contained questions designed to determine her knowledge of salvation through atonement of Jesus Christ. Required was a declaration that she had been moved by the Holy Spirit to become a foreign missionary and willingness to make that her life work. Susan had to express an earnest desire to win souls to Christ, something she had done for thirteen years, and state her belief in the doctrines of the Methodist Episcopal Church. Another necessity was completion of a health form by a competent physician, attesting to the condition of her health.[736]

A description of her education, including courses taken and degree earned, her language proficiency and how she acquired it, and knowledge of vocal and instrumental music had to be completed. Explaining her business training, positions held, executive ability, management of financial matters, and teaching abilities completed the knowledge and skills section of her application. Essential personal demographics included full name, place and date of birth, residence, marital status, number of dependents, and any indebtedness.[737] She had to supply the names of at least ten references, including pastors, instructors, and others who could provide information relative to her Christian usefulness, adaptability to people and circumstances, and general fitness for missionary work.[738]

After Susan's paperwork was submitted and reviewed, she was interviewed by at least two members of the Branch Standing Committee. When these women deemed her application acceptable, they forwarded it to the Reference Committee, and a final decision of her worthiness, dedication, and abilities to become a foreign missionary was made.[739] Susan was one of twelve women accepted and appointed by that committee to become a missionary in 1901. The committee noted, "Miss Collins is the first colored woman sent out by the Society. She has spent several years in Africa and is represented as a most efficient worker."[740]

While she was in Pasadena and after her acceptance by the Pacific

Branch to serve as a foreign missionary, she raised money selling *Up from Slavery: An Autobiography* by Booker T. Washington.[741] Susan possibly met Washington during her furlough when he spoke at Iowa's Grinnell College in 1900.[742] She intended to use the profits from the book sales to purchase supplies for the Quessua school. The school had a continual financial challenge because it did not receive money from the ruling government.[743]

Susan attended the annual meeting of the Pacific Branch in Los Angeles in early fall 1901, one month after William McKinley became the third American president to be assassinated. She received her formal appointment to Quessua at this meeting. What a joy it must have been for Susan to have the opportunity to return to her beloved students and the work to which she had dedicated her life! Attending the conference provided Susan the occasion to become acquainted with other women who shared her passion for missionary service. Through their sponsorship, they pledged to cover her salary and expenses while she labored in Angola, thus easing her previous burden of seeking self-support.

These women realized that Susan's ability to speak Kimbundu and Portuguese and her prior years of missionary service had perfectly prepared her to again teach at Quessua. The Pacific Branch members felt blessed that her return was made possible through the deathbed bequest of Mrs. Frannie J. Crothers-Graham. Her sister, Mary Crothers, "was moved to send a missionary to Africa in memory of her beloved sister."[744] The gift of $1,325 was to pay Susan's salary for three years.[745] The branch members believed Susan's "long and faithful work for Africa is our assurance that results will come from this generous giving."[746] They complimented Susan's devoutness of spirit, strong common sense, readiness for emergencies, generous and unselfish heart, and her outstanding character. Amazement at Susan's good health despite having lived in Angola's fever-laden environment was expressed. Their positive opinions of Susan were enhanced when Hilda Larsen, one of her colleagues, wrote, "No better work was ever done on the continent of Africa, than that done by Susan Collins."[747]

While in California, Susan became better acquainted with Abbie Mills, whom she had met at the Chicago Training School in 1887 just prior to her first African departure. Possibly that is when Mills told Susan she had assisted Bishop Taylor with Michigan revival meetings during early 1882. Perhaps Mills and Bishop Taylor had both encouraged Susan to come to California to seek assistance. After one of their conversations, Abbie Mills described her admiration for Susan: "But such as she does not rest easily in a world where there is so much to be done on salvation lines. When it seemed doubtful whether she would be sent back to her work she prayed that she might be just as willing to stay as she had been to go, nevertheless when the way opened for her return there was a peculiar light in her eye and a smile that told how glad she was to go. With a light step and a hallelujah heart, she bade her friends goodbye, to undertake her long journey."[748]

Shortly after her appointment, Susan traveled east through the snowcapped Rocky Mountains and marveled at the golden aspen adding splendor on the lower elevations. She stopped in Des Moines to visit her cousin John A. Joiner and his family. Then she proceeded to Fayette, seeing friends who had supported her with their prayers, love, and material resources. Always in demand as a speaker, Susan spoke to members of the Baptist Mission Circle the week of October 1, 1901. During her presentation, she displayed fabric woven of grass by the native women, a beautiful work basket, a porcupine quill, and seashells she had collected. Susan showed them a type of bread the women make using cassava roots they dig, dry, and then pound to a pulp. When baked, it resembled white coral.[749]

Before her departure, she was honored at several Fayette events. Forty-three members of the local WFMS honored her at their meeting on October 19, 1901. The Society and Susan's community friends presented her with a silver spoon to show their admiration and respect for her work in Africa, specifically with the children.[750] The following Wednesday afternoon, the WFMS held a reception for Susan at Mrs. Benton's home.[751]

Shortly thereafter, she was in New York City observing the progress made on the city's subway system begun in 1900. With her fundraising and visits concluded, Susan left the city on November 13, 1901, again aboard the steamer *Oceanic*. Traveling with her were Mary Shuett and Reverend Charles Gordon. His daughter, Florence, remained in the United States with her grandparents. After stopping in Liverpool, their next stop was London. They departed London on November 27, proceeding to Lisbon, Portugal. While there, Susan wrote to Reverend and Mrs. Jason Paine, with whom she had stayed during her Fayette visit.[752] Susan and her party boarded a boat for Luanda on December 6.[753] Along the way, they stopped at the Barraka Mission in Liberia, finally arriving in Angola on New Year's Eve, December 1901.[754]

In May 1902, just months after Susan left Iowa, the Iowa Federation of Colored Women's Clubs (IFCWC) was formed. The national association had been chartered six years earlier by black middle-class women who recognized a need to address social, racial, and economic issues within their communities. Formation of these clubs was a response to increased racism in the late 1800s. African American club women identified needs and provided "services, financial assistance, and moral guidance to the poor."[755] Focusing on uplifting their race, the National Association of Colored Women adopted the motto "Lifting as We Climb."

I envision Susan as a staunch supporter and member if she had been living in Iowa near an organization branch. During the 1900s, these women began working on suffrage issues and continued until there was no longer a need. They focused on philanthropic endeavors, assisting African Americans in ways designed to help them improve the quality of their lives. Examples included cooperating with African American church groups, establishing nurseries and homes for the elderly, and raising funds for a residence at the University of Iowa to provide housing for female black students beginning in 1919. Susan would have been pleased, as that helped her younger cousins Iva Joiner McClain and her sister Marjorie.

Return to Angola: Needing Strength

When the WFMS had assumed management of the girls' home and school at Quessua in 1900, the expectation was that "Miss Hilda Larson and Miss Susan Collins would return to Africa as missionaries of the Women's Society."[756] Due to poor health, Larson did not return with Susan. Larson's death was reported at the Western African Conference meeting in 1902. Bishop Hartzell officially appointed Susan to Quessua in late 1901 to assist Josephine Mekkelson, sent there in 1900.[757]

One month after landing, Susan reached Quessua in late January 1902. Here she served in numerous roles until her 1920 retirement. During those nineteen years, she supervised a building project, facilitated an increase in student numbers, welcomed and oriented new coworkers, took care of the sick, traveled in Western Africa, corresponded with many people, and pursued her interest in gardening. Her positive attitude, abundant energy, and love for the children continued to flourish during those years.

To reach Quessua after eighteen months of absence, Susan traveled by boat to the headwaters of the Cuanza River. Once again, she used modes of transportation such as a donkey, bullock, or bicycle for some of her land travel.[758] During the last hundred miles, she was alone, with the exception of several indigenous people who walked slowly, carrying her to the mission in a hammock supported on a long pole and with a canvas top and bottom. Susan reported it was a long and tedious journey.[759]

Others who maneuvered the ridge trail to Malange and then Quessua prior to the railway completion in 1909 described a line of trading posts. Most posts we run by half-castes whose fathers were Portuguese and mothers native people. A few posts were run by Portuguese men.[760] Those stores contained poor-quality fabrics, small quantities of trading goods, guns and powder, and rum. Rum sales were profitable, and small amounts were sold for one cent. Alcohol use was heavy in the kraals though discouraged by the missionaries, who considered alcoholism one of the four evils to be conquered. Susan and other missionaries met carriers bringing cloth and goods to traders and felt the sadness of the trails used primarily for rum and slave traffic.[761] I've contemplated what feelings Susan experienced as she saw Africans forced to the shore to be sent away from their homes to serve others. Perhaps she thought of her parents, who had been indentured servants in their young lives.

After reaching Malanje, situated on a high plateau east of the jungle, Susan had to make her way six miles to the base of Quessua Mountain where the mission station was situated. The nearly four-thousand-foot elevation and the terrain contributed to healthfulness, limiting mosquito-breeding places and the likelihood of contracting either malaria or African fever.[762]

There were other dangers in the area. When Frank C. Laubach, an evangelical Christian missionary, made a trip similar to Susan's, he saw creatures of the jungle, such as a young buffalo trailed by a leopard and later a lion and frolicking deer.[763] Although Quessua's location was beautiful, it was isolated, and the presence of large snakes, hyenas, and other wild animals was a continuing concern.[764]

After her long journey and absence, Susan was welcomed with "great rejoicing." She worked in the village and helped everywhere.[765] Upon her arrival, she found Miss Josephine Mekkelson, who had come to Quessua in 1900, suffering from African fever. Soon after, Susan wrote, "I have had two or three little brushes of fever myself, but nothing serious, and am most thankful that I have been able to keep on my feet to care for others."[766] Several months later, she wrote that her health had been remarkably preserved after her initial bouts of fever.[767] Susan competently nursed Miss Mekkelson and other missionaries who contracted African fever.

Now in Quessua doing the work she had committed her life to, Susan was laboring under different guidelines and with predictable financial support. These changes diminished some of the stress, challenges, and hardships she had experienced in her attempts to meet Bishop Taylor's self-sufficiency expectations.

Finally a Salary: No Longer Self-Sustaining

For her devotion to the church and providing practical and religious education to the Angolan children, Susan eventually received a salary that reached $400 per year. Shortly prior to her retirement in 1920, it was raised to $600 per year, the amount paid to missionaries in Africa, Bulgaria, Burma, India, and the Netherlands.[768] Yearly missionary salaries in other countries ranged from $650 to $700.

The WFMS covered travel expenses to and from the field of labor and required Susan's signature on her first contract, stating her willingness to serve five consecutive years.[769] Succeeding renewal contracts were for six-year terms. After each term, the missionaries received an evaluation of their service. Upon acceptance for another term, they had to provide a new medical certificate, but no other papers required updating.[770]

Missionaries supported by the WFMS could neither adopt nor bring home foreign-born children. When an exception to that guideline was requested, the Field Services Committee members evaluated the case and made a final ruling.[771]

Even though Susan was an experienced missionary when she returned to Quessua, because she was beginning service with the WFMS, she was eligible to receive a minimum of $100 for personal outfitting along with $100 for furniture, if needed.[772] When missionaries left the service, their furniture and medical outfits became the property of the Society, which reserved the right to determine the disposition of these items.

All major expenses had to be authorized by the WFMS General Executive Committee.[773] That was a time-consuming and lengthy process for the missionaries in foreign countries because mail delivery was slow and unpredictable.

There were a number of administrative tasks and financial reports and records to manage. The Society expected the personnel of each mission to plan the first year of work for new missionaries based upon the mission's needs. That would have been Susan's task. Missionaries were supposed to set aside time to learn the language of the people with whom they were working, a high priority of the Society.[774] Susan had acquired these requisite linguistic skills listening to and speaking Kimbundu and Portuguese during her first eleven years in Angola.

Maintaining detailed financial records occupied more of Susan's time than she desired as she kept track of expenses and income required on the annual reports to the WFMS Conference treasurer. She had to use the Society's standardized reporting form and include an itemized account of receipts and disbursements, all donations and fees, and other sources of money obtained for the support of mission work. Expenses allowed and reported were for travel, teachers, scholarships, operating costs such as fuel and lighting, medicines, and minor expenses necessary to maintain the school.[775]

Another of Susan's duties was sending a quarterly report to the corresponding secretary of the Pacific Branch and to the superintendent in whose African district her work originated. Annual communication to patrons supporting special work and to the branch secretary of Special Work was expected. Names of women studying the Bible and scholarship students were part of the reports, which were to be available for transfer to the missionary's successor.[776] Besides these duties, Susan communicated with her home support system. She wrote to the Fayette chapter of the WFMS, the Jason Paine family, other friends, and her Joiner cousins in Des Moines.

Through good fortune, her outstanding reputation among

missionaries, and her network of friends, Susan had been able to return to the mission at Quessua and her beloved girls. With rested mind and body and a renewed spirit, she was eager to spread the message of God's love to the people many described as heathens. She had used that descriptor early in her time in Africa, but as she got to know the people, her attitudes changed. Her length of tenure was unknown when she returned, but she was determined to care for and educate as many girls as resources provided.

13

⚬⊶⊷⚬

Busy Days and Nights: Never Enough Time

Susan's Quessua Roles: Teacher, Mother, and Nurse

Life was not easy for Susan when she returned to Quessua. Missionaries succumbed to illness, and Susan nursed them until they either regained their health, returned to the States, or died. There was political unrest between the indigenous people and the Portuguese resulting in a 1902 revolt. Small pox swept over the province, causing many to die. The number of students at the mission increased, as did the expectations for evangelism within the local kraals. And there was a presumption that she would write to family, friends, and sponsors back home.

When missionaries and others were sick, Susan provided care and strove to bring them back to health. If they died, she would lay them out and comfort the living. All who knew her recognized her kindly ministrations to God's children.[777] While serving at the Canandua Children's Home in December 1896, she was called to Nhanque to care for Mrs. Withey, who was very ill and suffering greatly. The Witheys' two daughters became ill the next day and died several days after Susan's arrival. With their daughters buried, Reverend Amos Withey had his wife transferred to Pungo Andongo, where she rapidly improved.[778]

Susan had looked forward to working with Josephine Mekkelson in Quessua upon receiving her appointment in late 1901. But when she returned to the mission in early 1902, she found Josephine in frail health. A distressed Susan notified the WFMS branch secretary as quickly as she could and requested a transfer for her colleague to Southern Rhodesia, present-day Zimbabwe, where West African fever, now known as malarial hemoglobinuria, was not prevalent.[779] The transfer did not transpire. As Susan waited for a resolution, she attempted to nurse Josephine back to health, doing all she could to make her comfortable. Finally sent to Luanda to recover, the fever recurred, and Josephine died on July 5, 1902, at age thirty-one while lifting a prayer for Susan.[780] She was buried in Luanda in the English Cemetery. Her death left Susan alone with many responsibilities and a heavy workload, as noted by a Pacific Branch officer: "Miss Collins, 'Our Susan,' by the death of Miss Mekkelson has been left with the Quessua school on her hands. What a special Providence it was that God should put into the heart of Miss Crothers of San Jose to send Susan to Africa just when Miss Mekkelson needed her so much; and how well her thirteen years of former service in Africa fit her for the responsible position she has to fill! God moves in a mysterious way."[781]

A brief excerpt of Miss Mekkelson's last message follows: "To the Missionary Society (W.F.M.S.): I am so glad you let me come. Let not the work stop. These are precious lives. Whatever Miss Collins can find of mine she can dispose of as she thinks best. Let all be faithful. Most dear remembrance to all the missionaries: and above everything I exhort the girls to be true to God."[782]

Soon after Josephine Mekkelson's death, construction of a new cottage was begun. When completed, it provided safer housing for Susan and the increasing number of girls. An older building constructed by the Parent Board in 1899 at the cost of $1,250 had housed boarding school students and orphans. With accommodation for only fifteen girls, who thought of Susan as their mother, the house had been outgrown.[783]

One of Susan's tasks was to complete a standard WFMS form, answering a series of questions about her situation. In the concerns section, Susan wrote she had held the Quessua Station alone since Josephine Mekkelson's death. It appeared the loss of her colleague and the burdens of managing the school, teaching, parenting, gardening, providing religions education, and managing finances had become stressful. Rather than directly asking for help, Susan described the situation as a concern. As teacher-in-charge, she received an appropriation of $400 to run the school for the 1902–1903 school year.[784]

Soon after Susan was back at Quessua, but farther south and inland from the coastal town of Benguela, the Ovimbundu people had made their last attempt to resist Portuguese colonization. They were recognized as the most important traders in the southern half of Africa. Known as the Bailundu Revolt of 1902, it was initiated due to a misunderstanding between a tribal chief and a military officer. Other contributing factors included declining rubber prices, slave trade issues, and pitting rival traders against each other. The revolt, put down on September 6, caused Portugal major financial troubles and bankruptcy. By 1904, the Benguela Highlands were effectively occupied, and the Benguela Railroad was under construction. That revolt and uprisings of other indigenous people made it more difficult for some missionaries to conduct their teaching and evangelism.[785] Because Susan and Methodist Episcopal missionaries were miles from the fighting, they were not directly affected. Traveling to bring news of the situation to Quessua was time-consuming and arduous.

The lack of missionary workers in Angola "to steadily pursue the direct work of evangelizing, or take the place of others who might," was expressed by William Dodson during the 1902 West Central Mission Conference.[786] He was concerned that some of the missionaries were due for furloughs in a year or two and the newer missionaries were not yet proficient in speaking Kimbundu and Portuguese and not able to effectively preach and teach.[787]

The year 1903 was challenging for the missionaries at Quessua. Susan had to "endure the strain and confusion of building and keep things in shape and homelike."[788] The numbers of girls at the school had increased, and more of the natives living nearby were interested in sending their daughters to be educated. The challenge for Susan was combining academic education with vocational education. Their WFMS building had been connected to the old mission house, boys' school, and to Malange, with a recently constructed road making it easier for students to attend the girls' school.[789]

The growing number of children in the school and orphanage increased Susan's workload in 1904. Recognizing this, Bishop Hartzell told the women of the Pacific Branch he "was trying to find a competent woman to send for the relief of Miss Collins in Quessua, Africa. She had twenty-three children and is need of an assistant."[790] Near her fifty-third birthday, Susan wrote to her benefactors, "My health has not been as good as in other years and I had to be in bed part of the time in the early summer months."[791]

Remembering Those at Home: Letter Writing

Susan wrote two letters each in 1904 and 1905 to John A. Joiner family members whom she had visited in the Des Moines area between her assignments. Those letters provided insight into her interests in extended family, children, education, and gardening.

In the spring of 1904, Susan wrote, "My Dear Little Cousin Iva," expressing delight over Iva's improved penmanship since they had seen each other in 1901. Contrasting educational opportunities in the United States and Angola, Susan explained to nine-year-old Iva, "It is a great blessing to live in a country like you are in where there are plenty of schools and good teachers. There are no schools in this country, only those made by missionaries. The schools are very far apart and there are hundreds of children in this land that will grow up without knowing how to read. Their fathers and mothers don't know how to read and usually more of them don't care about it."[792]

Susan, as she sat writing by candlelight, told Iva to be a good girl and learn all she could because God may have something for her to do someday. She explained while living in a "heathen land," she was teaching those who came to the mission school and hoping for a time when a few of her pupils would know how to read God's Word, inspiring other parents to value learning for their children.[793]

The same day Susan responded to Iva, she wrote to "My Dear Little Marjorie," age seven. Marjorie McClain had written describing her school experiences and the birthday parties their grandparents had for her and her sister Iva. Susan explained the children with whom she worked "never know anything about their birthdays so they never had birthday parties."[794] She did know the birth date of one young girl but didn't have a party for her, noting the children were quite happy without parties. One wonders if Susan liked birthday celebrations as a child and if her parents could manage to observe family birthdays. Susan may have enjoyed surprises, because she sometimes gave the children little presents as treats.[795]

She made it a practice to reward the children with a *mukuta*, a coin worth three cents, for every Bible chapter they memorized. Susan expressed pleasure that her youngest girl could repeat the Ten Commandments and the twenty-third Psalm in Kimbundu. She requested Marjorie to ask her Aunt Sadie to teach her those passages if she didn't know them.[796]

Susan acknowledged students who arrived on time for prayer each day for a month with another mukuta. Those who were sometimes tardy might receive only one and a half or two cents. She believed this incentive inspired them to change their behavior.[797]

Susan's letters revealed how deeply she treasured her own educational opportunities and her strong desire that Iva and Marjorie cherish their right to attend public schools. It is possible Susan's emphasis on school related to her parents' lack of a favorable environment to receive a formal education.

Corresponding with past and potential financial donors was expected of Susan.[798] Due to the volume of letters she received, Susan commented to "My Dear Cousin Sadie," age twenty-seven, "I am obliged to put a great many aside and wait for time."[799] On February 10, 1905, she acknowledged that she had put off writing to Sadie, "month after month, so long that I have at last resolved to write today." Susan expressed pleasure in gardening and described the beauty of the flowers she could enjoy this year because "the weather is never cold to freeze here."[800] Wanting to share the floral beauty, Susan sent Sadie Joiner flower seeds via a missionary who had departed from Quessua in May 1904. She advised Sadie to plant the seeds "as early as the ground is warm" so she would have beautiful flowers in a few months.[801] Perhaps Susan sent African daisy seeds that grow in Angola and are easy to cultivate. These large white flowers have mauve disklike centers surrounded by a ring of bright yellow stamens.

Susan clarified the seasonal differences between the Northern and Southern Hemispheres. Ever the teacher, she explained fall was approaching and the availability of food from the "useful garden" was disappearing. She wrote, "That seems strange doesn't it? It will be getting along toward spring in America when you receive this."[802] Susan informed Sadie she had subscribed to *The Woman's Home Companion* and asked her to accept it as a Christmas present.[803]

Concluding Sadie's letter, Susan wrote, "Oh, I have so much reason to thank God for his goodness to me. I have no coworker yet but that I can leave with Him, who has said, 'I will never leave thee nor forsake thee.' And surely he does not."[804] Slightly more than a year later in May 1906, Martha Drummer, a nurse missionary, arrived to assist Susan.[805] Before Martha came, Susan wrote, telling Sadie that "'she and God' performed all kinds of fine miracles"[806]

Soon after completing Sadie's letter, Bishop Hartzell visited Quessua and praised Susan's "beneficial garden" and the nineteen girls who maintained it. He admired the beautiful flowers, corn, and other valuable produce and commented on the great joy he received working with the girls harvesting pawpaws, lemons, guavas, pineapple, and other types of fruit.[807]

In a 1904 response to a letter from Iva, Susan praised her nice script, "It don't (sic) possible that it is the same little girl that thought she would never like school."[808] Susan encouraged Iva and Marjorie to "go on and make good scholars"[809] and expressed pride in them reaching fourth and third grades so quickly. She reminded them having good schools was a blessing, but not everyone experienced the same opportunity, including their grandparents. Susan explained, "My 21 girls all seem happy but they do not have a chance for school as you do. The most of them were poor children that had no good homes and no one to tell them that Jesus had died for them. I do the best I can for them and hope that they teach others by and by."[810]

Susan expressed to Iva her hope that one of her students would become a missionary teacher. That came to fruition when Florinda Bessa, who had grown up at the Luanda and Quessua missions, became a teacher at the day school in Luanda mission and later at Quessua. Florinda was seventeen in 1902 when she became a member of the mission staff in Luanda.[811] She was brought to the mission when her native mother died and her Portuguese father couldn't manage her care. When he died several years later, Florinda stayed at the mission, becoming a devout Christian and a charming young woman.[812]

During most of 1904, there were twenty-three girls in Susan's family.[813] That changed in October when the oldest girl married and one of the younger girls returned to the coast to be with relatives. Susan may have been feeling the strain of caring for these girls when she wrote to Sadie, "But that is not a very small family to look after, when you consider that I have to be school teacher as well as mother."[814] At the time Susan wrote, all of the children were well, and she felt her health was excellent. Pause for a moment and contemplate how teaching expectations differed for Susan compared to those in the early twenty-first century.

At the conclusion of her 1905 letters to Sadie and Iva, Susan sent love to Marjorie and her grandparents, John A. and Margaret Joiner.[815] The letters Susan wrote to her cousins in 1904 and 1905 are the only family communications I have discovered. They were taken to the State Historical Museum of Iowa by Marjorie McClain Kizer along with other family artifacts.

Expressing Needs: Students and Infrastructure

Susan welcomed and cared for the children at the mission as if they were her own. She expressed concern that girls were sold in markets and considered valuable property; therefore, they often had no opportunity to come to the mission school, the only education available. Those who came arrived under varied circumstances. As head of the school, Susan did all in her power to make it possible for the girls to remain under her tutelage.

Several children had come to Quessua with Susan from the Canandua school. One was Martha, ten years old when she arrived at Canandua. She had matured by the time Susan returned in 1902 and was Susan's dedicated helper and like a mother to the younger children. After ten years with Susan, she had become engaged and planned to leave the school after marriage.[816]

On New Year's Day 1903, a sixteen-year-old slave girl begged Susan to accept her at the school. Concerned about funds, Susan expressed unease. But wanting to help the desperate girl, Susan reviewed her accounts and found money. Susan's hope was to prepare her to take Martha's place after she married. Another bright girl for whom Susan expressed high expectations was the daughter of a native mother and a Scottish father, who paid her entire school support. Susan planned to guide that child to become a teacher.[817]

In early 1903, Susan wrote to her Pacific Branch sponsors describing the help the girls provided and the work she faced. "My health remains good and I am not at all discouraged. My school is growing and although I have not a helper, I have five girls who assist me in caring for the little ones and in cooking, doing general housework, sewing, and teaching a little. Of course, I would be glad to see a worker coming, but it makes me shudder to think how quickly the dear girls [Zentmire and Mekkelson] have gone who have tried to live here. I have been obliged to give up my village work, going only on Sabbath afternoons."[818]

Susan provided insights in an April 17, 1903, letter to the Pacific Branch secretary about the climate and conditions she and her students experienced at Quessua. She expressed her thankfulness for excellent health and then wrote, "We have been having what we call the later rains in March and April, and a great deal of them, but they will soon be over and we will have no more until October. From May until October is our cool season, but we never get frost."

In the same letter, she described their new abode. "I am quite settled in our new home; locks and hinges all on; a board floor in my room; glass windows in two rooms; and two panes of glass in each door of the middle room, which seems quite necessary as high winds soon will be upon us, and we are obliged to close the windows, makes the rooms very dark. The white ants are annoying us now. ... We are obliged to set everything up on blocks and watch them."

She concluded the letter describing their social life. "Each Wednesday evening, five missionaries living in Quessua meet at one of the three houses for Bible study and prayers for work and ourselves and then we take supper together. That is about all of the time I can spare, and sometimes I can hardly afford those two hours. I always think of how dear Miss Mekkelson would have enjoyed it."[819]

She mentioned Brother and Sister Ball had experienced fevers less frequently in the past three months and was hopeful they would recover. But within a year, Cora Lee Ayars Ball was dead. She and her husband, Reverend Hampton E. Ball, had arrived in Angola during April 1901 and were at the Malanje Mission Station located in the center of town. They were transferred to Quessua in June 1902 when Reverend Ball became the superintendent of the Mechanical Department of the mission.[820]

With the completion of the new cottage in 1903, living conditions improved, but other needs such as the scantiness and inconvenience of the water supply concerned Susan. She was apologetic when she requested funds for a cistern from the Pacific Branch members. "I am not in the habit of asking for things very much. I always tried to make the best of whatever I happen to have, but this seems a great necessity and I have faith to believe it will come. I am told it will cost between two and three hundred dollars, one large enough for washing and bathing through the year." She further explained, "When we were the only family in Quessua, the girls went to the river to wash their clothes and take their baths but since other families have moved here, they have no private place for bathing. I know of no better way than to try to get a cistern."[821]

The members responded to her request at their annual meeting and reported, "There is one comfort when we think of Miss Collins' toilsome, busy life—we know she wastes no time worrying. Her sunny temperament and her serene trust in God are her daily reinforcement of strength and hope. It will give us great pleasure to help make her much-needed well."[822]

In the same communication, Susan thanked the women for a Birthday Prayer Calendar she had desperately needed after struggling without one for many months. Susan expressed pleasure at the prospect of getting a girl nearly nine years old who she planned to call Charlotte. "We can support a girl now for $25 instead of $30 when there are so many together … feel assured of your prayers for our work here, and I trust that these dear girls will be as lights in the dark land, surrounded, as they are by so great superstitions."[823]

Girls were brought to the school for a variety of reasons. One eight-year-old orphan was conducted there by relatives who recognized her intellectual abilities. They could not read the Bible and wanted to learn what was in it, so they brought Mary Ann and their own daughter to learn to read. Susan renamed this girl Josephine in honor of Miss Mekkelson, whose mother and three aunts in Iowa had sent money to support the child.[824]

She again expressed compassionate feelings for the isolation Josephine

Mekkelson had experienced, reiterating grief over her colleague's death. When the Pacific Branch secretary suggested naming the school in Mekkelson's honor, Susan supported the idea, writing, "We are all glad to have it called by her name, for I feel that she really gave her life for it. God only knows what she went through here alone, with anxiety for the girls and the physical sufferings. It does not seem so hard to one who has been here as many years as I have been obliged to stay alone, but she was left alone in her first year."[825]

Susan blessed her good fortune and concluded reporting good health for herself and the children during 1903. She planned to give the students a break from school in October because the garden needed to be planted and they had been in classes since December 1902.[826]

In early 1904, Susan reported 1903 was an overall good year, as furnishings had been provided for the new building and the $300 cistern was nearing completion. She was delighted about the girls' spiritual and intellectual growth. Susan repeated her request for the help of a strong Christian woman to take charge of the school, so she could visit the people and find more girls who wanted an opportunity for an education.[827]

Large raindrops were pounding down on her roof and filling the cistern while Susan wrote to the branch members in April. She and the girls were joyous, as they no longer had to go to the nearby stream to get water for cooking, cleaning, and bathing. They relished the luxury of bathing privately in the dormitory and not in the river. Because the pump had not arrived, a pail was used to draw water from the cistern. When Susan expressed thanks for the pail, the branch secretary noted, "Blessed Susan! Nothing clouds her cheerful, thankful spirit."[828]

Missionaries throughout the world had to cope with slow communication. A letter took nearly two months to reach California from the west coast of Africa.[829] Susan felt the speed was good even though her requests for assistance were sometimes impeded due to sluggish mail service. She attributed that to the delayed arrival of the pump.

In a late 1904 letter, Susan shared a compelling story of a native practice and the almost tragic fate of a child. The young girl, while playing with another child, had fallen and broken that child's arm. According to custom, vengeance should be taken on the child causing the accident. A soldier cousin rescued Pambala Jona, who had caused the accident, and fled with her to the mission. Susan recognized how unjust the practice was and, always eager to advocate for children, sheltered her. Susan told the frightened girl her name meant Bellzebub John Goat and changed her name to Dorcas, which means gazelle. Even with these challenges, Susan was thankful and wrote her California sponsors, "The work the dear Lord has given me to do grows more and more precious and delightful to me every day."[830]

Within a few years after this incident and other children's names being changed, Bishop Hartzell strongly urged discontinuation of that practice. He felt it was improper to impose English names on the children and to deprive them of their given names if they had no evil significance.[831]

In addition to filling the cistern, water from crystal-clear mountain streams was used to irrigate the garden Susan and the girls tended. The men at the missionary-operated farm, situated across the stream from the girls' school, taught the boys and young men agricultural skills. To keep crops such as Indian corn and sugarcane growing during the dry season, the boys learned irrigation techniques that allowed water to flow into the orchards and fields.[832]

The days of 1904 passed quickly, and the routine of Susan's many responsibilities began to wear on her. She became sick in June and had to rely on the four teenagers at the mission for help. Those girls cared for the little children and a new baby. By Angolan spring, two of the teenagers were no longer at the mission. Martha had married in October, and Josephine had returned to Luanda to attend school. This left Susan with twenty-one in her family. Through all of these challenges and changes, she reflected her strong belief and optimism, writing, "I want to sound a note of praise to our Heavenly Father for good health and countless other blessings that come to me daily."[833]

During her early years at Quessua, Susan had projected good cheer regarding the results of her efforts. "We have many things to encourage us as we watch these children year after year, many of them are promising and we pray that all of them may accept Jesus and by their influence cause many others to accept him."[834] Even as she expressed optimism, there was a sense of isolation among the adults who lived at the mission station.[835]

Other than the few months Josephine Mekkelson was with Susan in early 1902, she had labored alone at Quessua Girls' School for three years. Each of the growing girls brought her own talents and challenges. They felt blessed to be receiving an education and to have a new, secure home, with Susan acting as their advocate and mother. Some of them realized the convenience of having the cistern was due to Susan's persistence, faith, and her rapport with the women of the Pacific Branch. Susan prayed and advocated for the help she knew she needed with her expanding workload.

14

⸙⸙⸙

Envisioning Growth: Bishop Hartzell Facilitates

Help Arrives: Prayers Are Answered

Between 1905 and 1910, Susan was faced with numerous tests to her endurance. She desperately needed another missionary's assistance with the increasing number of girls. The three-room house Susan shared with twenty-three girls was extremely crowded, deteriorating, and becoming a health hazard. Bishop Hartzell recognized the situation and provided resources for a new house. Susan soon found herself in charge of its construction and experienced delays due to an early rainy season and a financial panic in the United States that affected funding.

When Susan's income became predictable, she began planning for her retirement and had a portion of her quarterly salary sent to Reverend Jason Paine. He facilitated a Fayette house purchase for her in December 1905 with the money she had saved.[836]

Earlier in 1905, the Pacific Branch secretary reported, "Miss Collins, the only representative of the Woman's Foreign Missionary Society of African descent, is in charge of the Orphanage at Quessua, Africa and has not lost an hour of sickness since June 1904."[837] That year when WFMS members commented on Susan's race but not others, W. E. B. DuBois founded the Niagara Movement, where he was advocating for immediate equality for all aspects of life. Identifying one's race in those reports did not seem either necessary or equitable.

Susan strongly believed her wants and needs would be answered through prayer. That seemed true when a Pacific Branch member who knew of Susan's need and desire to have an assistant commented, "I cannot spare a dime beyond my dues."[838] But later when that woman saw the branch secretary, she exclaimed, "I told the Lord all about the matter of Miss Collins and He sent me three dollars and here it is!"[839] The secretary then entreated other branch members to relate to Jesus as a friend and ask his help when they earnestly desired to aid his cause. That 1905 plea and prayers yielded a pledge of $200 from the San Francisco District dedicated toward a helper for Susan.[840] By 1906, the branch had enough money to support a nurse missionary in Quessua. What a relief Susan must have felt receiving the news, because she alone had conducted a daily program of prayer, school, work, and play for the children for three years. In addition, she nursed the sick, kept house, managed finances and records, and maintained correspondence.[841]

The 1905 Mission Conference Report recognized Susan's good work. Fellow missionaries expressed concern for the heavy burden caused by the large numbers of students in her school. They knew it was too much for one woman and expressed regret for her lack of help. The complexity of her duties was recognized because they went beyond raising and educating the girls who would be the prospective mothers of the next generation. The goal was to educate them in church doctrine to apply in their future homes. It was hoped they would "have strenuous admonitions to get above the level of life out of which they came as can only be had when there is a full time and full force of workers. The girls are increasing in numbers and the Woman's Foreign Missionary Society will have to keep up with its growth. The impression seems to prevail with some of their authorities that Quessua is a deadly place. Truly they have experienced sad losses here, but there is a reason, and this is not altogether due to the place, as the experience of others for years proves."[842]

After Susan's long and patient wait for relief, help was on the way thanks to the California women who had committed to sponsoring

Martha Drummer. They described her as "well educated and fitted in every way for this work among people of her own race ... We thanked the Great Missionary that at last, 'Our Susan' was to have the much-needed help and such an efficient one."[843] Martha departed for Africa in February 1906, traveling on board the steamship *Majestic*. Her journey to Luanda took seven weeks and five days. Upon her arrival, she was asked to remain a month in the city due to heavy rains and danger of exposure that created unhealthy travel conditions. Frustrated by the delay, she remained hopeful and cheerful, expressing great desire to be in Quessua with Susan.[844]

At last, Martha Drummer, ill since her arrival in Angola, traveled to Quessua in May. She was shocked when she saw her mode of transportation, sedan seats carried by Africans. Martha attempted to walk to prevent what she considered cruel treatment for her carriers. When she discovered the hot sun burned and the tall, rough grasses cut her skin, she allowed herself to be carried. Upon her arrival, Susan welcomed Martha with great rejoicing and relief. Upon meeting, these women may have been surprised by the many similarities in their early lives. Both were born in rural areas, Martha in a little Georgia town, Susan in the Illinois countryside. They came from poor and struggling families. Each one had limited opportunities for school early in life. But later, schooling opened their minds to larger possibilities and a desire for additional education. Ministers paved the way for them to enter a university, Upper Iowa for Susan and Clark in Atlanta for Martha. Both lived and worked for a family during part of their college experience to help defray expenses. And eventually they became foreign missionaries expressing a desire to serve in Africa, and finally they met.[845]

Susan patiently and lovingly spent several months nursing Martha back to health. Living arrangements were inadequate, and Martha experienced "an onset of deadly tsetse flies and limited resources with which to carry out her duties."[846] Conditions had improved only slightly since Susan's return in 1902. Susan helped Martha Drummer settle quickly into the new and challenging environment, much different from Georgia and her work in the northeastern United States.

When Bishop Hartzell visited Quessua in conjunction with the 1906 annual conference, he acknowledged the taxing environment. His vision included improving and expanding missions in Angola through training native workers, especially teachers, educated in the best modern methods.

He desired to place schools in locations where people had not heard the Gospel.[847] The bishop wanted supplies for each school to include a clock, a bell, blackboards, paper, and other simple necessities, as well as a corn mill to grind meal for food, primarily porridge. Because the children often lacked clothing, except perhaps a loincloth, he suggested all children receive two suits of simple clothing each year.[848]

Bishop Hartzell envisioned spreading the Gospel through providing limited assistance in outlying areas by constructing native houses and a separate building to serve as a church and school.[849] His plan included teaching fifteen to twenty native girls and boys and gradually having Christian native families settled near each new center. His dream was to permanently plant the light of the church in Angola.[850] From that humble beginning to which Susan contributed, the Quessua-Malange area later became the center of the church's evangelistic, medical, and agricultural work.[851]

A high point for Susan during the bishop's visit was the baptism of seven of her girls and witnessing eleven of the older girls brought into the church on probation. The girls, all of whom lived at the mission, were expected to do the housekeeping while attending school.[852]

The unique characteristics and life experiences of those under Susan's care were described in her letters. One girl named herself Sarah Lake because she knew her support came from the Lake Avenue Auxiliary in Pasadena. Sarah was the youngest in the family and told Susan she had the most beautiful name of all the children at the mission.[853]

Prior to Bishop Hartzell's prohibition on name changing, a talented eight-year-old girl, Dominga, had come to the school during December 1907. Susan renamed her Nancy and struggled to find a patron to support her. When an older student, Jessie Benjamin, married early the next year, the patron transferred her support to Nancy. Later that year, another girl married and set up a Christian home, pleasing Susan and Martha. They believed that required disciplined housekeeping, meal planning, and childcare plus conversion to Christianity[854] and expressed delight when some of the couples began doing valiant missionary work.[855] Those marriages left twenty-seven girls residing at the mission.[856]

Bishop Hartzell's vision began to come alive with the expansion of the Quessua site through building construction and increasing numbers of children living and learning there. Erecting a two-story structure became possible in 1907 upon receipt of funds totaling $1,750 raised by the WFMS. Susan patiently supervised most of the construction, knowing everyone would be more comfortable in the expanded housing. Set upon a five-acre plot Bishop Hartzell had deeded to the girls' school during his 1906 visit, he projected the building could house a family of fifty girls.[857]

Facilities Are Added: Construction Challenges

Uncertain delivery times for building materials sorely tested Susan's patience in 1907. Obtaining structural iron was a long and laborious task. Brought from Angola's west coast on the backs of men struggling over rough trails, it took days to reach Quessua. At seventy-two pounds per man, it required many men to complete the delivery.[858] It was difficult to find carriers, as Portugal was at war with several native groups, including the Dembos, who lived ninety-four miles northeast of Luanda. The Portuguese subdued the Dembos in 1910.

Martha described the men's challenges in delivering the materials to Quessua prior to the completion of a crucially needed railroad: "There will be a great time of rejoicing when we shall not have to wait five weeks to get a 'man load' of anything from the coast. Thirty men have gone down to bring up the last of our supplies for the building. One of them fell sick and died on the way and the others are very long going and coming."[859]

While Susan and Martha were waiting for supplies, missionary friends John and Helen Springer visited them prior to John's first furlough late in 1907. Struck by Quessua's beauty, Helen described the mission setting. "It is almost ideal for that mission. For a background there is a long mountain whose steep sides afford splendid exercise for our lady missionaries and it is to be hoped they take advantage of it. Just as the foot of this mountain is the girls' school, whose teachers Miss Collins and Miss Drummer are supported by the Pacific Branch. A steep path in front of the school leads down to a beautiful brook of bountiful water which takes its rise in the mountain. This path continues up another steep incline on the other side of the boys' school."[860]

Due to crowded conditions at the girls' school, Helen Springer attended Sunday services at the boys' school, stayed the night, and then spent all day Monday with Susan. Impressed with Susan's energy, she wrote admiringly, "Although she has been in Africa for about twenty-two years, she is as nimble and lively as a girl. She is busy superintending the building of a much-needed dormitory for her large school."[861] Susan was fifty-six.

The Springers had been at the Old Umtali, Industrial Mission in Rhodesia since 1901. Umtali is now called Old Mutare, and the mission continues to serve people. Helen noted the differences between working in the two countries and the effect of the Portuguese rule of Angola. Before she met John Springer, she had served in Angola. Later, she commented, "It is all but impossible to realize the fearful atmosphere of immorality, which completely envelops that whole province of Angola, one of the very best garden spots in all of Africa, yet everywhere marred by the trail of the serpent. It is no wonder that sometimes the missionaries there get discouraged and wonder if it is worthwhile to struggle against the tide much longer." Helen Springer continued, "Thank God for the one bright spot at Quessua where a few girls may live clean lives and be trained up as Christian wives … Thank God, I say again for the two noble women at Quessua."[862] She was, of course, referring to Susan and Martha.

Susan did not attend the 1908 West Central Africa Mission Conference in Luanda between February 8 and 13. However, she, along with Martha, Mary Shuett, Ray Kipp, and presiding elder Charles H. Schreiber were appointed to the board of supervision of the Girls' School. The appointment was the result of a recommendation by William Dodson, noting that the schools should be supervised by a board to assure quality management in order "to secure good and useful and happy lives for the girls."[863]

When William Dodson summarized the work at the Quessua mission, he lauded Susan and Martha, calling them noble women. He commented, "The outcome for good in such a school as that is hard for an outsider to estimate. Every real success in that work means more than tongue can tell. They have their sorrows and their successes. It was something to hear about twenty-five of the girls following each other in prayer at evening. Miss Collins has done tremendous work with their new house." And then he added, "Miss Drummer has had good health after quite a suffering time last year and is diligently teaching. Her aim, in which she seems to be succeeding, is to make the girls think rather than committing to memory what they do not understand."[864]

Dormitory construction continued throughout most of 1908 and required much of Susan's time and energy as the year progressed. Lack of materials and excess rain had delayed moving forward in 1907. On June 5, 1908, Susan wrote explaining the situation to John Springer and his wife, Helen, on furlough in New Jersey. "I was not able to finish the building last year. The rains came very early in Sept. I am about to resume work again and I hope to have it finished soon. I felt the disappointment keenly when we were oblige [sic] to stop work last fall. The roof was put on the dormitory and we got along very well ... Let me thank you for your kindness to us."[865]

Three days earlier, Martha had written expressing concern about the building's completion due to lack of money. She observed, "I suppose the financial depression in America has not helped the missionary funds any."[866] Martha was referring to the Panic of 1907, which resulted in the contraction of the United States economy from May 1907 through June 1908 when stock values dropped. In her September 29, 1908, letter to Helen Springer, Martha joyously noted, "Four of the girls have married since I came here and each one seems happy in their homes."[867]

During and after the building process, members of the Fayette chapter of the WFMS expressed continued interest in Susan's work. Based upon a 1908 inquiry from a Fayette resident, Susan wrote, "The cottage is used at present for a school and dining room. The two-story building is being used for private rooms and sewing room and girls' dormitory."[868] Moving from their village huts to living in the new adobe structure was a frightful experience for the thirty-two girls, and they were "afraid to even attempt to climb stairs."[869] There were six rooms on the ground floor and three upstairs dormitory rooms.

Attitudes of WFMS members and the needs of Susan and Martha were expressed in the secretary's 1908 annual report. "Here our two missionaries, Miss Susan Collins and Miss Martha Drummer are earnestly and lovingly working to win from darkness to light these people of their own race ... Miss Collins is our faithful treasurer and mother to the girls, while Miss Drummer, besides teaching the school, frequently takes some of the larger girls with her to sing gospel in the surrounding towns where sacred song has never been heard. In this way she wins the hearts of many people who listen gladly while she reads and explains the Bible to them." Martha had reported this:

> The school is constant and the children are doing nicely with their studies. The outside trips are made on Saturdays and occasional afternoons during the dry season. Our native Christians have turned away from the witch-doctors and come to me so often for simple remedies which I do not have and cannot afford to purchase.

Transportation had become more difficult for Susan and Martha, and they along with the district superintendent pleaded with the Pacific Branch women "for a hundred dollars to buy a 'ricksha,' which is a one-wheeled, purely African conveyance, and would be a wonderful help to their work and a real economy as well, for many of their necessities have to be carried a long distance on the backs of the native men or in hammocks. Medicines and a conveyance are therefore the main needs now at this station."[870]

Martha Drummer described one of her numerous trips into the bush in 1908. She traveled twenty miles to reach the people who were fascinated with her, and she described her experience in this way: "As the people in that section had never seen a negro woman in full dress, large numbers came to see me and to their great surprise and delight I not only wore shoes and a dress but spoke to them in their own language." When visiting the tribes, she realized she was among warriors who valued fighting, and she learned each boy was given a large knife at an early age. Both men and women were wearing long braids shaped into a corkscrew. Dipping them in peanut or palm oil helped retain the corkscrew shape. Their wardrobes were sparse and often limited to a very small piece of cloth if available.

When four kings came to visit, "I told them of our school but each seems to think his own little circle is the world, and they do not care to hear about the school. I am praying that we may get some girls from that district. The people have the finest herds of cattle I ever saw and could easily support their girls if the Lord should melt their hearts to send them to school. Many of the women and girls came to see me on Sunday and the Lord was present in the little service I had with them."[871]

Other times during the dry seasons, Martha took twenty of the twenty-nine children to a village one mile distant to sing to the king and interest him in the Gospel. Dorcas, one of Susan's first students, had become known as an Angolan Bible woman and accompanied Martha to the village.[872] Reward for their efforts occurred when one king began coming to church. Later he invited Martha and the children to return to the village, where they read the Bible and taught his people one afternoon every week.[873] Village visits ceased during the rainy season when roads became inaccessible, and then Martha helped Susan operate the orphanage.

One of the challenges Susan and Martha encountered with the local people was overcoming their numerous superstitions. Many were related to witches, with women, children, and birds being accused of sorcery causing drought, illness, hunger, and other disasters. The natives told children if they swept the floor, they would have uninvited guests; if they put their hats on their beds, illness would strike; and if a bag of flour was set on the floor, they would be poor.[874]

Florinda Bessa, one of Susan's former students teaching in Luanda, shared several instances when her kindergartners cited superstitions as reasons not to attend school. Sometimes one would come and say, "Mamma says I must not come any more to this school because when I get sick I cannot go to the witch doctor and I will die. She says, 'The people of the mission do not go to the witch doctor and that they will die.' Another would say, 'We have the spirit of divination in our family and if I come here I shall lose it and my people want me to divine and take care of the family gods when I grow up.'"[875]

Frequently the natives made sacrifices to their ancestors' spirits. They believed evil spirits precipitated illness and returned to haunt you if you treated a living person badly. Many accepted the presence of spirits in natural objects, such as hollow trees, large rocks, deep forests, ravines, caves, and along riverbeds. Fear caused the natives to circumvent those areas, creating great inconvenience to themselves and the missionaries they were transporting through a particular region. Avoidance of locations such as graveyards, where they thought evil spirits lived, was common.

Witch doctors used fetishes to control and strengthen their power over the natives, who believed fetishes had religious significance and magical powers.[876] The power of the witch doctors made it difficult for Susan and other missionaries to guide their students in Christian beliefs. Eventually, they made inroads, and one Sunday, several women brought their fetishes to Sabbath school, wanting to show their desire for a better life.[877] Another woman frequently brought fetishes to Quessua after those she had been teaching gave them up as false.[878]

The Sasswood Ordeal was a native practice that appalled the missionaries. A man in a village near Quessua believed his wife was a witch, much like the Salem Puritan witch hunters. To determine the truth, at daybreak he gave her a drink made of the poisonous sasswood bark and other herbs. It was believed the witches' power was weakest at this time and only the guilty would die from drinking the potion. Those who vomit the mixture were deemed innocent. The man's wife died. Because many of the villagers were Christians, he was not killed but expelled from the village.[879]

Susan and Martha frowned upon these practices but always trusted they could make a difference in the lives of the girls and their families. They were convinced the girls should pursue meaningful work. In early 1908, Martha described a fall scene. "I wish you could see the girls with the short-handled hoes digging and making ridges for the garden. It is what the horses do in America, but each girl goes about it cheerfully They raise a large patch of corn, beans, potatoes, okra, and tomatoes but they soon go down the throats of so many."[880] Shortly after the rains, the girls were busily slicing their hoes though the black earth, killing weeds. It was a constant battle if they wanted their crops to thrive.

Another threat to the garden was the neighbors' pigs and goats who enjoyed the tasty produce. To thwart them, Susan made plans to construct a fence. Posts were made and paid for, and the fence was completed prior to the October 1909 planting season.[881] After that, they had more corn and beans than usual because all the goats could do was look longingly through the wire fence at the vegetables.[882]

Years later, they were still trying to teach girls gardening skills, but maintaining a garden remained a constant struggle. In 1922, a missionary identified one of the trials nature provided. "Gardens, a great essential to a successful girls' school, could be made only with great difficulty and much unnecessary labor. And the mountain was full of monkeys, porcupines, and other hungry animals that harvested the little garden we did manage to raise before we got a chance at it."[883]

Several goods things happened to Susan and her Quessua colleagues in 1909. One was the completion of the house whose construction she had been superintending. The first-year rain delays had caused a seven-month wait before she could continue in 1908 to complete the house that could accommodate fifty girls. She reported in 1909, "The house has a good stone foundation, 18 by 60 feet. The walls are made of adobe (sun dried brick); they are three feet thick. It has three rooms below and three above, in the main part; there are two rooms 10 by 15 feet in the back, and a hall between. There is a front veranda both below and above. The foundation of the back rooms is full as wide as that of the main part; so upper rooms can be added at any time when they are needed. We are very thankful to be at last settled in our new house and have plenty."

Susan expressed gratitude to male missionary colleagues Shields, Schreiber, and Miller. With the assassination of the Portuguese king, getting their foreign checks cashed and changed to Portuguese money in Malange had become very difficult. Robert Shields and Schreiber helped her get the money changed into copper. At various times, Miller had lent her money if he could spare it. She was relieved that it was always possible to pay the construction crew and she didn't have to halt the building progress. When the construction concluded, they had thirty-five girls and two boys who were temporarily housed with them. One boy's father was a soldier.

Susan concluded her report optimistically, describing the progress she felt they were making with the local people regarding their daughters' education. In the past, many of the girls were from distant villages, but that had changed. There were either eight or ten from nearby villages. She believed the natives had begun to trust them and that the Lord was winning their hearts. Susan concluded, "We think of the possibilities of the girls who come to us, and the advantage that it gives them over the women of the village. I feel compelled to take the children at whatever age we can get them. Some of them are so nearly grown that they stay but a few short years, but we know that however short the time is, it changes their lives, and they in turn become adherents. Some we are obliged to take in helpless babyhood in order to get them; then a number of years must pass before they reach school age."[884] Her ultimate hope was parents would value the experience for their daughters and send them to school.

With the house ready for occupancy and help from Martha, Susan was able to focus increased attention on the children in her mission family and their education, while hoping numbers would grow.[885] And even more importantly than keeping the animals out of the garden with the new fence was the completion of the railroad to Malange. Susan and Martha received good news when a box arrived via rail early in 1909. It contained materials they had requested from their Pacific Branch supporters, along with the *Daily Bulletin* of the branch's executive meeting held the previous fall. Upon reading it, they were overjoyed that money had been approved for the rickshaw they so desperately needed to ease their travels among the kraals.[886]

Closing out the Decade: Celebration and Growth

Bishop Hartzell had organized an African Diamond Jubilee for 1909. That event brought attention to the needs of the missionaries in Africa and locations they desired for future openings. The jubilee served as a way to obtain five-year pledges for expansion. President Theodore Roosevelt gave a major address to the attendees on January 8, 1909, in Washington, DC. He commented that Christian missionaries had made profound contributions to the physical, intellectual, and moral condition of African natives. Unfortunately, he only recognized the work of male missionaries and did not mention the efforts of female missionaries, particularly their roles in nurturing young children and teaching them home-management skills. However, when he appealed for both financial and service support, he explained that many missionaries, both women and men, had needs. He concluded, declaring, "The number of those who go as missionaries to Africa will increase; and it is not unreasonable to suppose that a large share of the leadership for the evangelization of the continent will be furnished from among our own colored in America."[887]

Susan was at the forefront of that concept and a role model for African American women and men who became missionaries. She was loyal to those who supported her. In one of her regular letters to the branch secretary, she explained that during 1909, Bishop Hartzell had given her and Martha the opportunity to contribute to the Diamond

Jubilee Celebration. They declined, and Susan explained, "After much consideration Miss Drummer and I both thought it would be better for us to send our mites to the Woman's Foreign Missionary Society seeing they have taken a large share in, so I will ask you to take $50 of my second quarter's salary for that purpose."[888] That equaled one-twelfth of the annual base salary missionaries in Africa were receiving that year. The generous gifts of Susan and Martha demonstrated the significance and eagerness with which the jubilee efforts were supplemented by missionaries in the field directly helping their WFMS causes.

With the jubilee underway, the house completed, and everyone settled into it, Susan spent three weeks in Luanda to rejuvenate and purchase necessary furnishings.[889] That was the first time in seven and a half years she had gone to the coast to rest. Traveling by train was a relaxing change from the long, tedious hammock and boat journeys of earlier years. Susan explained the productivity of her trip: "While I was in Loanda I borrowed from the district superintendent $100 on my fourth quarter's salary and bought a new stove and sewing machine. I had faith to believe that the money would come to pay for it. But I confess my surprise at a letter coming not long after my return from Miss Carnahan of the Philadelphia Branch saying they were about to send me $100 for the very things I bought. What do you think of that?"[890]

Susan's strong faith seemed to reward her with amazing frequency. Alternatively, perhaps it was her reputation of devotion and caring that earned her the respect of women throughout the Woman's Foreign Missionary Society, thus yielding those gifts. In addition to the Philadelphia Branch monetary gift, their members wanted to do more to aid Susan, whom they held in high esteem. They requested the name of a little girl to support. Susan was delighted and complied.[891]

During 1909, a key moment in African American history occurred in New York City. The National Association for the Advancement of Colored People was founded by leading black and white intellectuals and headed by W. E. B. Du Bois. Its inception was due partly to the continuing practice of lynching. For the next fifty years, it was America's more influential civil rights organization. Perhaps Susan became a member upon her return to the States in 1920.

Susan made a second trip to Luanda later in 1909 and brought back five very young girls. That raised the number in the family to forty, creating added demands. Susan explained, "I then settled down as house mother to look after and teach these little ones, for seven or eight were under school ages; so it has been necessary for me to look after them morning till night. While I have enjoyed this work myself, each day has been so much like the previous one that the report of such work is not very interesting to listen to. I have sewing school with the larger ones in the afternoon." All children except the very young ones participated in morning and evening prayer meetings, and on Thursday evenings, after prayers concluded, class meetings were held.[892]

All the girls helped and welcomed 1910, expressing thankfulness and appreciation for their new housing. They no longer felt like bees swarming around in the old, small dwelling. Soon they were preparing for a wedding and wondering what the bride's dress would be like. A delighted Susan wrote, "Yes, in one month more Dorcas is to be married to one of the boys from the boys' school. We pray that their lives may be lights for God in this land of darkness."[893]

In a later communique, Susan explained that Dorcas's groom was twenty-one, and she was much younger. Following their wedding, they had moved to a little house in Quessua.[894] Dorcas had come to the school in 1904 after being rescued by her uncle. In adulthood, she had become a Bible expert and an excellent teacher for younger children and had made Susan very proud.

Not all students' lives had the happy outcome Dorcas experienced. One teenager, Martinna, who was part of Susan's household, had given up her idols, attended church, and wanted to become a Christian. But one day her mother and four angry women came, took her by force, and sold her into slavery. Susan was powerless to rescue Martinna, who left shedding tears and knowing she would suffer as a slave. Other than the shock and sadness of that crisis, Susan, Martha, and the girls were doing well. Christian education was continually stressed in an effort to spur the girls to create loving homes when they left the mission.[895]

Susan was joyful and expressed thankfulness to her California friends when the rickshaw arrived in mid-1910 after being stored at the coast for nearly two years. At age fifty-nine, the prospect of sometimes riding rather than walking was becoming more appealing. Martha emphasized different news in her July letter. "Our girls are a happy lot and it is restful to look at them in their study, work, and play so great a contrast to their untrained neighbors. The softening influence of the blessed gospel is very manifest. Winter is upon us, the signs are the falling leaves, cool winds, and smoke from the burning grass plains, otherwise it is as pleasant as September in America. I can't tell you how delighted we are with our new stove. We ate so many ashes while trying to bake with the old one to say nothing of the smoke!"[896]

The reappearance of Halley's Comet in April 1910 was exciting, fascinating, and disquieting. Observers could see it with the naked eye, especially on May 10 when it made its closest pass to the earth. Someone in West Africa described it "like a flaming sword with a jeweled hilt!"[897] Over the centuries, the comet has been blamed for many things, including fires, wars, and deaths. Perhaps there were native superstitions to explain the passage of the comet. No correspondence from either Susan or Martha was available to describe how the African children and their relatives reacted to the comet and how that astronomical phenomena was explained to them.

Susan spent Christmas of 1910 in Luanda with German missionary Miss Hedwig Graf in her small iron house at the mission station. While there, Susan attended the long-delayed seventh session of the West Central Africa Mission Conference. She and others sang the hymn at the opening service in Kimbundu and listened as Isaiah, chapter 55 was read in Portuguese. The chapter offers the opportunity to receive the blessings of God if we listen to him as he gives pardon and peace. Prayers were given in Portuguese and English. Use of all three languages continued throughout various aspects of the conference.

It was reported at a later session that the fence begun in 1909 had been extended five hundred yards, enclosing the girls' school and garden. The expansion provided space to raise sweet potatoes and cassava. While the girls gardened, the boys' agricultural curriculum provided experience in raising corn, beans, bananas, and other fruit contributing to their self-support. Though these projects, the missionaries were striving to instill a work ethic in the children from a young age.[898]

Susan expressed delight that all family members had been healthy and over a year had passed since any girl had died. She noted eleven people had been received as probationers into the church the previous June, and all who had understood made the choice to live for Jesus.[899]

To explain some of the opposition Susan and Martha experienced, Martha described a young girl who wanted to learn more about Jesus. The girl "asked her mother if she could come to the Mission school, whereupon she was told by her people if she went to the Mission she would die in three days. Of course, this withered the girl's fond hopes. This is only one case out of hundreds, for in the heathen thought education is a bad thing for women; while the Christian world knows that an intelligent motherhood is the foundation of all true civilization."[900]

At the conclusion of the conference, it was mentioned finances were stretched. That was when Susan and others each contributed five dollars to help cover deficits in publishing the minutes for 1909 and 1910. And Susan willingly volunteered to serve as reporter for the *Woman's Missionary Friend*.[901]

In his closing comments, Bishop Hartzell emphasized the strong presence of the WFMS in Angola, I imagine, much to Susan's delight. To make a point, he again stressed to attendees the importance of letting the native children retain their given names as long as they had no evil significance.[902]

In 1911, Susan sent details of the 1910 conference to her sponsors. She shared her thrill at witnessing the first ordination in the West Central African Conference. Bishop Hartzell's secretary had chosen to be ordained in Africa rather than in the United States. She was jubilant when a king attending for the second time brought his brother. Susan felt he was a power for good and observed in the king's village, "At the ringing of the bell every day his people gather at his house for a family prayer." She continued, "We pray that scores of such men may be brought to the kingdom, they have such an influence over their people."[903]

Her communique concluded on an optimistic note, illustrating the progress missionaries were making in converting native people. "A goodly number of our young people have recently taken their stand for Jesus and also a number of older men and women, which is an unusual thing. One man and his wife, who have been attending meetings a long time, have accepted the Lord. The man is the father of three girls in our school."[904]

Listening to conference reports helped Susan realize the missionary efforts were making a difference in the lives of the Angolan people. While with Miss Graf, Susan observed the construction of a new girls' dormitory at the Luanda mission. She compared the workers at Luanda to those she had recently dealt with at Quessua. They had caused many delays and tested her patience, and she wrote, "If the dear people at home only knew with what speed or lack of it the Portuguese and natives work in this country, they would not be surprised at the length of time it takes to build a house or do anything else they undertake."[905]

Often the Pacific Branch women expressed their affection for Susan, calling her "the mother of our school," and "Our Susan."[906] Recognizing the many faceted expectations of her work, in November 1910, the branch secretary asserted, "Susan has the joy and comforts of missionary life as well as the cares and responsibilities and the financial statistics so necessary to know and meet."[907]

With the conclusion of 1910, Susan and Martha had worked together for almost five years. They had sheltered girls fleeing from forced marriages, rescued abandoned children, and protected others from difficult living situations. Susan had superintended a major building project and helped Martha learn about life in the plateau area of north-central Angola. Martha assumed many of Susan's nursing responsibilities and used her oratorical skills to guide an increasing number of girls and their families to believe in the Lord and to disavow their idols. Those who met Susan responded to her confidence, intellect, and drive, helping her whenever possible, sometimes sacrificing to do so. Based upon their reports and correspondence, the latter half of the first decade in the twentieth century had concluded on an optimistic note.

15

Fewer Missionaries: Increasing Workloads

Colleagues Take Furloughs: Continuing Changes

Susan did not know when she welcomed the 1911 new year she would be in Quessua to greet the beginning of nine more years in Angola. She knew there would be more girls to nurture and educate, new colleagues to greet and orient to life in this Portuguese colony, and additional building projects to supervise. Perhaps she was surprised by the retirement age requirements developed by the Woman's Foreign Missionary Society and delighted when a retirement fund was begun by the Society. Susan and her missionary colleagues had to cope with unrest in Angola due to famine resulting from drought, the shortage of missionaries, and lack of supplies caused by World War I.

While Susan had been in Luanda, the school received a new, larger chalkboard, making teaching easier. Martha had kept the girls busy tending the garden and developing skills considered necessary for their proper industrial education.[908] Upon Susan's January 1911 return from the Angolan coast, the girls welcomed her as they sang in English "Trying to Walk in the Steps of the Savior."[909] Martha was proud they had mastered the song. Refreshed from her time away, Susan commented that Miss Graf had "two important requisites for a missionary, *health and patience.*"[910] New missionaries learned quickly that the threat of malaria, blackwater fever, and other West African illnesses required their constant vigilance if they were to remain healthy. All of the teaching missionaries had to practice patience and tolerance, as the girls were not used to a disciplined schedule and work expectations.

Susan wrote to Lima, Iowa, friends on March 31, 1911, reflecting on her life and work in Africa and the future of evangelizing on that vast continent. "It was twenty-four years last night that I left Chicago for New York and I sailed from there for Africa the 6 of April. There will probably be greater progress made in the Christianizing of Africa in the next twenty-four years than in the last twenty-four. Bishop Hartzell and Bishop Wilson are expected here in May for special meetings at Quessua during the week, when the District Superintendent is with us. Twenty joined the church on probation with five of them being from our school."[911]

When the bishops arrived for the conference, Susan and Martha entertained them in their home while parenting thirty-six girls, most of whom were orphans. The men were delighted with Susan's southern cooking, a skill she acquired from her mother. Susan regretted the bishops could not extend their stay. Martha emphasized the school's need for modern equipment, including new desks and blackboards.[912] She felt the bishops' visit had worked wonders with the Africans and remarked, "The people who have saved their only clean loin cloths for their funerals take them out for this auspicious occasion."[913]

Martha went on furlough in July 1911, her first since arriving in Africa five years earlier. Due to a recent strike, she had the choice of taking either a third-class accommodation or waiting four to six weeks to secure an upgrade on another ship to America. She selected third class, traveled on the steamship *Olympic*, and was in New York City on September 5.[914] After visiting family in Atlanta, Georgia, she attended the WFMS General Executive Meeting in St. Louis.

Martha shared information and reported thirty-two of their forty girls were of school age. Sadly, on February 8, one of their best students, who had been converted to Christianity the previous June, died after a severe weeklong illness. Those who heard were consoled, believing she was with Jesus. Soon, a village girl took her place at school. Classes included three and a half hours of study and recitation and two hours of sewing. A portion of recitation was learning Portuguese, but it was often necessary to use Kimbundu for the girls to grasp the concepts. Martha described their school breaks, "Our vacation periods are the last two weeks in May, the month of October for gardening, and sometimes two weeks at Christmas time."[915]

Keeping the girls in school was frustrating and difficult. But Susan and Martha strongly believed if children didn't have educated mothers, conditions would not improve. They prayed the girls would rise above the prevailing attitude that girls didn't need an education.[916]

A continuing challenge was girls marrying non-Christian men their parents had selected. Susan was greatly disturbed in 1911when only one of three girls married a Christian. She expressed joy in everyone's good health, academic progress, and stable student numbers.[917] Other good news was the waning of native customs evidenced when more fetishes were brought to be burned.[918]

Susan's Iowa friends recognized her long-term efforts on Thursday, July 4, 1911, in a Lima news piece articulating pride in the four missionaries who had grown up in their tiny farming community. The writer reflected, "Miss Susan Collins is rounding out twenty-five years of fruitful toil in the continent of Africa."[919]

As necessary, Susan traveled between Quessua and Luanda, where she may have been during the first African demonstration to request Portuguese policy changes in Angola. The peaceful demonstration was led by Antonio Joaquim de Miranda, who was attempting to create a system of educational equity for all. Within a year, he was transferred to Malange to be a tax collector. If Susan hadn't heard of the demonstration in Luanda, she likely appreciated his refusal to collect a hut tax on the people in the interior. For that inaction, he was sent north to Cabinda, a Portuguese province, now a province of Angola and separated from it by a narrow strip of territory belonging to the Democratic Republic of the Congo.

When people couldn't pay the hut tax begun in 1907, they were forced into contract work for businesses owned by settlers. In 1919, the hut tax was replaced by a "native tax." Those taxes enabled the wealthy Portuguese to create a forced labor system for private employers. That system was eventually abolished by the Portuguese government in 1916 after the outbreak of war for independence.[920]

With no other adult to assist her in teaching and managing the school, Susan wrote in mid-1912 of experiencing financial anxieties and domestic cares.[921] With those heavy demands, she was thankful the older girls helped care for the younger children as their numbers continued to increase. The branch secretary commented, "But she is equal to it all, and like a wise house mother, is adjusting to everything to the satisfaction of all."[922] Susan's limited communication to Pacific Branch members that year reflected her heavy workload.

In 1912, planning was advanced by the WFMS, affecting Susan's eventual retirement. After five years of research and discussion initiated in 1907 by the corresponding secretary of the Baltimore Branch, the Society had begun a pioneering retirement program for their missionaries. The organization's astute leaders had recognized the meager annual salaries female missionaries received, ranging from $500 to $750, would not allow for setting aside funds for retirement. That salary range was based upon the missionary's location. Salaries dropped to $450 annually during furloughs.[923]

The WFMS created their retirement endowment fund from two sources. One was an annual assessment of one cent per auxiliary member of each branch. Gifts from individuals were the second source. The goal was to provide a $300 maximum yearly allowance for each retired missionary.[924] The funds Susan received were of great benefit to her due to economic stress in the country soon after she retired.

The formal announcement stating the age limit at which the missionaries must retire came in November 1916, with the rule going into effect on January 1, 1917. It required each missionary to enter upon "the retired relation at the furlough nearest her sixty-fifth birthday."[925] Executive board members had recognized that might trigger hardship in individual cases but felt the overall policy would be advantageous to both the work and the workers.[926] They knew the retirement fund would help ease financial burdens.

The WFMS Executive Board rethought the retirement age requirement because in 1919 the bylaws read, "The missionary shall be automatically retired at the end of the furlough nearest her sixty-seventh birthday.

Missionaries may be retired earlier by a three-fourths vote of the Foreign Department."[927] The change may have occurred because fewer and fewer women were entering the missionary field, leaving existing missions unattended.

Excitement was high in Quessua when a new church was completed in 1912. Susan and her students were among the first to attend services. Sermons preached in Kimbundu attracted and pleased the native people.

Upon completion of her furlough, Martha left New York on August 22, 1912, bound for Quessua four months after the *Titanic* hit an iceberg and sank. She arrived at the mission well rested and reported a pleasant furlough and delightful journey. Communication was sparse for the remainder of the year and the beginning of 1913.

In mid-July 1913, Martha described a surprise birthday party she hosted for Susan on July 3. They presented her with a cake celebrating her sixty-two years of life. Two new girls who arrived that day enjoyed the dessert. Hence, the next day, they asked for *doces*, meaning sweets in Portuguese. They learned quickly eating cake was not a daily occurrence but a treat for special occasions. At that time, all forty-nine girls, Martha, and Susan were in good health and considered that a blessing.[928]

The next month, Susan and Martha attended the mission conference in Quiongua, each pledging six dollars for the publication of the 1911–1912 minutes. Martha reported for both of them, announcing a record number of fifty-three girls at the home. Finances were helped because three fathers were paying all of their daughters' expenses. She lamented once again the difficulty of getting villagers to recognize the need to send girls to school and for people in Christian lands to understand those attitudes.[929] Martha shared the following example to illustrate the point.

> Old customs die hard. A man came several days' journey last year and brought two of his daughters. This year he brought two more. He seemed so anxious and happy to bring them here. I was touched by his fatherly interest in just girls. So I asked him his motive for bringing them. This is his answer: "My brother brought a girl here and when she went home she could read books, sew, and write letters, and the man who married with her gave her father

eight hundred mukutas ($24) more than the usual gift for women. Now if you will whip mine and teach them everything until they grow up I will be worth more than my brother. I have finished (mahezu). So you see he has at least a business interest in our school.[930]

In early August, many of the girls became ill. The doctor diagnosed it as "bilious fever of the gastro-intestinal type, of which one precious little girl died on the 12th."[931] The fever was likely caused by malaria. An exhausted Martha disclosed, "From being on duty twenty hours out of the twenty-four my flesh has reason to be weary as I write this, though the spirit is willing to continue to fight the disease. I know the clouds will lift and His grace is sufficient. This, as all years has been full of opportunity for service, and I have enjoyed good health until now."[932]

At nearly the same time, with the beginning of the fall 1913 academic year in the United States, Susan's "dear little cousin Iva," whom she had encouraged to study hard and be a good student in 1905, enrolled as a freshman at the University of Iowa in Iowa City. Imagine how proud Susan must have been! Iva Joiner McClain was encouraged by Des Moines, Iowa, attorney Joe Brown when she expressed an interest in obtaining a degree. Mr. Brown, an African American, graduated from the university in 1898 and was instrumental in helping her receive a scholarship and obtain lodging in Iowa City with a faculty member. He and his wife entertained Iva and other area African America students before they departed from Des Moines for college in the fall.[933] These students could not yet live in university residence halls.

While Iva was a college freshman, some of the mission girls were getting married. According to Susan, they were "being sorely tried and tested but they are true to their Christian principles. Our Christians here need the whole armor to fight Satan's agents."[934] Having young women and men from the two mission schools set up Christian homes when they married was mentioned frequently, illustrating how important those marriages were to Susan and Martha.

When new school desks arrived in late 1913, the children were alive with excitement and delight. And anticipation was high as they awaited the receipt of a Christmas box.[935] When it finally came on February 18, 1914,

Martha wrote, "A box arrival is a great event in Quessua and our neighbors came out in the rain to see the wonderful 'foreign babies' that could open and shut their eyes."[936] Oh, to know if the women of the Pacific Branch sent black dolls first made by American companies in the early 1900s or if the dolls were white. Martha's comments suggest they were white, as she described them as "foreign babies."

About mid-1914, two of their girls became engaged, and Susan happily reported they planned to have Christian-centered homes. And Dorcas was now a Bible woman doing excellent work among her people.[937] Susan, Martha, and the girls were eager to share that news with Bishop Hartzell when he made his much-anticipated visit in October.[938]

Susan was sixty-three in July. A while later, Martha penned, "Miss Collins seems just as young as when she first came to Quessua. And I tell you she could wear out two or three of me."[939] Susan had begun serving at Quessua in 1898. With more than fifty-one children under her care, a challenge for a younger woman, Susan wrote, "The Lord has given me wonderful health. Quessua is so like home and the children are so dear to me that I am in no hurry to leave them but will be ready to go when the society calls me home."[940]

Drought and War: Challenging Times in Angola

There was unrest in Europe, and after Archduke Franz Ferdinand and his wife were shot in Sarajevo on July 28, 1914, Austria-Hungary declared war on Serbia. World War I had begun, and it became difficult for missionaries to travel safely between the United States and Africa.

Susan's communication to branch members in 1913 and 1914 was sparse, but she did find time to write to her friends in the Fayette WFMS. The secretary recorded, "Mrs. Paine gave us many interesting items concerning Miss Collins and her work in Angola. This was of great interest-especially because Miss Collins spent much of her girlhood in Fayette."[941]

A great famine threatened the lives of many Africans in 1913 and 1914. Portions of Angola were affected, and hundreds of thousands on the continent died. It was said those who were starving tore down ant hills to get grain and chaff the ants had stored. Factors contributing to the famine were climate instability, drought, locusts, and cattle plague.[942] "In the early twentieth century malnutrition continued to be the most widespread problem of Angola's Africans and on occasions drove them to revolt."[943] Those in southern Angola were affected more than those in the plateau where Susan lived. However, that drought situation had an effect on Susan, her cohorts, their students, and the students' families. At Quiongua Station, located between Luanda and Pungo Andongo, lack of rain beginning in May 1913 caused severe food shortages for the schools. With no rain in the fall and scorching sun, crops were sparse; people were hungry and scavenged for food. The situation was dire, as one missionary explained the natives' low crop yield. "The natives, being less active and alert, got far less in proportion than we, and through the twenty-one months of drought have eaten what little they have and have long since been calling on us for help. Instead of helping them we are obliged now to send their children out of school to their homes of sin and darkness as well as hunger. This is almost more than our hearts are able to endure."[944]

The drought was so severe that for the first time, the river near them was dry, making their new irrigation system useless and limiting winter garden production. In some tribes, there was resistance to irrigation because the people believed rivers were sacred and spirits lived near the edges limiting the water flow. It took much convincing from the missionaries to assure them that was not true.[945]

There has been a history of drought and small pox cycles in Angola since the seventeenth century. During that time, small pox and sleeping sickness epidemics spread through Angola, increasing Susan's and Martha's workloads as they nursed the afflicted. Due to World War I, many Angolans were out of work and did not have proper nutrition, and health risks increased. The war caused turmoil in the county, and hundreds of carriers from Susan's area were forced into service in southern Angola. Their responsibility was to transport ammunition and provisions to the advance outposts.[946] During that time, the governor general proclaimed the end of slavery. This meant all slaves were set free and could leave their former owners.[947]

Fire danger was high during the 1913–1914 drought, and the home of a Quessua missionary partially burned. The fire was subdued once but caught again on a section of the thatched roof that had not been replaced with zinc. After living in their roofless house for several days, Susan and Martha insisted that Ray Kipp and his family move into their home until roof repairs were made. The repairs were completed six days later.[948]

After Christmas 1914, the missionaries at Quessua begin final preparations for the Annual West Central Mission Conference to be held in March 1915. Social responsibilities fell upon Susan and Martha. To ready the house, Susan had lime removed from the exterior and then ordered the walls plastered, oiled, and painted. That treatment kept the house in good condition for many years, eliminating the need for annual whitewashing.[949]

The conference came quickly, and on March 23, Bishop Hartzell spoke about the global situation caused by World War I. He described the war's bleak influence on mission finance and the missionaries. The secretary summarized, "He now returned to the subject, touched upon the unrest, uprisings, and border warfare in the Province, the drought, food scarcity, high prices, almost total loss of cattle by the pest, shrinking of our financial resources, and depletion of the number of missionaries, as several will need to go home. It was evident we were entered upon a period of enforced retrenchment in which we could hardly hope to more than just hold the fort at our central stations."[950]

While at the conference, Bishop Hartzell dedicated the newly completed church and baptized eight converts to Christianity. Susan was overjoyed at his presence. But her joy was tempered when a mad dog bit one of her girls, who later died of hydrophobia, known as rabies. Vaccine for the cure was first tested in France by Louis Pasteur and two of his colleagues on July 6, 1885, but was not available in Quessua. Susan lamented the death of the young girl who suffered terribly because she couldn't swallow food or water.[951]

Years later in December 1929, missionary Susan Wengatz, who had been in Angola with her husband, John, since 1910, was bitten by a mad dog when working in her Quessua garden. Dr. Alexander Kemp, also at Quessua, did all in his power to get the serum to treat her. Not locally available, it was flown from Cape Town but did not arrive in time. Portuguese officials denied rabies existed in Angola.[952]

During the 1915 conference, Quessua Mission superintendent Ray Kipp complimented Susan and Martha in an atypical manner, "I have one criticism of these esteemed fellow workers; and this is, their extreme modesty in telling of their own work."[953] He concluded his comments noting lack of protective field and garden fencing continued to be an issue because hungry natives and animals stole bananas needed by missionaries and children.

Susan's and Martha's responsibilities decreased slightly several months after the conference when Cilicia Cross arrived in midyear to help ease their burdens. She assumed the role of school principal. One of her first acts was having the schoolhouse painted inside and out, making it more sanitary within, improving its appearance, and providing some protection from the annual beating rains.[954]

Cilicia's presence relieved Susan of teaching duties, enabling her to focus on managing the boarding school and serving as housemother to the seventy girls residing there in late 1915. That year, several new girls had come under Susan's care when one of the parent board missionaries and his wife returned to the United States on furlough. Susan was concerned that if these girls with scholarships went home, they would not return to school, even though they had adapted well to their new situation.[955]

Within a few months after getting the new girls, Susan needed to take two other girls back to their Luanda homes. The mother of one of the girls died, and the father wanted his daughter with him. Based on the country's norms at that time, he possibly expected his daughter to either assist with homemaking or to marry in order to financially benefit him from the bride price. Susan and Martha felt the second girl had grown wayward and feared she would have a negative influence on the other girls.[956] Susan wisely reflected, "With such a family of girls we cannot expect smooth sailing all of the time and we are thankful that it has been no worse."[957]

The plight of some children disturbed Susan, especially girls who had a Portuguese father and an African mother. Often, those fathers had been banished to Angola and could not return to their homeland to work and provide for their children. The missionaries found it difficult to care for their daughters and preferred not to accept them but did. Many of the fathers were very poor but tried to look after their children with varying degrees of success. In some instances, the fathers were dead and the mothers had no resources to support their children. When that happened, the women often had sold their daughters to Portuguese men.

The practice dismayed Susan, and she made every effort to keep the girls at the orphanage as long as possible. She hoped they would either marry a Christian boy or learn enough to become a self-supporting Bible woman.[958]

Susan expressed concern about World War I during its second year. Even though the war had not directly disturbed them, the high prices of goods had. In a letter to the Pacific Branch women, Susan bemoaned, "Everything seems 'tinctured by war.'"[959] And indeed it was. Costs of operating missions had increased due to rising prices of food, labor, clothing, and transportation of supplies and missionaries. Therefore, allowances for missionary support were boosted. Missionary travel was hampered by new and stringent passport restrictions. As Martha discovered, there were limited ships for ocean crossings because the number of steamship lines had been reduced. Securing passage to travel across either the Pacific or the Atlantic Ocean was nearly impossible. With war heating up in the Northern Atlantic, missionary travel was closed; however, the Southern Atlantic route was an option. Arriving missionaries disembarked in Cape Town, South Africa, and traveled north by train or other means.[960]

Thousands of Africans were mustered into service by the colonial powers, and thousands were killed. Between 1914 and 1918, more than 450,000 indigenous African troops, including Western Africans, were deployed in Europe.[961] Most of those soldiers fought in the French Army. More than a million Africans died on their continent due to starvation. Those who survived were catalysts for changing sociocultural traditions in remote African areas and villages.[962] I have wondered what Susan's thoughts were about the ravages of the war.

Cecelia Cross's presence made it easier for Martha to continue her evangelistic work in the surrounding area that required traveling over rough and often muddy roads in the rickshaw. It was pulled by two boys she called her "gospel team" because their singing voices helped attract attention to her preaching. Martha set up little schools in villages and was inventive when using her limited supplies. She made visual aids by pasting paper over postcards and writing the alphabet and numbers to ten for the children.[963] Martha's outreach inspired more families to send their children to school, creating the need for a large new building with modern equipment.

In Iowa, the Reverend Jason Paine family continued to assist Susan from a distance as she served the Angolan children. When renters moved out of her Fayette cottage, they found new ones.[964] By late August 1915, the Gilbert family moved out, and within a month, the Glen Thomas family was living in Susan's house.[965]

The years between 1911 and 1915 had challenged Susan with many difficult issues, including housing the increased number of children at the Quessua school and orphanage. Funds to promote mission work were decreasing due to World War I. Fewer people were selecting that as an occupation, putting more stress on missionaries in the field. Drought-caused food insecurity, leading to compromised immune systems and a small pox epidemic in Angola, put the missionaries in more danger. Susan remained staunchly dedicated to her girls even though she was approaching retirement age. Trips to Luanda for respite and to obtain resources for her Quessua children invigorated her. Train travel eased the early burdens and dangers of trudging through grass that towered over her head and walking across rickety bridges and along narrow, rocky paths where she might plunge to her death. Her faith sustained her during these upheavals in Angola and on the world stage.

16

∞∞∞

Concluding an Era: Susan Leaves Quessua

Facing Retirement: But When?

Susan celebrated her sixty-fifth birthday on July 3, 1916, in Quessua, knowing she was approaching the Woman's Foreign Missionary Society's stipulated retirement age of sixty-seven. World War I officially had ended on November 11, 1918. Two years later, Susan would leave her beloved students, many of whom she saw attain her dream of becoming Christian homemakers, respected teachers, and esteemed Bible women. The 1920s and 1930s became a time of passage for Susan, as she was again among friends and adapting to a quieter life and new technologies. These decades were a time of transition for African Americans as they migrated north and were faced with different cultural and work expectations.

During 1916, the Angolan natives continued to be upset and rebellious over the earlier government-imposed hut tax. They felt oppressed and frightened, making it difficult for Susan and Martha to spread the Gospel in their villages. The villagers feared they might be spies who reported their numbers of goats, pigs, and cattle to government officials. But soon those fears subsided, and the missionaries once again proved their conscientious intentions of helping the day-school children and their families.[966]

Susan and Martha pressed on throughout the year and were cheered as more natives sought and accepted the Word of God. Budget limitations continued. They requested more Sunday school cards and cancelled postcards from the Pacific Branch members. With these, they made numerical and word flashcards used in games to spur student learning.

While Susan's students were mastering arithmetic and English words, Iva Joiner McClain was studying for her bachelor of arts degree at the University of Iowa. She received that degree in June 1917, modeling her mother, Mary Joiner McClain's, accomplishment as a graduate of Parkland College in Des Moines.[967] Two years later, Iva earned her master of arts degree, being the first young woman of her race in Iowa to attain that degree at the University of Iowa. Her thesis topic was "Public Education of the Negro in the United States."[968] While pursuing her degree, Iva assisted in organizing a sorority, Delta Sigma Theta, for African American women. It was the first chapter in Iowa.[969] After completion of her master's degree, she took a position as teacher of English and Domestic Science at Roanoke College in Roanoke, Alabama. Later, she accepted a similar position at Langston University, Oklahoma's only Historically Black College and University, where she remained until fall 1923.[970] Components of the domestic science curriculum, food preparation, sewing, and childcare, were similar to the skills Susan taught.

By New Year's Day 1917, sixty girls were squeezed into the Quessua dormitory built to house fifty.[971] The number of girls fluctuated yearly, making planning difficult. By 1918, sixty-eight lived there because more families decided their daughters needed an education.[972] When word of the overcrowded living conditions reached the WFMS, the women initiated a fundraising effort with the youth groups of the Methodist Episcopal Church. These youth contributed enough money to replace the facility.[973]

Even though more girls were attending the mission's primary school, during its history, very few stayed long enough to reach the American equivalent of sixth grade.[974] Their time spent at the school was typically short unless they came to the school when they were toddlers. Susan expressed regret their parents or other relatives frequently took them from school as soon as they were marriageable age, often at twelve years.[975]

One notable exception was Florinda Bessa, who at age nine was brought by her stepmother to the Luanda Mission, where she grew to womanhood.[976] Later she came to Quessua, met Susan, who treated her like a daughter, and developed great appreciation for all Susan did for her girls. Florinda dedicated her life to teaching at the Quessua and Luanda missions, helping her mother's people. While at Luanda, she was appointed class leader for the native Christian women of the church and had oversight of the village "Dorcas School," for young girls.[977] Born in 1880, Florinda died at age 108 in Luanda.[978] Three years prior to her death, she spoke at the one hundredth anniversary celebration recognizing the 1885 arrival of Methodist Episcopal missionaries in Angola. She shared recollections of how these missionaries had changed her life.[979]

Florinda's experiences and successes were atypical. African families placed many demands on their daughters. A missionary described their lives thus: "Of real girlhood there is so pitifully little. The girls began work in their villages at preschool age in the garden and carry produce or sticks for firewood. Each chapter of the girls' lives is alike, work, work, work."[980]

In 1917, missionary Fisher detailed contrasts between education in the bush and at Quessua. Although not explicitly stated, the bush school education appeared related to the rites of passage for females and males as they matured from childhood to adulthood. Many Africans believed females were inferior to males, but conditions of girls' social life varied from tribe to tribe. Female children, considered an article of trade in Angola, had some value due to the practice of wife buying. Women were the breadwinners and bread makers and became slaves to the men. At the Quessua mission school, the girls studied an academic curriculum and practical arts, including personal and clothing care. Fisher felt those opportunities transformed them from unclad to clothed, unkempt to groomed, and unclean to clean when necessary resources were provided.[981]

Many of these children had been raised with religious fetishes that caused them to be fearful. One day, terror struck them when they heard a box playing music and said it was crying. Thinking it was a fetish, they attributed magical powers to it and asked, "What makes the box cry?"[982] Likely, it was a music box Susan received from her American friends.

Geta Kirby described what these children were like when coming to school from the bush. They "had never seen a slate or pencil, never had a book of their own and did not know one letter from another. It has been interesting to me to work on such raw material. They are very eager to learn, and in a very short time can manipulate a pencil, write letters, and figure correctly and read words. Before long they will be reading the word of God."[983]

To better understand what their missionaries in Africa were experiencing, the WFMS began a two-year study of the continent to increase their knowledge of its people and their cultures. Those WFMS members realized that Susan and Martha were sympathetic to the women and children in the villages and had made them sisters "under the covenant."[984] For her empathy, successful work, and dedication, Susan was recognized in 1917 by her branch sponsors. One year later, at the annual meeting of the WFMS, Susan was lauded as "the real pioneer and continuously faithful representative missionary at Quessua."[985]

John Springer, attending the March 1917 Congo Mission Conference, also expressed sympathy regarding the low status of women who lived under the practice of heathenism. He felt there was limited opportunity for them to learn to live a pure and modest life and be treated fairly. With their low status, white men coming to the country took the native women as temporary concubines. These men wanted to remain childless and expected the women to prevent pregnancies from their unions. Springer wrote, "We wish to enter our strong protest against this practice and against the tolerance that is given to it in this country. One cannot be surprised at the great brazenness that manifests itself in the native women connected to this way of life. We also deplore the developing class of professional prostitutes, native women, within the European towns, and even in the native villages."[986]

He was troubled when he saw little girls in young native families being exposed to these behaviors through observation and family conversations. The hope was they could be secured as boarders for the mission schools, and their mothers would "have the opportunity for instruction and spiritual care."[987] He then made a plea for finding single women who would come to the mission field under the auspices of the WFMS and provide those services.

Those concerns were still paramount with the missionaries in 1918 when Susan was to retire with high honors. However, two reasons kept her in Africa until 1920. First, no one was available to fill her position because the missionary candidate committee members found applicants were not qualified. They discovered "there had been no provision for a detailed study of the manners and customs and community and family life of the people to whom they were to go."[988]

Second, both Martha and Cilicia were on furlough in the United States. That timing seems unfortunate, as Susan had her sixty-seventh birthday while she was single-handedly caring for the children and attempting to teach them. That seems an unrealistic expectation for someone her age, but she persevered. Given these circumstances, the Foreign Department of the Society voted to retain Susan, giving her a two-year extension despite the retirement age rules.[989] The numerous demands on her time limited Susan's letter writing to her cousins, the Paines, and other Fayette friends.

As the war effort ramped up, more Americans were needed on the frontlines. Thus, in 1917, the US Army began its first officer candidate class for African Americans at Ft. Des Moines and also brought African American recruits to Camp Dodge in central Iowa. Those camps were established in Iowa because no other state would accept African Americans.[990] "Iowa's selection for both posts was due at least in part to the remarkable evolution of racial attitudes among the majority of its white citizens."[991] However, some racial stereotyping occurred at the camp, usually by military officers not from Iowa.[992] The Knights of Columbus donated one of its halls for African American Camp Dodge troops to use. Several prominent Des Moines residents attended the dedication ceremony.[993]

While more Americans were being trained for war, Susan had sixty-five girls living at the mission in 1918. Entertaining Bishop and Mrs. Eben S. Johnson added to her responsibilities during annual conference, but she considered it an honor. She was enthusiastic about evangelizing results and reported, "On the Sabbath the bishop baptized thirty-two and received eleven in full membership and eleven on probation. Since that day eleven more have been received on probation. Three of the girls in the school have been married during the year and have set up Christian homes."[994]

One of the ways people became interested in the church was through women's prayer meetings. Louise Shields, another missionary, shared a glimpse of one held in a native woman's home. "During a recent visit of Bishop and Mrs. E. S. Johnson, Mrs. Johnson attended with me a native women's prayer meeting held in a little grass hut. The family had to borrow white coverings for the dingy table and bed and had put a new mat on the grass floor. Our lantern added much light for all they had was a narrow-necked bottle of oil with a rope wick, which gave out a smoking light." She described how everyone, including the bishop's wife, adapted to the simple shelter. "There was not enough space for all of us to kneel on the floor, so Mrs. Johnson knelt on her chair the only one in the room. She spoke tenderly and sympathetically to the women of the new life in Christ Jesus and her words will be long remembered."[995]

Susan spent the early months of 1919 managing the girls' school and faithfully caring for the children while her colleagues were still on furlough.[996] Martha remained with Pacific Branch members for several months and later spoke in Chicago. She used these opportunities to describe the needs of the mission and ways those women could contribute to Quessua programs.[997] Cilicia visited family in Milnor, North Dakota, and mounted similar requests.[998]

There was disappointment at Quessua in October 1918 when Miss Clara Ault, Susan's replacement, did not appear as scheduled. Susan had eagerly anticipated her arrival, but lengthy travel delays caused Clara to wait in Yokohama, Japan, and Bombay, India, for transportation. She finally made her appearance in May 1919.[999] Her presence helped relieve Susan, but Clara, still learning Portuguese and adjusting to life in Quessua, required Susan's mentoring.

Clara attended the West Central Africa Conference meeting in Luanda two weeks after her arrival in Quessua. Her conference reports provide insight into Susan's workload. "I have not taken up any work at the school yet. Since the departure of Miss Cross last June, Miss Collins has had charge of the Quessua Girls' School. While it has been necessary to abandon some of the classes, during that time some elementary instruction has been given. The religious training consists of morning and evening devotions and classes in Scripture study and Catechism. The girls are all enrolled in Sunday School classes on Sunday afternoons." Ault concluded, mentioning the effects of the Spanish flu at the mission: "During the past year the school has had an enrollment of sixty-five, but during the recent epidemic of Spanish Influenza, many were called to their homes and have not returned yet, but we hope to have the full enrollment again soon."[1000]

While Susan was struggling to maintain a disciplined life for the girls at the mission, a series of conferences were taking place in France at the Palace of Versailles. These conferences between January 1919 and January 1920 were part of the negotiations that officially ended World War I and the signing of the Treaty of Versailles. Representatives of fifty-five countries met and hammered out the formation of the League of Nations, the predecessor to the United Nations. Those peace efforts eased ocean transportation problems for missionaries and others traveling between the continents.

In 1919, Susan and Martha were recognized for their struggles and accomplishments in the *Jubilee Story of the Women's Foreign Missionary Society* when Isham described Africa as "The Pagan Land!" "Quessua, barely opened at the end of the last decade, was purchased by the death of two—Miss Zentmire (Mrs. Brewster) and Miss Mekkelson. Miss Collins and Miss Drummer were appointed, and there in the jungle, made a garden, in heathenism planted the seed of the Kingdom which was growing in young hearts and blossoming in clean young lives."[1001]

When Susan was endeavoring to keep a positive Christian environment for the mission girls, African American women in Iowa were operating a statewide campaign to raise enough money to purchase a dwelling in Iowa City to house female African American students. These women were prohibited from living in campus dormitories between 1913 and 1946. That is why Susan's cousin Iva Joiner McClain lived with a faculty member in 1913 after she enrolled at the University of Iowa. Procurement of a house on Market Street was made possible by the financial help and encouragement of the Iowa Federation of Colored Women's Clubs (IFCWC).[1002] After the nine students obtained the house, they organized themselves into a club. Iva was elected president.[1003]

In 1920, world conditions and those at Quessua were favorable for Susan to return home after almost nineteen consecutive years in Angola. Susan's last months in Africa were filled with many emotions, ranging from joy to be freed from duties and to sadness because she was leaving all of the girls whom she had nurtured and loved.

Susan had changed the lives of the girls she parented, worshipped with, and taught. She was proud of the Christian homes they started either near the mission or in their kraals away from the mission environment. One admirer wrote of Susan, "The children of many homes will rise up and call her blessed because of the way their mothers were, as children, taught by her to love the lord, thus becoming good homemakers."[1004]

Another testimony to Susan's influence was from Florinda Bessa, who followed Susan as a teacher at Quessua in the 1920s. One of Florinda's tasks was to develop leadership among the native people. During that time, 175 girls were receiving instruction at the Quessua school and raising and preparing much of their own food. One accomplishment was setting out 1,400 pineapple plants.[1005]

While at Quessua as a girls' school teacher, Florinda wrote to Fayette's Reverend John Clinton, responding to a May 19, 1937, article he wrote for *Zion's Herald*. Clinton's piece, "We Have Our Negro Member," described Susan's life and work in Africa and featured a picture of her with Bishop G. Bromley Oxnam. A thrilled Florinda Bessa wrote to Reverend Clinton, "I have been so happy since I saw dear Miss Collins' picture. We are all glad all of us who knew her. I showed the picture to one of her old school girls and she wept for joy just to see her in a picture even. It has been so long since any of us have heard from her that we thought she was already with our Lord." Florinda continued, "We have a very large girls school now even larger than she ever had for she had to pay the girls to come to the school and now they are sorry not to have the money to pay many of them who would like to come to school. This truly is a new day."[1006]

Florinda closed her letter requesting Clinton send her as many pictures of Susan as the two dollars she had enclosed would purchase. They were for "some who love her as mother that she was to many a poor motherless child."[1007] Learning of this request, Susan provided the pictures as gifts.[1008] No one has calculated the number of lives Susan influenced, but it must have been thousands.

These tributes confirm Susan's colleagues and the girls loved, respected, and missed her, but evidence of farewell events for Susan is lacking. Susan did not want to leave Africa and "refused to quit work and expressed little interest in retirement. She argued that her thirty something years in this country gave her the right to be buried here."[1009] Florinda Bessa recalled, "Everyone knew how she felt and wished it were possible, but she needed to return to America where she could receive the care and support that her condition required." My research did not reveal what Susan's health situation was at that time.

Florinda said it was difficult to convince Susan to return to the United States. The day she departed was a sad occasion. Florinda closed her letter explaining, "Like her good friend, Martha Drummer, she did not want to leave the land that had given her so much joy. The last few nights of her stay in Angola were spent in prayer for the people who had become like family. I helped her pack her meager belongings and accompanied her to the ship and waved goodbye until she was out of sight. I never saw her again."[1010]

Among Susan's belongings were some African bowls and spoons taken to the State Historical Association of Iowa by her cousin Marjorie McClain Kizer. These artifacts may have been gifts Susan brought for her Joiner relatives.

Leaving the vast and evolving African continent was difficult for Susan. She had spent almost half of her adult life there, and she had become close to many children as they grew to adulthood. After working and praying together for fourteen years, Susan and Martha certainly felt a sisterhood bond. Possibly there were promises and plans to meet again after Martha retired. Susan looked forward to continuing to share stories of her missionary experiences with friends in Northeast Iowa, settling into her home, tending her garden, and visiting her Joiner cousins in Des Moines.

Final Ocean Voyage: Traveling Home

Prior to departure, Susan was required to complete an emergency passport application at the American consulate in Luanda, Angola. That document, typically valid for six months, confirmed Susan had been in the Belgian Congo from 1887 to 1890, in Angola from 1890 to 1900, and back in Angola on December 31, 1901, until her final return to the United States. She signed the application, including an oath of allegiance, on May 28, 1920, which was witnessed by Reed Paige Clark, the consulate representative.[1011]

As a general rule, US citizens were not required to have a passport until 1941. Exceptions were during the Civil War from August 19, 1861, to

March 17, 1862, and during World War I. The war requirement began on May 22, 1918, and continued until the formal termination of the war by treaties in 1921.[1012] Susan's return to the United States in 1920 was the first and only time during her international travels a passport was necessary.

The application showed she planned to travel to the Madeira Islands and then Portugal en route to New York City. She wrote to Fayette friends from the islands[1013] on August 9, 1920. Susan arrived in the United States on the *Canada*, which had departed from the Port of Ponta Delgada, St. Michaelus, Azores on July 30.[1014] The passenger list did not reveal Susan's passage type.

As Susan's steamship eased into New York Harbor, the Statue of Liberty came into focus. The torch symbolizing enlightenment applied to much of Susan's life, dedicated to awakening the girls and women of Angola to greater happiness and possibilities through academic, practical, and religious education. The copper statue had developed a greenish patina between Susan's first vision of it in 1887 and her final return.

Lady Liberty stands on a broken shackle and chains, with her right foot raised to represent moving away from oppression and slavery. After observing the treatment of Angolan slaves and having knowledge of her parents' indenture, that symbol of freedom likely evoked strong emotions for Susan. Scanning the horizon, Susan would have viewed buildings forty to forty-five stories high, looking like palaces compared to the thatched roof huts in the African kraals.

She was only one of the tens of thousands of people on one of the hundreds of vessels arriving daily at the harbor. It must have taken awhile to adjust to the earsplitting din after life on the Angolan mountain plateau with many fewer people and no mechanized machinery. Adding to the frenzy of the city were the elevated railways, electric signs, and cars moving rapidly down smooth roads, along with the nearly six million residents going about their daily lives. Immigrants flooded the city, trying to find work in the center of manufacturing and commerce, creating the need for larger and more apartment buildings. The decade of the Roaring Twenties had begun, and disarmament and pacifism became major issues for the Methodist Episcopal Church.[1015]

Susan had left the United States in 1887 to find meaningful life's work. Now in the 1920s, African Americans were migrating north in large numbers with the same motivation. Between 1917 and 1925, approximately two hundred thousand African Americans moved to New York, looking for jobs and to benefit from the cultural life of Harlem. Many were migrating to Chicago, Los Angeles, and other northern cities to escape continued oppression and the low wages in the South due to the recession of 1920–21. Their destinations were often dependent either upon the most direct railroad line out of their state or where relatives or friends had settled.

Soon after arriving in New York City, Susan departed for Iowa. She was filled with awe, wonder, and amazement as the train sped westward. Possibly she thought of her father and his stories of his Civil War train trips across the northern states fifty-five years earlier. While the train groaned through the Pennsylvania mountains, she could imagine her father sitting in an open-air car and shivering in the cold on a misty morning. Later when the train bounced and lurched across Illinois, perhaps she thought of her time spent in Chicago preparing to become a missionary. With her mind awash with memories, she likely compared crossing the Mississippi River on the Rock Island Truss Swing Bridge to the upstream ferry ride in late 1865.

Upon her arrival in Fayette on August 18, nine days after her ship had landed, she was welcomed warmly by local residents anticipating her return. They were concerned that Iowa's cold winter months would be daunting for Susan after thirty-three years of living near the equator.[1016] She stayed at the home of Mrs. Jason Paine because her house was rented.[1017] The rent, an additional source of income for Susan when she was in Angola, continued for two more years.

The WFMS had allocated $350 to retiring missionaries to cover travel expenses upon returning home. Any unused balance was applied to their retirement benefits.[1018] The year Susan retired, the annual salary for missionaries in Africa had reached $950.[1019] That was commensurate with the elementary school teachers' wages in Iowa during the same timeframe.[1020] Susan was considered on furlough for her first two years in the States, possibly because she had not taken any during her nineteen years with the WFMS. By 1920, salaries for those on furlough had risen to $600 for the first twelve months.[1021]

Retirement allowances began two years after the missionaries had completed active service in the field.[1022] Susan benefitted from the retirement fund begun in 1912 by the WFMS for single or widowed women missionaries. Those on the retired list were to receive an annual allowance of fifteen dollars for each year of service up to and including the twentieth year.[1023] Based on this, Susan should have received annually $285 for her nineteen years of service sponsored by the WFMS. She also had annuity income from investments Reverend Jason Paine had made using money from the salary she received from the WFMS.[1024] Even with her house paid for, she had to live frugally to subsist on these income sources. Average per-person earnings in 1916 were $708 and $1,303 in 1924.[1025] Gardening and canning skills enabled her to produce and preserve much of her food, decreasing her living expenses.

So on a warm August day in 1920, Susan was ready to begin new chapters in her life. What these chapters would contain and how long they would last, she did not know. She was back in the location of her youth and with trusted, longtime friends. Travel between Fayette and Des Moines had become easier with better roads, so she could see her Joiner cousins more frequently. Reflecting on her life in Africa, she knew she had done what she could in her pioneering missionary role as mentor, mother, nurse, teacher, fundraiser, and construction project manager.

17

∞∞∞

Completed Circle: Return to Iowa

Adapting: Climate, Pace, Conveniences

Changes between Susan's departure to the Dakota Territory in 1882 and her return to Fayette thirty-eight years later required acclimation. Numerous friends and family members had either moved or died. Children she had cared for were grown and living in other parts of Iowa and the United States. Her cousin John A. Joiner, while living in Sully County, South Dakota, had died in April 1916. Traveling had become easier with railroad expansion and the advent of cars. Many improvements in utility service and infrastructure were visible in Fayette. African Americans were migrating from the south in large numbers, changing the demographics, particularly in large northern cities. Susan adapted to these changes while leading an active life.

People on both sides of the Atlantic cherished Susan and benefitted from her love and care. Those feelings were reciprocal. Perhaps that was she why she had decided to settle in Fayette after her missionary career was completed. She had the support and longtime friendship of Mrs. Jason Paine, wife of Reverend Paine, and their children, Amy Leigh, Margaret, Louie Bell, Charles, and Edward; members of the Fayette WFMS chapter; and friends in Fayette and the neighborhood where she had grown to womanhood.

An example of her friendship with the Paine family was demonstrated after she had begun receiving a salary from the WFMS. She sent most of her earnings back to Reverend Paine, who opened a bank account for her. Later, she asked him to use a portion of her savings to purchase land and a house for her.[1026] He honored her request, and on December 4, 1905, the warranty deed conveyed Lots 1, 2, and 3 Block 11 of the S. H. Robertson Addition to Susan.[1027] Reverend Paine managed and rented the house for Susan until his death in 1912, when his wife, Margaret Kent Fletcher Paine, assumed the responsibility.

When Susan returned, most rural Americans either walked everywhere or rode horses. Those who could, about one in fifty people, purchased Model T Fords. In 1924, one car cost $290, and an average family income was $1,303.

There were no cars at the Quessua mission when Susan retired, but by 1922, the missionaries had a Model T truck and a car. Those vehicles replaced the hammocks and rickshaws used primarily by Susan during her years in Angola. Rudimentary Angolan roads had been constructed, and car usage had shortened a two-day trip to three and a half hours by the time the missionaries traveled to a February 1922 conference at Quiongua Mission. Challenges still abounded, and rains often washed out bridges, causing workers to be sent ahead to make repairs.[1028]

Susan was fascinated with the car Mrs. Jason Paine owned.[1029] But she worried Margaret and her children would be hurt when they went driving. Margaret noted when her oldest daughter was learning to drive, "Susan finally went with us and now she would rather ride than eat."[1030]

Susan quickly overcame her fear of riding in a car. Less than six weeks after returning home, she traveled with Margaret 103 miles to Eldora, Iowa, to visit her son Charles.[1031] Susan was eager to see the man she had cared for as a young boy in Monticello and Fayette when working for his parents.[1032] Charles is the father of Samuel Collins Paine, possibly so named to honor Susan.

Upon Susan's return home, conveniences were still limited throughout the country. Only 30 percent of families had telephones, and fewer had radios. Fewer than 20 percent of homes had a range, and a lesser number had the luxury of a refrigerator instead of an icebox.[1033] People had to carefully manage their expenses because the wartime boom had collapsed and the number of jobs had decreased.

After more than three decades in Africa, there were many things requiring adjustment in Susan's life other than riding in a car. One change was the availability of utilities in Fayette. Some homeowners enjoyed electric lights after the city received a franchise for light, heat, and power in September 1914.[1034]

By December 1914, the Fayette County Municipal Telephone Company was at work putting up poles and lines for residents living on both sides of the Volga River.[1035] Using a telephone was starkly different from drums and wooden mallets Africans beat in code to communicate the arrival of missionaries and other visitors to their villages.[1036]

Fayette installed water lines in 1903 and completed the sanitary sewer system in 1919.[1037] Susan had a cistern on her property and hand-pumped water as needed.[1038]

How different having a house completely to herself must have been for Susan after sharing her four-room residence in Africa with twenty-five girls and later being the matron for up to seventy babies and girls. Envision Susan's amazement if she could see the more recent additions to her house. Still standing at the corner of Alexander and State Streets, she wouldn't recognize her small, white, single-story frame house with a slightly sloping roof built in 1902. It had one bedroom about thirteen by fourteen feet, a living room with a rock-walled cellar underneath, and a kitchen.[1039] It did not resemble the large, square, two-story houses common in the Fayette area. A recent addition of a three-car garage has nearly doubled its size.

At the time Susan purchased her house, there was either a heating or a cookstove in every room. Eventually, a woodburning furnace installed in the partial basement replaced the individual room stoves. The wood supply was thrown down a chute placed at the outside entrance to a small cellar and then put into a bin. Later, the heating system was converted to an oil furnace.[1040] Eventually, that outside entrance was replaced with an inside door and stairs after the enlargement of the cellar.[1041]

Soon after her arrival, Susan explored new buildings on the Upper Iowa campus, visited the aging Fayette House where she had worked as a young woman, and walked across the new bridge spanning the Volga River. Possibly she continued east to view the changes on the property her father once owned. Now seeing fox and wildcats was atypical. Fording the river had been a necessity when Susan was a teenager. The Stone School

House had closed in the spring of 1920, and the students living northeast of Fayette attended the newly constructed school in town. The grist and sawmills no longer operated. Tractors had replaced oxen, and the use of horses had declined in many farming operations.

When Susan departed for Africa in 1887, women did not have the right to vote or run for public office. But changes had occurred slowly in her absence with much effort from hundreds of women. On April 2, 1917, the first woman, Jeanette Rankin from Montana, was elected to the United States House of Representatives. In 1919, Iowa became one of six states through legislative enactment to secure presidential suffrage. Within days after Susan's return to the United States, ratification of the Nineteenth Amendment to the Constitution occurred on August 20, 1920. In Iowa, African American women were granted the right to vote by this amendment.[1042] However, women of color were not enfranchised to vote if they lived in states where men were disenfranchised because of their race. That included African American men who lived in the Jim Crow South, Native Americans, and Chinese Americans.[1043] Even though Susan could have voted, there is no record of her voting either that fall or in later years.

Evolution and expansion of women's roles and employment during Susan's lifetime was slow. By the 1890s, there were increasing numbers of women in politics and the workforce. Decrease in family size and increase in labor-saving devices contributed to those changes. Percentages of women working for pay rose slowly: 1890, 18 percent; 1900, 20 percent; and 1930, 26 percent.[1044] Percentages for numbers of working African American women were fairly constant at 43 percent prior to 1940. In the south, most African American women were confined to work as domestic servants in homes of white people. Those workers were the first to lose their jobs with the onset of the Depression in 1929. At the end of the nineteenth century, women worked primarily in service or manufacturing occupations. By 1930, clerical occupations were becoming more prevalent. Those numbers do not include farm women's, boardinghouse keepers', and industrial homemakers' unpaid work.[1045] During Susan's lifetime, more women were finding employment teaching in elementary and high schools, but they were paid less than men. Other popular career choices included nurse or librarian.

Discovering so many changes in America and rural Iowa must have seemed both strange and amazing to Susan. As she adjusted, she continued to do what she did best, serving the church and helping people.

At the October 1 meeting of the Fayette WFMS chapter at the home of Mrs. J. W. Dickman, "Miss Collins gave a very interesting talk on work in Africa. She shared many pretty articles from Africa."[1046] These items included examples of baskets and embroidery work created by her students. As a souvenir, she gave those present an African porcupine quill.[1047] They are collected and used in basketry and artwork by the indigenous people. Those sharp, banded brown and white quills, between eight and sixteen inches long, are cylindrical and stout. African tribesmen once used them as darts or arrow tips.[1048]

The following Sunday, Susan and Margaret Paine drove 140 miles to Muscatine, Iowa, spending a week with Reverend and Mrs. George Blagg. Mrs. Blagg was the former Louie Belle Paine, who Susan cared for as an infant. From Muscatine, Susan traveled by train to the Philadelphia area and participated in the fifty-first annual general executive meeting of the WFMS.[1049] During the meeting from October 29 to November 2, held at the First Methodist Episcopal Church in Germantown, actions were adopted to increase the salaries of the missionaries in the field and the allowances for retired missionaries.[1050]

Susan was one of fifty-one furloughed missionaries honored. Their aggregate years of service totaled 691 years and an average of 13.5 years in the mission field. Susan's thirty-three years were likely one of the longest tenures. During the ceremony honoring the furloughed and forty-seven newly commissioned missionaries, they sang their rallying song, "I Love to Tell the Story."[1051] Quite possibly, Susan served as a mentor to the new missionaries and shared stories with the others who were on furlough.

The conference planners put more than usual emphasis on foreign mission work. Several programs featured Africa. Maude W. Williams described many incidents of "Prayer Answers in Africa," and Dr. Willis. S. Rowe presented a stereopticon lecture that "brought out the lights and shadows of Christian endeavor in that great continent."[1052]

After her Pennsylvania travels, Susan left for California to avoid drifting snow, cold winds whipping out of the north, and icy sidewalks. Susan knew the harshness of Iowa winters and needed time to adjust before staying permanently in Fayette. Women of the Pacific Branch were eagerly awaiting the arrival of "our Susan."[1053] They honored her and invited her to stay in their homes for extended periods. In January 1921, Susan was living on Locust Street in Pasadena with Mrs. S. F. Johnson, the branch corresponding secretary.[1054] Later, she was in Los Angeles from May 1921 until her return to Fayette in September, where she again resided with Mrs. Jason Payne [sic] Paine.[1055] Susan moved to her own house just two blocks east of the Paines' home in mid-1922 when the renter's lease expired.[1056]

Perhaps it was Susan's influence during her stay with Mrs. Johnson that precipitated the women of the Pacific Branch contributing a share of their annual Thank Offering to the cost of homes for missionaries in Quessua and Mutambara, Africa.[1057] The female students at those locations were continuing to acquire domestic science skills, learning how to do laundry, iron, make beds, clean, mend, and sew. They also practiced simple food preparation techniques.[1058] Those were subjects Susan had taught throughout her missionary career.

The trip to California helped Susan transition to a less hectic pace while being nurtured by her hosts. Imagine the adjustments she had to make leaving her busy life in Quessua and the students to whom she had been a devoted mother figure. Susan missed the girls and wrote to them when time permitted. Their joy in receiving Susan's letters was described when Miss Clara Ault, her replacement, wrote, "On the last mail, Miss Collins sent a letter to the girls' [sic] and they were glad to get it. Now three weeks later, we see one and then another reading it again. They did love Miss Collins as do all her know her. I hope she is happy in America."[1059]

While in Angola, Susan would have observed the annual terror the natives experienced from the middle of March until the end of April. Martha Drummer described the frightful experience in *Woman's Missionary Friend* the fall Susan returned to Fayette from California. "This is the time of year the tall grass has reached the limit of growth, which is taller than any man and headhunters are supposed to be waiting in every convenient nook, hidden by the grass by every trail, in the gardens, up in the trees, at the spring, and so on."[1060]

Martha continued, "The terror of headhunters is so deep in the natives souls it will not be educated or laughed out of the present generation."[1061] Everyone had an enemy, and because it was likely unknown, the natives' lives were "a nightmare of fear." Martha elaborated that people walking alone were met with violence, but the motive was revenge and not robbery. She described a situation where a woman was attacked while in a garden near Malanje. The attacker was an enemy from her village who was settling an old feud. Soldiers and villagers identified him and took him to prison, where he soon died. The attackers concealed their sin under the mask of the *kifumbe*. Martha explained that when these things happened, it was useless to ask a man or boy to go alone for the mail or any other errands. For protection, they traveled with someone who had a spear or in caravans. She concluded, expressing pity for the villagers, "For they are grievously tormented. Pray that they may have perfect love for Him who casteth out fear."[1062] What a test of faith for Martha and Susan as they walked so many dangerous paths during their missionary work!

Participating in Activities: Church and the Community

Perhaps immersing herself in Fayette organizations helped Susan forget those distressing aspects of life in Angola and focus on the positive facets of her retirement. She remained active, engaged, and vibrant, exhibiting the strong faith she had shown in Africa. Information in the Fayette United Methodist Archives, local newspapers, and personal recollections provided glimpses of Susan's service to the church and community during the last twenty years of her life. Among these sources are secretaries' and treasurers' reports of the Fayette Chapter of the Woman's Foreign Missionary Society (WFMS).

When able, Susan attended church, taking an active part in both the Sunday-morning and evening services. As an avid seeker of knowledge, she read widely, keeping up with news of the day, including world affairs.[1063] Susan's sources included the local newspaper, a Methodist Church publication, and mission periodicals. Fiction was not a priority for her.[1064] Miss Margaret Paine admired Susan's biblical knowledge and considered her a wonderful student of the Bible.[1065]

Purchasing *The Picture Bible* for herself on February 11, 1933, enhanced Susan's delight in personal study. The 583 colorful illustrations of the Bible stories helped create reader interest. In 1975, Bertha Medberry Yearous, the little girl who had sat on Susan's lap more than seventy earlier, gave that Bible to the Fayette UMC. Presented on the December Day of Dedication, the Bible is prominently displayed in the church foyer along with one of Susan's African thumb pianos. Inscribed inside the Bible is Yearous's notation that Susan had given the Bible to her mother, Charlotte Medberry.

Members of the church often asked Susan to speak to various groups, especially before she became too frail.[1066] Well known throughout the area were her wonderful prayers, a talent that once paid for new glasses. At the conclusion of an eye appointment, the doctor, when asked for the bill, replied, "If Miss Collins will say the Lord's Prayer in Kimbundu, as we in the waiting room stand, the bill will be paid."[1067] She recited the prayer in her strong, confident voice.

In early January 1922, Susan once again shared her knowledge of Africa with local members of the WFMS. She used a map to illustrate the locales where she had served, including Quessua.[1068] Her topic was timely, appropriate, and persuasive, resulting in generous giving to the thank offering fund for missionaries in Quessua and Mutambara, Zimbabwe,[1069] just as the Pacific Branch women had done.[1070] In October, she inspired congregants at a Sunday-evening Lima Church service.[1071] Late in the year, she motived WFMS members to raise one hundred dollars toward the purchase of an automobile for Miss Mildred Simonds, a Fayette missionary serving in India.[1072]

During the fall of 1922, when maple and oak leaves carpeted the ground, Susan and two other women were elected to serve as delegates at the October WFMS Branch meeting in Waterloo, Iowa.[1073] She filled that role again in spring 1923.[1074] Susan graciously led devotions at local meetings in December 1925[1075] and September 1926, when she highlighted aspects of her thirty-three years of missionary service.[1076] Her energetic role in the adult Bible class resulted in her selection as one of six to serve on the church membership committee.[1077]

Susan's desire to remain involved in mission-related activities was strong as she strove to inspire young women and men to become missionaries. She spread the word in neighboring towns, including Hawkeye[1078] and Oelwein,[1079] enthusiastically sharing her gratifying experiences with members of the WFMS and Woman's Home Missionary Society (WHMS). In October 1933, she attended a missionary society meeting at the Wadena home of Mrs. Maggie Johnson. The twenty-one attendees savored a lunch featuring African foods and commented about the intriguing African craft objects Susan showed to enhance her lecture.[1080]

Susan hadn't learned to drive, so friends taking her to meetings were faced with challenges navigating the dirt roads prevalent in Iowa in the 1920s and 1930s. Rain-slick roads often caused cars to zigzag across muddy surfaces while the drivers tried to retain control and avoid watery ditches. The unfortunate ones who slid into a ditch had to walk through shoe-grabbing mud and find a farmer with a team of horses to pull them out.

Skill was required to avoid puddles of unknown depths and large clumps of flying dirt spattering across the windshield decreasing visibility. Staying on the planks covering mudholes demanded intense concentration. Falling off sometimes resulted in a damaged vehicle and injured passengers. Years later, graveled roads decreased the danger. But it wasn't until hard surfaced roads were laid down that Susan and her friends were assured of arriving safely and punctually for her presentations.

Throughout much of her retirement, Susan was a dues-paying member of the WFMS and WHMS. She contributed to specific needs, among them the annual thank offering fund and scholarships for students in India and to Miss Mildred Simonds.[1081]

On June 9, 1923, Susan deeded her house and three lots to the Pacific Branch of the WFMS of the Methodist Episcopal Church.[1082] That act demonstrated Susan's appreciation for the financial support and confidence Miss Crothers and other branch members had provided between 1902 and 1920 when she was in Quessua. The gift enabled Susan to express her gratitude for their belief in her abilities and devotion to missionary service at a time when the Methodist Episcopal Church hierarchy had not believed she should return to Angola.

Susan communicated with the faculty at the Chicago Training School, sharing appreciative memories of her experiences as a student. In 1925, she wrote just prior to the school's October 20 Founder's Day. "The very thought of Founder's Day brings very pleasant memories. I'll light my candle and send out a prayer for CTS."[1083]

In November 1929, the Fayette chapters of the WFMS, WHMS, and the Woman's Christian Temperance Union (WCTU) held a reception. Those closely linked organizations honored Susan and Joan Davis, another missionary with local roots, for their years of service promoting Christian ideals.[1084] The WCTU was founded early in the women's club movement in 1874 and quickly became the largest women's organization in the United States. Their fight against alcohol influenced the beliefs of the Methodist Episcopal Church when they made changes in the *Book of Discipline* in 1880. They declared, "Let none but pure, unfermented juice of the grape be used in administering the Lord's Supper, whenever practicable."[1085]

In the fall of 1935, the Fayette church sought funds to purchase new hymnals at a cost of one dollar each. Lists of contributors appeared in the Sunday-morning bulletins leading up to December 24, the due date of the publishing company bill. Susan generously donated ten dollars while those with more resources contributed enough for only one book.[1086]

Susan's interests and support extended beyond missions and the church. The threat of a proposed merger of their beloved Upper Iowa with another university caused spirited Fayette citizens to join forces and mount a publicity campaign during the spring of 1928. Susan actively sought donations and was among those who helped raise over $1,000 to stave off the merger.[1087] She staunchly exhibited her loyalty to causes she believed in through contributions of her services and limited financial resources.

Susan's contentment and secure environment were not the lot of many African Americans who were leaving the south due to continued racial and economic inequality. Their exodus was partly due to better modes of transportation as they moved from south to north and from farms to cities after World War I (WWI). Another factor was increased industrialization that provided attractive work opportunities. African Americans wanted to benefit from new jobs just as whites were. Their honorable service during WWI had proven their abilities. They had overcome enlistment discrimination and unequal treatment at training camps and in assignments. The first African American officer candidate school was at Fort Des Moines in Iowa. Men from Yale, Harvard, Tuskegee, and Howard Universities were among the 1,250 candidates who trained there. They received their commissions on October 15, 1917. Some remained in the Des Moines area and had basic training at Camp Dodge. While WWI had a direct impact on many African American families, it may have ultimately created a tragic event unrelated to the war in the family of Susan's cousin, John A. Joiner.

Of the 350,000 African Americans who had served during the war, most were in labor battalions rather than combat units. But some serving with French combat units had demonstrated heroic actions. Consequently, the French honored seventy-one African American soldiers of the 370th regiment with the French Crois de Gurre. Twenty-six received the Distinguished Service Cross.[1088]

While serving in Europe, the African Americans' unit bands played blues and jazz, which became popular. Their music was partially responsible for the Harlem Renaissance, a cultural revolution in the 1920s.[1089]

With the end of the war in November 1918, especially in the south, whites feared the returning African American veterans would demand equality, which they rightly felt they had earned. Racial tensions resulted in the deaths of more African American men, even some while in uniform.[1090]

The next year, twenty-six cities experienced antiblack riots. Susan was in California during the time when many believe "the single worst incidence of racial violence in American history," the Tulsa Race Riot, burst out on May 31, 1921, and continued into the next day.[1091] Tulsa was a troubled town with a vigilante mentality. A white mob formed outside the courthouse the evening of the thirty-first after an African American man had been jailed and accused of attacking a white woman. Twice, African American men, many of whom were WWI veterans, living in the Greenwood District of Tulsa went down town and volunteered to assist the sheriff. Both times, their offer was refused. The second time, "a white man tried to disarm a black veteran, and a shot was fired. The riot began."[1092] The number of deaths, mostly by gunfire, was estimated to have been thirty-six. Hundreds of homes and businesses in the Greenwood District were demolished by fire. The residents fought hard to save their property, but they did not have the numbers. The African American man was exonerated, but the all-white jury placed the blame for the riots on the African Americans. No whites were punished for their actions that caused massive death and destruction. Many African Americans had to live in tents during the winter while they rebuilt their community. Eventually, those remaining in Tulsa were repatriated for their losses.[1093]

Even though African Americans had supported their country and fought valiantly in WWI, they still weren't fully accepted into American culture and society as full citizens. Housing was controlled in cities through racial covenants resulting in segregated neighborhoods. In many states, African Americans had to use separate hotels, restaurants, school, water fountains, and public transportation. Attempts were made to keep them from voting by saying they could vote only if their grandfathers had voted. In 1915, the Supreme Court ruled these grandfather laws null and void because they violated the Fifteenth Amendment to the Constitution.

Susan, an avid reader, was appalled by those events and situations, feeling deeply about the injustices being wrought upon those of her race. The African Americans in rural Northeast Iowa were considered part of the pioneer stock and had become considered as equals. However, life wasn't always comfortable for those in Black Hawk, Polk, and Scott Counties, where the cities with the largest concentration of African Americans were located. Even though the Iowa Civil Rights Act of 1884 was the first of its kind in the United States, it did not remedy the discrimination that it was passed to eliminate. "A few individuals were successful in criminal prosecutions of civil damage suits, but the great bulk of discriminatory acts had no practical remedy."[1094] It had been noted that "the concentration of African-American residents occurs not only by county but within counties as well,"[1095] indicating that segregated areas existed in Iowa throughout Susan's life.

By the time Susan returned from Africa, Des Moines had become the hub of African American life in Iowa.[1096] The family of her cousin and Civil War veteran John A. Joiner was well known and respected throughout the area for their farming endeavors and their beautiful farm site.[1097] His son-in-law's second wife, Jessye McClain, was active in Order of the Eastern Star (OES) and the Iowa Federation of Colored Women's Club (IFCWS) initiatives in Des Moines. John A. Joiner's daughter Mary, John McClain's first wife, had died two years after their second child, Marjorie, was born. Jessye was mentioned as a leading woman in the Des Moines area when she attended the ninth annual meeting of Electa Grand Chapter of OES in May 1915 in the capacity as past worthy matron. Other leading citizens were Sue M. Brown, grand lecturer, and her husband, attorney Joe Brown.[1098] Attorney Brown had facilitated Iva's enrollment at the University of Iowa.

In 1916, Jessye McClain was the recording secretary for the IFCWC.[1099] She likely had been a part of the group that was instrumental in obtaining a house for African American female students at the University of Iowa. Among them was her stepdaughter Iva Joiner McClain.

Between 1900 and 1940, the year Susan died, the African American urban population in Iowa increased from 8,097 to 15,343.[1100] Conversely, the rural African American population decreased from 4,596 to 1,351. Most were farmers residing in rural areas. Over 50 percent of Iowa's urban African American men were working either in "manufacturing and mechanical industries" or in "domestic and personal service" jobs when the 1920 and 1930 United States Federal Census data were collected.[1101] Just as Susan had done early in her life, the majority of African American women were employed in "domestic and personal service," both in 1920 and 1930, with the percentage increasing from 80 to 90 during those years.[1102] Even though there were positive changes, equality for African Americans was still not a reality for many of them during the last twenty years of Susan's life.

Throughout the Great Depression, the WFMS suffered from decreased contributions and membership. Missionaries in the field had to postpone furloughs, new building projects were cancelled, and there was a 15 percent reduction in yearly operating appropriations. Allowances for retired missionaries were cut 5 percent, with the decrease continuing through 1934.[1103] It would be only conjecture as to how this affected Susan's level of living and giving, but she contributed through service and financially to causes important to her. Church members appreciated her knowledge of Africa and mission work and her ability to speak so they felt as if they were in Angola. Thus, she was sought as a featured lecturer, keeping her presence known in Fayette and surrounding communities and perhaps helping those residents better understand the struggles of African Americans moving to the north. Susan was persistent in demonstrating her commitment to education and to God.

18

∞∞∞

Comfortable in Fayette: Savoring Past and Present

Reconnecting with Friends: At Home and Away

Susan's relationships with the Paine family members, friends, and former colleagues remained strong, and she welcomed many of them into her home. Perhaps her hardest moments were related to the murder of a dear relative during her first decade back in the States. As a loyal Christian friend, she believed maintaining communication was important. Susan spoke to church youth groups and women's clubs and displayed her musical talents upon request. People treated her with respect, recognized her accomplishments, and honored her pioneering efforts as an educator in Africa. She continued to embrace life.

The long-standing relationship between Susan and members of the Reverend Jason Paine family flourished until Susan's death. They remembered Susan on various occasions, including her 1926 birthday celebration hosted at their home. Fifteen neighbors and friends valued the pleasure of sharing that milestone.[1104] At age seventy-five, Susan had lived seventeen years beyond the average life expectancy for females in the United States.

Three years after returning home, Susan journeyed to Atlanta, Georgia, to comfort a seriously ill friend,[1105] likely Martha Drummer, her missionary colleague for fourteen years. Susan had nursed Martha to health shortly after her arrival at Quessua in 1906. Martha took an early furlough in 1923 after contracting an illness in Angola the previous year.[1106] When she came home for medical care, Susan nursed her back to health. Martha returned to Africa, where she served until 1926 when her health failed again. She was fifty-five and lived another eleven years, dying in 1937 three years before Susan.[1107]

Life in Atlanta in 1923 was vastly different from life in Northeast Iowa where African Americans were not expected to defer to whites. Segregation that had begun in the South after the Civil War was still disenfranchising African Americans, many of whom were poor, when Susan traveled there. "Under Jim Crow, black Georgians suffered from a system of discrimination that pervaded nearly every aspect of life; they were denied their constitutional right to vote, encountered discrimination in housing and employment, and were refused access to public spaces and facilities."[1108]

Under the separate but equal laws "Blacks and whites attended separate schools, drank from separate water fountains, worshipped at separate churches, rode in separate railroad cars, and visited separate parks and recreational facilities."[1109] Sometimes African Americans were not allowed entrance to hotels and restaurants and weren't able to vote or to serve on juries.[1110] One wonders how Susan reacted to these differences and if she followed those constraints when in the south or felt safe enough to ignore them.

While Susan was still in Angola, her cousin Marjorie McClain, one of the 'little cousins" to whom she had written in 1904 and 1905, married Robert J. Harris in Des Moines on May 4, 1919. Robert was a World War I veteran and a soldier in the 163rd Depot Brigade, the first to form at Camp Dodge north of Des Moines.[1111] He likely met Marjorie while in training. By 1920, they were living in Greenfield, Iowa, with his parents, where he worked as a mechanic.[1112] Several years later, they settled in Des Moines.

In late 1924, a tragedy involving Marjorie and her older sister Iva occurred, haunting Susan the remainder of her life. The Harrises had traveled from Des Moines to Kansas City to spend the Christmas holiday with Iva, who was teaching at Lincoln High School.[1113] On the morning of December 29, a domestic quarrel broke out between Iva and Robert while the three of them were in Iva's home on Grove Street. The quarrel escalated, and Robert shot Iva and then committed suicide. Iva died a few days later on January 3, 1925, in Kansas City General Hospital.[1114] Her services were held at St. Paul A.M.E. Church on January 7 in Des Moines, where she is buried in Glendale Cemetery near her father and stepmother.[1115]

In her letters, Susan had encouraged Iva and Marjorie to be good scholars while emphasizing the importance of education for all students. Clearly, Iva took this to heart as she followed in Susan's footsteps teaching African American students in two southern universities and then in Kansas City. Iva's death was a devastating loss to Susan, Marjorie, and other cousins in the John A. Joiner family. Losing her only sibling, whom she adored, and her husband must have seemed unbearable to Marjorie, who lived until 1993. Both she and their aunt Sadie are buried in the Pine Hill Cemetery in Des Moines.[1116]

Sometime prior to 1930, Susan invited Nellie Valentine Crosswhite to live with her as a housemate. Perhaps the idea germinated when Nellie visited Susan in Fayette during January 1923.[1117] Nellie helped Susan maintain her home, and they shared expenses during the Great Depression that had begun on October 29, 1929.[1118]

Born in Wisconsin in 1855, Nellie was four years younger than Susan. She was the daughter of Robert Valentine's brother John who lived in Janesville. The roots and formation of the women's friendship probably occurred during their childhoods in Wisconsin when the brothers' families saw one another in Quincy. Nellie, nearly age eighty, died on May 10, 1935, and was buried at Pleasant Hill Cemetery north of Fayette and across the road from where the Stone School House had stood.[1119] Susan was now alone in her home.

Those who lived through the Depression didn't forget the hardships and deprivations. People often felt helpless and useless. Families in rural areas were frequently able to raise livestock, perhaps a few cattle, pigs, and chickens to help sustain themselves. If they had a garden, they could either eat or preserve the vegetables and harvest fruit such as cherries and apples from their orchards. Others likely picked wild gooseberries and blackberries in the summer and gathered walnuts and hickory nuts in the fall, all plentiful in Iowa woodlands and prairies. Many who experienced these difficult years practiced frugality during their lifetimes, passing those acquired behaviors on to their children.

To help people without work, President Franklin Roosevelt and his cabinet created several work relief programs, including the Works Progress Administration (WPA) in May 1933. That program along with the Civilian Conservation Corps (CCC) put unemployed men and women to work, for which they received temporary financial assistance. Thirty percent of the ten million jobless men in the United States in 1935 were assisted by the WPA. In Iowa, many of the WPA projects were related to community services and public works. Women made clothes in WPA sewing workshops.[1120] That funding enabled Iowa regionalist painter Grant Wood to create two murals in Parks Library on the Iowa State University campus. The murals titled "Breaking the Sod" and "When Tillage Begins, Other Arts Follow," representing rural Midwestern life, are the largest murals in the nation.

In the fall of 1934, Susan and Nellie, both still actively embracing life, participated in an event sponsored by the Twentieth Century Club to honor older settlers. Entertainment featured Reverend John Clinton addressing the topic "Pioneer Days, Past and Present." Guests shared recollections along with the state, month, and date of their births and then excitedly drew a gift from a grab bag, wondering what the small treasure was.[1121] Visualize Susan animatedly entertaining the nearly ninety attendees as she described the challenges in Wisconsin when her father was in the Civil War, their rigorous trip to Iowa in the fall of 1865, and her experiences in the unsettled Dakota Territory operating her own laundry.

Reverend Clinton, who served the Fayette Methodist Episcopal Church from 1925 to 1940, liked to share stories about Susan. One story may have been about a neighborhood child who spotted a fire on Susan's property. Thinking quickly, the boy turned in an alarm, and the Fayette Volunteer Fire Department was there in minutes, discovered rubbish burning in her yard, and extinguished the flames.[1122] That responsible child prevented Susan's home from being damaged and was briefly a local hero.

Another Clinton story described Susan's experience becoming a member of the Fayette church. Even though she had joined the Methodist

Episcopal Church in Huron many years earlier, she had not formally affiliated with the Fayette church. In January 1930 when Clinton held a membership campaign, Susan officially became a member. He explained the situation that occurred the Sunday she joined: "The church is 80 years old and we all found 80 people to join and Susan had been left to sit there and in her modesty she said she didn't know if they wanted her."[1123] A surprised Clinton made it clear the congregation wanted her as a full-fledged member, and she immediately joined the other incoming members at the front of the church.

Several years earlier in 1923, Upper Iowa personnel had presented a Diamond Jubilee Pageant, charging a one-dollar entry fee. Clinton recalled that, upon Susan's arrival for the second night, a thoughtful citizen, thinking the fee was too much for Susan, told her the pageant was the same both nights and expressed concern that the air might be too cold for her. She responded, "When I'm thru with life, I'll be quiet for a long while, so I'm going both nights, it's such a good pageant.[1124] These stories illustrate how people of all ages in the community treated Susan thoughtfully and respectfully.

Susan participated in Sunday school and the adult Bible class. She attended a class stunt party where she was the hit of the evening.[1125] When it was her turn to do a stunt, "She very demurely stood up and putting her hands behind her back recited in a child's voice:

> You'd scares expect one of my age
> To speak in public on the stage
> And if perchance, I fall below
> Demosthenes and Cicero,
> Don't view me with a critic's eye
> But pass my feeble blunders by."[1126]

In addition to showing her pluck at that event and participating in Sunday school and women's meetings, Susan was involved in other church activities as her time and energy permitted. Between late 1925 and early 1926, a basement was dug under the church building. Male members volunteered time to complete digging and hauling the dirt away in wheelbarrows. Reverend Clinton was an active participant in the process.

Space was created for a kitchen, fellowship hall, and Sunday school rooms to meet the needs of their growing congregation.

Susan and six other older women lovingly braided carefully cut strips of woolen rags into rugs to cover the cold, concrete basement floor the men had poured. One of the four oval rugs made from more than 1,600 feet of rags had a completed size of seven feet long and four and a half feet wide. It weighed about twenty pounds. Susan braided the initial two rounds for the rug's center using wool material she had contributed. The sight of her effort inspired Reverend John Clinton to write, "The heart of the rug was braided by a little elderly retired missionary. There is love at the heart of that rug."[1127] Collection of additional wool material occurred at an August church service, and admittance was by "rag only."[1128]

Susan had a bout with illness in the spring of 1931, and Mrs. Susan King took care of her. Near the end of April, she was feeling much better.[1129] By 1935, Susan's health had begun to decline. After Nellie's death in May, Margaret Paine arranged for Susan to live in the country northeast of Fayette with childhood friends, the three Graham siblings: Harriett Graham Lewis, Julia Graham Stepp, and Ervin Graham.[1130] The farm originally owned by their father is located approximately two miles from where Susan lived during her teenage years and later as she cared for her dying mother. It has been said the Graham and Collins children were schoolmates and church friends while growing up in the African American enclave. Their home seemed a logical place for Susan to spend her last years, as "Hattie Lewis was known for miles around as the one who would help in time of trouble. Many told they owed their life to her nursing. A wonderful woman."[1131]

An evening pastime of farm families was listening to their radios to stay attuned to local, state, national, and world events. Local news frequently consisted of high school sports results, farm commodity prices, and weather reports and forecasts. In 1936, much reporting focused on Iowa's extremely hot and dry summer and its effect on crops. The following winter, news concentrated on the frigid temperatures and heavy snows creating hazardous travel conditions, frozen water pipes, and dangers to livestock.

State-level newscasts included sporting events at the three state-supported colleges, proceedings in the Iowa legislature, and an overview of national and international events. Susan and the Grahams were likely pleased that during the 1930s, a small but increasing number of African Americans were earning PhD degrees. In 1935, Jesse Jarue Mark became one of the first African Americans to earn a PhD in botany. His degree was from Iowa State College, now a university. In 1938, Marguerite Thomas Williams graduated from Catholic University of America with a PhD in geology.[1132]

Attune to national events, Susan and the Grahams listened with interest to the political news related to the presidential campaigns and elections of 1932, 1936, and 1940 won by Franklin D. Roosevelt. Radio news provided information about government programs designed to aid the unemployed, including farmers suffering from the ravages of the dust bowl caused by the prolonged drought of 1933. Ervin and Harriett may have participated in the Soil Conservation and Domestic Allotment Act of 1936, designed to decrease the number of farm acres in production and to be used for conservation. To attain the goal of preventing future dust bowls, farmers were encouraged to plant trees, native grasses, and shrubs that would prevent soil erosion. The Social Security Act of 1935 did not benefit them because agricultural laborers were excluded.

They would have learned that millions of American were still unemployed at the conclusion of the 1930s. But events on the world stage were creating change. News broadcasts informed them of Hitler's appointment as chancellor of Germany in 1933 and führer in 1934. With complete control of Germany's government and military, he began moving to annex European countries into the Third Reich. On March 15, 1939, Czechoslovakia surrendered to Hitler, and on September 1, he invaded Poland. Two days later, Great Britain and France were at war with Germany, and on September 5, war had broken out in Europe. The war escalated in 1940, and on the day Susan died, the British evacuated more than 338,000 soldiers from France. The United States, favoring isolationism, had not yet entered World War II, but by October, men between the ages of twenty-one and thirty-six were required to register with the draft board.

While Susan lived at the farm, it was the destination for the Fayette Boy Scout Troop's annual pancake hike organized by Reverend Clinton. Harriett and Ervin were beekeepers, and they provided tasty honey for the pancakes devoured by the scouts and their leaders.[1133] Susan entertained them playing her African thumb piano while everyone ate. According to one scout, the piano was "about the size of home plate with a row of rattles along the bottom, and sounds something like a mouth harp with a tambourine on the side."[1134] The keys were flat, iron nails of varying lengths up to eight inches.[1135]

One of the songs Susan played was "Jesus Loves Me." She sang the first verse in her "Thin, true voice," using the Kimbundu words as follows:

Jesu ungesola, Jesu ungesola
Kidi ungesola, May Ami Makanbi.[1136]

After Reverend Clinton's death, his daughter June inherited that piano. With the author's encouragement, she presented the piano to the First United Methodist Church in Fayette during a June 2009 Sunday service. That fall, the author had the opportunity to closely examine the piano now on display in the church. Made from a solid piece of wood, the burned interior was hollowed out with a sharp tool that left visible marks. Thick brass tacks placed at each corner add a decorative element. The piano has a dark stain, much of which is worn off the bottom.

Twenty-three of the original twenty-six metal keys remain. They have pointed ends flattened into shape with a hammer. Fastened across the width of the instrument, the keys are elevated about seven-eighths of an inch above the wooden base. A rod of twisted metal attached to one end of the piano runs through six cylindrically shaped metal pieces and is used as a rattle. Attached to the bottom of the piano were the Kimbundu words for "Jesus Loves Me."

Recognizing Susan: Visitors and Honors

Even before Susan moved from her home to live with the Graham siblings, people realized this stalwart woman was aging. Friends and former colleagues began coming from far and near to visit and honor her. On July 1, 1930, two days prior to her seventy-ninth birthday, Reverend and Mrs. Austin J. Gibbs and their daughter, home on furlough from Quessua, visited Susan.[1137] She was eager to hear news they brought from her mission field friends and former students.

Mrs. Gibbs, the former Clara Ault, had come to Quessua in May 1919 as a new missionary to help Susan at the mission school. Her husband had begun his Angolan missionary work in the fall of 1907. Austin and Clara were married in Cape Town, South Africa, on November 26, 1921, with Bishop Eben S. Johnson performing the ceremony.[1138] Possibly they wrote from there to tell Susan of their wedding, thus explaining the source of the Suid Afrika (South Africa) stamp found in her New Testament.

Likely Clara told Susan of the severe challenges she and Cilicia Cross experienced soon after her return to the United States. Both of them became ill in 1921 due to the stress of living and working in crumbling buildings and with the increasing numbers of girls at the school. Clara went to Cape Town to recover from a nervous breakdown, and Cilicia contracted black water fever. She experienced symptoms including rapid pulse rate, rapidly developing anemia, high fever, and chills. The name originated because the urine turns black or dark red as red blood cells are destroyed by malarial parasites. The fever rarely appears until a person has had at least four attacks of malaria. Between 25 and 30 percent of those who contract it die, even with treatment.[1139] It took months for Cilicia to recover, which is typical, so Martha gave up her evangelistic work and taught. When Martha and an assistant became ill in February 1922, they had to close the school and send the girls home, causing bitter disappointment.[1140]

Six years later in 1936, Cilicia Cross, while on furlough, traveled to Fayette to visit Susan. She had come to Quessua in 1915 after two years in Luanda, so they had many stories to share. Each of them had been responsible for the construction of buildings at the Quessua mission site. Susan was involved in building projects over a decade before Cilicia. Those structures had become too small and not suited to the current needs in their crumbling condition. Cilicia described the condition of the building in 1922 thus: "The roof leaked in a dozen different places and the rain came in under the doors and made rivers across the kitchen and dining room floors at least once a day during the rainy season. The girls sometimes fell through the ant-eaten floors upstairs and last Christmas eve while we were enjoying a Christmas tree in another building, the ceiling gave way and let pieces of ant clay, some weighing no less than one hundred and fifty pounds down on the dining room table where we had been eating less than two hours before." Continuing, she expressed frustration of the length of time the building project had taken: "The work is being pushed as fast as it is possible in this land of 'tomorrow.' Every mason and carpenter that crosses my path is captured and set to work. The work is progressing and the buildings are going up rapidly. A Ford has arrived from America just in time to be a big factor in pushing the work."[1141]

When Susan was managing the construction, the materials were hauled from the coast in "man loads," and their arrival was unpredictable and weather dependent. Imagine Susan listening intently and then sharing some of the frustrations she had experienced when directing her building projects. She empathized when Cilicia described her challenges during the time six new mission buildings were constructed. The buildings were "a three-roomed school house, a nine-roomed two-story missionary home, two dormitories for the girls each sixty-six by twenty feet and planned to house two hundred girls, a large dining hall and a four-roomed building that will be used as a garage, store rooms, and laundry. ... All of the buildings are of adobe but with cement foundations to make them proof against the eternal invasion of white ants which up to the present time has been the bane of our lives." She elaborated, saying, "The floors are of tile or cement and the roofs are to be tiled thus making a much pleasanter and cooler house than the present ones of rough stone floors laid in mud, and corrugated iron roofs. And the screened verandahs will make them as near mosquito proof as can be made."[1142]

During her visit, Cilicia attended a church banquet honoring Susan. She admiringly described Susan's accomplishment for single-handedly managing the Quessua girls' school while she and Martha were on furlough. And then she complimented her for being an education pioneer in Africa.[1143]

A distinguished guest, Bishop G. Bromley Oxnan of Omaha, Nebraska, visited Susan in April 1937. He spoke to the Methodist Episcopal Church congregation, encouraging them to support missionaries. When the bishop expressed a desire to visit Susan, Reverend Clinton drove him to the farm, where they were warmly welcomed. Susan agreed to have her picture taken with the bishop as they stood on the lush front lawn, using the large, well-kept white farmhouse as a backdrop. Wearing her trademark long, starched white apron, she posed holding her well-thumbed Bible.[1144] Perhaps it was the *Pictorial Bible* she had purchased in 1923. Although no longer belonging to the Graham family, the farmhouse was still inhabited in 2019.

Several months after the bishop's visit, Susan had guests from Quessua. Dr. Alexander Kemp, his wife, Winifred Farmer Kemp, and their four daughters were home on furlough and wanted to see Susan. Delighted to meet Winifred, Grace, Lois Anne, and Martha, she listened to news from the mission, including updates on the school. Dr. Kemp shared stories of those he treated, likely people mauled by lions and leopards and a man whose face was torn away by a crocodile. He mentioned natives walking along the trails after dark, stepping on poisonous snakes and being bitten. The bites were often fatal because he didn't have antivenom.[1145]

Dr. Kemp described the escalating political tensions forced labor had caused. Some of the natives were treated badly, and violence occurred when they failed to follow the rules set by Portuguese officials regarding food production and sales. By 1926, missionaries, including the Kemps, had no longer remained quiet. When he began speaking out about those practices, the Portuguese government labeled him a troublemaker. Because he was being watched, the only time he wrote his opinions was in letters sent to the States. To protect himself, he developed a code that got past censors. When Cilicia Cross went on furlough, he sent a letter with her describing the situation. She mailed it after leaving Angola. Those dangerous and appalling conditions resulted in fewer missionaries going to Angola for years.[1146]

Throughout his career in Western Africa, Dr. Alexander Kemp's goal was to educate people that medicine, not witch doctors and evil spirits, cured illnesses. When he began showing native evangelists and converts germs magnified under a microscope, they started to comprehend the real cause of disease. That strategy convinced them it was hospital treatments and medicine that cured ailments and not charms or fetishes.[1147] During his years at Quessua Mission, Dr. Kemp dedicated much of his life to developing a medical education program for the local people.[1148]

While the Kemps were in Fayette, they along with Susan were honored at a supper held in the church Broad Room, the very room where the rug

Susan had begun braiding covered the floor. The evening program was a slideshow presented by Dr. Kemp. Centered in one of his pictures was a very young native boy recently christened and given the name Collins.[1149] Susan's dedicated service and influence had reached forward nearly twenty years to that namesake described by Dr. Kemp. What a heartwarming moment for Susan!

The fall after Dr. Kemp's visit and his summer request for cloth to make bandages at the Quessua hospital, Reverend Clinton held a worship service with the theme "White Cloth for White Fields." Again Susan's positive influence was felt and honored, as many congregates supplied cloth for Dr. Kemp, who had supervised building the hospital after Susan retired.[1150]

At a Sunday-evening service in early July 1937, Reverend Clinton's sermon, "Taking it to the Lanes and Fields," focused on the missionaries who had represented the Fayette church throughout the world. Prior to hanging Susan's picture in the west transept of the church, the congregation honored her with a special church service.[1151] Her picture was hung with those of twenty-four missionaries who had connections with the church, including Dr. John R. Mott, a Nobel Peace Prize winner. Besides Susan, two people from the church had served in Africa, while others had carried their Christian faith, love, joy, hope, and knowledge to Burma, Chile, China, India, Malaysia, and Palestine.[1152] I wish that, as a teenager who participated in Sunday school classes in the transept, I had taken a keener interest in those pictures. Sadly, they disappeared from the church archives when that building was demolished in 1962.

One of the women who went to India was Allie Bass, a descendent of the Basses who came to the county in the 1850s. Her father was the younger Sion Bass. Allie graduated from Fayette High School in 1919 and likely met Susan after her return to Fayette. Perhaps Susan inspired Allie to become a missionary. Allie earned a bachelor's degree in education from Iowa State Teachers College, now the University of Northern Iowa, and a master's degree from the University of Iowa. Then for sixteen years, she was an instructor in the boys' school in Moradabad, India. She wrote to my grandmother Emma Bennington in January 1929, requesting funds for her mission work by describing a typical day at the Parker Branch School.[1153] I have been told my grandmother willingly sent funds to that neighborhood friend because she was impressed with the excellent description of her work. Allie concluded her missionary career as the business manager at a college in India.[1154]

Perhaps the longest lasting honor and one involving the most people in the Fayette congregation was the construction, installation, and dedication of Susan's Star during the 1937 Christmas holidays. As a world traveler, Susan saw stars shining over three continents: North America, Europe, and Africa. To show their affection and demonstrate their high esteem and respect for Susan, the congregation created and dedicated a star to spotlight Susan's devotion to children fifty years after her first departure to Africa. Children in the Sunday school classes raised $12.76, mostly in nickels, to provide a tangible recognition for her life dedicated to the service of others, especially children.[1155]

Reverend John Clinton initiated construction of a nine-inch electric star to be installed at a point over the lectern on the east side of the church sanctuary. The star was to be lit primarily during Sunday-evening and Christmas services.[1156] Supplies to create the star made of satin finished aluminum and from a white translucent raised glass cost $8.23.[1157] It was fashioned by a church member, the local blacksmith Lysle Wooldridge, and hung by the scout master. Names of the contributors were placed in a sealed envelope and encased in the metal framework of the star. Donation of Wooldridge's services freed the remainder of the money to prepare the church bulletins used at the dedication on Sunday, December 19, 1937.[1158]

The congregation sang "Silent Night" as the meditation to open the service, followed by "There's a Star in the Sky." The minister intoned, "Dearly Beloved, we learn from the holy scriptures that devout men have set much in the stars. Their fixity reminded of God the Creator; their splendor and the variety of it, reminded of the loyalties of Men; and their clearness reminded of the full and clear knowledge of Christ. We therefore assemble here for the purpose of dedicating this Star as a 'beacon to God' and to the 'love and loyalty' of Susan Collins."[1159]

After the call to worship and the scripture reading describing the wise men following the star to Bethlehem, Reverend Clinton continued, "We present this star for dedication, the gift of the classes of the Sunday School, for the glory of God and in honor of Susan Collins."[1160] He affirmed, "We dedicate this star in appreciation of the men of old who loyally followed the Star, and also to those who from among us have followed a vision of service out into the world, especially Susan Collins in Africa."[1161] During the dedication, Reverend Clinton emphasized Susan's active participation in the Sunday school classes that continued, when she was able, until early 1940. The service concluded as the congregation sang "O Thou Who Dost the Vision Send."

That evening after the star's dedication, church members presented a biblical tableau. Following the presentation, a young couple was married under Susan's Star. Honoring their request, Susan sang and played "Jesus Loves Me" on her thumb piano while sitting under the star. When she finished, a member of the congregation was quoted as saying, "That's just plain unforgettable."[1162] And Reverend Clinton concluded the service simply saying, "This we know."[1163]

For years following the installation of Susan's Star, the church Christmas tree was placed beneath it. It was as if there was a star that crowned the tree.[1164] Some of the children wanted to know why the star was there, and the author was one of them. Unfortunately, this star dedicated to Susan was either lost or destroyed during the 1962 demolition of the church building.[1165] A newer church structure now stands on that site.

"Jesus Loves Me" was Susan's signature song. During an Armistice Day rally hosted by the Epworth League members in 1939, one hundred young adult attendees asked Susan to sing her song, and she willingly did. "She came through in flying colors singing in African dialect, 'Jesu mange zola' both verse and chorus."[1166] The audience, ages eighteen to thirty-five, honored Susan as an elder member of the congregation.

Later in November, members of the Rust College Singers shared the program with Susan, who sang "Jesus, Lover of My Soul" in Kimbundu. Young people representing seventeen Fayette area churches attended.[1167] Rust College was founded in 1866 by northern missionaries with a group called the Freeman's Aid Society, an organization of the Methodist Episcopal Church. It is one of the oldest colleges in the United States for Africa Americans and is located in Holly Springs, Mississippi.

Susan continued to participate in local and church activities while living in the country. During November 1939, she attended the church service honoring Golden Agers. As the oldest person in attendance at age eighty-eight, she was honored as First Lady of the occasion, receiving a silver framed picture of Elizabeth Alexander, a leading force in the establishment of Upper Iowa University.[1168] What a fitting tribute, as both women were strong advocates promoting the education of young women. Susan had benefitted from Alexander's early actions when she attended Upper Iowa. While working in Africa, "It was Susan's belief that once young women possessed a strong faith and a good education, they would want to return to their home villages to teach other young women. She was convinced that a generation of educated mothers would transform their world."[1169]

The final mention of church activities honoring Susan during her lifetime occurred in September 1939. Melon Monday, an evening event, was held on the west lawn of the church grounds by the stone fireplace. "A Half a Melon for Half a Dime" was the slogan, with half the proceeds to "go to Africa to the school established by Miss Susan Collins many years ago."[1170] Atrus Stepp, a prominent African American farmer and melon producer, who lived in the neighborhood where Susan had grown to womanhood contributed the melons. Stepp's father-in-law was one of the pioneer farmers in Fayette County. His mother, Julia Stepp, and his aunt Harriet Lewis were the women with whom Susan was living at the time of the event. Susan, a few months earlier, had helped them host a Sunday-afternoon service at their home for the congregation as part of a series called the Friendship Tour.[1171]

Quite likely, Susan continued to communicate with the remaining descendants of her cousin John A. Joiner's family either via letter or family visits until her death. His son John William and daughter Sarah Josephine lived in Sully County, South Dakota, at the time of the 1935 state census.[1172] Sometime after that, they returned to the Des Moines area and were listed there in the 1940 United States Federal Census.[1173] Marjorie remained in Des Moines after Iva's death and married a Mr. Kizer prior to 1930. John W. died in 1954, and Sarah "Sadie" Josephine in 1967. The last living member of Susan's cousin John A. Joiner's family I've been able to trace was Marjorie, who died on December 14, 1993, in Des Moines at the age of ninety-eight.

Susan remained active, engaged, and vibrant during her retirement years, exhibiting the strong, unwavering faith she demonstrated for thirty-three years as a missionary. We will never know precisely how, when, or why Susan received the vision to serve and to bring enlightenment and love through the Gospels to unknown numbers of children and adults in Western Africa. We do know she made a difference as twice she faithfully followed the stars across America, the Atlantic Ocean into Africa, and back again to America during her missionary career. Susan sowed seeds of compassion, grace, hope, and love. By example, she taught many they could make a difference regardless of their circumstances. After retiring, she continued to serve as a positive influence to young and old, blacks and whites, and "The name Susan Collins is revered in Fayette."[1174]

19

Surrounded by Friends: Cherished by Many

Susan's Final Days: Receiving Loving Care

Realizing her health was failing rapidly, Susan dictated and signed a document on April 19, 1940, expressing her gratitude to Margaret Paine and other members of the family for looking after her business affairs and for the many favors they had extended to her over the years. She requested that both her name and Margaret's remain on her account at the State Bank of Fayette and gave Margaret full power to deposit and withdraw funds. These funds were to be for Susan's use and comfort and other purposes Margaret thought wise throughout the duration of Susan's life.[1175]

During Susan's last few months of life, Margaret's sister Amy Leigh Paine drove them out to see her nearly every day. On one visit, they took Susan ice cream because she was very fond of it. As Susan lay in bed, Margaret tried to feed her some, but she would only take a little. Margaret said, "Take a mouthful for me, Susie," which she did. Susan showed her playfulness a little later when Margaret said, "Can't you take another spoonful for me, Susie?" She replied, "No, I took the last one for you."[1176]

In May, friends put an item in the Fayette newspaper reporting that Susan's failing health during the winter had not improved.[1177] Upon receipt of that information, members of the Woman's Society of Christian Service, a combination of the former WFMS and WHMS, and local friends began taking turns visiting Susan at the farm. Those social calls helped Susan's days pass more quickly and provided her admirers the opportunity to pay their respects for all the contributions she had made to the church, the community, and the larger world. I imagine many tears were shed during those visits, but also much laughter was heard ringing across the countryside.

On Thursday, June 6, Susan was reported very ill.[1178] Susan died the next day at age eighty-eight years, eleven months, and four days. When her battle with uterine cancer ended, Susan was in the presence of her lifelong friends, Harriett and Julia.

Reverend H. W. Mitchell conducted the funeral service on Saturday afternoon, June 8, at the Fox Funeral Home, as requested by Susan prior to her death.[1179] Reverend John Clinton, her admirer and friend for fifteen years, was on vacation and unable to return to perform the service. The funeral home, large for a town of Fayette's size, was packed. "Four white men, who were leading citizen together with two colored men, acted as bearers. Everyone in town was her friend. Yes, the negroes were friends and proud to know her."[1180] Two of Susan's favorite songs, "Rock of Ages" and "Jesus, Lover of My Soul," were sung with the organ accompaniment by church members Mrs. R. R. Erion and Mrs. Willis Walker.[1181] The Erion family, friends of Susan, lived south across State Street from her in the house owned by Mrs. Walker's mother-in-law.

After the service, I visualize the funeral procession slowly making its way across the Volga River bridge and along the tree-lined, curving, dusty gravel road to the Lima Cemetery situated six miles northeast of Fayette. With the fragrance of red clover blossoms wafting across the river valley, Susan was buried beside her mother, sister Maranda, and brother William. Immediately south of their gravestone is Martha Indiana Collins Thompson's stone, Susan's only sibling known to have married. The Collins family lived near that beautiful country cemetery at the time Susan's mother and siblings died.[1182] A number of white pioneers, who were neighbors, including the Everett, Hensley, Holtzman, Lambert, Oelberg, Stern, and Thorp families, are interred here.

The Burial Ground Association was formed in 1865 and laid out the cemetery on a hill north of the Volga River. At the time the Collins family arrived, there were large stands of hickory, maple, and oak trees near the river, and the silt-deposited soil provided good crop land.

Margaret Paine was appointed executrix of Susan's estate.[1183] One of the four areas Susan had outlined for the disbursement of her funds in the April 19 document was payment for a suitable grave marker. Margaret purchased the gray, polished-front granite gravestone that stands under the protective branches of a stately white pine tree. It is inscribed, "Susan Collins, 1851–1940, She served 33 yeas as a missionary in Angola, Africa." Susan did serve that many years in Africa, but two of these years were in the region of the Congo River Delta.

Susan had stipulated that at least one hundred dollars be paid to the girls' school she had helped found in Quessua, Angola. An undated letter verifies the fulfillment of this request.[1184] Susan's third stipulation was "To pay the Pacific Branch of the Woman's Foreign Missionary Society, the sum of ONE HUNDRED DOLLARS, this amount to be placed in the pension fund of said Society. This may be paid during my lifetime and before September 1, 1940 if the said Margaret E. Paine finds it is wise to do so."[1185] This wording suggests Susan knew her death was rapidly approaching.

The final stipulation contained three areas for the equal disbursement of the remainder of Susan's estate. Harriett Lewis, her childhood friend and caregiver during her final years, was to receive one-third of the residue. Another third was to go to Margaret Paine for being "such a good friend and who has spent so much time looking after me and my business affairs."[1186] The final third was to be used by Margaret to conduct Christian work Susan had discussed with her at different times. That document had been witnessed by Julia Stepp, Amy Leigh Paine, and Harriett Lewis.[1187]

In an attached codicil witnessed by Alma Fussell and Harriett Lewis, Susan requested that her "household belongings including clothes, contents of all closets, drawers, cupboards, trunk, and boxes be undisturbed until such time as Margaret Paine can dispose of same."[1188] Susan's wording in the document clearly illustrated the long, trusting friendship between her and the Paines.

Filing of the deed record for Susan's home occurred one day after her death.[1189] That act completed the transfer of her real estate property to the Pacific Branch of the Woman's Foreign Missionary Society for one dollar and other valuable considerations.[1190] Susan's home was valued at $2,000 in the 1930 United States Federal Census. However, due to deflation in the 1930s, the value likely had decreased by the time she willed it to the WFMS. The society sold the home to the John Bahl family,[1191] who modernized it and made it a very attractive cottage.[1192]

The Fayette Methodist Episcopal Church received her quill pen and a Bible, and Upper Iowa University inherited her personal books. Included were a two-volume set of Emerson's complete works; Hammerton's *Outline of Great Books* in three volumes; *The American Scrap Book*; and *European Scrap Book*. Those works are still housed in the university library. Thirty-three dollars from her estate provided a resource for the university library staff to acquire books including topics on United States history and American fiction.[1193]

Within a year after Susan's death, the Paine sisters used a portion of her estate residual to purchase an oak baptismal font in her honor for the church. They thought it was a fitting symbol of Susan's life and work in bringing the Gospel to the native people of north-central Angola and those living near the mouth of the Congo River. Dedication of the font occurred during a Sunday-morning service conducted by Reverend Arthur Kindred, who said of Susan's life, "No matter how inauspicious a beginning, no matter how humble the heritage, no matter how lacking in material possession along the way, SUCH A LIFE gathers about it a solid halo of things which bring to shadows of life a light of hope, inspiration and joy which is a source of blessings to those whom it touches."[1194]

Reverend Kindred concluded: "For a third of a century she told the story of the Master, more through her life than by vocal eloquence, and gradually built up one of the most effective mission stations throughout Africa. Therefore it is most appropriate that there should be presented in her memory a baptismal font, a symbol of the forgiving grace and cleaning power of God's love which is a bond that ties all Christians in one great brotherhood throughout the whole wide earth."[1195]

Unfortunately, the location of that baptismal font is unknown. Perhaps it was either discarded when the church building was demolished or given to another church. It exists in my mind because my mother told me it was used when I was baptized as a baby shortly after it was dedicated. It was still being used when my older daughter was baptized at the church in June 1961.

Memories of Susan: Church Members' Recollections

Several people who were teenagers during Susan's later years shared their memories enhancing my picture of her. Merle Sternberg recalled watching Susan as she pulled a small shopping cart past her home on the way to Main Street five blocks west. Main Street had four grocery stores where Susan could shop, with one of them having a dry goods section. On Sundays, she observed Susan dressed for church and briskly walking two blocks west along State Street and one block south on North Street to the Methodist Episcopal church. Tall, stately popular trees lining the sidewalks along State Street made soothing, whispering sounds as Susan went on her daily walks. She walked with purpose but took time to talk with people mowing their lawns, gardening, or sweeping their sidewalks. Susan's garden was weed-free with straight rows of corn, green beans, peas, beets, zinnias, and other vegetables and flowers. She had a small patch of strawberries.[1196]

Audrey Hurmence described Susan as small boned, five feet tall, with a ready smile and a twinkle in her eyes. She usually wore light-colored print dresses to church in the summer, topping her ensemble with a nice yellowish straw hat featuring a turned-up brim. Her winter wardrobe consisted of darker-hued wool dresses, often in navy blue or black and reaching her ankles.[1197] Plain black shoes with a little heel completed her ensemble. To protect her clothing, Susan often wore a white, starched, long apron that tied in the back. Her simply styled hair was parted in the middle and pulled back into a bun. She wore wire-rimmed glasses.[1198]

Each Sunday, the congregation could expect to see Susan near the back of the church. She sat on the east side in the second of three raised pews.[1199] When queried about the possibility Susan sat there due to prejudice, Hurmence responded there were not black-white issues in the church, and there were other African American members, including the Atrus

Stepp family, who sat elsewhere. June Clinton Rutt supported Hurmence, writing, "Susan, as far as I know was treated VERY well by the residents of Fayette and esp. the church,"[1200] Rutt stated her parents and siblings accepted Susan like a family member and expected her to have Sunday dinners with them. Feeling the community's acceptance, Susan was very social, conversing easily with everyone. Rutt mentioned as Susan aged, she did not get around very well, thus limiting her church attendance, perhaps because a ride from the Graham farm was not always available.

Russell Erion, a church member and Susan's neighbor, shared with one of Rutt's sons a conversation he had with Susan. He recalled her telling him that if a page or section of a book would become loose, she would get out her needle, thread, and thimble and stitch the sections together. Susan did that with her New Testament. A repair of that type was necessary because Scotch tape wasn't invented until 1930.[1201] Susan was able to make do throughout her life. But in doing so, she left rich memories for those who knew her.

Susan was a devout woman who had followed numerous stars throughout her life. Perhaps it was the North Star that had guided Susan, her parents, and siblings from Illinois to Wisconsin and then to Iowa in 1865. Their exact motivations for moving to Iowa remain a frustrating mystery. Other stars provided light and direction as she ventured, possibly alone, to the Dakota Territory, where her father later joined her for six months until his death. We do not know which stars, other than those in her eyes, guided her to Chicago, New York, Liverpool, and western Africa, where she began her missionary career in 1887. Stars shown and twinkled for Susan during her thirty-three years of loving service at various mission stations near the mouth of the Congo River and in Angola. Other stars provided direction as she made her way across the Atlantic in 1900 to New York, California, and back to Quessua, Angola, in early 1902. After those eighteen years of service at Quessua as a head mistress and teacher of a girls' school, she returned to view the stars of her teenage and young adult years in Northeast Iowa.

When she could no longer see the stars with earthly eyes, her star still shown with vibrancy in the First Methodist Episcopal Church built in 1876, the year Susan started classes at Upper Iowa University. The cross-shaped church was the oldest of that architectural style west of the Mississippi River until it was demolished. Susan's Star had provided light and hope for those who felt they were in a dark place. Even though the star is gone, Susan's memory and legacy continue to live in various ways. The brave and dedicated manner in which she lived her life can serve as a role model for current and future generations. She did not let her humble beginnings limit her life, one that was dedicated to service, first to God and then to God's children. Susan had become a citizen of the world.

Afterword

Susan's Story: Its Importance to Me

You may ask why telling Susan Angeline Collins's life story was important to me. My initial reasons weren't grand. One was curiosity that had surfaced during my childhood, and the second was to respond to a request from my mother's friend who remembered Susan from her childhood. Merle Sternberg wanted me to explore Susan's life and missionary legacy. I thought I could compose a ten- to twelve-page paper and be finished quickly with Merle's request. But the more information I found about Susan, the more I wanted to know how it was possible for this single African American woman to become a missionary when all I had seen as a child were white missionaries who spoke at our church. As I teenager, I had contemplated becoming a missionary, but life decisions and circumstances prevented it. So I thought I could live vicariously through Susan. I had not realized how unique and remarkable she was.

It was easy for me to romanticize missionaries' work until I started delving into articles, letters, and reports about their lives during the years Susan was in Africa from 1887 to 1920. I had no idea of the rigor, danger, sacrifice, and exhaustion they experienced. My original thought was it would be an effective way to travel and see the world while helping others.

As I've gotten to know Susan, I believe her story will inspire others. It is timeless, illustrating the important roles religion, family, friends, and community play in our lives. I wanted to learn what influence Fayette had on Susan's life. Discovering that has helped me appreciate the values I acquired living there during my childhood. Her story illustrates the benefits of having advocates and mentors such as Reverend Jason Paine, his wife, Margaret, and Bishops William Taylor and Joseph Hartzell.

Telling Susan's life story is important because too often women serve in support roles and aren't identified and recognized for their accomplishments. They are socialized to be modest. I have dedicated my time to telling Susan's story so she is recognized for the sacrifice, success, and service in her chosen career even though many would not consider her famous.

Examining Susan's life and the story that unfolded was important to me because it revealed much about nearly 150 years of the African American experience in America. The racial injustice and hatred in some institutions and sections of the country were more deeply ingrained than I knew. Conversely, the caring, support, and love in other places, such as the Fayette area, were more prevalent than I realized. Those feelings came from deep within the mind and heart.

As I became acquainted with Susan, I discovered a woman who had amazing mental, physical, and religious strength in adverse situations. Susan went to West Africa when the indigenous people were still being captured and sold as slaves. She didn't take no for an answer but found ways to advance her causes.

There are still many unknown facets about Susan's compelling life that will likely always remain a puzzle. It was important for me to find and put as many puzzle pieces together as possible and help others recognize what an awe-inspiring human being she was. Susan's story and Fayette's story are intertwined in part because of the strong missionary history of the Fayette United Methodist Church.

Fayette members of the WFMS recognized Susan was in her declining years and knew she merited rest and good care after her thirty-three years in the mission field.[1202] Her years of service were unrivaled by the twenty-four other missionaries from Fayette and the surrounding area, quite a large number for a town with a population of slightly more than one thousand from 1890 until 1940.[1203]

Susan's story illustrates the importance of inclusiveness and the effect that has had on a community for generations. I am proud of the missionary legacy the church of my youth began with their devotion to a single African American woman in 1887. Those early members answered her call for assistance, and present-day members have followed in that service pathway.

The history of supporting missions and missionaries has continued to the present at the Fayette United Methodist Church. Committed individuals and one couple have served in both domestic and international locations. Their scope of work has been diverse but always dedicated to engaging citizens in a manner that helps them become more self-sufficient through their faith and education. But without the dedication at the local Fayette level, these people would not have been captured by the spirit to serve and continue the legacy Susan unknowingly initiated. The names of Kaye Bergholt, Jean Martin, Dorothy Langerman, and Vivian Orr stand out for their many recent years of devoted local service. Women serving earlier were my mother, Mildred Bennington, Sue Dohrman, Elma Hofmeyer, Dorothea Odekirk, and Merle Sternberg. A sampling of their UMW mission-based projects include volunteering at food distributions, making school bags, donating clothing and supplies for formerly incarcerated women seeking employment, building Habitat houses, and aiding recovery efforts in tornado- and hurricane-damaged towns.

Domestic mission locations have been in Chicago, Des Moines, New Orleans, New York City, and Red Bird Mission in the plateau area of Southeastern Kentucky. It was my joy to spend a week at Red Bird in July 2017 as a small way to honor Susan's work. A Fayette friend, Rick Hofmeyer, has been there several times and to southern Mississippi six times. Shelley Wagener worked in Chicago at Cabrini-Green with Community Youth Creative Learning Experience (CYCLE). Later, she spent time at Red Bird and on the Lower East Side in Manhattan. After completing seminary, she served as a pastor and is now working in hospice care in Oregon.

International mission locations have included Bolivia, Costa Rica, Dominican Republic, Ethiopia, India, Mexico, Nicaragua, Russia, Spain, Thailand, Ukraine, Zambia, and Zimbabwe. Length of stays have varied from two weeks to Heidi and Bill Janecke's seventeen years in Santa Cruz, Bolivia. Heidi served at a children's home, Talita Cumi, which houses thirty boys and girls at a time. Those children had been abandoned, neglected, and abused. They lived at Talita Cumi until they were given homes or became self-sufficient. During her years there, more than seven hundred children were helped. Bill, a veterinarian, worked with subsistence farmers in remote areas using the train-the-trainer model to teach animal health, pasture management, diversification, and discipleship. They continue to serve as associates for the Christian Veterinary Missions and travel to Bolivia supporting the work they left.[1204]

Steve Popenhagen taught math in Choma, Zambia, from 1979 to 1982. After he returned to Fayette and while earning a master's degree, he set his sights on becoming a missionary in Russia. The US government would not allow him to evangelize, fearing it would upset the Soviet government. He was a driver for the US consulate in Moscow when the Soviet government fell. Due to illness, he returned to the States. He was treated and then signed up for two weeks of mission work in Khabarovsk, Far East Russia. He died of colon cancer at age forty-two, before he could fulfill that commitment. His Fayette High School friend, Rick Hofmeyer, willingly went in his place and helped convert a metallurgical lab on a former naval base to a residence hall for a Baptist college.[1205]

In 2010, a young woman from the church traveled to Barcelona, Spain, where she shared the Gospel on the streets. During the spring of 2011, she was in Santo Domingo, Dominican Republic, working with a local church, where she shared the Gospel with other college students. Two years later, she was experiencing life on the Burma-Thailand border. The church group she traveled with was partnering with a local nonprofit organization to meet the physical and spiritual needs of the Karen refugees through sharing stories of Jesus. Trips to Mae Sariang, Thailand, in 2014 and 2015 provided the opportunity to deepen relationships with the youth at an orphanage that serves children ages four to teenage. Emphasis was on building a foundation for the Gospel and discipleship and helping the girls develop sewing and crocheting skills.[1206]

Caren Collins's missionary work has taken her to Costa Rica, Ethiopia, India, and Ukraine. From 2005 to 2011, she was involved for various periods with Costa Rican mission work at Paraiso, in a remote southern jungle close to the Panamanian border. She and her group did various assignments for a pastor and coffee farmer who was ministering to the Guaymi people relegated to a reservation. At times, the pastor's life was in danger due to local prejudice against the Guaymis. Their work involved numerous construction projects, including building a house for the pastor, a schoolhouse, and bridges. They taught at an elementary school and repaired the playground.

In 2008, she served a short time in Ethiopia, working for Food for the Hungry (FFH), an international nonprofit that helps donors sponsor children in different countries. Their mission was to support the local workers and assist with the children. India was her 2014 destination, where she volunteered for a ministry called the India Gospel League (IGL). She and other Kansas City women traveled to southern India, where the IGL has a large compound that includes a children's home, primary school, nursing school, hospital, farm, and other ministries. That was much like the Quessua Mission Station where Susan spent her last eighteen years of service in Africa. While in India, Caren spoke at two conferences, one at Orissa and the other a Panjab. Her topic was the "Name of God, Elohim." These were the first conferences held by the IGL, and for safety reasons, Caren and her group could not divulge their location. She met women who had been persecuted for their Christian beliefs and learned that some had been killed. One woman at the conference was inspired to become a pastor despite a series of difficult life circumstances.

Ukraine with Campus Crusade was Caren's 2015 destination, where she participated in their first SpeakOut Program. In the morning, she helped teach English and met one-on-one with both Ukrainian and American missionaries. Afternoons were spent discussing their faith and sharing the Good News. The evening hours were for fun and relaxation.

Caren wrote, "My heart for other cultures and Jesus and the mission field is where I am called to go."[1207] As a lawyer, she spent the majority of her career as the lead attorney for the Protecting Immigrant Families Program at a nonprofit law firm in Kansas City. She has been a member of Teach for America and taught English in an underserved, low-income school in Kansas City. The school population is diverse, with more than twenty-one languages spoken. Because most of the refugee children are from the Democratic Republic of Congo (DRC), Caren learned Swahili to enhance communication with them. The DRC borders Angola to the southwest. It is almost as if the work of missionaries growing up in Fayette has come full circle. Susan's mission work began along the Congo River and concluded in Angola. Caren has educated Congolese children. Currently, she is attending divinity school.

In late October and early November 2018, I had the opportunity to spend ten days at Africa University, begun by the United Methodist Church and opened in 1992 in Zimbabwe. Our group served in various ways at the university and across the valley at the Old Mutare Mission, begun in 1895 by Bishop Hartzell. Each moment of service was rewarding as it opened my mind to the needs of the people. Those opportunities entailed helping at the Fairfield Children's Home with clothing repair, teaching a teenager to hem a skirt, and holding four-year-old Faith who needed cuddling. Being a conversation partner with three university students wishing to improve their English-speaking skills provided insight into their struggles, goals, and dreams for their futures. The circle of service continues, remaining unbroken, as the Fayette United Methodist Church women and men have built a strong legacy of encouraging the members to follow the Lord.

Influence of Mission Work in Angola: Susan's and the Church

It is difficult to answer the question, "What influence did Susan's life work have on the children in the Congo, Angola, and on Methodist missions between 1887 and 1940?" The difficulty is because there is no control study to illustrate what happened to a similar population that didn't have her influence.

Her students and colleagues saw daily demonstrations of her faith in the way she lived her life. For her, education had provided the path to a fuller, well-lived life. The education she gave her students was three pronged: religious, academic, and vocational. Susan intertwined the three areas into the students' daily lives. She saw education as a way to prepare the next generation of missionaries and Christian families. Beyond Bible study, church, and Sunday school, the students were expected to live Christian lives and to eventually establish Christian homes. Many of them did. Some of them became Bible women and taught at the mission schools or went into the villages to glorify God. The life of Florinda Bessa has provided an excellent example of Susan's success. Other girls married pastors, and by 1950, eighty of them were in parsonages throughout all of the districts. Crandall explained, "They carry on the services and work of the church without embarrassment when their preacher-husbands are away on other errands of the Kingdom. Their homes, filled with healthy, wide-awake children, are examples of Christian living. Thus the African woman is making her contribution to the building of the kingdom of God in her land."[1208]

Learning to read and write Portuguese allowed the students who passed the government tests to be considered full citizens. That increased their employment opportunities. Mastering reading and writing Kimbundu enabled students to study the missionary-translated Bible chapters and verses in their own language, moving them along the path to discipleship.

Susan and her colleagues guided the girls in the development of disciplined lives. The skills they acquired—childcare, cleaning, food preparation, gardening, home management, and sewing—when applied, helped create a healthier home environment, contributing to both physical and spiritual sustenance.

Susan gave the girls hope, protecting many from early marriage to much older men. The mission became a sanctuary, providing them the opportunity to experience childhood. Susan demonstrated how to be a loving adult and parent, transforming their lives and also their hearts. Her example of servanthood and tenderness touched the girls and her colleagues.

She was a role model for leadership. Susan saw and succeeded in her quest to start a children's home and school at a time when male missionaries were the decision makers. This did not discourage her, and soon she had a home for orphaned children. Later, she took charge of a major construction project. That involved ordering materials and supplies and directing male workers. These projects provided employment for local people and helped alleviate human suffering. The esteem accorded her was observed, and the African women with whom she worked were given courage to expect greater respect.

During her career, Susan recognized the importance of telling her mission story by writing letters to family and friends. Throughout much of her retirement, she was a staunch advocate for missionaries and their work. Susan educated Americans about Angolan arts, beliefs, culture, language, religion, and superstitions. In doing so, she raised funds for mission work and ultimately willed her home to the Pacific Branch of the WMFS so her work in Angola could be continued. In 1950, it was noted that her record had seldom been equaled in Africa. "She was a model of common sense, sweet nature, and faithful labor."[1209] Susan exceeded beyond what others might have imagined for her based upon her early life experiences and her parents' backgrounds and challenges. Most of all, I want Susan to be remembered for her unwavering character and love for all with whom she connected. She was part of the legacy that, "for more than a century, women in the Methodist and Evangelical United Brethren traditions have led a struggle for human rights and social justice. The generation of women who founded the early missionary societies developed powerful networks and organizational structures to help women attain full participation in the life of the church and society."[1210]

Susan and her missionary colleagues dealt with these issues even though they weren't identified using that terminology. In African regions where the United Methodist Church has been allowed to have a presence, missionaries have helped free people from the fears of myths and superstitions perpetuated by the medicine men. Medical treatments have extended lives, decreased the spread of diseases and infection, and provided scientific facts to alleviate fear. Students' lives improved through education that enhanced their employment opportunities. Some became entrepreneurs. The degree of respect and equity for girls and women has risen. Women acquired increased economic freedom through skill acquisition in the home arts. Some students who attended the mission schools became religious, education, or political leaders in their countries. For example, in Angola, "Antonio Agostinho Neto, son of a Methodist pastor, became president in 1975, when after fourteen years of intensive struggle the Portuguese accepted the idea of independent national political leadership. Bishop de Carvalho received his primary education at the Luanda mission school. Many of the other political and civil leaders received part of their initial schooling in the United Methodist educational program."[1211] All have found transformation through the power of the Holy Spirit.

When Susan retired in Fayette, she was considered an honored member of the community.[1212] Remembrance of her continues. In 1957, the Women's Society of Christian Service of the Fayette Methodist Episcopal Church honored Susan by naming one of their circles after her.[1213] At the Susan Collins Circle June 20, 1957, meeting, the woman leading devotions used Susan's Bible.[1214]

In 1984, during its annual Memorial Day Sunday-afternoon program, Lima Church friends gave tributes to the missionaries who had grown up in the area. "A tribute was given by Marian Oelberg in memory of Allie Bass; by Mrs. Parker Davis, Randalia, in memory of Joan Davis a missionary in India, and her sister, Sarah Davis, a missionary in the U.S.; and by Bertha Yearous, Fayette, in memory of Susan Collins, a missionary in Africa."[1215]

To continue Susan's legacy, Upper Iowa University annually awards the Susan Angeline Collins Memorial Scholarship begun in 2002. The scholarship was created in recognition of her indomitable spirit and amazing achievements, including treading in places no other African American woman had ventured. Susan and Martha Drummer were "able to go where few white workers would think of going."[1216] Scholarship recipients are African American women majoring in liberal arts with strong academic and extracurricular records. Susan's pioneering spirit was recognized during the inauguration of the twenty-first president of the university on October 11, 2013.

The life and work of Susan Angeline Collins and Susan's Star lived on in the minds and eyes of those who knew her, loved her, and admired her for her strength of character and humble courage. For those of us who did not have the opportunity to personally know her, she is an inspiration as we look to the stars shining in the heavens. We simply do not know which one is Susan's Star.

So Much Unknown: Questions I Would Ask Susan If I Could

If I could go back in time for a day to meet someone who lived in an earlier era, I would go to 1939 and visit with Susan. As I've studied her life, I've been unable to find definitive information for a number of questions I would like her to answer. I have ideas about possible answers, but I don't know if they are correct. Following are the questions I would ask.

1. Specifically where and when were your parents born? Was Dick your father's brother, and was your brother Richard named after him?
2. How did your family travel from Illinois to Wisconsin, and how long did it take?
3. Was your sister Mary still alive at the time you moved? Where, why, and when did she die? Where is she buried?
4. Who were your friends in Wisconsin?
5. Why did your father enlist in the Civil War? How was he treated by the men in his company?
6. What was it like for your family during the time he served in the war?
7. For what reasons did your family move to Iowa?
8. As a teen, how did you feel about another move and leaving your school friends?
9. What was your mode of transportation? How many days did you travel, and what were some of the obstacles?
10. Where did you live when you first arrived in Iowa? What was the house like? For whom did your father work?

11. How did your father finance the purchase of his sixteen and a half acres? Did he build a house and other buildings on that site?
12. How did Indiana meet William Thompson?
13. Where did you and your siblings attend school? Did Maranda attend school after the move to Iowa? Why or why not? When and why did she begin working for the Paine family?
14. Did you and your parents attend church services at the Stone School House? If not, where did you attend?
15. When did you first join a church, and what church was it?
16. Who were your friends and playmates? Who were John Moor and Adelia, whose names you wrote in your New Testament?
17. When did Julie, Harriet, and Ervin Graham become your friends and playmates?
18. Did you attend the Fayette Seminary prior to taking your Normal Training courses? How did you finance your education? Where did you live during that time?
19. What inspired you to attend college?
20. How were you received by the other students?
21. What are some of your best memories of those college years?
22. What was it like working at the Fayette House?
23. It appears that Captain Kingman had an influence on your desire to travel. Is that accurate?
24. Where did your father meet your stepmother, Hannah? Where was she born, and what was she like? Where were they married? Where is she buried?
25. In what other private homes, besides the Jason Paine home, did you work?
26. Why did you decide to move to the Dakota Territory? Who traveled with you?
27. Beadle County records do not support the story that you staked a land claim. Did you, and if so, where was it located? Were you able to prove it up?
28. What was your home like?
29. Why did you decide to open a laundry, and how profitable was it? What were the biggest challenges of having that type of business?

30. I have assumed you traveled by train when you brought your father back to Dakota. What was the train route? Where was Richard at this time?
31. Where in the Riverside Cemetery is your father buried? Is it with other Civil War veterans? What happened to the tombstone that was supposed to be placed there in his honor?
32. How would you describe your parents?
33. What did your brother Richard do after he stopped working at the Gaynor farm? Where and when did Richard die, and where is he buried?
34. Why did your father leave his property to Albert J. and not include you and Richard in his will? How did you and Richard feel about that?
35. What was your thought process as you made the decision to become a missionary?
36. Did you finance your Chicago Training School (CTS) education from the sale of your laundry, as has been said? What types of interactions did you have with Lucy Rider Meyer? Did you meet Jane Addams? In what ways did CTS prepare you for your missionary career?
37. There has been varied information as to why you selected Africa as your mission field. What were your reasons for going there?
38. What were your impressions of Bishop Taylor? Who, besides the Fayette members of the WFMS, helped provision you for your travels to Africa and during your first thirteen years there?
39. What were some of your most memorable experiences on your ocean voyage to the Congo Delta area? How were your treated by the missionaries with whom you traveled?
40. What were your first impressions of Africa?
41. What were your impressions of Amanda Berry Smith, and how many times did you see her? What did you learn from her?
42. How would you describe your journey up and down the Congo River?
43. How did Bishop Taylor treat you and the other missionaries?
44. What were the features of the Congo mission stations where you served and the people with whom you worked?

45. What was expected of you when you were in the Congo River Delta area? What Congolese languages did you learn? What was the state of your health while you were there?
46. Who made the decision that you would go to Angola? Upon what factors was that decision made?
47. What was it like traveling to the Angolan interior? Did other missionaries travel with you, and if so, who?
48. What were ways the missionaries worked together to make life easier in those remote stations?
49. What was it like adjusting to the Angolan climate? How did adjustments vary during the wet and dry seasons?
50. In what ways, if any, did your years in the Normal Training Program at Upper Iowa University help you in the Angolan environment and in teaching the children?
51. When did you learn to speak, write, and read Kimbundu, and were you fluent in Portuguese?
52. What were the most difficult survival challenges you faced working under Bishop Taylor's self-sufficiency model?
53. What inspired you to start the school in Canandua, and what were the challenges you faced?
54. When and what types of interactions did you have with Dr. Jennie Taylor, and what were your impressions of her?
55. During your first term of service in Angola, which colleagues did you most enjoy and why?
56. How independent were you able to be in running your school and orphanage?
57. Why did you return to the United States in 1900? Who arranged and paid for your travel? What was your return route, where did you stop, and how had the ships changed since your arrival in Africa? Did you have time to explore at these stops, and what were some of the more intriguing sights?
58. Upon your return home, what were some of the most dramatic changes you observed in the country and the people?
59. What was your schedule after you were back in the United States?
60. What were your reasons for traveling to California? When and how did you learn about the women of the Pacific Branch of the WFMS?

61. How did you happen to decide to sell the book *Life of Booker T. Washington*? Did you meet him in your travels? How much money were you able to raise in this endeavor, and how did you use it?

62. How did you feel about the Methodist Episcopal hierarchy being unwilling to continue your support in Angola? Would you have returned if you still had to operate under the self-sufficiency model? Why or why not?

63. Assuming Richard and Albert were still alive, did you see them while you were home?

64. What was travel like for you to California, back to Iowa, and then on to New York City and to Angola?

65. It appears you stopped in Des Moines to see your Joiner relatives. How would you describe their personalities? Who were other relatives with whom you communicated?

66. What experiences did you have on your second trip to Africa that you didn't have on the first trip?

67. What were some of the greatest challenges you faced when you managed the various construction projects at Quessua?

68. What special potential did you see in Florinda Bessa and Dorcus when you met them? How did you guide them and other students in development so they would become women of God and establish Christian homes?

69. Besides Madge Bender, the Paine family, and your cousins, to whom did you write personal letters? What types of support did you request?

70. What supplies could you have used at the school, but were unable to obtain?

71. How did you manage all of your roles—those of nurse, teacher, mother, building contractor, friend, and mentor?

72. What was your opinion of Martha Drummer, and how well did you get along?

73. You worked under the supervision of a number of different bishops. How were they alike and different, especially Bishops Taylor and Hartzell?

74. What types of support did you receive from the Fayette chapter of the WFMS and women of the Lima and Illyria churches?

75. In what ways did African superstitions affect your students and the ways in which you taught them?
76. What was your social life like at Quessua?
77. Did you travel to South Africa? What other African countries did you visit?
78. There was a South African stamp in your New Testament. Who did you correspond with there?
79. What were the similarities and differences of gardening in Quessua and Fayette?
80. Your continually expressed your strong belief in God. Do you feel you were ever let down, and if so, in what ways?
81. How did you spend your time when you visited Hedwig Graf in Luanda?
82. Why did you remain in Angola for eighteen years without taking any furloughs?
83. For Christmas 1913, a box arrived for the girls containing dolls. What did these dolls look like, and what did the girls think about them?
84. What, if any, challenges did you have in obtaining the emergency passport to come home in 1920?
85. What was your ocean route home on your final voyage, and how did your experiences compare to your earlier voyages? What were your feelings when you saw the Statue of Liberty?
86. Did you leave New York City immediately upon arriving, or did you explore it? Assuming you traveled by train, what was the route?
87. What were the most difficult adjustments you had to make upon your return home?
88. When did you first vote, and in how many elections did you vote?
89. Other than to escape the cold Iowa winter, for what other reasons did you go to California?
90. To whom did you give the baskets, embroidery work, and other items you brought home with you? Were these items the work of your students?
91. What can you tell me about the passages you underlined in your New Testament, and how were they significant to you?
92. What retirement activities gave you the greatest joy?

93. When and how did you learn to play the African thumb piano? How many did you bring back, and to whom did you give them other than Reverend Clinton?

94. Charles Paine's son was named Charles Collins, and there was a young boy named Collins in one of the pictures Dr. Alexander Kemp showed at the church in the summer of 1937. Were these boys named after you, and how did you feel about that?

95. I am assuming Martha Drummer was the friend you visited in Atlanta in 1923. How long did you stay with her, and what were the highlights of that reunion with your former colleague? What were your feelings about the lives of African Americans in Atlanta?

96. When and how did you first meet Nellie Valentine Crosswhite? When and why did you decide to become housemates?

97. What were your impressions of Bishop G. Bromley Oxnam, and which Bible were you holding in the picture taken with him in front of the Lewis home? What happened to that Bible?

98. What were your thoughts and feelings when church members created and mounted a star in the church in your honor?

99. How did you feel about living with the Graham siblings during the last years of your life? If you had a chance to live your life over, what would you change?

Acknowledgments

Merle Sternberg stimulated my interest in writing about missionary Susan Angeline Collins's life more than a decade ago. She connected me with June Clinton Rutt, whose father had become pastor at the Fayette First United Methodist Church five years after Susan retired and returned to Fayette. June graciously gave me pictures Susan had given her father. Those pictures were of Susan in Africa. She shared her recollections of Susan, many of which were gained during Susan's visits to their home. June also revealed her father had left some of his memorabilia at the church. That eventually led me to the church office, where I was greeted by longtime friend and church secretary Kathie Cybela. She and Pastor Jason Princer encouraged me to explore the contents of filing cabinets, cupboards, and bookshelves throughout the church. Of special value were Reverend Clinton's materials and the secretaries' minutes of the Woman's Foreign Missionary Society and Woman's Home Missionary Society, to which Jean Martin had directed me. Kathie graciously made copies of valuable items I found on my searches during periodic visits to my parents in Fayette. I extend thanks to them as well as the Sunday-morning church coffee group for sharing their recollections of church and community history. Each of them helped me move my research forward.

After Merle told me Susan had attended Upper Iowa University, I began to frequent their library when I was in town. I am indebted to Director Becky Wadian and her staff for the hours they spent gathering Susan-related documents and copying the sections I requested.

My Fayette roots provided a cadre of friends who supplied inspiration and tidbits of information that led to an ever-widening circle of facts and resources. Among those who willingly participated in my quest were Julie Ahrens, Pat Baumler, Connie Collins, David and Christie Dennis,

William J. Finch, Max Gross, Brenda Hildebrand, Rick Hofmeyer, Jean Karlson, Kip Knight, Terry Landsgaard, my sister Lois Llewellyn, Jean and A. W. Martin, Ruberta Paul, Joe Rhode, Louise Scott, Vera Stepp-Splinter, Judy Stalkfleet, Bonnie and Don Timmerman, and Barry Zbornik, a Fayette historian. Other friends beyond my Fayette circle who guided me in various ways were Gail and David Billings, Hugh Schultz, Linda Jakubowski, Adria Libolt, Colleen Reader, and Karen Schlue. My daughter Diane E. Kiss accompanied me to Taylor University and helped me search for information about Bishop Taylor and his work creating the Belgian Congo and Angolan missions. My son Andrew Van Buren kept nudging me forward when my enthusiasm waned, and daughter Jillian Van Buren was an encourager. Many thanks to each of you and apologies to those who I inadvertently omitted.

Fayette County Historical Center directors Frances Graham and Phyllis Holmstrom and many volunteers aided my search for country school information, especially for the Stone School House. Linda K. Adams, Fayette Public Library director, assisted in unearthing and copying local history documents. Fayette city administrator/clerk Christie Dennis and deputy clerk Anne Sellers were sources of early local utility information and town tax records. Staff in the Fayette County Recorder's Office graciously provided will, land records, and deed information.

Archivists deserving thanks are Frances Lyons, General Commission on Archives and History of the United Methodist Church, who provided documents and contacts; Becki Plunkett, State Historical Society of Iowa (SHSI), who supplied letters Susan Collins wrote in the early 1900s to her Joiner cousins; Sharon Avery (SHSI), who provided data supporting the link between Susan and her young Joiner cousins; and Laura Mummert and student associates, Taylor University, who generously gave of their time and provided a quiet workspace, enabling me to study contextual materials and the university's collection of Dr. Jenny Taylor's letters. The archivists at Africa University, Old Mutare, Zimbabwe, are to be commended for giving me their undivided attention during my short visit in October 2018. They found and then copied segments of documents related to Methodist Episcopal Church Africa conference meetings from the late 1880s to the 1930s.

Dr. Jaeyeon Chung, director, Styberg Library, Garrett-Evangelical

Theological Seminary, merits appreciation for searching archival boxes and files that yielded resources about the Chicago Training School and Susan.

Appreciation goes to Dr. Juanita P. Moss, who made a special trip to the National Archives to search for the Civil War records of Isaac Collins, father of Susan. Her findings provided insight into his birthplace and military service.

I am indebted to Vera-Stepp Splinter, Carmillo Stepp Woods, and Jan Shimek Coonrod, Vera's niece, who delved into family files and gave me Stone School House information, clippings, pictures, and a professional photograph of Susan. Vera drove me to sites where Susan had lived, and together we tramped fields and pastures searching for remnants of the country church Susan likely attended.

Emmett Van Buskirk merits a special thank you for granting me the privilege of using his watercolor sketch of Upper Iowa University's Alexander-Dickman Hall as it looked in 1857.

Family members who assisted were my mother, Mildred Stelzmiller Bennington, and my cousin Audrey Davis Hurmence. Mother's treasure trove of Fayette County historical documents and her amazing memory of local historical resources aided in closing gaps into my research. Audrey's memories of Susan were beneficial in developing a more complete understanding of Susan's personality and physical stature.

Members of my writing group deserve recognition for listening to and critiquing numerous iterations of Susan's story. Special thanks to Deena Linett and Barbara Dixon for their probing questions, resource suggestions, attention to details, and long-term encouragement.

As my writing progressed, Claudia Edwards, Carolyn Johnson, and Lilla Marigza enthusiastically provided ideas and resources that enabled me to enhance chapters describing the early training and education for female missionaries and the African American experience in the United States.

Deserving a medal for love, encouragement, and patience is my husband, Jim Boyle, who shared the highs and lows of my search for details of Susan's life. One search involved trudging through a meadow and forest in Iowa on two humid, ninety-degree July days. Another search in Huron, South Dakota, included spending hours in the Beadle County courthouse and the public library, and a later tramp through the James

River Cemetery on an equally hot day. He remained patient when I was late for the delicious dinners he had prepared and when I said, "I'll be there in a minute," which often meant more than sixty seconds. His patience was tried with my lack of computer skills. Those skills have been enhanced, as has my knowledge of legal documents. Thank you, my sweet, for your support and confidence in me.

Reading Group Guide

1. Reflect upon the lives of Susan's parents. What challenges did they face? What strengths did they exhibit?
2. Who do you think had more influence on Susan's life, her mother or her father? Explain your thinking.
3. How might Susan's life have been different if she had been born in the South?
4. What character traits did Susan possess that you would like to emulate? How did these traits contribute to her pioneering spirit?
5. What aspects of Susan's early life contributed to her successful missionary career?
6. What do you imagine are the reasons she went to the Dakota Territory in 1882?
7. Reverend Jason Paine, Susan's mentor, was instrumental in uplifting her. Why do you think he and his wife, and later their daughters, helped her? What role have mentors played in your life?
8. Bishop Taylor seemed eager for Susan to become one of his missionaries. Do you think he would have accepted her if she was not African American? Why or why not?
9. Susan left for Africa with a "hallelujah heart," leaving behind two younger brothers and dear cousins. Explain what you would have done in that situation.
10. What life circumstance propelled Susan toward serving the people of Africa, especially the children?
11. Susan seemed passionate about her desire to become a missionary in Africa. Do you think she had any idea her ancestors might have been brought from Angola to the United States in slave ships? Upon what do you base your answer?

12. What do you imagine Susan was thinking as she walked along the slave trails in Angola and observed Africans chained together and being marched to the coast?

13. How did the colonization of Africa and North America differ, and how have these differences affected people of different races?

14. For what reasons did the colonial powers in Africa allow missionaries to set up missions in their countries? What were the positive and negative aspects of the presence of missionaries in those countries?

15. In what ways did gender equity issues affect women serving their churches prior to, during, and after Susan's missionary service?

16. How did economics, race, religion, and politics differ in America and Africa during Susan's missionary years from 1887 to 1920?

17. In what ways did the lives of African Americans evolve during the time Susan was in Africa?

18. What might have been Susan's reasons for telling Florinda Bessa she wanted to die in Africa?

19. How do the challenges of Susan's early life compare to those young Africa Americans are experiencing today?

20. What lessons from Susan's life could you and others apply to life during current times?

Bibliography

"A Brief History of Halley's Comet." Accessed April 2, 2018. www.ianridpath.com/halley/halley7.htm.

"A New Study of Africa." *Woman's Missionary Friend*. September 1917. www.lib.umich.edu.

Adelman, William J. "The Haymarket Affair." (Chicago: Illinois Labor History Society). Accessed May 20,2020, www.illinoislaborhistory.org.

"African-American History in Madison County, Illinois." *Illinois Timeline and Statistics—1800s*. Assessed February 22, 2009. http://madison.illinoisgenbwe.org/black_history.html.

"African Superstitions." Accessed February 28, 2018. www.superstitionsof.com/african-superstitions.htm.

"Africa." In *Forty-Ninth Annual Report of the Woman's Foreign Missionary Society of the Methodist Episcopal Church*. Boston: Woman's Foreign Missionary Society, 1919. http://archive.org/stream/annualreportofwo00meth#page/138/mode/2up.

"Africa." In *Forty-Second Annual Report of the Woman's Foreign Missionary Society of the Methodist Episcopal Church*. Boston: Woman's Foreign Missionary Society, 1911. http://www.babel.hathitrust.org.

"Africa." In *Thirty-Fourth Annual Report of the Woman's Foreign Missionary Society of the Methodist Episcopal Church*. Boston: P. J. Walden, 1902–1903. http://books.google.com/books?id=wRMQAAAAIAAJ&pg=PA191&1pg=PA191&dq.

"Age Limit for Missionaries." *Woman's Missionary Friend*. Boston: Woman's Foreign Missionary Society, November 1916. http://babel.hathitrust.org/cgi?pt?id=mpd.3901502123955;view=1up;seq=988.

Aidoo, M., D. J. Terlouw, M. S. Kolczak, P. D. McElroy, F.O. ter Kuile, S. Kariuki, B.L. Nahlen, A. A. Lal, and V. Udhaykuma. "Protective Effect of Sickle Cell Trait against Malaria-Associated Mortality and Morbidity." *Lancet* 359 (April 13, 2002). 1311–1312. DOI:www.https://doi.org/10.1016/SO140-6736(02)08273-9.

Ajayi, J. F. Ade. "Africa at the Beginning of the Nineteenth Century: Issues and Prospects." In *General History of Africa—Vol. VI, Africa in the Nineteenth Century Until the 1880*. 1–10. Berkley, CA: University of California Press, 1989.

Andreas, A. T. *Andreas' Historical Atlas of Dakota*. Chicago: R. R. Donnelley & Son, the Lakeside Press, 1884. https://beadlecountysd.blogspot.com/2011/normal-0-microsoftinternetexplore.

"Angola—History & Background." Accessed May 20, 2017. http://education.stateuniversity.com/pages/32/Angola-History-Background.html.

"Angola." *Natural Wonders of Africa*, 1. Accessed May 20, 2017. http://naturalwondersofafrica.com/angola/.

Angola History& Background. Accessed May 20, 2017. http://education.stateuniversity.com/pages/32/Angola-History-Background.html.

"Angola." *Natural Wonders of Africa*. Accessed May 20, 2017. http://naturalwondersofafrica.com/angola/.

"Angola District." *Minutes of the West Central Africa Mission Conference, Quiongoa, Angola, Africa, October 12–17, 1905*, 30–31, n.p.: Methodist Mission Press, 1906. Missions Collection, Yokomo Yamada Library Archives, Africa University, Mutare, Zimbabwe, Africa.

"Annual Branch Meeting." *Woman's Missionary Friend*. February 1904. http://google.com/books?id=uX4zAQAAMAAJ&printsec=frontcover&source=gbs_ge_summary_r&cad=0#v=onepage&q&f=false.

"Annual Meeting." *Woman's Missionary Friend*. February 1902. http://books.google.com/books?id=JIAzAQAAMAAJ&lpg=PA741pg+PA74&dq.

"Appropriations for 1902–1903, Africa." *Thirty-Third Annual Report of the Woman's Foreign Missionary Society of the Methodist Episcopal Church, 1901–1902*. Boston: P. J. Waldon, 1902.

AP U.S. History Notes. *The South and the Slavery Controversy, 1793–1860*. Accessed June 8, 2019. www.apstudynotes.org/us-history/outlines/chapter.

Archivist, London School of Hygiene and Tropical. "Ross and the Discovery that Mosquitoes Transmit Malaria Parasites." Centers for Disease Control and Prevention, (9-16-2015). http://www.cdc.gov/malaria/about/history/ross.html.

Ault, Clara V. "Report of Clara V. Ault." *Minutes of the West Central African Mission Conference of the Methodist Episcopal Church, Loanda, Angola, Africa, June 5–11, 1919*, 55–56. Bristol, NH: Musgrove Printing House, n.d. Missions Collection, Yokomo Yamada Library Archives, Africa University, Mutare, Zimbabwe, Africa.

Baker, Frances J. *The Story of the Woman's Society of the Methodist Episcopal Church, 1869–1895*, Revised Ed. New York: Eaton & Mains, 1898.

Ball, Jeremy. *Oxford Research Encyclopedia of African History*, s.v. "The History of Angola." Oxford, England: Oxford University Press, November 2017. Abstract. DOI: 10.1093/acrefore/9780190277734.013.180.

Bancroft, Jane M. *Deaconesses in Europe and Their Lessons for America*. New York: Hunt & Eaton, 1890.

Barton, James L. "The Effect of War on Protestant Missions." *Harvard Theological Review* 12, no. 1 (January 1919): 1–35, www.jstor.org/stable/1507910.

Bays, Daniel H. "The Foreign Missionary Movement of the 19th and 20th Centuries," Part 2 (n.d.) 2. Accessed August 22, 2015. http://nationalhumanitiescenter.org.

Bernson, Sara L., and Robert J. Eggers. "Black People in South Dakota History." Yankton, SD: Yankton Area Chamber of Commerce Bicentennial Committee. Accessed August 22, 2015. https://www.sdhspress.com/journal/south-dakota-history.

Bessa, Florinda. "Kindergarten and Auxiliary in Loanda." *Woman's Missionary Friend.* October 1911. http://babel.hathitrust.org/cig/pt?id=mdp.39015021233765:view=1up:swq+423.

Biography.com Editors. *Harriet Beecher Stowe.* (A&E Television Networks, April 2, 2014). https://www.biography.com/people/harriet-beecher-stowe-9496479.

Biography.com Editors. *Sojourner Truth.* (A&E Television Networks). Accessed September 8, 2015. http://www.biography.com/people/sojourner-truth-9511284.

Birmingham, David. "Merchants and Missionaries in Angola." *Lusotopie* (February 1998): 345–355. http://www.lusotopie.sciencespobordeaux.fr/birmingham98.pdf.

"Bishop Taylor's Missionaries in Africa." *Gospel in All Lands.* March 1894. http://onlinebooks.library.upenn.edu/webbin/serial?id=gospall.

Boatner, Mark M. "Soldiers Pay in the American Civil War." In *Civil War Dictionary*, Philadelphia: David McKay Company, 1959. http://www.civilwarhome.com/Pay.htm.

Breaux, Richard M. "To the Uplift and Protection of Young Womanhood: African-American women at Iowa's Private Colleges and the University of Iowa, 1878–1929." *History of Education Quarterly* 50, no. 2 (May 2010): 159–181. http://www.jstor.org/stable/40648057.

Brekus, Catherine A. "Female Preaching in Early Nineteenth-Century America." Waco, TX: Baylor University Center for Christian Ethics, 2009. https://www.baylor.or.edu/conent/services/document.php/98579.pdf.

"Briefs." *Woman's Missionary Friend.* February 1902. http://www.babel.hathitrust.org/cgi/pt?id=mdp.67123839015039.

Bryan, Jami L. "Fighting for Respect: African-American Soldiers in WWI." Fort Belvoir, VA: National Museum of United States Army. January 20, 2015. http://armyhistory.org.

Buchanan, Thomas C. *Black Life on the Mississippi: Slaves, Free Blacks, and the Western Steamboat World.* Chapel Hill: University of North Carolina, 2004.

Bundy, David. "The Legacy of William Taylor." *International Bulletin of Missionary Research* (October 1994): 172–176. www.internationalbulletin.org/issues/1994-04/1994-04-172.bundy.pdf.

"By-laws." *Year Book, Woman's Foreign Missionary Society of the Methodist Church, Fiftieth Annual Report of the Society.* Boston: Woman's Foreign Missionary Society of the Methodist Episcopal Church, 1919. http://archive.org/stream/yearbookwomansfo01woma#page/n3/mode/2up.

"California Conference." *Woman's Missionary Friend*. May 1905. http://www.babel. hathitrust.org/cgi/pt?id=md.39015039671758.

Case Western Reserve University. "Settlement Houses." Cleveland, OH: Author. Accessed May 18, 2017. http://www.case.edu/ch/articles/s/settlement-houses.

Chamberlain, Logan. *History of Slavery in America*. Accessed July 21, 2020. www. infoplease.com/ … /history-of-slavery-in-America.

Chase, Hal. S. "You Live What You Learn." In *Outside In African-American History in Iowa, 1838–2000*, edited by Bill Silag, Susan Koch-Bridgford, and Hal Chase, 134–163. Des Moines: State Historical Society of Iowa, 2001.

Cheyenne Valley Heritage Road Tour. Accessed May 20, 2016, https://.www.travel-wisconsin.com/tours/cheyenne-valley-heritage-road-tour.

Civil War Soldiers Letters and Diaries Database. *The American Civil War Soldier*. Accessed November 17, 2009, http://www.soldierstudies.org/index.php?action=webquest_1.

Clarence-Smith, William Cervase, and John Kelly Thornton. *Encyclopaedia Britannica*, s.v. "Angola," Edinburgh, Scotland: Encyclopaedia Britannica, Inc., September 14, 2018. https://www.britannica.com/place/Angola.

Clarke, John Henrik. *The Kongo Nation and Kingdom*. Last modified March 13, 2017. www.dhwtyslearningcenter.com/2017 … /the-kongo-nation-and-kingdom-by-jon.ht.

Clinton, John D. *Servant of God*. Des Moines, IA: Wallace-Homestead Co., 1971.

———. "We Have Our Negro Member: Meet Susan Collins." *Zion's Herald*, May 19,1937.

"Congo Mission Conference." *Gospel in All Lands*, October 1897. http://books.google.com/books/about/The_Gospel_in_All_Lands.html?ie=RGwahoHLeTrer.

Collett, Margaret Jane, Amy Leigh Paine, and Edna Dorman Lee. *100th Anniversary, First Methodist Church, Fayette, Iowa*. n.p.: Fayette, IA, 1950.

Collins, Susan. "A King at Conference." *Woman's Missionary Friend*. October 1911. http://books.google.com/booksid=TafNAAAAMAA&printsec=frongcover&source+gbs_ge_summary_r&cad+0#v=onepage&q&f=false.

———. "Mulatto Girls in Africa." *Woman's Missionary Friend*. August 1915. http://babel.hathitrust.org/cgi/pt?id=mdp.39015021233955;view=1up;seq=476.

———. "News from the Field." *Woman's Missionary Friend*. April 1910. http://books.google.com/booksid=TafNAAAAMAA&printsec=frontcover&source+gbs_ge_summary_r&cad=0#v=onepage&q&f=false.

———. "Report of Miss Susan Collins." *Minutes of Congo Mission Conference June 9–15, 1897*, 70–71. New York: Eaton & Mains, 1897. Missions Collection, Yokomo Yamada Library Archives, Africa University, Mutare, Zimbabwe.

———. "Report of Miss Susan Collins of the Woman's Foreign Missionary Society." *Minutes of the West Central Africa Mission Conference, July7–11, 1909, Quessua Mission Station, Malange, Angola, Africa*, 44–46. London: A. Smith & Co.,

1910. Missions Collection, Yokomo Yamada Library Archives, Africa University, Mutare, Zimbabwe, Africa.

———. "Report of Miss Collins, Quessua." *Official Journal of the West Central Africa Mission Conference, December 21–26, 1910, Loanda, Angola, Africa*, 29, 35–36. Bedford, England: Rush & Warwick, 1911. Missions Collection, Yokomo Yamada Library Archives, Africa University, Mutare, Zimbabwe, Africa.

———. "Report of Miss Collins, Quessua." *Minutes of the West Central Africa Mission Conference of the Methodist Episcopal Church, Quessua, Angola, Africa, April 27–May 1, 1911*, 29. Bedford, England: Rush & Warwick, 1911. Missions Collection, Yokomo Yamada Library Archives, Africa University, Mutare, Zimbabwe, Africa.

———. "West Central Africa." *Woman's Missionary Friend*. July 1911. http://books. google.com/booksid=TafNAAAAMAA&printsec=frongcover&source+gbs_ge_summary_r&cad+0#v=onepage&q&f=false.

Constitutional Rights Foundation. "Wealth and Power," *Bill of Rights in Action* 16, no. 16 (Spring 2000): 1–3. http://www.crf-usa.org.

Cooper, Arnie. "A Stony Road: Black Education in Iowa, 1838–1860." *Annals of Iowa* 48, no. 3 (Winter 1986): 113. http://ir.wiowa.edu/annuals-of-iowa/vol48/iss3/2.

Copplestone, J. Tremayne. *Twentieth-Century Perspectives, The Methodist Episcopal Church, 1896–1939*. New York: Board of Global Ministries. United Methodist Church, 1973. https://archive.org/historyofmethodi04barc/historyofmethod-i04barc_djuv.text.

Cornell Report Staff. "First African-American Enrolled in 1870." *Cornell Report*, October 30, 2011. http://news.cornellcollege.edu/tag/cornell-report-fall-2011.

Costa, Dora L. "From Mill Town to Board Room: The Rise of Women's Paid Labor." *Journal of Economic Perspectives* 14, no. 4 (Fall 2000): 101–102. www.jstor.org/stable/2647077.

Council Bluffs Community Alliance. *Iowa's Progressive History*. Accessed January 5, 2018, https://councilbluffscommunityalliance.wordpress.com/iowa/iowas-progressive-history/.

Crandall, Violet. "Quessua's Fifty Years." *Methodist Woman*, January 1950.

Cross, Cilicia. "Report of Miss Cilicia Cross." *Minutes of the Angola Mission Conference of the Methodist Episcopal Church, Quessua, Angola, Africa, August 5-10, 1925 and Loanda, Angola Africa, November 25-December 1, 1926*, 5–6. Cape Town, South Africa: Samuel Griffiths and Co. Ltd. Printers, 1927. Missions Collection, Yokomo Yamada Library Archives, Africa University, Mutare, Zimbabwe, Africa.

———. "The Lady Builder," Woman's Foreign Missionary Society Work at Quessua." *South Africa Missionary Advocate* 1, no. 6 September–December. (1922): 7, 10. http://AD1715-15-8-12-001-jpeg.pdf.

Cruz de Silva, Teresa. *Oxford Research Encyclopedia of African History*, s.v. "Christian Mission and the State in 19th and 20th Century Angola and Mozambique." Oxford, England: Oxford Press, May 2017. DOI: 10.1093acreforce9780190277734.013.182.

Davies, Edward. *An Illustrated Handbook on Africa. Giving An account of Its People, Its Climate, Its Resources, Its Discoveries, and Some of Its Missions.* Reading, MA: Holiness Book Concern, 1886. OpenLibrary_editionOL6953058M.

———. *The Bishop of Africa: or the Life of William Taylor, D.D. With an Account of the Congo Country and Mission.* Reading, MA: Holiness Book Concern, 1885. http://www.openlibrary.org/ia/cu319240953193.

"Demographics of Chicago." Wikipedia. Accessed October 17, 2016. http://en.wikipedia.org/wiki/Demographics_of_Chicago.

Dexter, Darrell. "Slavery in Illinois, Freedom Trails: 2 Legacies of Hope." Accessed February 18, 2009. http://freedomtrails2legacies.org/slavery/htm.

Dhamaraj, Glory E. "Give Her the Fruit of Her Hands: An Ancient Order and Abiding House for the Deaconesses." 1–15. Paper presented at Scarritt-Bennett Center, Nashville, TN, August 2014. www.unitedmethodistwomen.org/ … /dhamarajiglory.pdf.

Dias, Jill R. "Famine and Disease in the History of Angola c. 1830–1930." *Journal of African History* (July 1981): 22–23. http:///www.cambridge.org/ … /journals/journal_of_African-history/ … /famine-and-disease.

Dodge, Ralph E. "Angola Methodists Celebrate a Hundred Years." *New World Outlook.* May 1985.

Dodson, Mrs. William P. "Report of Mrs. W. P. Dodson." *Minutes of the Congo Mission Conference June 9–15, 1897, 59.* New York: Eaton & Mains, 1897. Missions Collection, Yokomo Yamada Library Archives, Africa University, Old Mutare, Zimbabwe, Africa.

Dodson, William P. "Report of the Presiding Elders, Angola District." *Official Journal of the Congo Mission Conference, June 1–3, 1899,* 16. Monrovia, Liberia: Press of the College of West Africa, 1899. http://images.library.yale.edu/divinitycontent/dayrep/Methodist%20%Episcopal%20Church%20Congo%20Mission%20Conference%20%201899%203.pdf.

Dodson, W. P. "Angola District Report" *Minutes of the West Central Africa Mission Conference, May 30 to June 4, 1902,* 25. n.p.: Methodist Mission Press, 1902. Missions Collection, Yokomo Yamada Library Archives, Africa University, Mutare, Zimbabwe, Africa.

"Domestic Work." *Woman's Missionary Friend.* April 1922. http://babelhathitrust.org/cgi/pt?id=mpd.39015030140118;view=1up/seq=624.

Douglas, Bill. "Wartime Illusions and Disillusionment: Camp Dodge and Racial Stereotyping, 1917–1918." *Annuals of Iowa* 57, no. 92 (1998): 111–134. https://doi.org/10.17077/0003-4827.10154.

Drummer, Martha. "Africa News." *Woman's Missionary Friend.* May 1908. http://books.google.com/books?id=E6bNAAAAMAAJ&pg=PA418-IA5&1pg=-PA418-JA6&ots=ooNOpqYjnU4_&dq=woman%27+missionary+friend+1907.

———. "Comments at 1911 Executive Meeting." *Woman's Missionary Friend.* December 1911. http://books.google.com/booksid=TafNAAAAMAA&print-sec=frongcover&source+gbs_ge_summary_r&cad+0#v=onepage&q&f=false.

———. "Report of Miss Drummer, Quessua." *Minutes of the West Central Mission Conference of the Methodist Episcopal Church, Quessua, Angola, Africa, April 27–May 1, 1911,* 28–29. Bedford, England: Rush & Warwick, 1911. Missions Collection, Yokomo Yamada Library Archives, Africa University, Mutare, Zimbabwe, Africa.

———. "Report of Miss Drummer, Quessua." *Official Journal of the West Central Africa Mission Conference, December 21–16, 1910, Loanda, Angola, Africa,* 36. Bedford, England: Rush & Warwick, 1911. Missions Collection, Yokomo Yamada Library Archives, Africa University, Mutare, Zimbabwe, Africa.

———. "Report of Miss Martha Drummer." *Official Journal of the West Central Africa Mission Conference, August 26–31, 1913,* 59–60. n.p.: n.p., 1913. Missions Collection, Yokomo Yamada Library Archives, Africa University, Mutare, Zimbabwe, Africa.

———. "Six Weeks of Terror." *Woman's Missionary Friend.* September 1921. http://babel.hathitrust.org/cgi/pt?view=image;id=mdp.39015030140118;-size=125;page-r0.

———. "Traveling to the Villages." *Woman's Missionary Friend.* May 1908. http://www.babel.hathitrust.org.

Dykstra, Robert R. *Bright Radical Star: Black Freedom and White Supremacy on the Hawkeye Frontier.* Ames: Iowa State University Press, 1993.

"Early Chicago: Jean Baptiste du Sable." *Chicago's Black Metropolis.* Accessed May 25, 2016. http://www.interactive.wttw.com.

"Early Chicago: Old Settlers." *Chicago's Black Metropolis.* Accessed May 25, 2016. http://www.interactive.wttw.com/dusable-to-oboma/old-settlers.

Ellsworth, Scott. "Tulsa Race Riot." *Encyclopedia of Oklahoma History and Culture,* 1–3. Accessed May 15, 2018, www.okhistory.org.

Enlistment Age Distribution, All Years Union Army. Accessed November 24, 2012. http://museum.dva.state.wi.us?Res_CWRegiments.asp.

"Enrollment Rates." *120 Years of American Education: A Statistical Portrait,* edited by Tom Snyder. Washington DC: National Center for Educational Statistics, 1993.

Evenden, Edward Samuel. "Enrollment Rates." *Teacher Salaries and Salary Schedules in the United States, 1918–1919.* Washington, DC: National Education Association, 1919.

"Extracts from Foreign Letters." *Woman's Missionary Friend.* May 1903 and August 1906.

"Extracts from Missionary Letters." *Woman's Missionary Friend.* August 1902– November 1910. Nine assorted issues.

Fellows, Stephen Norris. *History of the Upper Iowa Conference of the Methodist Episcopal Church 1856–1906*. Cedar Rapids, IA: Laurance Press Co., Printers and Binders, 1907.

First Methodist Episcopal Church Bulletin. December 19, 1937. First United Methodist Church Archives, Fayette, IA.

Fisher, Lena Leonard. *Under the Crescent, and Among the Kraals A Study of Methodism in Africa*. Boston: Woman's Foreign Missionary Society, 1917.

Firkus, Angela. "Chasing the North Star: The Search for Black Opportunity in Wisconsin, *1850–1860*." Bachelor's Thesis, University of Wisconsin-Eau Claire, 2008.

Florida State College at Jacksonville. "Africans in the Low Country," Module 3: The Development of Indentured Servitude and Racial Slavery in the American Colonies." Accessed January 2, 2020. www.courses.lumenlearning.com/atd-fscj-african.

Foote, Virginia. *Amorette's Watch: A Civil War Widow and Her Granddaughter*. Berkley, CA: Regent Press, 2009.

"Fording to Conference in Angola." *South Africa Missionary Advocate*, Sept.–Dec. 22, 1922. Missions Collection, Yokomo Yamada Library Archives, Africa University, Mutare, Zimbabwe, Africa.

"Foreign Fields." *Woman's Missionary Friend*. May 1906. http://www.babel.hathitrust.org/cgi/pt?id=mdp.39015039671758.

"Foreign Items." *Woman's Missionary Friend*. May 1905. http://books.google.com/books?id=uZ4zAQAAMAAJ&printsec=frontcover&source=gbs_ge_summary_r&cad=0#v=onepage&q&f=false.

"Foreign News." *Woman's Missionary Friend*. October 1919. http://www.babel.hathitrust.org/cgi/pt?id=mpd.39015039671774.

"Former Missionaries Connected with the Congo and Angola Missions." *Woman's Missionary Friend*. December 1901. http://books.google.com/books?id=qhgFbOfTdP8C&oe-UTf-8.

Frese, Stephen. "From Emancipation to Equality: Alexander Clark's Stand for Civil Rights in Iowa." *Iowa Heritage Illustrated*," Fall 2010, www.ir.uiowa.edu/cgi/viewcontent.cgi?article=14274.

"From Our Missionaries." *Woman's Missionary Friend*, April 1910–November 1915. 7 assorted issues. http://www.babel.hathitrust.org.

"From the Foreign Field." *Woman's Missionary Friend*. November 1907–March 1916. 5 assorted issues. http://www.babel.hathitrust.org.

Gale, Thomson. "Black Women's Club Movement." *Encyclopedia of African-American Culture and History*. Accessed August 20, 2017. http://www.Encyclopedia.com.

George Washington Carver Collection: Biographical Note. Accessed November 6, 2015. https://digitalcollections.lib.iastate.edu/george-washington-carver.

Gilder Lehrman Institute of American History, "Statistics: The American Economy During the 1920's." Accessed April 16, 2018. http://www.gilderlehrman.org/content/statistics-american-economic-during-1920's.

Goc, Michael J. *From Past to Present: The History of Adams County*. Friendship, WI: Adams County Historical Society and New Past Press, Inc., 1999.

Goodwin, Cardinal. "The American Occupation of Iowa 1833 to 1860." *Iowa Journal of History & Politics* 17, no. 1 (1919): 83–102. http://Penelope.uchicago.edu/ … American Occupation of Iowa.

Goudy, Willis. "Selected Demographics, Iowa's African-American Residents, 1840–2000." In *Outside In: African-American History in Iowa, 1838–2000*, edited by Bill Silag, Susan Koch-Bridgford, and Hal Chase, 22–42. Des Moines: State Historical Society of Iowa, 2001.

Grant, Richard. "Bishop Taylor's African Missions." *Gospel in all Lands*. May 1887. http://books.google.com/books?id=Q7MmVFsFAkoC&oe=UTF-8.

Green, Richard Gleason. *The International Cyclopedia: A Compendium of Human Knowledge, Vol. 4*, New York: Dodd, Mead and Company, January 1890.

Hamburg, James E. "Railroads and the Settlement of South Dakota During the Great Dakota Boom, 1878–1887," 165–178. Pierre, SD: South Dakota Historical Society Press, 1975. www.sdhspress.com/journal/south-dakota-history-5.

Hammond, Lily Hardy. *In the Vanguard of a Race*. New York: Council of Women for Home and Missionary Education for the US and Canada, 1922. https://books.google.com/books/about/in_the_Vanguard_of_a_Race.html?id.

Hanna, William A. "St. Mark the Evangelist: Apostle, Martyr, and Behold of the Divine, The First Pope & Patriarch of Alexandria and the See of St. Mark." June 23, 2003. http://www.stmary-church.com/stmark_1,pdf.

Hansan, J. E. "Jim Crow Laws and Racial Segregation." *Social Welfare History Project*. Accessed August 8, 2018. http://socialwelfare.library.ucv.edu/eras/civil-war-reconstruction/jim-crow-laws-and-racial-segregation.

Hanson, Coriless V. *The Ivory Necklace*. Lacey, WA: Author, 2011.

Harper, Douglas. "Exclusion of Free Blacks in the North." *Abbeville Review*, December 23, 2014. www.abbevilleinstitute.org … /author/douglas-harper.

Hartzell, J. C. "The Methodist Episcopal Church in Africa." *The Gospel in All Lands*. June 1898.
http://books.google.com/books?id+3jODvSUevlwC&printsec=frontcover&source=gbs_ge_summary_r&ead=O#v=onepage&q&f=false.

Hartzell, Joseph Crane. "A New Mission Conference in South Central Africa." *Minutes of the Congo Conference, June 9–15, 1897*, 2–5. New York: Eaton & Mains, 1897. Missions Collection, Yokomo Yamada Library Archives, Africa University, Mutare, Zimbabwe, Africa.

Hartzell, Joseph C. "Bishop's Remarks." *Official Journal of the West Central Africa Mission Conference, December 21–26, 1910, Loanda, Angola, Africa*, 71–72.

Bedford, England: Rush & Warwick, 1911. Missions Collection, Yokomo Yamada Library Archives, Africa University, Mutare, Zimbabwe, Africa.

Hartzell, Joseph Crane. "Congo Conference Report." *Gospel in All Lands*. January 1900. http://books.google.com/books?id=hDPAAAAMAAJ&printsec=frontcover&source=gbs_ge_summary_r&cad=0#v=onepage&q&f=false.

———. "Glimpses of Our African Mission Field." *Woman's Missionary Friend*. April 1906. http://books.google.com/books?id=IzIzAQAAMAAJ7printsec=frontcover&dq=Woman's+missionary+friend+1908&1909&sirce=bl&ots=bl&ots.

———. "Naming of Children." *Official Journal, West Central African Mission Conference, December 21–26, 1910, Loanda, Angola, Africa*, 72. Bedford, England: Rush and Warwick, 1911. Missions Collection, Yokomo Yamada Library Archives, Africa University, Mutare, Zimbabwe, Africa.

Hartzell, Joseph. "The Work in Angola." *Northwestern Christian Advocate* 52, no.1 (May 25, 1904): 16. http://google.books.com.

Hatfield, Edward A. "Segregation." *New Georgia Encyclopedia*, s.v., accessed December 26, 2018. https://m.georgiaencyclopedia.org/articles/history-archeology:segregation.

Hawthorne, Frances E. *African Americans in Iowa, a Chronical of Contributions 1830–1992*. Des Moines: Author, 1992.

Heller, Cassandra. "The Modern Deaconess: Answering God's Call to Mission." *New World Outlook*. September/October 2005. http://gbgm-umc.org/global_news/full_article.cfm?articleid=3471.

Helpful Hints for Steamboat Passengers. (1855). www.iowahist.uni.edu/Frontier_Life/Steamboat_Hists/steamboat_Hints2.htm.

Hendricks, Rich. *The Rock Island Rapids*. (n.d.). Accessed October 10, 2012. www.bqu.wikispaces.com/The+Rock+Island+Rapids..

"Higher Education." *120 Years of American Education: A Statistical Portrait*, edited by Thomas D. Snyder, 64. Washington, DC: Center for Education Statistics. Accessed May 19, 2019. https://nces.ed.gov/pubs93/93442.pdf.

Hill, Kimberly Dejoie. "Careers Across Color Lines: American Women Missionaries and Race Relations, 1870-1920." PhD diss., University of North Carolina at Chapel Hill, 2008. http://cdr.lib.unc.edu/indexablecontent?id=uuid:5411504f-b78e-4ebd-87b8-8f9f9790458c&ds=DATAFILE.

History of Fayette County, Iowa. Chicago: Western Historical Company, 1878. Reproduced Evanston, IL: Unigraphic, Inc, 1974.

History of Prairie du Chien. (n. d). Accessed October 15, 2015. www.prairieduchien.org/history.

History of the First Methodist Church and Women who Supported the Church. No place: n.p., 1965. Fayette United Methodist Church Archives, Fayette, IA.

History Place. "Abraham Lincoln: The Dred Scott Decision." 1996. http://www.historyplace.com/lincoln/dred.htm.

Home Missions. Nashville: Woman's Missionary Council, Methodist Episcopal Church, South, 1930.

Homestead Act. Accessed January 21, 2009. www.nps.gov/homestead_act.htm.

Hooper, Florence. "Change in By-laws." *Forty-Ninth Annual Report of the Woman's Foreign Missionary Society of the Methodist Episcopal Church, Jubilee Number, 1918–1919*. Boston: Woman's Foreign Missionary Society, 1920. http://archive.org/stream/followinggreato01woman#page/246/mode/2up.

House, Christie R. "Martha Drummer Missionary to Angola." *Newworldoutlook.org*. Accessed April 18, 2012. http://gbgm-umc.org/global_news/full_article.cfm?Articleid=6186.

Hufstetler, Mark, and Michael Bedeau. *South Dakota's Railroads: An Historic Context*. Pierre: South Dakota State Historic Preservation Office, 2007. https://history.sd.gov/preservation/doc/SDRailroad.pdf.

Huston, Mrs. M. S. "Africa." *Thirty-Second Annual Report of the Woman's Foreign Missionary Society of the Methodist Episcopal Church 1900-1901*. Boston: P. J. Walden, 1902. http://books/google.com/books?id=wR-MQAAAAIAAJ&oe=UTF-8.

Iliffe, John. *The African Poor: A History*. New York: Press Syndicate of the University of Cambridge, 1987.

IM Staff, and Dr. Deborah Van Broekhoven. "Lulu Fleming, Born into Slavery." *International Ministries on Location*. Winter 2010. http://www.internationalministries.org/wp … /2017/OnLocation_2010_)1_winter.pd.

"In Lands Afar." *Year Book Woman's Foreign Missionary of the Methodist Episcopal Church, Fifty-Second Annual Report of the Society*. Boston: Woman's Foreign Missionary Society of the Methodist Episcopal Church, 1921. http://archive.org/stream/yearbookwomansfo1921woma#page88/mode/2up.

"In Lands Afar-Africa." *Jubilee Number, Forty-Ninth Annual Report of the Woman's Foreign Missionary Society of the Methodist Episcopal Church*. Boston: Woman's Foreign Missionary Society of the Methodist Episcopal Church, 1918. http://archive.org/stream/followinggreatco01woma#page/138mode/2up.

"Indian Removal in Iowa." *The Mesquakie Story*. Accessed January 5, 2015. http://www.iptv.org/iowapathways/mypath.cfm?ounid=ob_000120.

Ioway Cultural Institute. "Resources on Iowa or Ioway Indian Tribe for Students." Accessed January 5, 2012. www.iowanatives.org.

"Items, Pacific Branch." *Woman's Missionary Friend*. March 1919. http://babel.hathitrust.org/cgi/pt?id=mpd.39015039671744;view=lup;seq-403.

Jacobs, Sylvia M. "African-American Women Missionaries and European Imperialism in Southern Africa, 1880-1920." *Women's Studies International Forum* 13, no. 4 (1990): 381–394.

———. "Give a Thought to Africa: Black Women Missionaries in South Africa." In *Western Women and Imperialism: Complicity and Resistance*, edited by Nupur

Chaudhuri and Margaret Strobel, 207–228. Bloomington: Indiana University Press, 1992.

———. "Give a Thought to Africa: Black Women Missionaries in South Africa." In *We Specialize in the Wholly Impossible: A Reader's Guide to Black Women's History*, edited by Darlene Clark Hine, Wilma King, and Linda Reed, 110-111. Brooklyn, NY: Carlson Publishing Inc., 1995.

Johnson, Mary W. "Greetings from the Corresponding Secretary." *Woman's Missionary Friend*. February 1906. http://books.google.com/books?id=InIzAQAAMAA-J&printsec=frontcover&dq=Woman's+missionsary+friend+1906&hl=en&sa=X-&ei=q.

Johnson, Michael. "Teaching about Slavery." *Newsletter of FRPI's Wachman Center* 13, no. 14, (August 2008): 1–9. www.files.eric.ed.gov/fulltext/ED505491.pdf.

Johnson, Mrs. S. F. "Africa," *Thirty-Ninth Annual Report of the Woman's Foreign Missionary Society for the Methodist Episcopal Church*. Boston: Woman's Foreign Missionary Society, 1908. http://archive.org/details/thirtyninthannua0wom.

———. "Angola Mission Conference." *Year Book Woman's Foreign Missionary Society of the Methodist Episcopal Church, Fifty-First Annual Report of the Society*. Boston: Woman's Foreign Missionary Society of the Methodist Episcopal Church, 1920. http://archive.org/stream/yearbookwoma01woma#page83/mode/2up.

Katz, William Loren. *Black Pioneers: An Untold Story*. New York: Taylor & Francis, 1999.

Kelly, Martin. "Chinese-Americans and the Transcontinental Railroad." *ThoughtCo.*, February 11, 2020. www.://thoughtco.com/east-meets-west-104218.

Kemp, Alexander H. *Twenty Years of Medical Missionary Work in Africa*. n.p.: Privately Printed, n.d..

Kipp, Mr. and Mrs. Ray E. "Interrupted by Rain and Fire." *Official Journal of the West Central Africa Mission Conference, August 26–31, 1913*, 54–55. n.p.: n. p., 1913. Missions Collection, Yokomo Yamada Library Archives, Africa University, Mutare, Zimbabwe.

Kipp, Ray E. "Report of Quessua Mission Station." *Officials Journal of the West Central Africa Mission Conference, March 22–26, 1915*, 36. n.p.: n. p., 1915. Missions Collection, Yokomo Yamada Library Archives, Africa University, Mutare, Zimbabwe, Africa.

Kirby, Geta D. "Report of Geta D. Kirby." *Minutes of the West Central Africa Mission Conference of the Methodist Episcopal Church, Loanda, Angola, Africa, June 5-11, 1919*, 55. Bristol, NH: Musgrove Printing House, n.d. Missions Collection, Yokomo Yamada Library Archives, Africa University, Mutare, Zimbabwe, Africa.

Koller, Christian. *International Encyclopedia of the First World War*, s.v. "Colonial Military Participation in Europe (Africa). eds. Ute Daniel, Peter, Gatrell, Oliver

Janz, Heather Jones, Jennifer Keene, Alans Kramer, and Bill Nasson. Berlin: Freie Universitat Berlin, 2014. DOI: http://dx.doi.org/10.15463/ie1418.10193.

Kreutziger, Sarah S. " Social Work's Legacy: The Methodist Settlement Movement." In *Christianity and Social Work: Reading on the Integration of the Christian Faith and Social Work Practice*, edited by B. Hugen, 79–92. Botsford, CT: NACSW, 1998. www.nacsw.org/Download/CSW/Legacy.pdf.

Leach, Gene. Glimpses of Lincoln's Brilliance. *Connecticut Explored* (Fall 2005). https://www.ctexplored.org>ConnecticutHistory.

Linda Hall Library Staff. "Rail Cars of the 19th Century." Accessed August 22, 2015. https://railroad.lindahall.org/essays/rail-cars.html.

Lindgren, H. Ellen. "Ethnic Women Homesteading on the Plains of North Dakota," *Great Plains Quarterly* (Summer 1989): 157–173. http://digitalcommons.unl.edu/greatplainsquarterly/454.

Livingstone, David. *Life and Explorations of David Livingstone, L.L.D., D.C.L., The Great Missionary Explorer in the Interior of Africa: All His Extensive Travels and Discoveries as Detailed By His Diary, Reports and Letters, and Including His Famous Journals*. Philadelphia: John E. Potter and Co., 1874.

"Living the Legacy: The Continuing Journey of Women in Mission." *United Methodist Women*. Accessed May 26, 2018. http://unitedmethodist.women.org/

Loew, Patty. "Ho-Chunk Nation: A Brief Introduction." In *Indian Nations of Wisconsin*. Madison: Wisconsin Historical Society Press, 2001. www.wisconsinhistory.org/Records/Article/CS4337.

Lord Acton, Richard, and Patricia Nassif Acton. "A Legal History of African-Americans From the Iowa Territory to the State Sesquicentennial, 1838–1996." In *Outside In: African-American History in Iowa, 1838–2000*, edited by Bill Silag, Susan Koch, and Hal Chase, 60–89. Des Moines: State Historical Society of Iowa, 2001.

Lovino, Joe. "Methodist History: Controversary, Communion, & Welch's Grape Juice." Accessed April 19, 2018. http://umc.org.

Lufkin, Jack. "Higher Expectations of Ourselves, African-Americans in Iowa's Business World." In *Outside In: African-American History in Iowa, 1838–2000*, edited by Bill Silag, Susan Koch, and Hal Chase, 190–215. Des Moines: State Historical Society of Iowa, 2001.

Maps Angola. Assessed May 4, 2011. http://mapsof.net/uploads/static-maps/angola_topography.png.

Marshall, Colin. "The World's First Skyscraper: Chicago's Home Insurance Building." *Guardian*, no. 9 (April 8, 2015). Accessed April 10, 2019. www.theguardian.com/ … /history-cities-50-buildings.

Mason, Mary W. *Consecrated Talents: or The Life of Mrs. Mary W. Mason*. New York: Carlton & Lanahan, 1870.

Mastalio, Christine. *Women's Suffrage in Iowa: A Sneak Peek of a New Digital Collection.* Iowa City: Iowa Women's Archives, University of Iowa. Accessed May 21, 2018. http://sdrc.lib.uiowa.edu/exhibits/Suffrage.

McClain, Iva Joiner "Public Education of the Negro in the United States." Master's Thesis, University of Iowa, 1917. https://books.google.com/books?id=D30yAQAAMAAJ.

McEllenney, John C. "The 'Archbishop of Deaconesses' Who Took on the Fundamentalists 1849–1922." Accessed May 5, 2015. http://www.gcah.org/site/apps/nlnet/content3.aspx?c=ghKJIOPHIoE&B3637669&ct=451

McRae, Bennie, Jr. *Lest We Forget African-American Military History*, "General Orders No.323." Accessed February 15, 2013. http://lestweforget.hamptonu.edu/page.cfm?uuid+9FEC3FE4-94C9-77A2-49FA5C465660FEDF.

Mead, Samuel J. "From S. J. Mead, Malange, Angola, Africa, May 28, 1888." *African News 1.* Vineland, NJ: T. B. Welch & Son, 1889. William Taylor Collection, Taylor University Archives, Upland, IN.

———. "Mission Work in Malange, South Central Africa at Malange." *Gospel in All Lands.* February 1891. http://books.google.com/books/about/The_Gospel_in_All_Lands.html?id=qw761-Wkqc1C.

Medary, Marjorie. *Each One Teach One, Frank Laubach, Friend to Millions.* New York: Longman's, Green, and Co. Inc. 1954.

Meehan, Amanda C. "Honoring Seven Special Women." *P.E.O. Record*, January-February, 2010.

Methodist Episcopal Church. *Seventy-First Annual Report of the Missionary Society of the Methodist Episcopal Church for the Year 1889.* New York: Cable Address, Missions, 1890. https://hdl.handle.net/2027.

———. *Seventy-Second Annual Report of the Missionary Society of the Methodist Episcopal Church for the Year 1890.* New York: Cable Address, Missions, 1891. https://hdl.handl.net/2027.

———. *Seventy-Fourth Annual Report of the Missionary Society of the Methodist Episcopal Church for the Year 1892.* New York: Cable Address, Missions, 1893. http://books.google.com/books?id+M7YPAAAAIAAJ&pg=PA1&dq=Seventy-fourth+annual+report+of+Missiionsary+Society+of+the+Methodist+Episcopal+Church+annual+report.

"Methodist Episcopal Missions in Angola and the Congo." *Gospel in All Lands.* June 1893. http://books/google/com/books?id+RGwahoHLeTrC&pg=PA270&dq+-Munhall+Mission+Station+In+Angola+Africa+named+for+Dr.+L.+W.+Munhall.

Meyer, Lucy Rider. 1885. "A Missionary Training School for Women." Paper presented at *Chicago Methodist Episcopal Ministers Meeting, June 15, 1885."* Chicago: Lucy Rider Meyer Personal Papers, Chicago Training School Collection, Series 1.1 Box 1 Folder 6, Archives, Styberg Library, Garrett-Evangelical Theological Seminary.

———. *Deaconesses, Biblical, Early Church, European, American, with the Story of the Chicago Training School for City, Home and Foreign Missions, and the Chicago Deaconess Home*. Chicago: The Message Publishing Co., 1889. http://www. archive.org/stream/deaconessesbib100meyegoog/deaconessesbib100meyegoog.

Mills, Abbie. "Notes from Los Angeles." *California Christian Advocate*, October 1901.

———. *Quiet Hallelujahs*. Boston: McDonald & Gill, 1886. www.worldcat.org/ title/quiet-Hallelujah-Abbie-Mills.dp/

Mills, Wallace G. "The Taylor Revival of 1868 and the Roots of African Nationalization in the Cape Colony." *Journal of Religion in Africa* 8, no. 2 (1976): 105–122. www.jstor.org/stable/1271866.

"Missionaries." *Gospel in All Lands*. December 1901. http://books,google.com/ books?id+5BHPAAAAMAAJ&pg=PA55&dq=Missionaries+Gospel+in- +all+lands+1901.

"Missionaries in Active Service." *Woman's Missionary Friend*. October 1919. http:// babel.hathitrust.org/cgi/pt?id=mdp.39015039671774;view+lup;seq-403.

"Missionary Letters-Extracts." *Woman's Missionary Friend*. November 1903. http:// babel.hathitrust.org/cgi/pt?id+mdp.39015039671238:view=1up:seq+247.

"Missionaries on Home Leave." *Woman's Missionary Friend*. 2 issues July 1919 and September 1921. http://babel.hathitrust.org.

Morain, Tom. "The Path to Statehood: The Northwest Ordinance." *Iowa Pathways*. Accessed February 9, 2018. www.iowapbs.org/iowapathways/mypath/ path-statehood.

"More or Less Personal." *Northwestern Christian Advocate*, February 1, 1922. https:// books.google.com/books?id=TcKYsum7asC.

Morris, William S. "Black Iowans in Defense of the Nation." In *Outside In: African-American History in Iowa:1838–2000*, edited by Bill Silag, Susan Koch-Bridgford, and Hal Chase, 90–133. Des Moines: State Historical Society of Iowa, 2001.

Mudge, James. "Bishop Taylor in Central Africa." *Gospel in All Lands*. June 1889. http://www.openlibrary.org/gospelinalllands08.socigoog/.

Nassau, Robert Hamill. *Fetishism in West Africa-Forty Years: Observation of Native Customs and Superstitions*. New York: Charles Scribner's Son, 1904.

"Native American Tribes of Iowa." Accessed December 4, 2012. http://www.ha-tive-languages.org/iowa.htm.

"New from the Field." *Woman's Missionary Friend*. August 1903. http://babel.hathi-trust.org/cgi/pt?id=mdp.3901503761238:view=1up:seq=247.

"New York Passenger Lists, 1820-1957." Accessed November 15, 2009. http://www. Ancestry.com.

"Next Needs." *Woman's Missionary Friend*. March 1922. http://babel.hathitrust.org/ cgi/pt?id=mdp.39015030140118;view=1up;seq=624.

Nielsen, Lynn E. "Civil Rights: Jim Crow Laws." *Iowa Pathways*. Accessed October 20, 2017. http://iptv.org/iowapathways/my/path/civil-rights.

Niger-Congo, Mbundu. Assessed July 10, 2017. www.dice.missouri.edu/.

Noble, Janie S. 2007. "A Calling to Fulfill: Women in the 19th Century American Methodism." Paper presented at Oxford Institute of Methodist Theological Studies, August 2007. https://oimts,files.wordpress.com/2013/04/207-3/noble.pdf.

Northwest Ordinance Primary Documents in American History. Accessed May 3, 2016. www.guides.lc.gov/norwest-ordinance.

Norton, William Bernard. *The Founding of the Chicago Training School for City, Home, and Foreign Missions*. Chicago: James Watson & Company, n.d. Archives, Styberg Library, Garrett-Evangelical Theological Seminary, Evanston, IL.

"Notes on Missionaries, Missions." *Gospel in All Lands*. September 1900. http://books.google.com/books?id=hDPAAAAMAAJ&printsec=frontcover&-source=gbs_ge_summary_r&cad=0#y=onepage&q&f=false.

Notson, G. T. "The Methodist Episcopal Church in South Dakota," In *History of South Dakota, Vol. 1*, edited by Doane Robinson, 511–544. Indianapolis: B. F. Bowden & Co. Publishers,1904. https://usgwarchives.net/sd/sdfiles.htm.

Nye, John A. *Between the Rivers – A History of Iowa United Methodism*. Des Moines: Commission on Archives and History, Iowa Annual Conference of the United Methodist Church, 1986.

O'Neal, Charlotte. "Pacific Branch." *Thirty-Third Annual Report of the Woman's Foreign Missionary Society of the Methodist Episcopal Church 1901–1902*. Boston: Miss P. J. Waldon, 1902. http://archive.org/stream/thirtythirdannuaO1woma#page/80mode/2up.

"On Home Leave." *Woman's Missionary Friend*. September 1921. http://babel.hathitrust.org/cgi/pt?id=mdp.39015030140118;view=1up;seq=459.

"Our Branch Missionaries." *Woman's Missionary Friend*. February 1902. http://books.google.com/books?id+JIAzAQAAMAAJ&lpg=PA74=PA74&dq.

Our History. Evanston, IL: Garrett-Evangelical Theological Seminary. Accessed September 10, 2015. http://www.garrett.edu/about-us/our-history.

"Our Mission Field and Missionaries: Africa." *Gospel in All Lands*. December 1888. http://archive.org/details/gospelinalllands02socigoog.

"Our Missionaries." *Woman's Missionary Friend*. November 1913 and August 1914. http://www.babel.hathitrust.org.

"Our Substitutes." *Woman's Missionary Friend*. February 1914. http://books.google.com/books?id+XanNAAAAMAAJ&printsec=frontcover#v=onepage&q&f=false.

Paine, Margaret Fletcher Kent. *My Ninety-five Milestones*. Chicago: Austin C. Murray, 1932.

Parker, Mary E. "Briefs." *Woman's Missionary Friend*. November 1902. http://books.google.com/books?id=JIAzQAAMAAJ&printsec=frontcover&source=gbs_ge_summer_r&cad=0#v=onepage&q&f=false.

"Personal and Church News," *Christian Advocate*, August 1904. http://catalog.hathitrust.org/Record?012370636.

Peterman, Thomas Draper. *Historical Sketches of Fayette County, Iowa in the Forties and Fifties*. Fort Dodge, IA: Walterick Printing Company, 1916.

Peters, Gerhard, and John T. Wooley. "Abraham Lincoln: Proclamation 116 – Calling for 500,000 Volunteers." Accessed September 10, 2012. http://www.presidency.uscb.edu/ws/?pid=69996.

Pierce, Lieut. S. W. *Battle Fields and Camp Fires of the Thirty-Eighth*. Milwaukee: Daily Wisconsin Printing House, 1866. http://www.archive.org/details/battlefieldscamp00pier.

Plant Resources in Tropical Africa, edited by D. Loupee, A. A. Oteng-Amoako, and M. Brink. PROTA Foundation, 72. Wageningen, Netherlands: Backhuys Publishers, 2008. http://books.google.com/books?isbn=9057822091.

Pond, Harry Robinson. *"The Old Stone Schoolhouse,"* n.d. Stone Schoolhouse File, Fayette County Historical Society, West Union, IA.

Pope-Levison, Priscilla. "A 'Thirty Year War' and More: Exposing Complexities in the Methodist Deaconess Movement." *Methodist History* 47, no. 2 (January 2009): 101–116. www.archives.gcah.org/ … /10516/221/methodist-History-2009-01.

Potter, Andrey A. *Ellen H. Richards (Foundress and Other Pioneers in Home Economics)*. Washington, DC: American Home Economics Association, February 1968.

Queen Nzinga (1583–1663). Accessed September 5, 2016. www.blackpast.org/gah/queen-nzinga-1583-1663.

"Quessua, Africa." *Woman's Missionary Friend*. June 1906. http://books.google.com/books?id=1z1zAQAAMAAJ7printsec+frontcover&dq=Woman's+missionary+-friend+1906&hl=en&sa=X&ei=q.

"Quessua, Africa." *Woman's Missionary Friend*. June 1918. http://guides.library.yale.edu/c.ph?g=296016&p=1976394.

"Questions to Missionary." *Thirty-Second Annual Report of the Woman's Foreign Missionary Society of the Methodist Episcopal Church 1900-1901*. Boston: Miss P. J. Waldron. http://books.google.com/books?id=wRMOAAAAIAAJ&PA191&1pg=PA191&dq.

Reconstruction Statistics. Accessed 12, 2017. http://www.shmoop.com/reconstruction/statistics.html.

Reddick, Andy. "The Athens of Iowa." *County Facts and Folklore*. Accessed May 26, 2018. http://iagenweb.org/vanburen/.

Regan, Stephen D. *Pioneering Spirit: Upper Iowa University Celebrating 150 Years, 1857–2007*. Cedar Rapids, IA: WDG Printing, 2008.

"Report of the Committee on By-laws." *Year Book Woman's Foreign Missionary Society of the Methodist Episcopal Church, Fifty-First Annual Report of the Society*. Boston: Woman's Foreign Missionary Society of the Methodist Episcopal Church, 1920. http://archive.org/stream/teachers/salaries00even/teacherssalaries00even_djuv.txt.

"Requirements of Missionary Candidates." *Thirty-Second Annual Report of the Woman's Foreign Missionary Society of the Methodist Episcopal Church 1900–1901*. Boston: Miss P. J. Waldon, 1902.

Richmond, Volney P. *The Wood River Massacre*. Accessed August 24, 2051. www.museum.state.il.us/ ... 1901/wood_20river_20massarce.html.

Robert, Dana L. 2010. "Faith, Hope, Love in Action: United Methodist Women in Mission Yesterday, Today, and Tomorrow." Paper presented at Mission Forward Symposium, St. Louis, MO, April 19, 2010. www.unitedmethdistwomen.org/what-we-do/ ...

Ross-Nazzal, Jim. *Our Story: An Ancillary to US History* (n.d.) Ch. 24, 1. Accessed February 28, 2021, https://www.ourstory.pressbooks.com.

Roosevelt, Theodore. 1909. "The Expansion of the White Races." Paper presented at the Celebration of the African Diamond Jubilee of the Methodist Episcopal Church, Washington, DC, January 18, 1909. www.english.illinois.edu/maps/poets/a-flespada/roosevelt.htm.

Rousselow, Jessica L., and Alan H. Winquist. *God's Ordinary People: No Ordinary Heritage*. Upland, IN: Taylor University Press, 1996.

Rubin, Michelle. "African-American Communities." *Goldfinch*, Summer 1995. www.iowapbs.org/ ... /mypath.african-american-communities.

———."Laws and African-American Iowans." *Goldfinch*, Summer 1995. www.iowapbs.org/ ... /mypath.laws-and-african-american-iowans.

Ruth, Amy. "One Room Schools in Iowa." *Goldfinch*, Fall 1994. www.eric.ed.gov/?id=ED380380.

Sapp, Peggy L. *Illinois Madison County Court Records, 1813–1818 and Indenture Records, 1805–1826*. Springfield, IL: Folk Works Research, 1993.

Savacool, H. H. "Herald of Christ." *Classmate* 59 (1952): 6–7.

"Seventh Session." *Official Journal of the West Central Africa Mission Conference, December 21–26, 1910, Loanda, Angola, Africa*, 64. Bedford, England: Rush & Warwick, 1911. Missions Collection, Yokomo Yamada Library Archives, Africa University, Mutare, Zimbabwe, Africa.

Shields, Mrs. Louise S. "A Prayer Meeting in Africa." *Woman's Missionary Friend*. August 1918. http://guides.library.yale.edu/c.ph?g=296016&p=1976394.

Shields, Mrs. Robert. "Report of Loanda Schools." *West Central Africa Conference Report of the Methodist Episcopal Church, Loanda, Angola, Africa, February 7–11, 1907*, 57–58. n.p.: Methodist Mission Press, 1907. Missions Collection, Yokomo Yamada Library Archives, Africa University, Mutare, Zimbabwe, Africa.

Shields, Robert. "Angola District, Report of the District Superintendent." *Official Journal of the West Central Africa Mission Conference, December 21–26, 1910, Loanda, Angola, Africa*, 12. Bedford, England: Rush and Warwick, 1911. Missions, Collection, Yokomo Yamada Library Archives, Africa University, Mutare, Zimbabwe, Africa.

———. "Work in Angola." *Minutes of the West Central Africa Mission Conference of the Methodist Episcopal Church, Quessua, Angola, Africa, April 27–May, 1911.* Bedford, England: Rush & Warwick, 1911. Missions Collection, Yokomo Yamada Library Archives, Africa University, Mutare, Zimbabwe, Africa.

Shillington, Keith. *Encyclopedia of African History.* New York: Taylor & Francis, 2005.

Slade, Ruth. "Congo Protestant Missions and European Powers before 1885." *Baptist Quarterly*, May 1956. https://doi.org/10.1080/0005576X.1956.11750936.

Smith, Amanda. *An Autobiography: The Story of the Lord's Dealing with Mrs. Amanda Smith, the Colored Evangelist.* Chicago: Meyer & Brother, 1893.

Smith, Eugene R. "African Missions of American Methodists." *Gospel in All Lands.* December 1893. http://books.google.com/books/about/The_Gospel_in_All_Lands.html?id=RGwahoHL.eT4C.

Snead, Mike, Sean Rorison, and Oscar Scafidi. *Angola.* Guliford, CT: Globe Pequot Press, Inc., 2013.

Soldier's Pay in the American Civil War. Accessed November 7, 2009, http://www.civliwarhome.com/Pay.htm.

South Dakota Guide. Accessed March 14, 2009, http://www.archive.org/stream/southdakotaguide00writmiss/southdakotaguide00writmiss.

South Dakota Historical Society. *Homesteading,* sec. Daily Life. Accessed January 21, 2009. http://www.sdhistory.org/mus/ed/ed%home2.html.

———. *Homesteading.* sec. Sod Houses. Accessed January 21, 2009. http://www.sdhistory.org/mus/ed/ed%home.html.

South Dakota History Timeline. Accessed March 3, 2009. www.ereferencedesk.com/ … /south-dakota.html.

Springer, Helen Emily Chapman. *Snap Shots from Sunny Africa.* New York: F. H. Revell Company, 1909.

Springer, J. M. "Women." *Journal of the First Session of the Congo Mission Conference, Methodist Episcopal Church, Kambove, Katanga, Belgian Congo, March 28–30, 1917,* 40. Bristol, NH: Musgrove Printing House, n.d. Missions Collection, Yokomo Yamada Library Archives, Africa University, Mutare, Zimbabwe, Africa.

Springer, John McKendree. *The Heart of Central Africa Mineral Wealth and Missionary Opportunity.* New York: The Methodist Book Concern, 1909.

Springer, Mrs. John M. "The Creoles of Angola, Africa." *Woman's Missionary Friend.* March 1909. http://books.google.com/books?id=TafNAAAAMAAJ7pg=P-P8&lpg+PP8&dq=Woman's+Missionary+Friend+1908-1909&sirce=bl&ots+bl&ots.

Springer, Mrs. J. M. "Quessua in Angola." *Woman's Missionary Friend.* May 1908. http://www.babel.hathitrust.org

Stone, Robert Benjamin. "The Legislative Struggle for Civil Rights in Iowa: 1947–1965." Master's Thesis, Iowa State University, 1990. https://lib.dr.iastate.edu/rtd;17319.

"Susan Collins." *Christian Advocate*, November 14, 1901. http://www.babel.hathi-trust.org.

Taylor, William. "A Conference on the Congo by Bishop Taylor." *Gospel in All Lands*. March 1888. http://books.google.com/books?id=mLPM OJeDwwC&oe=UTF-8.

———. *Bishop Taylor's Self-supporting Missions in Central Africa*. London: Hazell, Watson, & Viney, Ld., l885.

———. "From Pungo Andongo to Malange." *African News 2* (1889): 452–454. William Taylor Collection, Taylor University Archives, Upland, IN.

———."Methodist Episcopal Missionary Report." *Gospel in All Lands*. June 1891. http://books.google.com/books/about/The_in_All_Lands. html?id=qw761-WkqlC.

———."Missionary Self-support in Malange." *African News 3* (1890): 455. William Taylor Collection, Taylor University Archives, Upland, IN.

———. "Qualifications for Missionaries," *Report of Transit and Building Fund Society of Bishop William Taylor's Self-supporting Missions from November 1, 1889 to December 31, 1890*. New York: Palmer & Hughes, 1891. William Taylor Collection, Taylor University Archives, Upland, IN.

Taylor, Bishop William. "Report on African Missions." *Seventy-First Annual Report of the Missionary Society of the Methodist Episcopal Church for the Year 1889*. New York: Cable Address, Missions, 1890. http://books.google.com/books=id5m4F-4JmVdAC&pg=PA278&dq=seventy-one+annual+report.

———."Report on African Missions." *Seventy-Fourth Annual Report of the Missionary Society of the Methodist Church for the Year of 1892*. New York: Cable Address, Missions, 1893. http://books.google.com/books?id+M7YPAAAAIAAJ&pg=PA1&dq=Seventy-fourth+annual+report+of+Missionary+Society+of+the+-Methodist+Episcopal+Church+annual+report.

———."Report on African Missions." *Seventy-Second Annual Report of the Missionary Society of the Methodist Episcopal Church for the Year 1890*. New York: Cable Address, Missions, 1891. http://babel.hathitrust.org.

Taylor, Willian. "Sabbath Services in Our Chapel in Malange, Africa." *African News 4* (1889.): 457–461. William Taylor Collection, Taylor University Archives, Upland, IN.

———."To the Missionary Committee of the Methodist Church, in Session for 1889." *Report of Bishop Taylor's Self-supporting Mission from March 25th to October 31st, 1889*, 5–22. New York: Palmer & Hughes, 1890. William Taylor Collection, Taylor University Archives, Upland, IN.

———."William Taylor's Mission Work: Qualifications." *Report of Bishop Taylor's Self-supporting Missions from July 1st, 1884 to March 24th, 1888*, 23. New York: A. H. Kellogg, 1888. William Taylor Collection, Taylor University Archives, Upland, IN.

38th Wisconsin Infantry Regiment: Regimental History-Thirty-Eighth Infantry. Accessed November 3, 2009, http://www.secondwi.com/wisconsinregiments/38th_wisconsin_infantry.htm.

"Thank Offerings." *Woman's Missionary Friend*. May 1905. http://books.google.com?books?id=uZ4ZAQAAMAAJ&printsec=frontcover&source=gbs_ge_summary_r&cad=0#v=onepage&q&f=false.

The Free Library, S.v. The Other Pioneers: African Americans on the Frontier: Although They Rarely Made It Into the History Books, Black Men and Women Helped Shape the Old West. Accessed July 2, 2019. https://www.thefreelibrary.com/The+other+pioneers+African-Americans+on+the+Frontier%3a+although-they ... -a0141294059.

"The Pagan Land." *Woman's Missionary Friend*. June 1920. http://babel.hathitrust.org/cgi/pt?id=mdp.39015039671774;view=1up;seq=218.

"The Retirement Fund." *Woman's Missionary Friend*. March 1912. http://babel.hathitrust.org/cgi/pt?id=mdp.39015021233765;view=1up;seq=641.

Thompson, Derek. "America in 1915: Long Hours, Crowded Houses, Death by Trolley." *Atlantic*, February 11, 2016. http://www.theatlantic.combusiness/archives/2018/America-in-1915/4625601/.

Thompson, George. "The African Climate." *African News* 1 (1889): 240–241. William Taylor Collection, Taylor University Archives, Upland, IN.

"Timeline of UIU History." Upper Iowa University. Accessed November 14, 2017. https://uiu.ed/about/history.html.

Timeline of Women in Methodism. United Methodist Church. Accessed May 18, 2007. www.umc.org/who-we-are/timelline-of-women-in-methodism.

Titcomb, Caldwell. "Key Events in Black Higher Education: JBHE Chronology of Major Landmarks in Progress of African Americans in Higher Education." *Journal of Blacks in Higher Education*, no. 33, (n.d.): 92–101. Accessed August 23, 2017. http://www.jbhe.com/chronology/.

U. S. Department of State. Office of Historian. *Milestones in the History of the U. S Foreign Relations, Founding of Liberia,1847*. Assessed March 1, 2016. http://www.history.state.gov.

United States Provost Marshal General's Office. *Second Report of the Provost Marshal General to the Secretary of War on the Operations of the Selective Service System to December 1918*. "Appendix J Summary of Civil War Draft," (Washington, DC: Government Printing Office, 1919): 377. http://www.archive.org/details/secondreportpro00deptgoog.

Urofsky, Melvin. "Civil Rights Cases." *Law Cases* (1883). https://www.britannica.com/topic/Civil-Rights-Cases.

Veen, Alice Hoyt. "Iowa's African-American Heritage." *Prairie Roots Research*, February 2, 2014. http://www.prairierootsresearch.com/black-history-month/.

Walker, Eric Anderson. "Colonisation of Africa: Concepts and Conflicts." *Concise Encyclopeida of World History*, (Oxford, UK, 2002), 45–66. http://www.shodganga.inflibnet.ac.in.bitstreatm/10603/186385/7/07_chapter$202.pdf.

Waltz, Alan K. *A Dictionary for United Methodists*. Nashville: Abingdon Press, 1991.

Ward, Marilyn. "Must the Christian Church Condemn All Use of Military Force?: The Methodist Episcopal Church and the Endorsement of World War II." *Methodist History* 35, no. 3 (April 1997): 157–168. www.archives.gcah.org/handle/10516/2946.

Warner, Laceye. "Toward the Light: Methodist Episcopal Deaconess Work Among Immigrant Populations, 1885–1910." *Methodist History* 43, no.3 (April 2005): 169-182. http://dhl.handle.net/10516/6632MH-2005-April-Warner-pdf.

Washington, Reginald. "The Freedman's Savings and Trust Company and African American Genealogical Research." *Federal Records and African American History* 29, no. 2 (Summer 1997): 1–3. https://www.archives.gov/publications/prologue/1997/summer/freedman.

Wengatz, J. C. "Report of Quiongua Station," *Official Journal of the West Central Africa Mission Conference, Quessua, Angola, Africa, March 22–26, 1915*, 16. n.p.: n.p., 1915. Missions Collection, Yokomo Yamada Library, Africa University, Mutare, Zimbabwe, Africa.

Wengatz, Mrs. J. C. "Report of Quiongua Girls' School." *West Central Africa Mission Conference, Quessua, Angola, Africa, March 22–26, 1915*, 23. n.p.: n. p., 1915. Missions Collection, Yokomo Yamada Library, Africa University, Mutare, Zimbabwe, Africa.

Wheeler, Douglas C., and Diane Christensen. *The Rise with One Mind, The Bailundo War of 1902*. Accessed November, 10, 2015. http://run.edu.ng/media/1834181203243.pdf.

White, Jesse. "African-American Records: Genealogical Research Series Pamphlet No. 6." Accessed February 21, 2009. http://cyberdriveillinois.com/publications/ard131.pdf.

Wilkerson, Brenda. "Martha Drummer: A Woman of Courage," 2000. General Board of Global Missions New Archives, New York.

"Winnebago History." secs. Winnebago Location and Winnebago History. Accessed January 5, 2012. http://wwwdickshovel.com/in.htm.

Wisconsin Council of Churches. *Immigrants in Wisconsin in the 1800s*. Accessed March 16,2017. www.wcucc.org/wp-content/uploads/2017/02/BUC_1.

Wisconsin Historical Society. *Roster of Wisconsin Volunteers, War of Rebellion, 1861–1865*. Thirty-eighth Regimental Infantry, Roster of Company "H", 1914. www.wisconsinhistory.org/roster/search.asp.

Withey, A. E. "Angola District." *Minutes of the Liberia Annual Conference of the Methodist Church, January 22 to 28, 1896*, 21–23. New York: Press of Eaton & Mains, 1896. Missions Collection, Yokomo Yamada Library Archives, Africa University, Mutare, Zimbabwe, Africa.

———."Angola Missions." *Gospel in All Lands.* January 1900. http://books.google.com/books?id+hDPAAAAMAAAJ&printsec+frontcover&source+gbs_ge_summary_r&cad=0#v=onepage&q&f=false.

Withey, Herbert C. "Angolan Missions Report." *Minutes of the West Central Africa Mission Conference, Loanda, Angola, December 9–11, 1903*, 21–30. n.p.: Methodist Mission Press, 1904. Missions Collection, Yokomo Yamada Library Archives, Africa University, Mutare, Zimbabwe, Africa.

———. "Daily Proceedings, First Day, Monday March 22, 1915." *Official Journal of the West Central Africa Mission Conference, Quessua, Angola, Africa, March 22–26, 1915*, 61. n.p.: n.p., 1915. Missions Collection, Yokomo Yamada Library Archives, Africa University, Mutare, Zimbabwe, Africa.

———. "Malanje District." *Official Journal of the West Central African Mission Conference, Quessua, Angola, Africa, March 22–26, 1915*, 26. n.p.: n.p., 1915. Missions Collection, Yokomo Yamada Library Archives, Africa University, Mutare, Zimbabwe, Africa.

———."Sixth Day Conference Summary," *Official Journal of the West Central Africa Mission Conference, December 21–26, 1910, Loanda, Angola, Africa*, 66–67. Bedford, England: Rush & Warwick, 1910. Missions Collection, Yokomo Yamada Library Archives, Africa University, Mutare, Zimbabwe, Africa.

Withey, Hester Hartzell. Hester Hartzell Withey Papers, Collection 418 T1, Billy Graham Center, Wheaton University, Wheaton, IL. Assessed January 7, 2018. http://WWW2.wheaton.edu.

"Woman's Foreign Missionary Society General Executive Committee-Fifty-First Annual Meeting." *Christian Advocate*, November 11, 1920. http://books.google.com/books?id=KLo6AQAAMAAJ.

"Woman's Work." *Minutes of the West Central Africa Mission Conference, Loanda, Angola, February 8–13, 1908*, 18–19, n.p.: Methodist Mission Press, 1908. Missions Collection, Yokomo Yamada Library Archives, Africa University, Mutare, Zimbabwe, Africa.

"Woman's Work." *Northwestern Christian Advocate*, August 27, 1902. University of Illinois at Urbana-Champaign, Call #287.05 NO.

———."*Northwestern Christian Advocate*, September 13, 1905). http://babel.hathitrust.org/cgl/pt?id=mdp.39015084595456.

Yeager, Stuart A. "The Black Experience at Grinnell, 1863–1954." Master's Thesis, Grinnell College, 1984. Abstract, Grinnell College Library call number 73.65Y3b Vault.

Yearous, Bertha. "Susan Collins." In *Lima Friends*, edited by Peggy Strong, Ann Marie Dickinson, Eileen Fagle, Iola Standard, and Pat Baumler, 18. Fayette, IA: Lima Union Church, 1994.

"York." *Lewis and Clark, Inside the Corps.* Accessed April 4, 2016. www.pbs.org/lewisandclark/inside/york.html.

Notes

Chapter 1

1. "Database of Illinois Servitude and Emancipation Records," (n.d.) *Isaac Collins*, File ER, vol. 3, 32, accessed March 10, 2009, http://www.ilsos.gov/isa/servEmanSearch.do?nameNo=3179.

2. "Database of Illinois Servitude and Emancipation Records," (n.d.) *Sally Joiner*, File ER, vol. 2, 24, accessed March 10, 2009, http://.ilsos.gov/isa/serv/EmanSearch.do?nameNo=3048.

3. "Illinois Statewide Marriage Index," (n.d.) *Isaac Collins and Sarah Joiner* vol. 6, Lic. No. 00000355, Madison, assessed January 10, 2010, http://www.ilsos.gov/isavital/marriageSearch.do.

4. Declaration of Recruit Isaac Collins, Company H, 38th Regiment, Wisconsin Infantry, August 6, 1864, Film Number: M559, Roll 6, Civil War Records, Library of Congress.

5. Peggy L. Sapp, *Illinois Madison County Court Records, 1813–1818 and Indenture Records, 1805–1826* (Springfield, IL: Folk Works Research, 1993), 92.

6. Volney P. Richmond, *The Wood River Massacre*, (1901), 1–3, accessed August 24, 2015, www.museum.state.il.us/.../1901/wood_20river_20massacrehtml.

7. Darrell Dexter, "Slavery in Illinois, Freedom Trails: 2 Legacies of Hope," (n.d.), 1–6, accessed February 18, 2009, http://freedomtrails2legacies.org/slavery/htm.

8. Jesse White, "African-American Records: Genealogical Research Series Pamphlet No. 6." (n.d.), 1–2, accessed February 21, 2009, http://cyberdriveillinois.com/publications/ard131.pdf.

9. Dexter, "Slavery in Illinois," 4.

10. Dexter, "Slavery in Illinois," 5.

11. Dexter, "Slavery in Illinois," 5.

12. "African-American History in Madison County, Illinois," *Illinois Timeline and Statistics-1800's.* (n.d.), 1, accessed February 22, 2009, http://madison.illinoisgenbwe.org/black_history.html.

13. "African-American History," 1.

14   *1860 United States Federal Census*, Newark Valley, Adams, Wisconsin, Roll M 653_1399, page 118, accessed September 7, 2009, http://ersheritgequestonlline. com/hqoweb/library/results/image?surname=collins.

15   *1850 United States Federal Census*, Township 5NR8, W. Madison, Illinois, Roll M432_119, page 553A, Image: 446, accessed September 11, 2009, Ancestry.com.

16   *1850 United States Federal Census*, 553A.

17   *1850 United States Federal Census*. Name is spelled "Maranda" on her tombstone but "Miranda" on census page.

18   *1860 United States Federal Census*, 118.

19   Logan Chamberlain, *History of Slavery in America* (June 2020), 1, accessed July 21, 2020, www.infoplease.com/.../history-of-slavery-in-America.

20   The History Place, *Abraham Lincoln: The Dred Scott Decision* (1996), 1, accessed August 24, 2016, http://www.historyplace.com/lincoln/dred.htm.

21   *1860 United States Federal Census*, 118.

22   Thomas C. Buchanan, *Black Life on the Mississippi: Slaves, Free Blacks, and the Western Steamboat World* (Chapel Hill: University of North Carolina Press, 2004), 1–5.

23   Buchanan, *Black Life*, 1–5.

24   *1860 United States Federal Census*, 118.

25   *Helpful Hints for Steamboat Passengers*, (1855), 4–6, accessed October 10, 2012, www.iowahist.uni.edu/iowahist/Frontier_Life/Steamboat_Hints/Steamboat_Hints2_htm.

26   *Encyclopedia Dubuque Online*, s.v. "Steamboating," accessed August 30, 2015, www.encyclopediadubuque.org.

27   *Helpful Hints for Steamboat Passengers*, 4.

28   Rich Hendricks, *The Rock Island Rapids*, (n.d.), 1–5, accessed October 15, 2012, www.bqu.wikispaces.com/The+Rock+Island+Rapids.

29   Hendricks, *Rock Island Rapids*, 1–5.

30   *Helpful Hints for Steamboat Passengers*, 7.

31   *History of Prairie du Chien*, (n.d.), 1–5, accessed October 15, 2015, www. prairieduhien.org/history.

32   Wisconsin Council of Churches, *Immigrants in Wisconsin in the 1800's*, (n.d.): 1, accessed March 16, 2017, www.wcucc.org/wp-content/uploads/2017/02/BUC_1...

Chapter 2

33   Gene Leach, *"Glimpses of Lincoln's Brilliance," Connecticut* Explored (Fall 2005), 4, accessed January 15, 2018, https://www.ctexplored.org>ConnecticutHistory

34   *Northwest Ordinance, Primary Documents in American History*, Introduction, accessed May 3, 2018, www.guides.loc.gov/northwest-ordinance.

35   *Article X. Education*, Wisconsin Constitutional Convention, 1848. Constitution of the State of Wisconsin: adopted in convention at Madison, on the first day of February, in the year of our lord one thousand eight hundred and forty-eight. (Madison: Beriah Brown, 1848), accessed July 18, 2018, http:///www.wisconsinhistory.org/turningpoints/search.asp?id=1627

36   Michael J. Goc, *From Past to Present: The History of Adams County* (Friendship, Wisconsin: Adams County Historical Society and New Past Press Inc., 1999), 23–24.

37   Douglas Harper, "Exclusion of Free Blacks in the North," *Abbeville Review*, December 23, 2014, 5–6, accessed May 17, 2017, www.abbevilleinstitute.org.../author/douglas-harper.

38   Harper, "Exclusion of Free Blacks," 3.

39   Barry Zbornik, Email message to author, April 10, 2018.

40   Angela Firkus, "Chasing the North Star: The Search for Black Opportunity in Wisconsin, 1850–1860" (Bachelor's Thesis, University of Wisconsin-Eau Claire, 2008), 357, accessed December 2, 2010, http://digital.library.wisc.edu/1793/30661.

41   Goc, *From Past to Present*, 25–26.

42   *Adams County Chronology*, 140, accessed September 3, 1015, www.scls.lib.wi.us/acl/localhistory/past-present/images 00000026.pdf.

43   Goc, *From Past to Present*, 25–26.

44   Goc, *From Past to Present*, 27–28,1–2

45   White, "African-American Records," 6, 1–2.

46   White, "African-American Records," 6, 1–2.

47   Cheyenne Valley Heritage Road Tour, 1, accessed May 20, 2016, https://www.travelwisconsin.com/tours/cheyenne-valley-heritage-road-tour.

48   "Quincy," *Adams County Press*, January 1, 1876, 11, accessed April 21, 2016, http://www.genealogytrails.com/wis/adams/history.html.

49   Goc, *From Past to Present*, Introduction.

50   *Adams County Chronology*, 142.

51   "Quincy," *Adams County Press*, 11.

52   *1860 United States Federal Census*, 118.

53   "The South and the Slavery Controversy, 1793–1860," *AP U.S. History Notes*, chap. 16: 1–9, accessed May 27, 2016, www.apstudynotes.org/us-history/outlines/chapter.

54   "The South and the Slavery," 3.

55   "The South and the Slavery," 5.

56   Biography.com Editors, *Sojourner Truth*, (A&E Television Networks, n.d.), 1–4, accessed September 8, 2015, http://www.biography.com/people/sojourner-truth-9511284.

57   Biography.com Editors, *Harriett Beecher Stowe*, (A&E Television Networks, April 2, 2014), 1–2, accessed July 23, 2018, https://www.biography.com/people/harriet-beecher-stowe-9496479

58 "The South and the Slavery," 5.

59 Wisconsin Historical Society, *Roster of Wisconsin Volunteers, War of the Rebellion, 1861–1865.* Thirty-Eighth Regimental Infantry, Roster of Company "H" (1914) 649, accessed November 8, 2009, www.wisconsinhistory.org/roster/search.asp.

60 Wisconsin Historical Society, 649.

61 "Wake" spelled "Waik" in document.

62 Declaration of Recruit Isaac Collins.

63 Gerhard Peters and John T. Woolley, "Abraham Lincoln: Proclamation 116 – Calling for 500,000 Volunteers, July 18,1864." *The American Presidency Project*, accessed September 10, 2012, http://www.presidency.uscb.edu/ws/?pid=69996.

64 Company Muster Rolls for Isaac Collins, Company H, 38th Regiment, Wisconsin Infantry, September 1861 – April 1865. Civil War Records, Library of Congress.

65 Bennie McRae, Jr. *Lest We Forget African-American Military History,* "General Orders No. 323," accessed February 15, 2013, http://lestweforget.hamptonu.edu/page.cfm?uuid+9FEC3FE4-94C9-77A2-49FA5C465660FEDF.

66 *Adams County Chronology*, 143.

67 Goc, *From Past to Present: The History of Adams County*, 78–79.

68 Civil War Soldiers Letters and Diaries Database, *American Civil War Soldier*, 1–7, accessed November 17, 2009, http://www.soldierstudies.org/index.php?action=webquest_1.

69 *Reconstruction Statistics*, 2, accessed January 12, 2017, http://www.shmoop.com/reconstruction/statistics.html.

70 United States Provost Marshal General's Office, *Second Report of the Provost Marshal General to the Secretary of War on the Operations of the Selective Service System to December 1918.* "Appendix J Summary of Civil War Draft," (Washington, DC: Government Printing Office, 1919), 377, accessed May 12, 2012, http://www.archive.org/details/secondreportpro00deptgoog.

71 United States Provost Marshal, 377.

72 *Soldier's Pay in the American Civil War*, accessed November 7, 2009, http://www.civilwarhome.com/Pay.htm.

73 Declaration of Recruit Isaac Collins.

74 "Enlistment Age Distribution, All Years Union Army," accessed November 24, 2012, http://www.civilwardata.com/ca_demo2html.

75 "38th Wisconsin Infantry Regimental History–Thirty–Eighth Infantry," 1–7, accessed November 3, 2009, http://www.secondwi.com/winconsinregiments/38th_wisconsin_infantry.htm.

76 "38th Wisconsin Infantry." 1–7.

77 Lieut. S. W. Pierce, *Battle Fields and Camp Fires of the Thirty-Eighth* (Milwaukee: Daily Wisconsin Printing House, 1866), 54, accessed December 17, 2010, http://www.archive.org/details/battlefieldscamp00pier.

78 Pierce, *Battle Fields and Camp Fires of the Thirty-Eighth*, 55–56.

79   Pierce, *Battle Fields*, 57.

80   Pierce, *Battle Fields*, 59–60.

81   Pierce, *Battle Fields*, 61–64.

82   Pierce, *Battle Fields*, 66.

83   Pierce, *Battle Fields*, 71.

84   "American Civil War Recipes Union Hardtack and Confederate Johnnie Cakes," assessed November 7, 2011, http://americancivilwar.com/tewn/civil_war_cooking.html.

85   "American Civil War Recipes."

86   Pierce, *Battle Fields*, 117.

87   Pierce, *Battle Fields*, 124–127.

88   Pierce, *Battle Fields*, 128.

89   Emmanuel Dabney, "City Point during the Civil War," accessed November 25, 2012, http://www.encyclopediavirginia.org/Dabney-John-ca-1829-1900.

90   Pierce, *Battle Fields*, 133.

91   Pierce, *Battle Fields*, 136.

92   Pierce, *Battle Fields*, 137.

93   Pierce, *Battle Fields*, 134.

94   Pierce, *Battle Fields*, 137–138.

95   Pierce, *Battle Fields*, 138–139.

96   Pierce, *Battlefields*, 136.

97   Virginia Foote, *Amorette's Watch: A Civil War Widow and Her Granddaughter* (Berkley, CA: Regent Press, 2009), 33–34.

Chapter 3

98   Council Bluffs Community Alliance, *Iowa's Progressive History*, 1, accessed January 5, 2018, https://councilbluffscommunityalliance.wordpress.com/iowa/iowas-progressive-history.

99   Council Bluffs Community Alliance, 1.

100   Seven 1958–1961 Fayette, Iowa High School graduates, Personal communication with author, May–June 2017.

101   Ed Hines, "Iowa's Negro Farm Families Have Pioneer History," *Des Moines Register*, February 7, 1965.

102   The Ioway Cultural Institute, "Resources on the Iowa or Ioway Indian Tribe for Students," 1–2, accessed January 5, 2012, www.ioway.native.org.

103   Cardinal Goodwin, "The American Occupation of Iowa 1833 to 1860," *Iowa Journal of History & Politics* 17, no. 1 (Jan. 1919): 83–84, accessed June 4, 2016, www.penelope.uchicago.edu/...American_Occupation_of_Iowa.

104   Goodwin, "The American Occupation," 84.

105   Goodwin, "The American Occupation," 85–86.

106 John A. Nye, *Between the Rivers – A History of Iowa United Methodism*, (Des Moines: Commission on Archives and History, Iowa Annual Conference of the United Methodist Church, 1986), 7–8.

107 Stephen Norris Fellows, *History of the Upper Iowa Conference of the Methodist Episcopal Church 1856–1906* (Cedar Rapids: IA: Laurance Press Co., Printers and Binders, 1907), 34.

108 Fellows, *History of the Upper Iowa*, 33.

109 Fellows, *History of the Upper Iowa,* 72.

110 "Native American Tribes of Iowa," 1, accessed December 4, 2012, 1, http://www.native-languages.org/iowa.htm.

111 "Winnebago History," sec. Winnebago Location, accessed January 5, 2012, http://wwwdickshovel.com/in.htm.

112 Patty Loew, "Ho-Chunk Nation: A Brief Introduction," *Indian Nations of Wisconsin*. (Madison: Wisconsin Historical Society Press, 2001), 1–2, accessed December 4, 2018, www.wisconsinhistoryorg/Records/Article/CS4337.

113 "Winnebago History," sec. History.

114 "Indian Removal in Iowa," sec. The Mesquakie Story, accessed January 5, 2012, http://www.iptv.org/iowapathways/mypath.cfm?ounid=ob_000120. Current spelling for the tribe is "Meskwaki."

115 Stephen Frese, "From Emancipation to Equality: Alexander Clark's Stand for Civil Rights in Iowa." *Iowa Heritage Illustrated* (Fall 2010): 117, accessed January 22, 2015, www.ir.uiowa.edu/cgi/viewcontent.cgi?article=1427&.

116 Stephen Frese, "From Emancipation to Equality," 117.

117 Tom Morain, "The Path to Statehood: The Northwest Ordinance," *Iowa Pathways* (n.d.): 1–2, accessed February 9, 2018, www.iowapbs.org/iowapathways/mypath/path-statehood.

118 United States Census Bureau, "Iowa-race and Hispanic Origin: 1840 to 1890," Table 30, accessed February 10, 2009, http://www.census.gov/population.www.documentation/twps0056/tab30.pdf.

119 United States Census Bureau, Table 30.

120 Frese, "From Emancipation to Equality," 119.

121 Frese, "From Emancipation to Equality," 120.

122 Frese, "From Emancipation to Equality," 118.

123 Frese, "From Emancipation to Equality," 118.

124 Frese, "From Emancipation to Equality," 119.

125 Frese, "From Emancipation to Equality," 119.

126 Frese, "From Emancipation to Equality," 119.

127 Christine Mastalio, *Women's Suffrage in Iowa: A Sneak Peek of a new Digital Collection*. [PowerPoint slides]. Iowa City: Iowa Women's Archives, University of Iowa, (August 2010), accessed May 21, 2018, http://sdre.lib.uiowa.edu/exhibits/Suffrage.

128 Michelle Rubin, "Laws and African-American Iowans," *Goldfinch* 16, no. 4 (Summer 1995): 15, accessed January 5, 2017, www.iowapbs.org/iowapaths/mypath/path-statehood.

129 Thomas Draper Peterman, *Historical Sketches of Fayette County, Iowa in the Forties and Fifties* (Fort Dodge, IA: Walterick Printing Company, 1916), 77.

130 Peterman, *Historical Sketches of Fayette County*, 77.

131 Goodwin, "The American Occupation," 85.

132 "Dunham Grove Cemetery," Plot 10 David Watrous, accessed November 30, 2010, https://iowagravestones.org/cemetery-list.php?CID=33cName=Dunham+Grove.

133 "Rev George H Watrous," accessed November 30, 2010, https://www.findagrave.com/memorial99479879.

134 Robert R. Dykstra, *Bright Radical Star: Black Freedom and White Supremacy on the Hawkeye Frontier*, (Ames: Iowa State University Press, 1993), 19.

135 William Loren Katz, *Black Pioneers: An Untold Story*, (New York: Taylor & Francis, 1999), 131.

136 Sion Bass, BLM Document # 79869, accessed September 2, 2015, https://www.blm.gov/services/land-records.

137 Dykstra, *Bright Radical* Star, 19.

138 Katz, *Black Pioneers*, 131.

139 Dykstra, *Bright Radial Star*, 20.

140 Barry Zbornik, "Agriculture: Breaking Prairie Land Described," extracted from *Chats with Old Timers*, Oliver William Stevenson, (Fayette County Leader, Fayette, Iowa 1938–1943), accessed October 21, 2013, http://.angelfire.com/ia/z/sitemap.html.

141 Dykstra, *Bright Radical Star*, 20.

142 Dykstra, *Bright Radical Star*, 20.

143 Katz, *Black* Pioneers, 131–132.

144 Peterman, *Historical Sketches of Fayette County*, 78.

145 Michael Johnson, "Teaching about Slavery." *Newsletter of FRPI's Wachman Center* 13, no. 14, (August 2008): 1–3, accessed April 10, 2018, www.files.eric.ed.gov/fulltext/ED505491.pdf.

146 Johnson, "Teaching about Slavery," 3.

147 Peterman, *Historical Sketches of Fayette County*, 78.

148 Michelle Rubin, "Laws and African-American Iowans," 14.

149 "The Story of the Ku Klux Klan in America and in Iowa," *Iowa Pathways*, 1, accessed August 15, 2018, www.iptv.org/iowapatahways/mypath/story-ku-klux-lkan-america-and-iowa.

150 "Local News Notes," *Elkader Register*, September 10, 1925, accessed August 3, 2018, www.iowaoldpress.com/IA/Clayton/1925.html.

151 "The Ku–Klux–Klan at Ridler's Hall," *Oelwein Daily Register*, October 5, 1923, Fayette County Historical Society, West Union, IA.

152 Barry Zbornik, Email message to author, March 25, 2010.

153 Deed Record Book 28, 448, Fayette County Recorder's Office, West Union, IA.

154 Deed Record Book 31, 15, Fayette County Recorder's Office, West Union, IA.

155 *1870 United States Federal Census*, Illyria Township, Fayette County, Iowa, Series M593, Roll 391, page 109, accessed September 6, 2011, http://persi.heritagequestonline.com/hqoweb/library/do/census/results/image?surname=collins.

156 *1870 United States Federal Census*, Illyria Township, 109.

157 Dykstra, *Bright Radical* Star, 20.

158 Vera Stepp-Splinter, Personal communication with author, June 14, 2012.

159 Albany no longer exists.

160 Zbornik. Agriculture.

161 Zbornik, mail message to author, March 25, 2010.

162 "Enrollment Rates," *120 Years of American Education: A Statistical Portrait*. Ed. Tom Snyder, National Center for Educational Statistics, 1993), 1, accessed April 10, 2015, http://www.nces.edu.gov.

163 Arnie Cooper, "A Stony Road: Black Education In Iowa, 1838–1860." *Annals of Iowa* 48, no. 3: (Winter 1986): 113, accessed March 28, 2010, http://ir.wiowa.edu/annals-of-iowa/vol48/iss3/2.

164 Cooper, "A Stony Road," 114.

165 Cooper, "A Stony Road," 119.

166 Cooper, "A Stony Road," 129.

167 Cooper, "A Stony Road," 132.

168 Zbornik, Email message to author, March 25, 2010.

169 Peterman, *Historical Sketches of Fayette* County, 79.

170 "Notice," *Iowa Postal Card,"* October 24, 1890.

171 "Spring Valley and Frog Hollow," *Fayette Reporter*, October 24, 1912.

172 Frances E. Hawthorne, *African Americans in Iowa, a Chronical of Contributions: 1830–1992.* (Des Moines, IA: Author, 1992), 1–3.

173 Amy Leigh Paine to M. Dorothy Woodruff, 1 September 1961, Mission Biographical Reference Files, 1880s–1969, Susan Collins 1468-3-1:22, General Commission on Archives and History of the United Methodist Church, Madison, NJ.

174 Zbornik, Email message to author, November 30, 2010.

175 Susan Collins Response to Roll Call for Missionaries (n.d.), Mission Biographical Reference Files, 1880s–1969, Susan Collins 1468-3-1:22, General Commission on Archives and History of The United Methodist Church, Madison, NJ.

176 Harry Robertson Pond, *The Old Stone Schoolhouse*, Stone Schoolhouse File, Fayette County Historical Society, West Union, IA.

177 "Hearts of Gold," *Iowa Postal Card*, June 22, 1899.

178 Peterman, *Historical Sketches of Fayette County*, 79.

[179] Amy Ruth, "One Room Schools in Iowa," *Goldfinch* 16, no. 1 (Fall 1994): Abstract, www.eric.edu.gov/?id=ED380380.

[180] William J. Finch, Email message to author, April 20, 2009.

Chapter 4

[181] *1870 United States Federal Census*, Illyria Township, 110.

[182] "Upper Iowa University: A Mother of Missionaries," *Fayette Reporter*, June 18, 1908, 1.

[183] Zbornik, Email message to author, May 14, 2018.

[184] Gravestones, Lima Cemetery, east of Fayette, Iowa.

[185] Zbornik, Email message to author, April 20, 2009.

[186] Mark 14: 8 (English Standard Version).

[187] Margaret Fletcher Kent Paine, *My Ninety-five Milestones*, (Chicago: Austin C. Murray, 1932), 104.

[188] John D. Clinton, "Susan–A Fayette, Iowa Star," *Upper Iowa Press*, March 20, 1975, 4.

[189] *Catalogue of the Officers and Students of the Upper Iowa University for 1876–1878*, (Dubuque, IA: Palmer, Winall & Co., Printers and Binders, 1878), 5.

[190] G. T. Notson, "The Methodist Episcopal Church in South Dakota," in *History of South Dakota Vol. 1*, ed. Doane Robinson, (Indianapolis: B. F. Bowen & Co. Publishers, 1904), 545, accessed October 10, 2017, http://usgwarchives.net/sd/sdfiles/htm.

[191] Fellows, *History of the Upper Iowa Conference*, 72.

[192] Fellows, *History of the Upper Iowa Conference*, 205.

[193] Nye, *Between the Rivers*, 174.

[194] Nye, *Between the Rivers*, 175–176.

[195] "Obituary of Rev. Jason L. Paine," *Fayette Reporter*, December 5, 1912, 1.

[196] Bertha Yearous, "Susan Collins," in *Lima Friends*, eds. Peggy Strong, Ann Marie Dickinson, Eileen Fagle, Iola Standard, and Pat Baumler, (Fayette, IA: Lima Union Church, 1994), 18.

[197] "Timeline of UIU History," Upper Iowa University, 1, accessed November 14, 2017, https://uiu.edu.about/history.html.

[198] "Higher Education," *120 Years of American Education: A Statistical Portrait*, ed. Thomas D. Snyder (Washington DC: National Center for Education Statistics), 64, accessed May 19, 2019, https://nces.ed.gov/pubs93/93442.pdf.

[199] Andy Reddick. "The Athens of Iowa," *Country Facts and Folklore*, accessed May 26, 2018, http://iagenweb.org/vanburen/.

[200] Richard M. Breaux. "To the Uplift and Protection of Young Womanhood: African-American Women at Iowa's Private Colleges and the University of Iowa, 1878–1928." *History of Education Quarterly* 50, no. 2 (May 2010): 159–160, accessed February 12, 2012, http://www.jstor.org/stable/4aa0468057.

201 Hal S. Chase. "You Live What You Learn," in *Outside In*: *African-American History in Iowa, 1838*–2000, eds. Bill Silag Susan Koch-Bridgford and Hal Chase (Des Moines: State Historical Society of Iowa, 2001), 135.

202 Stuart A. Yeager, "The Black Experience at Grinnell, 1863–1954," (Master's Thesis, Grinnell College, 1984), Abstract, Grinnell College Library call number 73.65Y3b Vault.

203 Cornell Report Staff. "First African-American Enrolled in 1870," *Cornell Report*, (October 30, 2011), 1–2, Accessed May 20, 2016, https://news.cornellcollege.edu/tag/cornell-report-fall-2011.

204 George Washington Carver Collection: *Biographica* Note. 1–2, accessed January 20, 2019, https://digitalcollections.lib.iastate.edu/george-washington-carver.

205 Breaux, "To the Uplift and Protection of Young Womanhood," 160.

206 Breaux, "To the Uplift and Protection of Young Womanhood," 165, 173–178.

207 Breaux, "To the Uplift and Protection of Young Womanhood," 181.

208 "Obituary of Iva Joiner McClain," *Daily Iowan*, January 18, 1925, 7, accessed October 28, 2016, http://www.dailyiowan.lib.uiowa.edu.

209 Breaux, "To the Uplift and Protection of Young Womanhood," 164.

210 Breaux, "To the Uplift and Protection of Young Womanhood," 175.

211 JBHE Research Department, "Key Events in Black Higher Education: JBHE Chronology of Major Landmarks in the Progress of African Americans in Higher Education," *Journal of Blacks in Higher Education*, accessed August 23, 2017, http://www.jbhe.com/chronology/.

212 JBHE Research Department, "Key Events."

213 Stephen D. Regan, Pioneering Spirit: *Upper Iowa University Celebrating 150 Years, 1857–2007* (Cedar Rapids, IA: WDG Printing, 2008), 3.

214 Ronald F. Kocher to Dorothy Woodruff, 11 December 1962, Mission Biographical Reference Files, 1880s–1969, Susan Collins 1468–3–1:22, General Commission on Archives and History of the United Methodist Church, Madison, NJ.

215 *Catalogue of the Officers and Students of the Upper Iowa University for 1876–1878*, (Dubuque, IA: Palmer, Winall & Co., Printers and Binders, 1876), 22.

216 Regan, *Pioneering Spirit*, vii.

217 Regan, *Pioneering Spirit*, 4.

218 Regan, *Pioneering Spirit*, 4.

219 *Catalogue of Upper Iowa University for the Academic Year, 1878–1879*, (Dubuque, IA: Palmer, Winall & Co., Printers and Binders, 1879), 14.

220 *Catalogue of Upper Iowa University*, 10.

221 *Catalogue of Upper Iowa University*, 10.

222 George Capell, Personal communication with author, June 2, 2009.

223 Regan, *Pioneering Spirit*, 4.

224 Breaux, "To the Uplift and Protections of Young Womanhood," 161.

225 Amy Leigh Paine to Miss Woodruff, 4 September 1961, obtained copy July 30, 2018, from Jan Coonrod, Marion, IA.

226 *1880 United States Federal Census*; Census Place: Westfield, Fayette, Iowa; Roll: 340; Page: 205D, Enumeration District: 209, accessed January 15, 2008, http://www:search.ancestryheritagequest.com.

227 *1880 United States Federal Census*; Census Place: Smithfield, Fayette, Iowa, Series T9, Roll; 399: Page: 195, accessed June 19, 2011, http://persi.heritage questonline.com/hqoweb/librarydo/census/results/image?surname=collins&givenname=Richard&serices=10&state=17&countyid=637&hitcount=1&p=1&urn=urn3Aproq.

228 *History of Fayette County, Iowa*, (Chicago: Western Historical Company, 1878) reproduced (Evanston, IL: Unigraphic, Inc, 1974), 457–458.

229 *History of Fayette County, Iowa*, 453–456.

230 Alice Hoyt Veen, "Iowa's African-American Heritage," *Prairie Roots Research*, (February 2, 2014): 2–3, accessed October 20, 2017, http://www.prairierootsresearch.com/black-history-month/.

231 Jennifer Lee, "New York and the Panic of 1873," *New York Times*, October 14, 2008, https://cityroom.blogs.nytimes.com/2008/10/14/learning-lessons-from-the-panic.

232 Reginald Washington, "The Freedman's Savings and Trust Company and African American Genealogical Research," *Federal Records and African American History* 29, no. 2 (Summer 1997): 1–3, https://www.archives.gov/publications/prologue/1997/summer/freedman.

233 Lynn E Nielsen, "Civil Rights, Jim Crow Laws," *Iowa Pathways*, 1, accessed October 20, 2017, http://iptv.org/iowapathways/mypath/civil-rights.

Chapter 5

234 John D. Clinton, "Susan–A Fayette, Iowa Star," 4.

235 O. W. Stevenson, "Chats With Old Timers," *Fayette County Leader*, reprints beginning regularly March 17, 1938.

236 "Fayette House Memories Still Live On," *Fayette Leader*, July 13, 1961, 1–2.

237 Amy Leigh Paine to Miss Woodruff, 1 September 1961.

238 Breaux, "To the Uplift and Protection of Young Womanhood," 161.

239 Breaux, "To the Uplift and Protection of Young Womanhood," 161.

240 Breaux, "To the Uplift and Protection of Young Womanhood," 161.

241 South Dakota History Timeline, 3, accessed March 3, 2009, www.ereferencedesk.com/.../south-dakota.html.

242 James E. Hamburg, "Railroads and the Settlement of South Dakota During the Great Dakota Boom, 1878–1887," (Pierre: South Dakota State Historical Society, 1975), 165, accessed July 10, 2018, www.sdhspress.com/journal/south-dakota-history-5.

243 Hamburg, "Railroads and the Settlement of South Dakota," 166.

244 South Dakota History Timeline, 5.

245 South Dakota History Timeline, 5.

246 South Dakota History Timeline, 5.

247 G. T. Notson, "The Methodist Episcopal Church in South Dakota," 545.

248 Notson, "The Methodist Episcopal Church in South Dakota," 545.

249 Notson, "The Methodist Episcopal Church in South Dakota," 646.

250 South Dakota History Timeline, 3.

251 Hamburg, "Railroads and the Settlement of South Dakota, 167.

252 Hamburg, "Railroads and the Settlement of South Dakota," 168.

253 Hamburg, "Railroads and the Settlement of South Dakota," 168.

254 Hamburg, "Railroads and the Settlement of South Dakota, 168–169.

255 A. T. Andreas, *Andreas' Historical Atlas of Dakota*, (Chicago: R. R Donnelley & Sons, The Lakeside Press, 1884), 146, accessed March 29, 2012, https://beadlecountysd.blogspot.com/2011/normal-0-microflintexplore.

256 Mark Hufstetler and Michael Bedeau, *South Dakota's Railroads: An Historic Context*, (Pierre: South Dakota State Historic Preservation Office, 2007), 8–10, accessed July 11, 2010, https://history.sd.gov/preservation/docs/SDRailroad.pdf.

257 Amy Leigh Paine to Miss Woodruff, 1 September 1961. Mission Biographical References Files, 1880s–1969, Susan Collins 1468-3-1:22, General Commission on Archives and History of The United Methodist Church, Madison: NJ.

258 Hamburg, "Railroads and the Settlement of South Dakota," 176.

259 Martin Kelly, "Chinese-Americans and the Transcontinental Railroad," *ThoughtCo.*, (February 11, 2020): 1–2, accessed April 2, 2020, www://thoughtco.com/east-meets-west-104218.

260 Robert Benjamin Stone, "The Legislative Struggle for Civil Rights in Iowa: 1947–1965" (Master's Thesis, Iowa State University,1990), 13–14.

261 History from the 1883 Huron City Directory, Compiled by Chas. N. Campbell, (Huron, Dakota: Huronite Auxiliary Publishing House, 1883), accessed June 20, 2020, https://sdgenwebcom/beadle/hist1883.htm.

262 Linda Hall Library Staff, "Rail Cars of the 19th Century," Transcontinental Railroad Home, Linda Hall Library, accessed August 22, 2015, https://railroad.lindahall.org/essays/rail-cars.html.

263 "York," *Lewis and Clark. Inside the Corps*, (n.d.), 1, accessed April 4, 2016, www.pbs.org/lewisandclark/inside/york.html.

264 Sara L. Bernson and Robert J. Eggers, "Black People in South Dakota History," (Yankton, SD: Yankton Area Chamber of Commerce Bicentennial Committee, 1977), 242, accessed August 22, 2015, https://www.sdhspress.com/journal/south-dakota-history.

265 Bernson and Eggers, "Black People in South Dakota," 242.

266 Bernson and Eggers, "Black People in South Dakota," 243.

267 Bernson and Eggers, "Black People in South Dakota," 244.

268   The Free Library, S. v. The Other Pioneers: African Americans on the Frontier: Although They Rarely Made It Into History Books, Black Men and Women Helped Shape the Old West, 1, accessed July 2, 2019, https://www.thefreelibrary. com/The+other+pioneers+African-Americans+on+the+Frontier%3a+although+ they...-a0141294059.

269   United States Census Bureau, "Negro Population: 1790–1915," *Table 13.-Populaton by States: Negro and White at Each Census, 1790–1910, Indian and other, 1910 and1900—Continued*, 44, accessed November 30, 2016, https:// www.census.gov/library/publications/1918/.../negro-population-1790-1915ht.

270   H. Elaine Lindgren, "Ethnic Women Homesteading on the Plains of North Dakota," *Great Plains Quarterly*. Paper 454, (Summer 1989): 162–166, accessed November 29, 2016, http://digitalcommons.unl.edu/greatplainsquarterly/454.

271   United States Census Bureau, "Negro Population: 1790–1915," 44.

272   Bernson and Eggers, "Black People in South Dakota," 247–248.

273   Bernson and Eggers, "Black People in South Dakota," 249.

274   Bernson and Eggers, "Black People in South Dakota," 249–259.

275   Spelled "Joyner" incorrectly in Bernson and Eggers.

276   Bernson and Eggers "Black People in South Dakota," 251.

277   Sharon Avery, Email message to author, November 11, 2016.

278   "Alumni Notes," *Daily Iowan*, January 18, 1925, 7.

279   "South Dakota Guide, (n.d.), 114, accessed March 14, 2009, http://www. archive.org/stream/southdakotaguide00writmiss/southdakotaguide00writmiss.

280   "South Dakota Guide," 114.

281   Jim Ross-Nazzal, *Our Story: An Ancillary to US History* (n.d.) Ch. 24,1, accessed February 28,2021, https://www.ourstory.pressbooks.com.

282   John D. Clinton to Dorothy Woodruff, 17 June 1961. Mission Biographical References Files, 1880s–1969, Susan Collins 1468-3-1:22, General Commission on Archives and History of The United Methodist Church, Madison: NJ.

283   Audrey D. Hurmence, Telephone conversation with author, February 24, 2009. Hurmence stated Susan Collins had a laundry in Huron.

284   Coriless V. Hanson, *The Ivory Necklace*, (Lacey, WA: Hanson self-published, 2011) 174.

285   *Homestead Act*, accessed January 21, 2009, 1, www.nps.gov/homestead_act.htm.

286   South Dakota State Historical Society, *Homesteading*, sec. Sod Houses, accessed January 21, 2009, http://www.sdhistory.org/mus/ed/ed%home2html.

287   Andreas, *Andrea' Historical Atlas of Dakota*, 146.

288   South Dakota Historical Society, *Homesteading*, sec. Daily Life, accessed January 21, 2009, http://www.sdhistory.org/mus/ed/ed%/home2.html.

289   Sometimes called "sad irons".

290   Hurmence, Telephone conversation with author, February 24, 2009.

291   Andreas, *Andreas' Historical Atlas of Dakota,* 146.

292 Hurmence, Telephone conversation with author, February 24, 2009.

293 Andreas, *Andreas' Historical Atlas of Dakota*, 146.

294 Melvin Urofsky, "Civil Rights Cases," Law Cases (1883): 2–3, accessed August 17, 2018, https://www.britannica.com/topic/Civil-Rights-Cases.

295 John D. Clinton to Dorothy Woodruff, 17 June 1961.

296 "Upper Iowa University: A Mother of Missionaries."

297 Abbie Mills, "Notes from Los Angeles," *California Christian Advocate* 31 (October 1901): 8.

298 Andreas, *Andreas' Historical Atlas of Dakota*, 147.

299 Andreas, *Andreas' Historical Atlas of Dakota*, 147.

300 "Hannah Collins," *Iowa, County Death Records, 1880–1992*, GS Film Number 001018347, Digital Folder Number 004708019, Image Number 00519, accessed November 10, 2017, https://familysearch.org/ark:/61903/1:1:QVMF-TPM5:29October2015.

301 *Card Records of Headstones Provided for Deceased Union Civil War Veterans, 1879–1903*, [database on-line]. Provo, UT, accessed February 15, 2010, Ancestry.com., Isaac Collins.

302 *Kimball Graphic*, "Dakota Territorial News," November 28, 1884, 1.

303 Isaac is buried in Lot Number E2, Block Number 8, accessed January 22, 2009, http://apps.sd.gov/applications/DT58Cemetery/Default.aspx.

304 *Card Records of Headstones*.

305 Amy Leigh Paine to M. Dorothy Woodruff, 1 September 1961.

306 Clinton, "Susan–A Fayette, Iowa Star," 4.

Chapter 6

307 "History of Chicago," *Wikipedia*, 2, accessed April 10, 2017, http://en.wikipedia.org.

308 "Demographics of Chicago," *Wikipedia*, 1, accessed November 11, 2011, http://en.wikipedia.org/wiki/demographics_of_Chicago.

309 Colin Marshall, "The World's First Skyscraper: Chicago's Home Insurance Building," *Guardian*, no. 9 (April 8, 2015): 1, accessed April 10, 2019, www.theguardian.com/.../history-cities-50-buildings.

310 "Early Chicago: Jean Baptiste du Sable," *Chicago's Black Metropolis* (Wednesday, May 25, 2016), accessed May 26, 2017), http://www.interactive.wttw.com.

311 "History of Chicago," 2–4.

312 "History of Chicago." 2–4.

313 "Early Chicago: Old Settlers," accessed May 25, 2016, http://www.interactive.wttw.com/dusable-to-obama/old-settlers.

314 Cassandra Heller, "The Modern Deaconess: Answering God's Call to Mission," *New World Outlook* (September/October 2005): 17, accessed September 10, 2011, http://gbgm-umc.org/global_news/full_article.cfm?articleid=3471.

315 Mary W. Mason, *Consecrated Talents: or The Life of Mrs. Mary W. Mason* (New York: Carlton & Lanahan, 1870), 82, accessed May 21, 2019, www. protectourcoastline.org/mary-mrs-mason.html.

316 Sarah S. Kreutziger, Social Work's Legacy: The Methodist Settlement Movement. *Christianity and Social Work: Readings on the Integration of Christian Faith and Social Work Practice*, ed. B. Hugen (Botsford, CT: NACSW, 1998), 85.

317 "Demographics of Chicago," 3.

318 William J. Adelman, "The Haymarket Affair," (Chicago: Illinois Labor History Society), 1, accessed May 20, 2020, www.illinoislaborhistory.org.

319 Adelman, "The Haymarket Affair," 2.

320 Adelman, "The Haymarket Affair," 2.

321 Adelman, "The Haymarket Affair," 2.

322 *Home Missions*, (Nashville: Woman's Missionary Council, Methodist Episcopal Church, South, 1930), 1–2.

323 Cookie Steponaitis, "Meet Lucy Rider Meyer: A Vermont Educator and Missionary," *Valley Voice*, November 30, 2010, 1, accessed September 11, 2011, http://www.vvoice.org/?module=displaystory&story_id=2192&format=html.

324 Glory E. Dhamaraj, "Give Her the Fruit of Her Hands: An Ancient Order and Abiding House for the Deaconesses," 3, paper delivered at Scarritt-Bennett Center, Nashville, TN, August 2014, accessed March 8, 2016, www. unitedmethodistwomen.org/.../dharmarjajglory.pdf.

325 William Bernard Norton, *The Founding of the Chicago Training School for City, Home, and Foreign Missions*, (Chicago: James Watson & Company, n.d.), 7, Chicago Training School Collection, Box 1, Archives, Styberg Library, Garrett-Evangelical Theological Seminary, Evanston, IL.

326 Daniel H. Bays, "The Foreign Missionary Movement in the 19th and 20th Centuries," Part 2, (n.d.): 2, accessed August 3, 2010, http://nationalhumanitiescenter.org.

327 Breaux, "To the Uplift and Protection of Young Womanhood," 168.

328 Alan K. Waltz, "Glossary: Christmas Conference," *A Dictionary for United Methodists*, (Nashville, TN: Abingdon Press, 1991), accessed October 25, 2011, www.umc.org/what-we-believe/glossary-christmas-conference.

329 Alan K. Waltz, "Glossary: Methodist Episcopal Church, South," *A Dictionary for United Methodists*, (Nashville, TN: Abingdon Press, 1991), 1, accessed September 10, 2011, http://archives.umc.org/interior. asp?mid=258&GID=341&GMOD=VWD&GCAT=M.

330 Amanda C. Meehan, "Honoring Seven Special Women," *P.E.O. Record* 123, no. 1 (January-February, 2011): 10.

331 Lucy Rider Meyer, *Deaconesses, Biblical, Early Church, European, American, with the Story of the Chicago Training School for City, Home and Foreign Missions, and the Chicago Deaconess Home*, (Chicago: The Message Publishing

Co., 1889), 109, accessed June 3, 2011, http://www.archive.org/stream/deaconessesbib100meyegoog/deconessesbib100meyegoog.

332 Lucy Chung, Personal communication with author, September 23, 2011.

333 Rider Meyer, *Deaconesses, Biblical*, 109.

334 Norton, *The Founding of the Chicago Training School*, 31.

335 Lucy Rider Meyer, "A Missionary Training School for Women: A Paper Read before the Chicago Methodist Episcopal Ministers Meeting, June 15, 1885." 14. Chicago: Lucy Rider Meyer Personal Papers, Chicago Training School Collection, Series 1.1 Box 1 Folder 6, Archives, Styberg Library, Garrett-Evangelical Theological Seminary.

336 Norton, *The Founding of the Chicago Training School*, 25.

337 Meyer, *Deaconesses, Biblical*, 110–111.

338 Meyer, *Deaconesses, Biblical*, 110–111.

339 Norton, *The Founding of the Chicago Training School*, 45.

340 *Training School Pamphlet* (1898), 1, Chicago Training School Collection, Box 1, Archives, Styberg Library, Garrett-Evangelical Theological Seminary.

341 *Training School Pamphlet*, 1.

342 Meyer, *Deaconesses, Biblical*, 112–113.

343 Meyer, *Deaconesses, Biblical*, 112–113.

344 Meyer, "A Missionary Training School for Women." 7–8.

345 *Training School Pamphlet*, 2.

346 *Training School Pamphlet*, 2.

347 Stephonaitis, "Meet Lucy Rider Meyer," 1.

348 Stephonaitis, "Meet Lucy Rider Meyer," 1.

349 John G. McEllenney, "The 'Archbishop of Deaconesses' Who Took on the Fundamentalists 1849–1922," (n.d.) General Commission on Archives and History, The United Methodist Church, 2, accessed May 5, 2015, http://www.gcah.org/site/apps/nlnet/content3.aspx?c=ghKJIOPHIoE&B=3637669&ct=451.

350 Meyer, "A Missionary Training School for Women." 6.

351 Laceye Warner, "Toward the Light: Methodist Episcopal Deaconess Work Among Immigrant Populations, 1885–1910," *Methodist History* 43, no. 3 (April 2005): 177, accessed January 21, 2009, http://hdl.handle.net/10516/6632MH-2005-April-Warner.pdf.

352 Warner, "Toward the Light," 174–175.

353 Meyer, *Deaconesses, Biblical*, 137.

354 Meyer, Deaconesses, *Biblical, 137.*

355 Lucy Chung, Email message to author, September 23, 2011.

356 Warner, "Toward the Light," 172.

357 Janie S. Noble, "A Calling to Fulfill: Women in 19th Century American Methodism." Paper for the Oxford Institute of Methodist Theological Studies, (August 2007): 14, accessed August 11, 2010, https://oimts.files.wordpress.com/2013/04/207-3-noble.pdf

[358] Norton, *The Founding of the Chicago Training* School. 39.

[359] Warner, "Toward the Light," 170.

[360] Rider Meyer, *Deaconesses, Biblical*, 232.

[361] *Our History*, Evanston, IL: Garrett-Evangelical Theological Seminary, 1–2, accessed September 10, 2015, http://www/garrett.edu/about-us/our-history.

[362] Foote, *Amorette's Watch*, 118.

[363] Foote, *Amorette's Watch*, 119.

[364] Norton, *The Founding of the Chicago Training School*," 48.

[365] Norton, *The Founding of the Chicago Training School*," 48.

[366] Warner, "Toward the Light," 181.

[367] 367 Case Western Reserve University, "Settlement Houses," Cleveland, OH: Author, n.d.), 1–2, accessed May 18, 2017, http://www.case.edu/ch/articles/s/settlement-houses.

[368] Case Western Reserve University, "Settlement Houses," 1–2.

[369] Andrey A. Potter, *Ellen H. Richards (Foundress and Other Pioneers in Home Economics)* (Washington, DC: American Home Economics Association, February 1968), 5.

[370] Jane M. Bancroft, *Deaconesses in Europe and Their Lessons for Americans*, (New York: Hunt & Eaton, 1890), 60.

[371] Priscilla Pope-Levison, "A "Thirty Year War" and More: Exposing Complexities in the Methodist Deaconess Movement," *Methodist History* 47, no. 2 (January 2009): 105, www.archives.gcah.org/.../10516/221/Methodist-History-2009-1.

[372] *Timeline of Women in Methodism*. United Methodist Church, accessed May 18, 2017, www.umc.org/who-we-are/timeline-ofwomen-in-methodism.

[373] Warner, *Toward the Light*, 177.

[374] Pope-Levison, "A "Thirty-year War' and More", 106.

[375] Dharmaraj, "Give Her of the Fruit of Her Hand," 7.

[376] Catherine A. Brekus, "Female Preaching in Early Nineteenth-Century America," (Waco. TX: Baylor University: Center for Christian Ethics, 2009), 22, accessed August 14, 2017, https://www.baylor.or.edu/content/services/document.php/98579.pdf.

[377] Brekus, "Female Preaching in Early," 22–23.

[378] Brekus, "Female Preaching in Early," 23.

[379] *Timeline of Women in Methodism*.

[380] *Timeline of Women in Methodism*.

[381] Carrie L. Cokely, "Declaration of Sentiments," Encyclopaedia Britannica Online, 1, accessed September 7, 2018, https://www.britannica.com/topic/Declaration-of-Sentiments.

[382] "National Association of Colored Women's Clubs," Encyclopaedia Britannica Online, 1–2, accessed September 7, 2018, https://www.britannica.com/topic/National-Association-of-Colored-Women's-Clubs.

[383] J. E. Hansan, "Jim Crow Laws and Racial Segregation," *Social Welfare History Project*, (2001), 1, accessed August 28, 2018, http://socialwelfare.library.vcu.ed/era/civil-war-reconstruction/jim-crow-laws-and-racial-segregation.

[384] David Bundy, "The Legacy of William Taylor," *International Bulletin of Missionary Research*, Note 10, (October 1994): 176, accessed June 18, 2017, www.internationalbulletin.org/issues/1994-04/1994-04-172.bundy.pdf.

[385] A. Mills, "Notes from Los Angeles," 8.

[386] "Upper Iowa University: A Mother of Missionaries," 8.

[387] Hanson, *The Ivory Necklace*, 174.

[388] Edward Davies, *An Illustrated Handbook of Africa. Giving an Account of Its People, Its Climate, Its Resources, Its Discoveries, and Some of Its Missions*, (Reading, MA: Holiness Book Concern, 1886), 63, accessed July 16, 2020, Openlibrary_ Edition OL6953058M.

[389] William Taylor, "Qualifications for Missionaries," *Report of Transit and Building Fund Society of Bishop William Taylor's Self-supporting Missions from November 1, 1889 to December 31, 1890*, (New York: Palmer & Hughes, 1891), 6. William Taylor Collection, Taylor University Archives, Upland, IN.

[390] Bundy, "The Legacy of William Taylor," 172–176.

[391] "William Taylor's Mission Work: Qualifications," *Report of Bishop Taylor's Self-supporting Missions from July 1st, 1884 to March 24, 1888*," (New York: A. H. Kellogg, 1888), 23. William Taylor Collection, Taylor University Archives, Upland, IN.

[392] "William Taylor's Mission Work," 23.

[393] "William Taylor's Mission Work," 23.

[394] "Upper Iowa University: A Mother of Missionaries," 8.

[395] "William Taylor's Mission Work: Qualifications," 23–24.

[396] Edward Davies, *The Bishop of Africa: or the Life of William Taylor, D. D With an Account of the Congo Country and Mission*, (Reading, MA: Holiness Book Concern, 1885), 385, accessed May 23, 2010, http://www.openlibrary.org/ia/cu31924050953193.

[397] Vera Stepp-Splinter, Personal communication with author, August 10, 2011.

[398] A. Mills, "Notes from Los Angeles," 8.

[399] A. Mills, "Notes from Los Angeles," 8.

[400] A. Mills, "Notes from Los Angeles," 8.

[401] Abbie Mills, *Quiet Hallelujahs*, (Boston: McDonald & Gill, 1886), 243, accessed May 15, 2011. https://books.google.com/books?id=6CpaAAAAMAAJ.

[402] Amanda Smith, *An Autobiography: The Story of the Lord's Dealing with Mrs. Amanda Smith, the Colored Evangelist* (Chicago: Meyer & Brother, Publishers, 1893), 464–465.

[403] Sylvia M. Jacobs, "Give a Thought to Africa: Black Women Missionaries in Southern Africa," in *We Specialize in the Wholly Impossible, A Readers Guide to*

Black Women's History, eds. Darlene Clark Hine, Wilma King, and Linda Reed (Brooklyn, NY: Carlson Publishing, Inc., 1995), 110–111.

404 "Woman's Work," *Northwestern Christian Advocate*, (August 27, 1902), 28, University of Illinois Urbana-Champaign, Call # 287.05 NO.

Chapter 7

405 David Birmingham, "Merchants and Missionaries in Angola," *Lusotopie*, (February 1998): 348, assessed May 23, 2016, http://www.lusotopie. sciencespobordeaux.fr/birmingham98.pdf.

406 "William Taylor's Mission Work: Qualifications," *Report of Bishop Taylor's Self-supporting Missions from July 1ˢᵗ, 1884 to March 24, 1888* (New York: A H. Kellogg, 1888), 10. William Taylor Collection, Taylor University Archives, Upland, IN.

407 Birmingham, "Merchants and Missionaries in Angola," 349.

408 Birmingham, "Merchants and Missionaries in Angola," 350.

409 David Bundy, "The Legacy of William Taylor," *International Bulletin of Missionary Research* (October 1994): 172.

410 Bundy, "The Legacy of William Taylor," 172.

411 Bundy, "The Legacy of William Taylor," 174.

412 Bundy, "The Legacy of William Taylor," 174.

413 William A. Hanna, "St. Mark the Evangelist: Apostle, Martyr, and Behold of the Divine, The First Pope & Patriarch of Alexandria and the See of St. Mark," (June 23, 2003): 3–5, accessed September 5, 2016, http://www.stmary-church. com/stmark_1.pdf.

414 *Timeline of Christian Missions*, "Early Christianity," 1, accessed March 5, 2016, https://en.wikipedia.org/wiki/Timeline_of_Christian_missions.

415 *Timeline of Christian Missions*, "1000–1499," 6, accessed March 5, 2016, https:// en.wikipedia.org/wiki/Timeline_of_Christian_missions.

416 Editors of Encyclopaedia Britannica, "Alfonso I King of Kongo Kingdom," *Encyclopaedia Britannica*, 1–2, accessed September 5, 2016, http://www. britannica.com/biography.com/biography/Alfonso-I-king-of-Kongo-kingdom.

417 "Henrique (Dom)," *Dictionary of African Christian Biography*, 1, March 22, 2016, https://dacb.org/storeies/democratic-republic-of-congo/henrique-dom/.

418 Also spelled "Kwanza."

419 "Queen Nzinga (1583–1663), 1–2, accessed September 5, 2016, www.blackpast. org/gah/queen-nzinga-1583-1663.

420 *Timeline of Christian Missions*, "1700–1799," 18, accessed March 5, 2016, https:// en.wikipedia.org/wiki/Timeline_of_Christian_missions.

421 *Timeline of Christian Missions*, "1800–1849," 18, accessed March 5, 2016, https:// en.wikipedia.org/wiki/Timelline_of_Christian_missions.

422 David Livingstone, *Life and Explorations of David Livingstone, L.L.D., D.C.L., The Great Missionary Explorer in the Interior of Africa: All His Extensive Travels and Discoveries as Detailed By His Diary, Reports, and Letters, and Including His Famous Journals* (Philadelphia: John E. Potter and Co., 1874), 116.

423 Livingstone, *Life and Explorations of David Livingstone*, 603–604.

424 Emily Conroy-Krutz, *U. S. Foreign Mission Movement, c. 1800–1860* (Oxford Research Encyclopedia of Religion, February 2017), Summary and Keywords, accessed April 20, 2017, DOI: 10.1093/9780199340378.013.389.

425 Keith Shillington, *Encyclopedia of African History* (New York: Taylor & Francis, 2005), 79.

426 Wallace G. Mills, "The Taylor Revival of 1868 and the Roots of African Nationalization in the Cape Colony," *Journal of Religion in Africa* 8, no. 2 (1976): 105, accessed March 16, 2016, www.jstor.org/stable/271866.

427 Jessica L. Rousselow and Alan H. Winquist, *God's Ordinary People: No Ordinary Heritage*, (Upland, IN: Taylor University Press, 1996), 57.

428 Davies, *The Bishop of Africa*, 385.

429 "Turkey red" is a dye color made from the root of the rubia plant and was used on cotton fabric in the 18th and 19th centuries.

430 "Drill," depending upon its weight, is used for blouses, shirts, safari jackets, work clothing, and uniforms. It is a very durable cotton fabric with a diagonal weave.

431 An "octavo sheet" is usually six by nine inches and made from printer's sheets folded into eight leaves.

432 Davies, *The Bishop of Africa*, 385.

433 W. Mills, "The Taylor Revival," 106.

434 Davies, *The Bishop of Africa*, 77.

435 U. S. Department of State, Office of the Historian, *Milestones in the History of U. S. Foreign Relations, Founding of Liberia, 1847*, 1–2, accessed March 1, 2016, http://www.history.state.gov.

436 Eric Anderson Walker, "Colonisation of Africa: Concepts and Conflicts, *Concise Encyclopedia of World History*, (Oxford, UK, 2002), 51, accessed September 6, 2017, http://www.shodhganga.inflibnet.ac.in/bitstream/10603/186385/7/07_chapter$202.pdf.

437 Walker, "Colonisation of Africa," 58.

438 Angola – History & Background, accessed September 6, 2017, http://education.stateuniversity.com/pages/32/Angola-History-Background.html.

439 Angola – History & Background.

440 Angola – History & Background.

441 Teresa Cruz e Silva, *Oxford Research Encyclopedia of African* History, s. v. "Christian Mission and the State in 19th and 20th Century Angola and Mozambique," (Oxford University Press, May 2017), accessed July 20, 2017, DOI: 10.1093/acrefore/9780190277734.013.182.

442 Jeremy Ball, *Oxford Research Encyclopedia of African History*, s. v. "The History of Angola," (Oxford University Press, November 2017), accessed December 3, 2017, DOI: 0.1093/acrefore/9780190277734.013.180.

443 Ball, *Oxford Research Encyclopedia*.

444 William Cervase Clarence-Smith and John Kelly Thornton, *Encyclopaedia Britannica*, s. v. "Angola," (September 14, 2018), accessed September 22, 2018, https://www.britannica.com/place/Angola.

445 William Taylor, *Bishop Taylor's Self-supporting Missions in Central Africa*. (London: Hazell, Watson, & Viney, Ld., 1885), 388. William Taylor File, Taylor University Archives, Upland, IN.

446 W. Taylor, *Bishop Taylor's Self-supporting Missions*, 388.

447 Davies, *The Bishop of Africa*, 387.

448 Davies, *The Bishop of Africa*, 387.

449 Taylor, *Bishop Taylor's Self-supporting Missions*, 388.

450 Taylor, *Bishop Taylor's Self-supporting* Missions, 390.

451 Davies, *The Bishop of Africa*, 387.

452 Davies, *The Bishop of Africa*, 387.

453 Davies, *The Bishop of Africa*, 387.

454 Davies, *The Bishop of Africa*, 387.

455 Florida State College at Jacksonville, "Africans in the Low County," Module 3: The Development of Indentured Servitude and Racial Slavery in the American Colonies, accessed January 2, 2020, www.courses.lumenlearning.com/atd-fscj-african.

456 Aidoo, et al. "Protective Effect of Sickle Cell Trait against Malaria-Associated Mortality and Morbidity," *Lancet* 359, (April 13, 2002): 1311–1312, accessed August 27, 2016, https://www.cdc.gov/malaria/about/biology/sickle_cell.

457 Aidoo, "Protective Effect," 1311–1312.

458 Davies, *An Illustrated Handbook*, 56

459 Davies, *An Illustrated Handbook*, 56.

460 Davies, *An Illustrated Handbook*, 56.

461 Davies, *An Illustrated Handbook*, 56.

462 Davies, *An Illustrated Handbook*, Preface.

463 "His Labors in Africa: A talk with Bishop Taylor of the Methodist Episcopal Church," *New York Times*, May 11, 1895, accessed February 20, 2009, http://query.nytimes.com/gst/abstracttml?res=940CE4DD173CE433A257521A9639C94649ED7CF.

464 "His Labors in Africa."

465 W. Taylor, *Bishop Taylor's Self-supporting Missions in Central Africa*, 452.

466 "His Labors in Africa."

467 Davies, *An Illustrated Handbook on Africa*, Preface.

468 Davies, *An Illustrated Handbook on Africa*, 66.

469 Davies, *An Illustrated Handbook on Africa*, 67.

470   Davies, *An Illustrated Handbook on Africa*, 67.

471   Davies, *An Illustrated Handbook on Africa*, 67.

472   Davies, *An Illustrated Handbook on Africa*, 67.

473   Taylor, *Bishop Taylor's Self-supporting Missions in Central Africa*, 453.

474   Taylor, *Bishop Taylor's Self-supporting Missions in Central Africa*, 453.

475   Taylor, *Bishop Taylor's Self-supporting Missions in Central Africa*, 454.

476   Davies, *An Illustrated Handbook on Africa*, 68.

477   Davies, *An Illustrated Handbook on Africa*, 204.

478   Davies, *An Illustrated Handbook on Africa*, 204.

479   Davies, *An Illustrated Handbook on Africa*, 204.

480   Davies, *An Illustrated Handbook on Africa*, 204.

481   Davies. *An Illustrated Handbook on Africa, 205.*

482   Davies, *An Illustrated Handbook on Africa*. 205.

483   Davies, *An Illustrated Handbook on Africa*, 205.

484   Davies, *An Illustrated Handbook on Africa*, 205.

485   Davies, *The Bishop of Africa*, 388.

486   Constitutional Rights Foundation, "Wealth and Power," *Bill of Rights in Action*, 16, no. 2 (Spring 2000): 1–3, accessed July 19, 2017, http://www.crf-usa.org.

487   Ruth Slade, "Congo Protestant Missions and European Powers before 1885," *Baptist Quarterly* 16, no. 5 (1956): 202, accessed July 18, 2017, https://doi.org/10.1080/0005576X.1956.11750936.

488   Slade, "Congo Protestant Missions," 203.

489   Slade, "Congo Protestant Missions," 205.

490   Slade, "Congo Protestant Missions," 207.

491   IM Staff and Dr. Deborah Van Broekhoven, "Lulu Fleming, Born into Slavery," *International Ministries On Location*, (Winter 2010): 1, 5, accessed December 1, 2017, http://www.internationalministries.org/wp.../2017/OnLocation_2010_)1_winter.pd.

Chapter 8

492   "Farewell to Missionaries," *New York Times*, April 4, 1887, 5, accessed February 27, 2009, http://query.nytimes.com/men/archive=free/pdf?_r=1&res=9203EEB1630EA2575COA9629C94669FDFC7.

493   Susan Collins, "Report of Miss Susan Collins," *Minutes of the Congo Mission Conference June 9–15, 1897, 70–71.* New York: Eaton & Mains, 1897. Missions Collection, Yokomo Yamada Library Archives, Mutare, Zimbabwe, Africa.

494   William Taylor, *Bishop Taylor's Self-supporting Missions in Central Africa*. 397.

495   W. Taylor, *Bishop Taylor's Self-supporting*, 397.

496   W. Taylor, *Bishop Taylor's Self-supporting*, 397.

497   W. Taylor, *Bishop Taylor's Self-supporting*, 397.

498   W. Taylor, *Bishop Taylor's Self-supporting*, 397.

499 Richard Grant, "Bishop Taylor's African Missions," *Gospel in All Lands*, May 1887, 236, accessed March 1, 2009, http://books.google.com/books?id=Q7MmVFsFAkoC&oe=UTF-8.

500 Grant, "Bishop Taylor's African Missions," 236.

501 H. H. Savacool, "Herald of Christ," *Classmate* LVIV (1952): 6–7.

502 Savacool, "Herald of Christ," 6–7.

503 "Farewell to Missionaries," 5.

504 Grant, "Bishop Taylor's African Missions." 236.

505 "Doctor, Dentist, Missionary. Miss Taylor Goes to Africa with her Uncle to Do Many Kinds of Work," *New York Times*," December 5, 1893, accessed February 27, 2009, http://select.nytimes.com/gst/abstract.html?res=FAOC11FE3A5FIA738DDDAC984DA415B8385FOD3.

506 Jennie Taylor to Lizzie Akers, 12 December 1893, Jennie Taylor File, Taylor University Archives, Upland, IN.

507 Jennie Taylor to Lizzie Akers, 8 December 1893, Jennie Taylor File, Taylor University Archives, Upland, IN.

508 J. Taylor to Akers, 8 December 1893.

509 J. Taylor to Akers, 8 December 1893.

510 J. Taylor to Akers, 8 December 1893.

511 J. Taylor to Akers, 8 December 1893.

512 Jennie Taylor to Lizzie Akers, 22 December 1893, Jennie Taylor File, Taylor University Archives, Upland, IN.

513 J. Taylor to Akers, 22 December 1893.

514 Jennie Taylor to Lizzie Akers, 4 January 1894, Jennie Taylor File, Taylor University Archives, Upland, IN.

515 J. Taylor to Akers, 4 January 1894.

516 J. Taylor to Akers, 4 January 1894.

517 J. Taylor to Akers, 4 January 1894.

518 J. Taylor to Akers, 4 January 1894.

519 J. Taylor to Akers, 4 January 1894.

520 "Bishop Taylor's Missionaries in Africa," *Gospel in All Lands* (New York: Hunt & Easton, March 1894), 142, accessed October 22, 2009, http://onlinebooks.library.upenn.edu/webbin/serial?id+gospall.

521 Jennie Taylor to Lizzie Akers, 8 March 1894, Jennie Taylor File, Taylor University Archives, Upland IN.

522 J. Taylor to Akers, 8 March 1894.

523 J. Taylor to Akers, 8 March 1894.

524 Jennie Taylor to Lizzie Akers, 6 April 1894, Jennie Taylor File, Taylor University Archives, Upland, IN.

525 "Natomba" is sometimes spelled "Natumba."

526 J. Taylor to Akers, 6 April 1894.

527 William Taylor, "A Conference on the Congo by Bishop Taylor," *Gospel in All Lands* (New York: A. D. F. Randolph, March 1888), 144, accessed October 1, 2009, http://books.google.com/books?id=mLPM_OJeDwwC&oe=UTF-8.

528 J. Taylor to Akers, 6 April 1894.

529 "Former Missionaries Connected with the Congo and Angola Missions," *Gospel in All Lands* (New York: Hunt & Eaton, December 1901), 571, accessed October 3, 2009, http://books.google.com/books?id=qhgFbOfTdP8C&oe=UTF-8.

530 J. Taylor to Akers, 6 April 1894.

531 Jennie Taylor to Lizzie Akers, 9 April 1894, Jennie Taylor File, Taylor University Archives, Upland, IN.

532 Jennie Taylor to Lizzie Akers, 2 May 1894, Jennie Taylor File, Taylor University Archives, Upland, IN.

533 J. Taylor to Akers, 2 May 1894.

534 J. Taylor to Akers, 2 May 1894.

535 A. Smith, *An Autobiography*, 332.

536 A. Smith, *An Autobiography*, 454.

537 George Thompson, "The African Climate," *African News* 1, (1889): 240–241, William Taylor Collection, Taylor University Archives, Upland, IN.

538 Thompson, "The African Climate," 240–241.

539 Thompson, "The African Climate," 240.

540 Thompson, "The African Climate," 240.

541 Archivist, London School of Hygiene and Tropical Medicine, "Ross and the Discovery that Mosquitoes Transmit Malaria Parasites," Centers for Disease Control and Prevention, 9-16-2015, accessed October 23, 2016, https://www.cdc.gov/malaria/about/history/ross.html.

542 Thompson, "The African Climate," 241.

543 Thompson, "The African Climate," 241.

544 Frances J. Baker, *The Story of the Woman's Society of the Methodist Episcopal Church, 1869–1895*, Revised Ed. (New York: Eaton & Mains, 1898): 393, accessed August 10, 2010, http://nationalhumanitiescenter.org.

545 Baker, *The Story of the Woman's Society*, 393.

546 Niger-Congo, Mbundu, 2, accessed July 10, 2017, www.dice.missouri.edu/.

547 Niger-Congo, Mbundu, 3.

548 Livingstone, *Life and Explorations of David Livingstone*, 97.

549 Livingstone, *Life and Explorations of David Livingstone*, 127–130.

Chapter 9

550 A. Smith, *An Autobiography*, 465.

551 James Mudge, "Bishop Taylor in Central Africa," *Gospel in All Lands* (New York: Methodist Episcopal Church Missionary Society, June 1889), 249–250, accessed October 21, 2009, http://www.openlibrary.org/gospelinalllands08socigoog/.

552 "Farewell to Missionaries."

553 William Taylor to Susan Collins, 31 October 1887, in possession of author.

554 W. Taylor to Collins, 31 October 1887.

555 W. Taylor to Collins, 31 October 1887.

556 Eugene R. Smith, "African Missions of American Methodists," *Gospel in All Lands*, (New York: Eaton & Mains, December 1893), 450, accessed November 14, 2010, http://books.google.com/books/about/The_Gospel_in_All_Lands.html?id=RGwahoHLeT4C.

557 William Taylor, "To the Missionary Committee of the Methodist Episcopal Church, in Session for 1889," *Report of Bishop Taylor's Self-supporting Mission from March 25th to October 31st, 1889* (New York: Palmer & Hughes, 1890), 10–16. William Taylor Collection, Taylor University Archives, Upland, IN.

558 J. Taylor to Akers, 9 April 1894.

559 Davies, *An Illustrated Handbook on Africa*, 54.

560 J. Taylor to Akers, 6 April 1894.

561 J. Taylor to Akers, 6 April 1894.

562 William Taylor, *Report of Bishop Taylor's Self-supporting Missions from July 1st, 1884 to March 24th, 1888* (New York: A. H. Kellogg, 1888), 22–24. William Taylor Collection, Taylor University Archives, Upland, IN.

563 Taylor, "To the Missionary Committee of the Methodist Episcopal Church," 10–16.

564 "Our Mission Field and Missionaries: Africa," *Gospel in all Lands*, (New York: A. D. F. Randolph, December 1888), 561, accessed January 3, 2011, http://archive.org/details/gospelinalllands.02socigoog.

565 Susan Collins to unidentified friend, January 4, 1888, "A Letter from Africa," *Daily Huronite*, April 10, 1888, accessed June 10, 2011, Newspaper Archives.org.

566 Collins to friend, January 4, 1888.

567 Richard Gleason Green, *The International Cyclopedia: A Compendium of Human Knowledge, Vol. 4* (New York: Dodd, Mead and Company, January 1890), 239, accessed February 10, 2013, http://book.google.com/books?id=9nUWAAAAYAAJ.

568 John Henrik Clarke, *The Kongo Nation and Kingdom*, (March 13, 2017), 10–12, accessed May 18, 2017, www.dhwtyslearningcenter.com/2017/.../the-kongo-nation-and-kingdom-by-john.ht.

569 Clarke, *The Kongo Nation*, 10–12.

570 Clarke, *The Kongo* Nation, 13.

571 "Death of Miss Collins," *Oelwein Daily Register*, June 12, 1940, 6.

572 W. Taylor, "To the Missionary Committee," 10.

573 W. Taylor, "To the Missionary Committee," 10.

574 J. Taylor to Akers, 6 April 1894.

575 J. Taylor to Akers, 6 April 1894.

576   Susan Collins, "Report of Miss Susan Collins," *Minutes of the Congo Mission Conference, June 9–15,1897.* 70–71. (New York: Press of Eaton & Mains, 1897). Missions Collection, Yokomo Yamada Library Archives, Africa University, Mutare, Zimbabwe, Africa.

Chapter 10

577   Hester Hartzell Withey Papers, Collection 418, T1, Billy Graham Center, Wheaton University, Wheaton, IL, accessed January 7 2018, http://WWW2. wheaton.edu.

578   Joseph Hartzell, "The Work in Angola," *Northwestern Christian Advocate* 52, no. 1 (May 25, 1904): 16, accessed January 20, 2018, http://google.books.com.

579   Jennie Taylor to Lizzie Akers, May 2, 1894, Jennie Taylor File, Taylor University Archives, Taylor University, Upland, IN.

580   J. Taylor to Akers, May 2, 1894.

581   Mike Stead, Sean Rorison and Oscar Scafidi, *Angola* (Guilford, CT: Globe Pequot Press, Inc., 2013), 118.

582   Stead, Rorison and Scafidi, *Angola*, 118.

583   Stead, Rorison and Scafidi, *Angola*, 118.

584   Bengo River, accessed January 22, 2017, http://en.wikipedia.org.

585   Hanson, *The Ivory Necklace*, 175.

586   Ralph E. Dodge, "Angola Methodists Celebrate a Hundred Years," *New World Outlook*, May 1985, 16.

587   Dodge, "Angola Methodists Celebrate a Hundred Years," 20.

588   Helen Emily Chapman Springer, *Snap Shots from Sunny Africa* (New York: F. H. Revell Company, 1909), 153, accessed November 10, 2016, https://archive. org/details/snapshotsfromsun00spri.

589   H. Springer, *Snap Shots*, 153–155.

590   W. Taylor, "To the Missionary Committee," 10.

591   W. Taylor, "To the Missionary Committee," 10.

592   Hanson, *The Ivory Necklace*, 176.

593   W. Taylor, "To the Missionary Committee," 10.

594   W. Taylor, "To the Missionary Committee," 10.

595   Susan Collins, "Report of Miss Susan Collins," 70–71

596   Davies, *An Illustrated Handbook of Africa*, 54.

597   Birmingham, "Merchants and Missionaries in Angola," 350.

598   Jennie Taylor to Lizzie Akers, 6 September 1894, Jennie Taylor File, Taylor University Archives, Upland, IN.

599   J. Taylor to Akers, 6 September 1894.

600   W. Taylor, "To the Missionary Committee," 10.

601   W. Taylor, "To the Missionary Committee," 10.

602   W. Taylor, "To the Missionary Committee," 10.

603 "Angola," *Natural Wonders of Africa*, 1, accessed May 20, 2017, http://naturalwondersofafrica.com/angola/

604 Jennie Taylor to Lizzie Akers, 26 September 1894, Jennie Taylor File, Taylor University Archives, Upland, IN.

605 "Angola," *Natural Wonders*, 1.

606 J. Taylor to Akers, 2 May 1894.

607 Bishop William Taylor, "Report on African Missions," *Seventy–First Annual Report of the Missionary Society of the Methodist Episcopal Church for the Year 1889* (New York: Cable Address, Missions, 1890): 32, accessed November 12, 2011, http://books.google.com/books?id=5m4F-4JmVdAC&pg=PA278&lpg=PA278&dq=seventy-one+annual+report+of+the+Missionary+Society+of+the+Methodist+_episcopal+church+for+year+1889&sc.

608 W. Taylor, "Report on African Missions," 32.

609 W. Taylor, "Report on African Missions," 32.

610 Bishop William Taylor, "Report on African Missions," *Seventy–Second Annual Report of the Missionary Society of the Methodist Episcopal Church for the Year 1890* (New York: Cable Address, Missions, 1891), 26, accessed November 12, 2011, http://babel.hathitrust.org.

611 W. Taylor, "Report on African Missions," *Seventy–First Annual Report of the Missionary Society*, 32.

612 William Taylor, "From Pungo Andongo to Malange," *African News* 2 (1889): 452, William Taylor Files, Taylor University Archives, Upland, IN.

613 W. Taylor, "From Pungo Andongo to Malange," 452.

614 W. Taylor, "From Pungo Andongo to Malange," 452.

615 W. Taylor, "From Pungo Andongo to Malange," 453.

616 W. Taylor, "From Pungo Andongo to Malange," 453.

617 J. Taylor to Akers, 26 September 1894.

618 Maps Angola, accessed May 4, 2011, http://mapsof.net/uploads/static-maps/angola_topography.png.

619 W. Taylor, *Report of Bishop Taylor's Self-supporting missions from July 2nd, 1884 to March 24th, 1888*, 12.

620 Hanson, *The Ivory Necklace*, 176.

621 Birmingham, "Merchants and Missionaries in Angola," 350.

622 Jacob Festus Ade Ajayi," Africa at the Beginning of the Nineteenth Century: Issue and Prospects," in *General History of Africa, VI Africa in the Nineteenth Century until the 1880's*, ed. J. F. Ade Ajayi (Berkley, CA: University of California Press, 1989), 8, accessed December 11, 2017, https://www.sahistory.org.za/sites/defaultIV/files/...general_historyorg_africa_VI.pdf.

623 W. Taylor, "To the Missionary Committee of the Methodist Episcopal Church, in Session for 1889," 16.

624 William Taylor, "Missionary Self-Support in Malange," *African News* 3 (1890): 455, William Taylor Collection, Taylor University Archives, Upland, IN.

625 Rousselow and Winquist, *God's Ordinary People*, 71.

626 Rousselow and Winquist, *God's Ordinary People*, 71

627 Dodge, "Angola Methodists Celebrate a Hundred Years," 16.

628 W. Taylor, *Seventy–First Annual Report of the Missionary Society*, 31.

629 W. Taylor, *Seventy–First Annual Report of the Missionary Society*, 31.

630 W. Taylor, *Seventy–First Annual Report of the Missionary Society*, 31.

631 W. Taylor, "Missionary Self–support in Malange," 455.

632 Birmingham, "Merchants and Missionaries in Angola," 350.

633 Davies, *An Illustrated Handbook on Africa*, 54.

634 Florinda Bessa to Reverend John D. Clinton, n. d., estimate 1937 based on content. First United Methodist Church Archives, Fayette, IA.

635 W. Taylor, *Report of Bishop Taylor's Self–supporting Missions*, 12.

636 W. Taylor, *Report of Bishop Taylor's Self–supporting Missions*, 12.

637 Hanson, *The Ivory Necklace*, 177.

638 "His Labors in Africa," *New York Times*, May 11, 1895, accessed June 8, 2009, Newspaper Archives.com.

639 William Dodson, "Report of William Dodson," *Minutes of the Congo Mission Conference June 9–15, 1897.* (New York: Eaton & Mains, 1897), 57-58. Missions Collection, Yokomo Yamada Library Archives, Africa University, Mutare, Zimbabwe, Africa.

640 Bundy, "The Legacy of William Taylor," 174.

Chapter 11

641 Probate Book 21, 238–239. Fayette County Recorder's Office, West Union, IA.

642 Deed Record Book 97, 165. Fayette County Recorder's Office, West Union, IA.

643 Iowa Census 1895, Iowa, State Census Collection 1836–1925 [database on-line] Provo, UT, USA. Accessed November 7, 2011, www.ancestry.com.

644 Birmingham, "Merchants and Missionaries in Angola," 351.

645 Birmingham, "Merchants and Missionaries in Angola," 351.

646 Dodge, "Angola Missions Celebrate a Hundred Years," 16.

647 W. Taylor, *Report of Bishop Taylor's Self-supporting Missions*, 12.

648 *Plant Resources in Tropical Africa*, eds. D. Loupee, A. A. Oteng-Amoako, M. Brink, PROTA Foundation, (Wageningen, Netherlands: Backhuys Publishers, 2008), 472, accessed March 29, 2018, http://books.google.com/books?isbn=9057822091.

649 W. Taylor, "From Pungo Andongo to Malange," 453.

650 W. Taylor, "From Pungo Andongo to Malange," 453.

651 Samuel J. Mead, "Mission Work in Malange, South Central Africa at Malange," *Gospel in All Lands*, (New York: Hunt & Eaton, February 1891): 93–94, accessed

November 10, 2010, http://books.google.com/books/about/The Gospel in All Lands.html?id=qw761-WkqclC.

652 Mead, "Mission Work in Malange," 93–94

653 W. Taylor, *Report of Bishop Taylor's Self-Supporting missions*, 12.

654 W. Taylor, "Missionary Self-support in Malange," 454.

655 Samuel J. Mead, "From S. J. Mead, Malange, Angola, Africa, May 28, 1888," *African News*, 1 (1889): 29–30. William Taylor File, Taylor University Archives, Upland, IN.

656 W. Taylor, "Missionary Self-support in Malange," 455.

657 Mead, "From S.J. Mead," 29–30.

658 William Taylor, "Sabbath Services in Our Chapel in Malange, Africa." *African News*, 4 (1889): 457. William Taylor Collection, Taylor University Archives, Upland, IN.

659 Samuel H. Williamson, "Measuring Worth, Purchasing Power of Money in the United Stated from 1774 to Present," Measuring Worth, 2019, accessed January 10, 2019, www.measuringwortj.com/ppowerus/.

660 W. Taylor, "Missionary Self-Support in Malange," 455.

661 W. Taylor, *Report of Bishop Taylor's Self-sustaining Missions*, 12.

662 Mead, "Mission Work in Malange," 94.

663 W. Taylor, "Sabbath Services in Our Chapel," 457–458.

664 W. Taylor, "Sabbath Services in Our Chapel," 458.

665 W. Taylor, "Sabbath Services in Our Chapel," 458.

666 W. Taylor, "Sabbath Services in Our Chapel," 458–459.

667 W. Taylor, "Sabbath Services in Our Chapel," 460.

668 W. Taylor, "Sabbath Services in Our Chapel," 461.

669 Mead, "Mission Work in Malange," 94.

670 Mead, "From S. J. Mead, Malange," 29–30.

671 Mead, "From S. J. Mead, Malange," 29–30.

672 Mead, "From S. J. Mead, Malange," 236.

673 Hal S. Chase, "You Live What Your Learn," in *Outside In African-American History in Iowa, 1838–2000*, eds. Bill Silag, Susan Koch-Bridgford, & Hal Chase (Des Moines: State Historical Society of Iowa, 2001), 137–138.

674 W. Taylor, "Report on African Missions," (1891), 26.

675 William Taylor, "Methodist Episcopal Missionary Report," *Gospel in All Lands* (New York: Hunt & Eaton, June 1891), 281, accessed November 10, 2010,http://books.google.com/books/about/The Gospel in All Lands.html?id=qw761-WkqlC.

676 Mead, "From S. J. Mead, Malange," 236.

677 *History of the First Methodist Church and Women who Supported the Church*, (Fayette, IA: Fayette United Methodist Church, 1965), 2.

678 Collins, "Report of Miss Susan Collins," 70–71.

679 *Seventy–Fourth Annual Report of the Missionary Society of the Methodist Episcopal Church for the Year 1892*, (New York: Cable Address Missions, 1893), 74,

22, accessed November 18, 2012, http://books.google.com/books?id+M7YP
AAAAIAAJ&pg=PA1&1pg=PA1&dq=Seventy-fourth+annual+report+of+the+
Missionary+Society+of+the+Methodist+Episcopal+Church+annual+report+for
the+year+1892.

680 Collins, "Report of Miss Susan Collins," 74.

681 Collins, "Report of Miss Susan Collins," 71.

682 Collins, "Report of Miss Susan Collins," 71.

683 Jennie Taylor to Lizzie Akers, 23 November 1894, Jennie Taylor File, Taylor
University Archives, Upland, IN.

684 Jennie Taylor to Lizzie Akers, 26 September 1894, Jennie Taylor File, Taylor
University Archives, Upland, IN.

685 J. Taylor to Akers, 23 November 1894.

686 Eugene R. Smith, "African Missions of American Methodists," 450.

687 Jacobs, *Give a Thought to Africa: Black Women Missionaries in Southern Africa*,
110–111.

688 A. E. Withey, "Angola District," *Minutes of the Liberia Annual Conference of the
Methodist Church, January 22 to 28, 1896* (New York: Press of Eaton & Mains,
1896), 21–23, Missions Collection, Yokomo Yamada Library Archives, Africa
University Archives, Mutare, Zimbabwe, Africa.

689 Withey, "Angola District," 23.

690 Withey, "Angola District," 21.

691 J. Taylor to Akers, 23 November 1894.

692 "Missionary Starts Girls' School in Angola," *Iowa State Bystander*, December
24, 1897, 4.

693 Joseph Crane Hartzell, "A New Mission Conference in South Central Africa,"
Minutes of the Congo Conference June 9–15, 1897, 2, Mission Collection, Yokomo
Yamada Library Archives, Africa University Archives, Mutare, Zimbabwe, Africa.

694 Hartzell, "A New Mission Conference," 4.

695 J. Tremayne Copplestone, *Twentieth-Century Perspectives, The Methodist
Episcopal Church, 1896-1939* (New York: Board of Global Ministries, United
Methodist Church, 1973), 569–570.

696 Hartzell, "A New Mission Conference," 4.

697 "Upper Iowa University: A Mother of Missionaries."

698 A. Smith, *An Autobiography*, 464.

699 J. Taylor to Akers, 26 September 1894.

700 J. Taylor to Akers, 26 September 1894.

701 Livingstone, *Missionary Travels and Researches in South Africa*, 112, 218.

702 J. Taylor to Akers, 23 November 1894.

703 Dodge, "Angola Methodists Celebrate a Hundred Years," 16.

704 Fellows, *History of the Upper Iowa Conference of the Methodist Episcopal Church
1856–1859*, 73–74.

705 Secretaries' books, First United Methodist Church Archives, Fayette, IA.

706 *Oelwein Daily Register,* "Death of Miss Collins."

707 Yearous, "Susan Collins," 18.

708 Paine, *My Ninety-five Milestones*, 23.

709 *History of the First Methodist Church and Women who Supported the Church*," 4.

710 Yearous, "Susan Collins," 18.

711 "Congo Mission Conference," *Gospel in All Lands* (New York: Eaton & Mains, 1897), 485, accessed November 14, 2010, http://books.google.com/books/about/The_Gospel_in_All_Lands.html?ie=RGwahoHLeTrc.

712 Joseph Crane Hartzell, "The Methodist Episcopal Church in Africa, *Gospel in All Lands*(NewYork:Eaton&Mains,1898),256,accessedAugust10,2013,http://books. google.com/books?id+3jODvSUcvlwC&printsec=frontcover&source=gbs_ge_ summary_r&cad=O#v=onepage&q&f=false.

713 Sylvia M. Jacobs, "African-American Women Missionaries and European Imperialism in Southern Africa, 1880– 1920," *Women's Studies International Forum* 13, no. 4, (1990): 387.

714 Dana L. Robert, "Faith, Hope, and Love in Action: United Methodist Women in Mission Yesterday, Today, and Tomorrow." *UMC Mission Studies*, (St. Louis, MO: Address to Mission Forward Symposium April 19, 2010), accessed June 15, 2018, www.unitedmethodistwomen.org/what-we-do/...

715 Report of Methodist Episcopal Missions for 1898," *Gospel in All Lands* (New York: Eaton & Mains, January 1899), 15, accessed March 20, 2011, https:// books.google.com/books/about/The_Gospel_in_All_Lands.html?id.

716 "Methodist Episcopal Missions in Angola and the Congo," *Gospel in All Lands* (New York: Hunt & Eaton, June 1893), 270, accessed March 25, 2011, http://books.google.com/books?id=RGwahoHLeTrC&pg=PA270&dq+ Munhall+Mission+Station+In+Angola+Africa+named+for+Dr.+L.+W.+Munhall.

717 Robert, "Faith, Hope, and Love in Action."

718 William P. Dodson, "Report of the Presiding Elders, Angola District," *Official Journal of the Congo Mission Conference, June 1–3, 1899* (Monrovia, Liberia: Press of the College of West Africa, 1899), 16, accessed May 21, 2012, http://images.library.yale.edu/divinitycontent/dayrep/Methodist%20 Episcopal%20Church%20Congo%20Mission%20Conference%20%20 1899%203.pdf.

719 A. E. Withey, "Angola Missions," *Gospel in All Lands* (New York: Eaton & Mains, January 1900), 3, accessed April 1, 2011, http://books.google.com/ books?id=hDPAAAAMAAJ&printsec+frontcover&source+gbs_ge_summary_ r&cad=0#v=onepage&q&f=false.

720 Dodson, "Report of William Dodson," 57.

721 Dodson, "Report of William Dodson," 58.

722 Joseph Crane Hartzell, "Congo Conference Report, *Gospel in All Lands* (New York: Eaton & Mains, January 1900, 4–5, accessed April 1, 2011, http://books. google.com/books?id=hDPAAAAMAAJ&printsec=frontcover&source=gbs_ ge_summary_r&cad=0#v=onepage&q&f=false.

723 Withey, "Angola Missions," 4–5.

724 "Notes on Missionaries, Missions, *"Gospel in All Lands* (New York: Eaton & Mains, September 1900), 432, accessed April 1, 2011, http://books.google.com/ books?id=hDPAAAAMAAJ&printsec=frontcover&source=gbs_ge_summary_ r&cad=0#v=onepage&f=false.

725 "Seventh Session," *Official Journal of the West Central African Mission Conference December 21–26, 1910*, (Bedford, England: Rush & Warwick, 1910), 64. Missions Collection, Yokomo Yamada Library Archives, Africa University Library, Mutare, Zimbabwe, Africa.

Chapter 12

726 "Randalia News," *West Union Gazette*, September 28, 1900, 1.

727 Carrie Gammons, "Minutes of Woman's Foreign Missionary Society Chapter," October 3, 1900, First United Methodist Church Archives, Fayette, IA. Last name is difficult to read so may be in error.

728 "County Correspondence," *Argo*, October 10, 1900, 1.

729 "County Correspondence," *Argo*, October 24, 1900, 8.

730 Yearous, "Susan Collins," 18.

731 Yearous, "Susan Collins," 18.

732 Yearous, "Susan Collins," 18.

733 "County Correspondence," *Argo*, November 14, 1900, 8.

734 "County Correspondence," *Argo*.

735 "Upper Iowa University: Mother of Missionaries." *Fayette Reporter*, June 18, 1908, 1.

736 "Questions to Missionary," *Thirty–Second Annual Report of the Woman's Foreign Missionary Society of the Methodist Episcopal Church 1900–1901* (Boston: Miss P. J. Waldon, n.d.), 229, accessed January 20, 2010, http://books.google.com/ books?id=wRMOAAAAIAAJ&pg=PA191&1pg=PA191&dq.

737 "Questions to Missionary," *Thirty–Second Annual Report*.

738 "Questions to Missionary," *Thirty–Second Annual Report*.

739 "Requirements of Missionary Candidates," *Thirty–Second Annual Report of the Woman's Foreign Missionary Society of the Methodist Episcopal Church 1900–1901* (Boston: Miss P. J. Waldon, n.d.), 242–243, accessed January 20, 2010, http:// books.google.com/books?id=wRMOAAAAIAAJ&pg=PA191&1pg=PA191&dq.

740 "Susan Collins," *Christian Advocate*, November 14, 1901, 1820, accessed November 18, 2011, http://wwwbabel.hathitrust.org.

741 Mrs. M. S. Huston, "Africa," *Thirty–Second Annual Report of the Woman's Foreign Missionary Society of the Methodist Episcopal Church 1900–1901* (Boston:

Miss P. J. Waldon, n.d.), 191–192, accessed January 20, 2010, http://books.google.com/books?id=wRMOAAAAIAAJ&pg=PA191&1pg=PA191&dq.

742 Hal S. Chase, "You Live What You Learn," 144.

743 Susan Collins to Madge Bender, n.d., based on content speculate written after 1905, Mission Archive File, Box 4 Individual Methodist Missions, Folder 1 Quessua, Angola; New York: Interchurch Center.

744 Charlotte O'Neal, "Pacific Branch," *Thirty–Third Annual Report of the Woman's Foreign Missionary Society of the Methodist Episcopal Church, 1901–1902* (Boston: Miss P. J. Waldon, 1902), 81, accessed February 19, 2011, http://archive.org/stream/thirtythirdannua01woma#page/80/mode/2up.

745 "Annual Meeting," *Woman's Missionary Friend* (Boston: Woman's Foreign Missionary Society of the Methodist Episcopal Church, February 1902), 72–73, accessed April 13, 2011, http://books.google.com/books?id=JIAzAQAAMAAJ&lpg=PA74lpg=PA74&dq.

746 "Briefs," *Woman's Missionary Friend* (Boston: Woman's Foreign Missionary Society of the Methodist Episcopal Church, February 1902), 74, accessed April 13, 2011, http://books.google.com/books?id=JIAzAQAAMAAJ&lpg=PA74lpg=PA74&dq.

747 "Briefs," *Woman's Missionary Friend*, 74.

748 A. Mills, "Notes from Los Angeles," 8.

749 "Baptist Mission Circle," *West Union Gazette*, October 11, 1901, 8.

750 Frances S. Walker, "Minutes of Woman's Foreign Missionary Society Chapter," October 19, 1901, First United Methodist Church Archives, Fayette, IA.

751 "County Correspondence," *Argo*, October 23, 1901, 8.

752 "County Correspondence," *Argo*, January 22, 1902, 8.

753 "Our Branch Missionaries," *Woman's Missionary Friend* (Boston: Woman's Foreign Missionary Society of the Methodist Episcopal Church, February 1902), 74, accessed April 13, 2011, http://books.google.com/books?id=JIAzAQAAMAAJ&lpg=PA74lpg=PA74&dq.

754 Susan Collins' Emergency Passport Application, May 28, 1920, accessed September 2, 2011, http://search.ancestry.com/cgi-bin/sse.dll?h=1992779&db=USpassports&indiv=try.

755 Thomson Gale, "Black Women's Club Movement," *Encyclopedia of African-American Culture and History*, s.v. accessed August 20, 2017, http://www.Encyclopedia.com.

756 "Missionaries," *Gospel in All Lands* (New York: Missionary Society of the Methodist Episcopal Church, December 1901), 551, accessed July 10, 2011, http://books.google.com/books?id=5BHPAAAAMAAJ&pg=PA55&dq=Missionaries,+Gospel+in+all+lands +1901.

757 Huston, "Africa," 191–192.

758 Lena Leonard Fisher, *Under the Crescent, and Among the Kraals A Study of Methodism in Africa* (Boston, MA: The Woman's Foreign Missionary Society,

1917), 45, accessed March 21, 2009, http://babel.hathitrust.org/cgi/pt?id=uc2. ark:/13960/t2f7a6gx1f:view=1up:seq=59.

759   "Woman's Work," 28.

760   John McKendree Springer, *The Heart of Central Africa: Mineral Wealth and Missionary Opportunity* (New York: The Methodist Book Concern, 1909), 207, accessed May 31, 2010, http://www.archive.org/details/heartofcentralaf00spri.

761   Springer, *The Heart of Central Africa*, 207.

762   Fisher, *Under the Crescent*, 107.

763   Marjorie Medary, *Each One Teach One, Frank Laubach, Friend to Millions*, (New York: Longman's, Green and Co. Inc., 1954).

764   Fisher, *Under the Crescent*, 108.

765   O'Neal, "Pacific Branch," 81.

766   Extracts from Missionary Letters, *Woman's Missionary Friend* (Boston: Woman's Foreign Missionary Society of the Methodist Episcopal Church, August 1902), 300, accessed March 5, 2009, http://books.google.com/books?id=JIAzAQAAMAAJpg=PA74&lpg=PA74&dq.

767   Extracts from Missionary Letters, *Woman's Missionary Friend* (Boston: Woman's Foreign Missionary Society, November 1902), 415–416, accessed March 5, 2009, http://books.google.com/books?id=JIAzAQAAMAAJ&pg=PA4&lpg=PA74&dq.

768   Florence Hooper, "Changes in By-laws," *Forty-Ninth Annual Report of the Woman's Foreign Missionary Society of the Methodist Episcopal Church, Jubilee Number, 1918–1919* (Boston: Woman's Foreign Missionary Society, 1919), 229–231, accessed November 10, 2011. http://arachive.org/stream/followinggreato01woma#page/246/mode/2up.

769   "By-laws," *Year Book, Woman's Foreign Missionary Society of the Methodist Church, the Fiftieth Annual Report of the Society* (Boston: Woman's Foreign Missionary Society of the Methodist Episcopal Church, 1919), 216–217, accessed November 11, 2011, http://archive.org/stream/yearbookwomansfo01woma#page/n3/mode/2up.

770   "By-laws," *Year Book*, 216–217.

771   "By-laws," *Year Book*, 216–217.

772   "By-laws," *Year Book*, 216–217.

773   "By-laws," *Year Book*, 216–217.

774   "By–laws," *Year Book*, 216–217.

775   "By-laws," *Year Book*, 216–217.

776   "By-laws," *Year Book*, 216–217.

Chapter 13

777   "Upper Iowa University: A Mother of Missionaries."

778   Mrs. William P. Dodson, "Report of Mrs. W. P. Dodson," *Minutes of the Congo Mission Conference June 9–15, 1897* (New York: Eaton & Mains, 1897),

59. Missions Collection, Yokomo Yamada Library Archives, Africa University, Mutare, Zimbabwe, Africa.

779 The fever was often seen in Caucasians when the treatment regime was not completed.

780 O'Neal, "Pacific Branch," 81.

781 Mary E. Parker, "Briefs," *Woman's Missionary Friend* (Boston: Woman's Foreign Missionary Society of the Methodist Episcopal Church, November 1902), 416, accessed May 23, 2011, http://books.google.com/books?id=JIAzAQAAMAAJ&printsec=frontcover&source=gbs_ge_summary_r&cad=0#v=onepage&q&f=false.

782 "Josephine Mekkelson," Connor Family Album, Alta, Buena Vista County, IA, accessed June 9, 2012, http://freepages.genealogy.rootsweb.ancestry.com/~yourfamilyhistory/Buena%20Vista%20Site/photos/page6.htm.

783 Susan Collins to Madge Bender, n.d.

784 "Appropriations for 1902–1903, Africa," *Third–Third Annual Report*, 193.

785 Douglas C. Wheeler and C. Diane Christensen, *The Rise with One Mind: The Bailundo War of 1902*, accessed October 13, 2016, http://run.edu.ng/media/1834181203243.pdf.

786 W. P. Dodson, "Angola District Report," *Minutes of the West Central Africa Mission Conference, May 30 to June 4, 1902* (n.p.: Methodist Mission Press, 1902), 25. Missions Collection, Yokomo Yamada Library Archives, Africa University, Mutare, Zimbabwe, Africa.

787 Dodson, "Angola District Report," 25.

788 Herbert C. Withey, "Angolan Missions Report," *Minutes of the West Central Africa Mission Conference, Loanda, Angola, Africa, December 9–11, 1903* (n.p.: Methodist Mission Press, 1904), 21–23. Missions Collection, Yokomo Yamada Library Archives, Africa University, Mutare, Zimbabwe, Africa.

789 Withey, "Angola Missions Report." 21–23.

790 "Extracts from Missionary Letters," *Woman's Missionary Friend* (Boston: Woman's Foreign Missionary Society of the Methodist Episcopal Church, November 1904) 415–416, accessed July 19, 2011, http://books.google.com/books?id=uZ4zAQAAMAAJ&printsec=frontcover&source=gbs_ge_summary_r&cad=0#v=onepage&q&f=false.

791 "Extracts from Missionary Letters," 415–416.

792 Susan Collins to Iva McClain, 15 April 1904, Susan Collins, Letters from Africa, 1904–1905, Special Collections, Des Moines: State Historical Society of Iowa.

793 Collins to I. McClain, 15 April 1904.

794 Susan Collins to Marjorie McClain, 15 April 1904, Susan Collins, Letters from Africa, 1904–1905, Special Collections, Des Moines: State Historical Society of Iowa.

795 Collins to M. McClain, 15 April 1904.

796 Collins to M. McClain, 15 April 1904.

797 Collins to M. McClain, 15 April 1904.

798 Susan Collins to Sadie Joiner, 10 February 1905, Susan Collins, Letters from Africa, 1904–1905, Special Collections, Des Moines: State Historical Society of Iowa.

799 Collins to Joiner, 10 February 1905.

800 Collins to Joiner, 10 February 1905.

801 Collins to Joiner, 10 February 1905.

802 Collins to Joiner, 10 February 1905.

803 Collins to Joiner, 10 February 1905.

804 Collins to Joiner, 10 February 1905.

805 Robert, "United Methodist Women in Mission."

806 Hanson, *The Ivory Necklace,* 174.

807 Joseph Crane Hartzell, "Glimpses of Our African Mission Field," *Woman's Missionary Friend* (Boston: Woman's Foreign Missionary Society of the Methodist Episcopal Church, April 1906), 116–117, accessed February 12, 2011, http://books.google.com/books?id=1zIzAQAAMAAJ7printsec=frontcover&dq=Woman's+missionary+friend+1906&hl=en&sa=X&ei=q.

808 Collins to I. McClain, 15 April 1904.

809 Collins to I. McClain, 15 April 1904.

810 Susan Collins to Iva McClain, 10 February 1905, Susan Collins, letters from Africa. 1904–1905, Special Collections, Des Moines: State Historical Society of Iowa.

811 Hanson, *The Ivory Necklace*, 174.

812 Mrs. John M. Springer, "The Creoles of Angola, Africa," *Woman's Missionary Friend* (Boston: Woman's Foreign Missionary Society, March 1909), 81–83, accessed Mary 29, 2011, http://books.google.com/books?id=TafNAAAAMAAJ7pg=PP8&lpg+PP8&dq=Woman's+Missionary+Friend+1908-1909&sirce=bl&ots=bl&ots.

813 Collins to Joiner, 10 February 1905.

814 Collins to Joiner, 10 February 1905.

815 *1900 United States Federal Census*, Saylor Township, Des Moines, Iowa, Roll 455, Page205D; Series T623, accessed August 3, 2013, http://persi.heritagequestonline.com/hqoweb/library/do/census/resu...neus%3816728821.

816 "Extracts from Missionary Letters," *Woman's Missionary Friend* (Boston: Pauline J. Walden, May 1903): 188-189, accessed December 10, 2011, http://babel.hathitrust.org/cgi/pt?id=mdp.39015039671238:view=lup:seq+247.

817 "Extracts from Missionary Letters," 189.

818 "Extracts from Missionary Letters," 189.

819 "News from the Field," *Woman's Missionary Friend* (Boston: Pauline J. Walden, August 1903), 302, accessed December 10, 2011, http://babel.hathitrust.org/cgi/pt?id=mdp.3901503671238;view=1up:seq:247.

820 "Personal and Church News," *Christian Advocate* 79, no. 8 (1904): 308, accessed November 15, 2017, http://catalog.hathitrust.org/Record?012370636.

821 "Missionary Letters–Extracts," *Woman's Missionary Friend* (Boston: Pauline J. Walden, November 1903), 417, accessed December 10, 2011, http://babel. hathitrust.org/cgi/pt?id+mdp.39015039671238:view=1up:seq+247.

822 "Annual Branch Meeting," *Woman's Missionary Friend* (Boston: Woman's Missionary Society of the Methodist Episcopal Church, February 1904), 72–73, accessed July 19, 2011, http://books.google.com/ books?id=uX4zAQAAMAAJ&printsec=frontcover&source=gbs_ge_summary_ r&cad=0#v=onepage&q&f=false.

823 "Missionary Letters–Extracts," 417.

824 "Extracts from Missionary Letters," *Woman's Missionary Friend*, (Boston: Woman's Foreign Missionary Society of the Methodist Episcopal Church, February 1904), 74, accessed July 19, 2011, http://books.google.com/ books?id=uX4zAQAAMAAJ&printsec=frontcover&source=gbs_ge_summary_ r&cad=0#v=onepage&q&f=false.

825 "Extracts from Missionary Letters," 74.

826 "Extracts from Missionary Letters," 74.

827 "Africa," *Thirty–Fourth Annual Report of the Woman's Foreign Missionary of the Methodist Episcopal Church,* (Boston: P. J. Walden, 1902–1903), 177, accessed January 8, 2012, http:// books.google.com/books?id=wRMQAAAAIAAJ&pg=PA191&lpg=PA191&dq.

828 "Extracts from Missionary Letters," *Woman's Missionary Friend* (Boston: Woman's Foreign Missionary Society of the Methodist Episcopal Church, August 1904), 302, accessed July 19, 2011, http://books/google.com/ books?id=uX4zAQAAMAAJ&printsec=frontcover&source=gbs_ge_summary_ r&cad=0#v=onepage&q&f=false.

829 "Extracts from Missionary Letters." February 1904, 74.

830 "Extracts from Missionary Letters," *Woman's Missionary Friend* (Boston: Woman's Foreign Missionary Society of the Methodist Episcopal Church, November 1904), 416.

831 Joseph Crane Hartzell, "Naming of Children," *Official Journal, West Central Africa Mission Conference, December 21–26, 1910,* (Bedford, England: Wawrick & Rush, 1910), 72. Missions Collection, Yokomo Yamada Library Archives, Africa University, Mutare, Zimbabwe, Africa.

832 Jacobs, "Give a Thought to Africa: Black Women Missionaries in South Africa," 110–111.

833 "Foreign Items," *Woman's Missionary Friend* (Boston: Woman's Foreign Missionary Society of the Methodist Episcopal Church, October 1905), 328, accessed July 19, 2011, http://books.google.com/ books?id=uX4zAQAAMAAJ&printsec=frontcover&source=gbs_ge_summary_ r&cad=0#v=onepage&q&f=false.

834 Collins to Bender, n. d.

835 Hartzell, "Naming of Children," 72.

Chapter 14

836 Town Lot Deed Record, No. 30, filed December 12, 1905, Recorder's Office, Fayette County, West Union, IA.

837 "Woman's Work," *Northwestern Christian Advocate* 53, no. 37 (September 13, 1905): 29, accessed October 21, 2011, http://babel.hathitrust.org/cgl/pt?id=mdp.39015084595456.

838 "Thank Offerings," *Woman's Missionary Friend* (Boston: Woman's Foreign Missionary Society of the Methodist Episcopal Church, May 1905), 188, accessed July 19, 2011, http://books.google.com/books?id=uZ4zAQAAMAAJ&printsec=frontcover&source=gbs_ge_summary_r&cad=0#v=onepage&q&f=false.

839 "Thank Offerings," 188.

840 "California Conference," 188.

841 "California Conference," 188.

842 "Angola District," *Minutes of the West Central Africa Mission Conference, Quiongoa, Angola, Africa, October 12–17, 1905*, (n.p.: Methodist Mission Press, 1905), 30–31. Missions Collection, Yokomo Yamada Library Archives, Africa University, Mutare, Zimbabwe, Africa.

843 Mary Johnson, "Greetings from the Corresponding Secretary," *Woman's Missionary Friend* (Boston: Woman's Foreign Missionary Society of the Methodist Episcopal Church, February 1906), 73, 75, accessed November 29, 2011, http://books.google.com/books?id=1n1zAQAAMAAJ&printsec=front cover&dq=Woman's+missionary+friend+1906&hl=en&sa=X&ei=q.

844 "Extracts from Foreign Letters," *Woman's Missionary Friend* (Boston: Woman's Foreign Missionary Society of the Methodist Episcopal Church, August 1906), 294, accessed November 29, 2011, http://books.google.com/books?id=1nIzAQAAMAAJ&printsec=frontcover&dq+Woman's+missionary+friend+1906&hl=en&sa=X&ei=q.

845 Lily Hardy Hammond, *In the Vanguard of a Race*. (New York: Council of Women for Home Missions and Missionary Education for the US and Canada, 1922), 131–135, accessed June 19, 2015, https://books.google.com/books/about/in_the_Vanguard_of_a_Race.html?id.

846 Brenda Wilkinson, "Martha Drummer: A Woman of Courage. (New York: GBGM News Archives, 2000), 2, accessed January 20, 2009, http://gbgm-umc.org/mission/news2000/gbgm21000bwbm.html/.

847 Hartzell, "Glimpses of our African Mission Field," 119.

848 Hartzell, "Glimpses of our African Mission Field," 119.

849 Hartzell, "Glimpses of our African Mission Field," 119.

850 Hartzell, "Glimpses of our African Mission Field," 119.

851 Dodge, "Angola Methodists Celebrate a Hundred Years," 20.

852 "Quessua, Africa," *Woman's Missionary Friend* (Boston: Woman's Foreign Missionary Society of the Methodist Episcopal Church, June 1906), 213, accessed November 29, 2011, http://books.google.come/books?id=1nIzAQ AAMAAJA&printcover&dq=Woman's+missionsary+friend,=1906&hl=en& sa=X&ei=q.

853 "Foreign Fields," *Woman's Missionary Friend* (Boston: Woman's Foreign Missionary Society of the Methodist Episcopal Church, May 1906), 188, accessed November 29, 2011, http://books.google.com/books?id=1nIzAQAAM AAJ&printsec=frontcover&dq=Woman's+missionary+friend,+1906&hl=en& sa=X&ei=q.

854 Kimberly Dejoie Hill, "Careers Across Color Lines: American Women Missionaries and Race Relations, 1870–1920" (PhD diss., University of North Carolina at Chapel Hill, 2008), 24, accessed November 28, 2014, http://cdr.lib.unc.edu/indexablecontent?id=uuid:54415 04f-b78e-4ebd-87b8-8f9f9790458c&ds=DATAFILE.

855 "Extracts from Missionary Letters," *Woman's Missionary Friend* (Boston: Woman's Foreign Missionary Society of the Methodist Episcopal Church, November 1910), 411, accessed December 6, 2011, http://books.google.com/ booksid=TafNAAAAMAAJ&printsec=frontcover&source=gbs_ge_summary_ r&cad=0#v=onepage&q&f=false.

856 "From the Foreign Field," *Woman's Missionary Friend* (Boston: Woman's Foreign Missionary Society of the Methodist Episcopal Church, August 1908), 291, accessed August 1, 2011, http://books.google. com/books?id+E6bNAAAAMAAJ&pg=PA418-IA&lpg=PA418- IA6&ots=NOpqYjinU4_&dq=woman%27=missionary+friend+1907.

857 Hartzell, "Glimpses of Our African Mission Field." 118.

858 "Extracts from Missionary Letters," *Woman's Missionary Friend* (Boston: Woman's Foreign Missionary Society of the Methodist Episcopal Church, August 1907), 294–295, accessed November 30, 2011, http://books. google.com/books?id=E6bNAAAAMAAJ&pg=PA418-IA5&lpg=PA418- JA6&ots=NOpqYjnU4_&dq=woman%27s+missionary+friend,+1907.

859 "From the Foreign Field," *Woman's Missionary Friend* (Boston, Woman's Foreign Missionary Society of the Methodist Episcopal Church, November 1907), 413, accessed November 30, 2011, http://books. google.com/books?id=E6bNAAAAMAAJ&pg=PA418-IA5&lpg=PA418- JA6&ots=ooNOpqYjnU4_&dq=woman%27s+missionary+friend,+1907.

860 Mrs. J. M. Springer, "Quessua in Angola," *Woman's Missionary Friend* (Boston: Woman's Foreign Missionary Society of the Methodist Episcopal Church, May 1908),153–154, accessed December 2, 2011, http://books.

google.com/books?id+E6bNAAAAMAAJ%pg=PA418-IA5&ipg=PA418-JA6&ots+NOpqYjnU4 &dq=woman%27s+missionary+friend,+1908.

861 Mrs. Springer, "Quessua in Angola," 153–154.

862 Mrs. Springer, "Quessua in Angola," 153–154.

863 "Woman's Work," *Minutes of the West Central Africa Mission Conference, Loanda, Angola, Africa, February 8–13, 1908* (London, England: A. Smith & Co., Printers, 1908), 18–19. Missionary Collection, Yokomo Yamada Library Archives, Africa University, Mutare, Zimbabwe, Africa.

864 William P. Dodson, "Report of Stations," *Minutes of the West Central Africa Mission Conference, Loanda, Angola, Africa, February 8–13, 1908* (London, England: A. Smith & Co., Printers, 1908), 31, Missions Collection, Yokomo Yamada Library Archives, Africa University, Mutare, Zimbabwe, Africa.

865 Susan Collins to John and Helen Springer, 5 June 1908, File 1000-1-6:4, General Commission on Archives and History of the United Methodist Church, Madison, NJ, accessed February 21, 2018, gcah@gcad.org.

866 Martha Drummer to John and Helen Springer, 2 June 1908, File 1001-1-7:2, General Commission on Archives and History of the United Methodist Church, Madison, NJ, accessed February 21, 2018, gcah@gcad.org.

867 Martha Drummer to Helen Springer, 29 September 1908, File 1001-1-7:8, General Commission on Archives and History of the United Methodist Church, Madison, NJ, accessed February 21, 2018, gcah@gcad.org.

868 Collins to Bender, n. d.

869 Fisher, *Under the Crescent*, 108.

870 Mrs. S. F. Johnson, "Africa," *Thirty–Ninth Annual Report of the Woman's Foreign Missionary Society of the Methodist Episcopal Church* (New York: Woman's Foreign Missionary Society, 1908), 182–183, accessed September 7, 2017, http://archive.org/details/thirtyninthannua01wom.

871 Martha Drummer, "Traveling to the Villages," *Woman's Missionary Friend* (Boston Woman's Foreign Missionary Society of the Methodist Episcopal Church, May 1908), 172–173, accessed December 2, 2011, http://books.google.com/books?id=E6bNAAAAMAAJ&pg=PA418-IA5&lpg=PA418-JA6&ots=ooNOpqYjnU4 &dq=woman%27s+missionary+friend,+1907.

872 Christie R. House, "Martha Drummer: Missionary to Angola," *Newworldoutlook.org*, 2, assessed April 18, 2012, http://gbgm-umc.org/global_news/full_article.cfm?Articleid=6186.

873 "From the Foreign Field," *Woman's Missionary Friend* (Boston: Woman's Foreign Missionary Society of the Methodist Episcopal Church, November 1908), 417, accessed December 2, 2011, http://books.google.com/books?id+E6bNAAAAMAAJ%pg=PA418-IA5&ipg=PA418-JA6&ots+NOpqYjnU4 &dq=woman%27s+missionary+friend,+1908.

[874] "African Superstitions," accessed February 28, 2018, www.superstitionsof.com/african-superstitions.htm.

[875] Florinda Bessa, "Kindergarten and Auxiliary in Loanda," *Woman's Missionary Friend* (Boston, Woman's Foreign Missionary Society of the Methodist Episcopal Church, October 1911), 359, accessed December 5, 2011, https://babel.hathitrust.org/cig/pt?id=mdp.39015021233765;view=1up;seq=423.

[876] Robert Hamill Nassau, *Fetishism in West Africa–Forty Years! Observation of Native Customs and Superstitions*, (New York: Charles Scribner's Sons, 1904), 223–224; 231–232, accessed March 30,2018, www.sacred-texts.com/afr/fiwa/fiwao6.htm.

[877] Mrs. J. C. Wengatz, "Report of Quiongua Girls' School," *West Central Africa Mission Conference, Quessua, Angola, Africa, March 22–26, 1915* (n.p.: n.p., 1915), 23, accessed November 25, 2011, http://images,library.yale.edu/divinity/content/dayrep/Methodist%20Church%20Angola%20Mission%20Conference%20201915.pdf.

[878] Herbert C. Withey, "Malanje District," *West Central Africa Mission Conference, Quessua, Angola, Africa, March 22–26, 1915* (n.p.: n.p., 1915), 26, accessed November 25, 2011, http://images,library.yale.edu/divinity/content/dayrep/Methodist%20Church%20Angola%20Mission%20Conference%20201915.pdf.

[879] Withey, "Malanje District, 26.

[880] Martha Drummer, "Africa News," *Woman's Missionary Friend* (Boston: Woman's Foreign Missionary Society of the Methodist Episcopal Church, May 1908), 173, accessed December 2, 2011, http://books.google.com/books?id=E6bNAAAAMAAJ&pg=PA418-IA5&lpg=PA418-JA6&ots=ooNOpqYjnU4 &dq=woman%27s+missionary+friend,+1907.

[881] "From Our Missionaries," *Woman's Missionary Friend*, (Boston: Woman's Foreign Missionary Society of the Methodist Episcopal Church, November 1911), 404, accessed August 10, 2011, http://babel.hathitrust.org/cgi/pt?id=mdp.39015021233765;view=1up;seq=535.

[882] "From Our Missionaries," *Woman's Missionary Friend* (Boston: Woman's Foreign Missionary Society of the Methodist Episcopal Church, May 1911), 187, accessed August 10, 2011, http://babel.hatitrust.org/cgi/pt?id=mdp.39015021233765;view=1up;seq=525.

[883] Cilicia Cross, "The Lady Builder, Woman's Foreign Missionary Society Work at Quessua," *South Africa Missionary Advocate* 1, no. 6 (September-December 1922): 7, 10, accessed May 3, 2018, http://AD1715-15-8-12-001-jpeg.pdf.

[884] Susan Collins, "Report of Miss Susan Collins of Woman's Foreign Missionary Society," *Minutes of the West Central Africa Mission Conference, July 7–11, 1909, Quessua Mission Station, Malange, Angola, Africa* (London, England: A. Smith

& Co., n.d.), 44–46. Missions Collection, Yokomo Yamada Library Archives, Africa University, Mutare, Zimbabwe, Africa.

885 J. Springer, *The Heart of Central Africa*, 207.

886 'From the Foreign Field," *Woman's Missionary Friend* (Boston: Woman's Foreign Missionary Society of the Methodist Episcopal Church, May 1909), 189, accessed December 4, 2011, http://books.google.com/books?id=TafNAA AAMAA&pg=PP8&lpg=PP8&dq=Woman's+Missionary+Friend,+1908-1909.

887 Theodore Roosevelt, "The Expansion of the White Races," January 18, 1909, 6, Washington, D. C., accessed February 5, 2018, www.english.illinois.edu/maps/ poets/a-flespada/roosevelt.htm.

888 "From the Foreign Field," May 1909, 189.

889 Martha Drummer to John and Helen Springer, August 1909, File 1001-1-7:8, General Commission and History of the United Methodist Church, Madison, NJ, accessed February 21, 2018, gcah@gcad.org.

890 "From our Missionaries," *Woman's Missionary Friend* (Boston: Woman's Foreign Missionary Society of the United Methodist Church, (May 1910) 180, accessed February 21, 2018, gcah@gcad.org.

891 "From Our Missionaries," 180.

892 Susan Collins, "Report of Miss Collins, Quessua," *Official Journal of the West Central Africa Mission Conference, December 21–26, 1910, Loanda, Angola, Africa* (Bedford, England: Rush and Warwick, 1910), 35–36. Missions Collection, Yokomo Yamada Library Archives, Africa University, Mutare, Zimbabwe, Africa.

893 Susan Collins, "News from the Field," *Woman's Missionary Friend* (Boston: Woman's Foreign Missionary Society of the Methodist Episcopal Church, April 1910), 137, accessed December 6, 2011, http://books.google.com/ booksid=TafNAAAAMAA&printsec=frontcover&source+gbs_ge_summary_ r&cad=0#v=onepage&q&f=false.

894 "From our Missionaries," *Woman's Missionary Friend* (Boston: Woman's Foreign Missionary Society of the Methodist Church, April 1910), 180, accessed December 6, 2011, http://books.google.com/ booksid=TafNAAAAMAA&printsec=frontcover&source+gbs_ge_summary_ r&cad=0#v=onepage&q&f=false.

895 "From Our Missionaries," *Woman's Missionary Friend* (Boston: Woman's Foreign Missionary Society of the Methodist Episcopal Church, August 1910), 297, accessed December 6, 2011, http://books.google.com/ booksid=TafNAAAAMAA&printsec=frontcover&source+gbs_ge_summary_ r&cad=0#v=onepage&q&f=false.

896 "Extracts from Missionary Letters," *Woman's Missionary Friend* (Boston: Woman's Foreign Missionary Society of the Methodist Episcopal Church, November 1910), 411, http://books.google.com/

booksid=TafNAAAAMAA&printsec=frontcover&source+gbs_ge_summary_r&cad=0#v=onepage&q&f=false.

897 A Brief History of Halley's Comet," extracts from *A Comet Called Halley*, accessed April 2, 2018, www.ianridpath.com/halley/halley7.htm.

898 Robert Shields, "Angola District, Report of District Superintendent," *Official Journal of the West Central Africa Mission Conference, December 21–26, 1910, Loanda, Angola, Africa* (Bedford, England: Rush and Warwick, 1910), 12. Missions Collection, Yokomo Yamada Library Archives, Africa University, Mutare, Zimbabwe, Africa.

899 Collins, "Report of Miss Collins, Quessua," 35–36.

900 Martha Drummer, "Report of Miss Drummer, Quessua," *Official Journal of the West Central Africa Mission Conference, December 21–26, 1910, Loanda, Angola, Africa,* (Bedford, England: Rush & Warwick, 1910), 36. Missions Collection, Yokomo Yamada Library Archives, Africa University, Mutare, Zimbabwe, Africa.

901 Herbert C. Withey, "Sixth Day Conference Summary," *Official Journal of the West Central Africa Mission Conference, December 21–26, 1910, Loanda, Angola, Africa*, (Bedford, England: Rush & Warwick, 1910), 66–67. Missions Collection, Yokomo Yamada Library Archives, Africa University, Mutare, Zimbabwe, Africa.

902 Joseph C. Hartzell, "Bishop's Remarks," *Official Journal of the West Central Africa Mission Conference, December 21–26, 1910, Loanda, Angola, Africa*, (Bedford, England: Rush & Warwick, 1910), 71–72. Missions Collection, Yokomo Yamada Library Archives, Africa University, Mutare, Zimbabwe, Africa.

903 Susan Collins, "A King at Conference," *Woman's Missionary Friend* (Boston, Woman's Foreign Missionary of the Methodist Episcopal Church, October 1911), 361, accessed December 7, 2011, http://books.google.com/booksid=TafNAAAAMAA&printsec=frontcover&source+gbs_ge_summary_r&cad=0#v=onepage&q&f=false.

904 Collins, "A King at Conference, 361.

905 Susan Collins, "West Central Africa," *Woman's Missionary Friend* (Boston, Woman's Foreign Missionary Society of the Methodist Episcopal Church, July 1911), 245, accessed December 7, 2011, http://books.google.com/booksid=TafNAAAAMAA&printsec=frontcover&source+gbs_ge_summary_r&cad=0#v=onepage&q&f=false.

906 "Extracts from Missionary Letters," *Woman's Missionary Friend* (November 1910), 411.

907 "Extracts from Missionary Letters," *Woman's Missionary* Friend (November 1910), 411.

Chapter 15

[908] "From Our Missionaries," *Woman's Missionary Friend* (Boston, Woman's Foreign Missionary Society of the Methodist Episcopal Church, May 1911), 187, accessed December 6, 2011, http://books.google.com/booksid=TafNAAAAMAA&printsec=frontcover&source+gbs_ge_summary_r&cad=0#v=onepage&q&f=false.

[909] "From Our Missionaries," 187.

[910] "From Our Missionaries," 187.

[911] "Susan B. Collins Completes Twenty-fourth Year as African Missionary," *Fayette Reporter*, June 1, 1911, 8. Middle initial should be "A".

[912] "Africa," *Forty–Second Annual Report of the Woman's Foreign Missionary Society of the Methodist Episcopal Church* (Boston: Woman's Foreign Missionary Society, 1911), 212, accessed December 10, 2011, http://www.babel.hathitrust.org

[913] Martha Drummer, "Comments at 1911 Executive Meeting," *Woman's Missionary Friend* (Boston: Woman's Foreign Missionary Society of the Methodist Episcopal Church, December 1911), 426, accessed December 6, 2011, http://books.google.com/booksid=TafNAAAAMAA&printsec=frontcover&source+gbs_ge_summary_r&cad=0#v=onepage&q&f=false.

[914] "From Our Missionaries," *Woman's Missionary Friend* (Boston: Woman's Foreign Missionary Society of the Methodist Episcopal Church, November 1911), 404, http://books.google.com/booksid=TafNAAAAMAA&printsec=frontcover&source+gbs_ge_summary_r&cad=0#v=onepage&q&f=false.

[915] Martha Drummer, "Report of Miss Drummer, Quessua," *Minutes of the West Central Africa Mission Conference of the Methodist Episcopal Church, Quessua, Angola, Africa, April 27–May 1, 1911*, (Bedford, England: Rush & Warwick, 1911), 28, Missions Collection, Yokomo Yamada Library Archives, Africa University, Mutare, Zimbabwe, Africa.

[916] Drummer, "Report of Miss Drummer, Quessua, 29.

[917] Susan Collins, "Report of Miss Collins, Quessua," *Minutes of the West Central Africa Mission Conference of the Methodist Episcopal Church, Quessua, Angola, Africa, April 27–May 1, 1911*, (Bedford, England: Rush & Warwick, 1911), 29, Missions Collection, Yokomo Yamada Library Archives, Africa University, Mutare, Zimbabwe, Africa.

[918] Robert Shields, "Work in Angola," *Minutes of the West Central Africa Mission Conference of the Methodist Episcopal Church, Quessua, Angola, Africa, April 27–May 1, 1911*, (Bedford, England: Rush & Warwick, 1911), 3, Missions Collection, Yokomo Yamada Library Archives, Africa University, Mutare, Zimbabwe, Africa.

[919] "Lima News," *Fayette Reporter*, July 4, 1911, 1.

[920] Jeremy Ball, *The History of Angola*, (November 2017): Abstract, accessed March 28, 2018, DOI: 10.1093/acreforce/9780190277734.013.180.

921 "From Our Missionaries," *Woman's Missionary Friend* (Boston: Woman's Foreign Missionary Society of the Methodist Episcopal Church, February 1912), 72, accessed December 10, 2011, http://babel.hathitrust.org/cgi/pt?mdp.39015021233755.view=1up:seq=641.

922 "From Our Missionaries," 72.

923 "The Retirement Fund," *Woman's Missionary Friend* (Boston, Woman's Foreign Missionary Society of the Methodist Episcopal Church, March 1912), 91–92, accessed December 10, 2011, http://babel.hathitrust.org/cgi/pt?id=mdp.39015021233765;view=1up;seq=641.

924 "The Retirement Fund," 91–92.

925 "Age Limit for Missionaries," *Woman's Missionary Friend* (Boston, Woman's Foreign Missionary Society of the Methodist Episcopal Church, November 1916), 392, accessed December 18, 2011, http://babel.hathitrust.org/cgi/pt?id=mdp.39015021233955;view=1up;seq=988.

926 "Age Limit for Missionaries," 392.

927 "By-laws," *Year Book Woman's Foreign Missionary Society of the Methodist Episcopal Church, Fiftieth Annual Report of the Society* (Boston: Woman's Foreign Missionary Society of the Methodist Episcopal Church, 1919), 216–217, accessed December 18, 2011, http://archive.org/.../yearbookwomansfo01woma/yearbookwomansfo01woma_djvu.t.

928 "Our Missionaries," *Woman's Missionary Friend* (Boston: Woman's Foreign Missionary Society of the Methodist Episcopal Church, November 1913), 24, accessed December 12, 2011, http://books.google.com/books?id=XanNAAAAMAAJ&printsec=frontcover#v=onepage&q&f=false.

929 Martha Drummer, "Report of Miss Martha Drummer, *Official Journal of the West Central Africa Mission Conference August 26–31, 1913*, (no place: n. p., n.d.), 59–60. Missions Collection, Yokomo Yamada Library Archives, Africa University, Mutare, Zimbabwe, Africa.

930 Drummer, "Report of Miss Martha Drummer," 59.

931 Drummer, "Report of Miss Martha Drummer," 59.

932 Drummer, "Report of Miss Martha Drummer," 59.

933 "Students and Teachers Entertained," *Iowa State Bystander*, September 4, 1914, 1, www.chroniclingamerica.loc.gov/lcon/sn85049804/1916....

934 "Our Missionaries," November 1913, 24.

935 "Our Substitutes," *Woman's Missionary Friend* (Boston: Woman's Foreign Mission Society of the Methodist Episcopal Church, February 1914), 70–71, accessed December 13, 2011, http://books.google.com/books?id=XanNAAAAMAAJ&printsec=frontcover#v=onepage&q&f=false.

936 "Our Missionaries," *Woman's Missionary Friend* (Boston: Woman's Foreign Missionary Society of the Methodist Episcopal Church, August 1914), 291–292, accessed December 13, 2011, http://books.google.com/books?id=XanNAAAAMAAJ&printsec=frontcover#v=onepage&q&f=false

[937] "Our Missionaries," August 1914, 291–292.

[938] "Our Missionaries," *Woman's Missionary Friend* (Boston: Woman's Foreign Missionary Society of the Methodist Episcopal Church, November 1914), 416, accessed December 12, 2011, http://books.google.com/books?id=XanNAAAAMAAJ&printsec=frontcover#v=onepage&q&f=false.

[939] "From Our Missionaries," *Woman's Missionary Friend* (Boston: Woman's Foreign Missionary Society of the Methodist Episcopal Church, May 1915), 178, accessed December 15, 2011, http://babel.hathitrust.org/cgi/pt?id=mdp.39015021233955;view=1up;seq=476.

[940] "From Our Missionaries," 178.

[941] Mrs. Skinner, Minutes of Woman's Foreign Missionary Society, October 2, 1914, First United Methodist Church Archives, Fayette, IA.

[942] John Iliffe, "Rural Poverty in Colonial Africa," *The African Poor: A History* (New York: Press Syndicate of the University of Cambridge, 1987), 155.

[943] Jill R. Dias, "Famine and Disease in the History of Angola c. 1830–1930," *Journal of African History*, (July 1981): 22–23, accessed May 23, 2017, https://www.cambridge.org/.../journals/journal-of-African-history/.../famine-and-disease.

[944] J. C. Wengatz, "Report of Quiongua Station," *Official Journal of the West Central Africa Mission Conference, March 22–26, 1915* (n.p.: n. p., 1915), 16, Missions Collection, Yokomo Yamada Library Archives, Africa University, Mutare, Zimbabwe, Africa.

[945] Wengatz, "Report of Quiongua Station," 7.

[946] Wengatz, "Report of Quiongua Station," 5.

[947] Wengatz, "Report of Quiongua Station," 5.

[948] Mr. and Mrs. Ray E. Kipp, "Interrupted by Fire and Rain," *Official Journal of the West Central Africa Mission Conference August 26–31, 1913* (n.p.: n. p., n. d.), 54–55. Missions Collection, Yokomo Yamada Library Archives, Africa University, Mutare, Zimbabwe, Africa.

[949] "From Our Missionaries," *Woman's Missionary Friend* (Boston: Woman's Foreign Missionary Society of the Methodist Episcopal Church, November 1915), 408, accessed December 15, 2011, http://babel.hathitrust.org/cgi/pt?id=mdp.39015021233955;view=1up;seq=476.

[950] Herbert C. Withey, "Daily Proceedings, First Day, Monday, March 22, 1915," *Official Journal of the West Central Africa Mission Conference, March 22–26, 1915* (n.p.: n. p., 1915), 61, Missions Collection, Yokomo Yamada Library Archives, Africa University, Mutare, Zimbabwe, Africa University.

[951] "From Our Missionaries," November 1915, 408.

[952] Hanson, *The Ivory Necklace*, 134.

[953] Ray Kipp, "Report of Quessua Station," *Official Journal of the West Central Africa Mission Conference, March 22–26, 1915*, (n.p.: n. p., n. d.), 36, Missions Collection, Yokomo Yamada Library Archives, Africa University, Mutare, Zimbabwe: Africa.

954 Herbert C. Withey, "Malanje District," 26.

955 "From the Foreign Field," *Woman's Missionary Friend* (Boston: Woman's Foreign Missionary Society of the Methodist Episcopal Church, March 1916), 105, accessed December 16, 2011, http://babel.hathitrust.org/cgi/pt?id=mdp.39015021233955;view=1up;seq=653.

956 Susan Collins, "Mulatto Girls in Africa," *Woman's Missionary Friend* (Boston, Woman's Foreign Missionary Society of the Methodist Episcopal Church, August 1915), 282, accessed December 15, 2011, http://babel.hathitrust.org/cgi/pt?id=mdp.39015021233955;view=1up;seq=476.

957 Collins, "Mulatto Girls in Africa," 282.

958 Collins, "Mulatto Girls in Africa," 282.

959 "From Our Missionaries," November 1915, 408.

960 James L. Barton, "The Effect of War on Protestant Missions," *Harvard Theological Review* 12, no. 1 (January 1919): 5, accessed December 15, 2017, www.jstor.org/stable/1507910.

961 Christian Koller, "Colonial Military Participation in Europe (Africa)," in *International Encyclopedia of the First World War*, s. v., eds. Daniel Ute, Peter Gatrell, Oliver Janz, Heather Jones, Jennifer Keene, Alan Kramer, and Bill Nasson, (issued by Freie Universitat Berlin, Berlin 2014-10-08), 2, 6–7, accessed May 20, 2018, https://encyclopedia.1914-1918 online.net/..../colonial military participation in euro. DOI: 10.15463/ie1418.10193.

962 Koller, "Colonial Military Participation," 6–7.

963 "From the Foreign Field," March 1916, 105.

964 "Fayette News," *Oelwein Daily Register*, August 12, 1915, 4.

965 "Fayette News," *Oelwein Daily Register*, September 30, 1915, 6.

Chapter 16

966 "From the Foreign Field, Quessua, Africa," *Woman's Missionary Friend*, (Boston, Woman's Foreign Missionary Society of the Methodist Episcopal Church, January 1916), 105, accessed December 16, 2011, http://babel.hathitrust.org/cgi/pt?id=mdp.39015021233955;view=1up;seq=653.

967 Sharon Avery, Email message to author, November 22, 2016.

968 Iva Joiner McClain, "Public Education of the Negro in the United States," (Master's Thesis, University of Iowa, 1917), title page. *Schedule of Dissertations of Approved Candidates for Advanced Degrees with Major and Minor Subjects, University of Iowa Studies, First Series*, 1, no.8 (April 1920): n.p. Iowa City: University of Iowa, accessed December 18, 2016, https://books.google.com/books?id=D30yAQAAMAAJ.

969 "Alumni Notes" *Daily Iowan*, January 19, 1925, 7, accessed December 10, 2016, http://www.dailyiowan.lib.uiowa.edu/DI/1925/di1925-o1-18.pdf.

970 "Alumni Notes," 7.

971 Fisher, *Under the Crescent*, 108.

972 "In Lands Afar-Africa," *Jubilee Number Forty–Ninth Annual Report of the Woman's Foreign Missionary of the Methodist Episcopal Church* (Boston, Woman's Foreign Missionary Society of the Methodist Episcopal Church, 1918), 141–142, accessed January 5, 2012, http://archive.org/stream/followinggreatco01woma#page/138/mode/2up.

973 In Lands Afar-Africa," 141–142.

974 Collins to Bender, n.d.

975 Collins to Bender, n.d.

976 Hanson, *The Ivory Necklace*, 57.

977 " Mrs. Robert Shields, "Report of Loanda Schools," *West Central Africa Conference Report of the Methodist Episcopal Church, Loanda, Angola, Africa, February 7–11, 1907* (n.p.: n. p., n. d.), 57–58, Missions Collection, Yokomo Yamada Library Archives, Africa University, Mutare, Zimbabwe.

978 Mrs. Shields, "Report of Loanda Schools," 57–58.

979 Hanson, *The Ivory Necklace*, 227-233.

980 Fisher, *Under the Crescent*. 108.

981 Fisher, *Under the Crescent*. 108.

982 Fisher, *Under the Crescent*. 108.

983 Geta D. Kirby, "Report of Geta D. Kirby," *Minutes of the West Central Africa Mission Conference of the Methodist Episcopal Church, Loanda, Angola, Africa, June 5–11, 1919* (Bristol, NH: Musgrove Printing House, n.d.) 55. Missions Collection, Yokomo Yamada Library Archives, Africa University, Mutare, Zimbabwe, Africa.

984 Kirby, "Report of Geta D. Kirby," 237.

985 "In Lands Afar-Africa," 138.

986 J. M. Springer, "Women," *Journal of the First Session of the Congo Mission Conference Methodist Episcopal Church, Kambove, Katanga, Belgian Congo, March 28–30, 1917* (n.p.: n. p., n.d.) 40. Missions Collection, Yokomo Yamada Library Archives, Africa University, Mutare, Zimbabwe, Africa University.

987 J. M. Springer, "Women," 40.

988 "A New Study of Africa," *Woman's Missionary Friend* (Boston: Woman's Foreign Missionary Society of the Methodist Episcopal Church, September 1917), 135, accessed December 17, 2011, https://guides.library.yale.edu/c.php?g=296016&p=1976394.

989 "In Lands Afar-Africa," 138.

990 William S. Morris, "Black Iowans in Defense of the Nation, 1863–*1991*," in *Outside In: African-American History in Iowa: 1838–2000*, eds. Bill Silag, Susan Koch-Bridgford and Hal Chase (Des Moines, IA: State Historical Society of Iowa, 2001), 106.

991 Morris, "Black Iowans in Defense," 107.

992 Bill Douglas, "Wartime Illusions and Disillusionment: Camp Dodge and Racial Stereotyping, 1917–1918," *Annals of Iowa* 57, no. 92 (Spring 1998): 119, accessed December 17, 2012, https://doi.org/10.17077/0003-427.10154.

993 Morris, "Black Iowans in Defense," 110–111.

994 "Quessua, Africa," *Woman's Missionary Friend* (Boston: Woman's Foreign Missionary Society of the Methodist Episcopal Church, June 1918), 221, accessed December 18, 20ll, https://guides.library.yale.edu/c.php?g=296016&p=1976394.

995 Mrs. Louise S. Shields, "A Prayer Meeting in Africa," *Woman's Missionary Friend* (Boston: Woman's Foreign Missionary Society of the Methodist Episcopal Church, August 1918), 431, accessed December 20, 2011, http://guides.library.yale.edu/c.php?g=29601&p=197694.

996 "Missionaries in Active Service," *Woman's Missionary Friend* (Boston: Foreign Missionary Society of the Methodist Episcopal Church, October 1919), 377–379, accessed December 20, 2011, http://babel.hathitrust.org/cgi/pt?id=mdp.39015039671744;view=lup;seq-403.

997 "Items, Pacific Branch," *Woman's Missionary Friend* (Boston: Woman's Foreign Missionary Society of the Methodist Episcopal Church, March 1919), 108, accessed December 20, 2011, http://babel.hathitrust.org/cgi/pt?id=mdp.39015039671744;view=lup;seq-403.

998 "Missionaries on Home Leave," *Woman's Missionary Friend* (Boston: Woman's Foreign Missionary Society of the Methodist Episcopal Church, July 1919), 266, accessed December 20, 2011, http://babel.hathitrust.org/cgi/pt?id=mdp.39015039671744;view=lup;seq-403.

999 "Foreign News," *Woman's Missionary Friend* (Boston: Woman's Foreign Missionary Society of the Methodist Episcopal Church, October 1919), 369–370.

1000 Clara V. Ault, "Report of Clara V. Ault," *Minutes of the West Central Africa Mission Conference of the Methodist Episcopal Church, Loanda, Angola, Africa, June 5–11, 1919*, (Bristol, NH: Musgrove Printers, 1919), 55–56, Missions Collection, Yokomo Yamada Library Archives, Africa University, Mutare, Zimbabwe, Africa.

1001 "The Pagan Land," *Woman's Missionary Friend* (Boston: Woman's Foreign Missionary Society of the Methodist Episcopal Church, June 1920), 200, accessed December 20, 2011, http://babel.hathitrust.org/cgi/pt?id=mdp.39015039671774;view=1up;seq=218.

1002 "Iowa City News," *Bystander*, November 23, 1917, 1, accessed November 29, 2016, https://www.newspapers.com/newspaper143682719/.

1003 "Iowa City News," 1.

1004 "Africa," *Jubilee Number, Forty-Ninth Annual Report of the Woman's Foreign Missionary Society of the Methodist Episcopal Church* (Boston: Woman's Foreign Missionary Society, 1919), 138–139, accessed December 15, 2011, http://archive.org/stream/annualreportofwo00meth#page/138/mode/2up.

1005 Cilicia Cross, "Report of Miss Cilicia Cross," *Minutes of the Angola Mission Conference of the Methodist Episcopal Church, Quessua, Angola, Africa, August 5–10, 1925 and Loanda, Angola, Africa, November 25–December 1,* 1926 (Cape Town, South Africa: Samuel Griffiths and Co., Ltd. Printers, n. d.), 55–56. Missions Collection,Yokomo Yamada Library Archives, Africa University, Old Mutare, Zimbabwe, Africa.

1006 Florinda Bessa to John D. Clinton, n.d. First United Methodist Church Archives, Fayette, IA:. Dr. Clinton did not meet Susan until 1925 when he became pastor at the Fayette Methodist Episcopal Church and served there for 15 years.

1007 Bessa to Clinton, n.d.

1008 John D. Clinton, "Fayette Picture Order to Africa," *Fayette County Leader,* September 9, 1937, 1.

1009 Hanson, *The Ivory Necklace,* 175.

1010 Hanson, *The Ivory Necklace,* 175.

1011 Susan Angeline Collins, *Passport Application.* (n.d.), assessed October 13, 2012, http://www.archives.gov/research/passport/index.html.

1012 Collins, *Passport Application,* n.d.

1013 "Aged Fayette Missionary Will Return from Africa," *Fayette County Leader,* July 29, 1920, 1.

1014 "New York Passenger Lists, 1820–1957," accessed November 15, 2009, http://www.Ancestry.com.

1015 Marilyn Ward, "Must the Christian Church Condemn All Use of Military Force?: The Methodist Episcopal Church and the Endorsement of World War II," *Methodist History* 35 no. 3 (April 1997): 162, www.archives.gcah.org/handle/10516/2946.

1016 "Aged Fayette Missionary Will Return from Africa," 1.

1017 "Neighborhood News Item," *Fayette County Leader,* August 19, 1920, 8.

1018 "By-laws," *Year Book Woman's Foreign Missionary Society of the Methodist Episcopal Church Fiftieth Annual Report of the Society* (Boston: Woman's Foreign Missionary Society of the Methodist Episcopal Church, 1919), 216–217, accessed January 11, 2012, https://archive.org/.../yearbookwomansfo01woma/yearbookwomansfo01woma_jkru.t.

1019 "Report of the Committee on By-laws," *Year Book Woman's Foreign Missionary Society of the Methodist Episcopal Church, Fifty-first Annual Report of the Society* (Boston: Woman's Foreign Missionary Society of the Methodist Episcopal Church, 1920), 131, accessed January 12, 2012, http://archive.org/stream/yearbookwomo01woma#page/130/mode/2up.

1020 Edward Samuel Evenden, *Teacher Salaries and Salary Schedules in the United States, 1918–1919,* (Washington, DC: National Education Association, 1919), accessed April 9, 2012, http://www.archive.org/stream/teacherssalaries00even/teacherssalaries00even_djvu.txt.

1021 "By-laws," 217.
1022 "By-laws," 221.
1023 "By-laws," 221.
1024 "Susan Angelina Collins," Upper Iowa University Archived Webpage, 19th century, *Collins, Susan Angelina-p2*. Her middle name is "Angeline."
1025 Gilder Lehrman Institute of American History, "Statistics: The American Economy During the 1920's," 1–3, accessed April 16, 2018, http://www.gilderlehrman.org/content/statistics-american-economc-during-1920's.

Chapter 17

1026 Margaret Paine, *My Ninety-five Milestones*, 104.
1027 Abstract of Title Number 32689, (1905), Fayette County Abstract Company, West Union, IA: 10.
1028 "Fording to Conference in Angola," *South Africa Missionary Advocate* 1, no.6 (Sept.–Dec. 1922): 8.
1029 Paine, *My Ninety-five Milestones*, 104.
1030 Paine, *My Ninety-five* Milestones, 105.
1031 "Neighborhood News Items," *Fayette County Leader*," September 30, 1920, 8.
1032 Roger Bowen to Dorothy Woodruff, 28 March 1960. Mission Biographical Reference Files, 1880's–1969, Susan Collins 1468-3-1:22, General Commission on Archives and History of the United Methodist Church, Madison, NJ.
1033 Derek Thompson, "America in 1915: Long Hours, Crowded Houses, Death by Trolley," *Atlantic*, February 11, 2016, 4, accessed April 16, 2018, http://www.theatlantic.combusiness/archives/2018/America-in-1915/4625601/
1034 Anne Sellers, Email message to author, November 19, 2010.
1035 "Telephone Co. Report," *Fayette County Leader*, December 3, 1914, 1.
1036 South Africa History Online, "The Oldest Forms of Human Communication," *Towards a People's History*, 1, www.sahistory.org.-za/article/oldest-forms-human...
1037 Christie Dennis, Email message to author, February 8, 2011.
1038 Merle Thompson Sternberg, Personal communication with author, August 21, 2011.
1039 Joe Rhode, Personal communication with author, July 23, 2013.
1040 Alma Aanes, Personal communication with author, August 21, 2011.
1041 Joe Rhode, Personal communication with author, August 21, 2011.
1042 Susan Cloud, Email message to author, July 7, 2020.
1043 Cloud, Email message to author, July 7, 2020.
1044 Dora L. Costa, "From Mill Town to Board Room: The Rise of Women's Paid Labor," *Journal of Economic Perspectives* 14, no. 4 (Fall 2000): 103, accessed November 10, 2017, www.jstor.org/stable/2647077.
1045 Costa, "From Mill Town to Board Room," 103.

[1046] Mrs. Frances S. Walker, Minutes of Woman's Foreign Missionary Society, October 1, 1920, First United Methodist Church Archives, Fayette, IA.

[1047] "W. F. M. S. Held Enjoyable Meeting," *Fayette Country Leader*, October 7, 1920, 1.

[1048] African Porcupine, accessed September 5, 2011, http://www.rollinghillswildlife. com/animals/p/porcupines/indexafrican.html.

[1049] "Fayette Area News," *Oelwein Register*, October 20, 1920, 5.

[1050] "Woman's Foreign Missionary Society General Executive Committee-Fifty-First Annual Meeting," *The Christian Advocate*, 46 (November 11, 1920): 1500, 1504, accessed May 20, 2018, http://books.google.com/books?id=KLo6AQAAMAAJ.

[1051] "Woman's Foreign Missionary Society," 1500, 1504.

[1052] "Woman's Foreign Missionary Society," 1504.

[1053] "Personals, " *Woman's Missionary Friend* (Boston: Woman's Foreign Missionary Society of the Methodist Episcopal Church, November 1920), 412, accessed December 20, 2011, http://babel.hathitrust.org/cgi/ pt?id=mdp.39015039671774;view=1up;seq=880.

[1054] "Missionaries on Home Leave," *Woman's Missionary Friend* (Boston: Woman's Foreign Missionary Society of the Methodist Episcopal Church, January 1921), 37, accessed December 20, 2011, http://babel.hathitrust.org/cgi/ pt?id=mdp.39015030140118.view=1upl.seq-549.

[1055] "On Home Leave," *Woman's Missionary Friend* (Boston: Woman's Foreign Missionary Society of the Methodist Episcopal Church, September 1921), 339, accessed December 22, 2011, http://babel.hathitrust.org/cgi/ pt?id=mdp.39015030140118;view=1up;seq=549.

[1056] "One Home Leave," *Woman's Missionary Friend* (Boston: Woman's Foreign Missionary Society of the Methodist Episcopal Church, September 1921), 37, accessed December 22, 2011, http://babel.hathitrust.org/cgi/ pt?id=mdp.39015030140118;view=1up;seq=549.

[1057] "Next Needs," *Woman's Missionary Friend* (Boston: Woman's Foreign Missionary Society of the Methodist Episcopal Church, March 1922), 104, accessed January 27, 2012, http://babel.hathitrust.org/cgi/ pt?id=mdp.39015030140118;view=1up;seq=624.

[1058] "Domestic Work," *Woman's Missionary Friend* (Boston: Woman's Foreign Missionary Society of the Methodist Episcopal Church, April 1922), 130, accessed January 27, 2012, http://babel.hathitrust.org/cgi/ pt?id=mdp.39015030140118;view=1up;seq=624.

[1059] "In Lands Afar," *Year Book Woman's Foreign Missionary Society of the Methodist Episcopal Church, Fifty-second Annual Report of the Society* (New York: Woman's Foreign Missionary Society of the Methodist Episcopal Church, 1921), 88, accessed January 25, 2012, http://archive.org/stream/ yearbookswomansfo1921woma#page88/mode/2up.

[1060] Martha Drummer, "Six Weeks of Terror," *Woman's Missionary Friend* (Boston: Woman's Foreign Missionary Society of the Methodist Episcopal Church, September 1921), 321–322, accessed January 25, 2012, http://babel.hathitrust.org/cgi/pt?view=image;id=mdp.39015030140118;size=125;page=ro.

[1061] Drummer, "Six Weeks of Terror," 321–322.

[1062] Drummer, "Six Weeks of Terror," 321–322.

[1063] Amy Leigh Paine to Dorothy Woodruff, 20 September 1961. Mission Biographical Reference Files, 1880's–1969, Susan Collins 1468-3-1:22. General Commission on Archives and History of the United Methodist Church, Madison, NJ.

[1064] Paine to Woodruff, 20 September 1961.

[1065] Paine to Woodruff, 20 September 1961.

[1066] Paine to Woodruff, 4 September 1961.

[1067] Paine to Woodruff, 4 September 1961.

[1068] Alice Billings, Minutes of Woman's Foreign Missionary Society, January 6, 1922, First United Methodist Church Archives, Fayette, IA.

[1069] When the gifts were made the country was Southern Rhodesia.

[1070] "Next Needs," *Woman's Missionary Friend*, (March 1922), 104.

[1071] "Lima News," *West Union Argo-Gazette*, October 25, 1922, 8.

[1072] *History of the First Methodist Church and the Women who Supported the Church*, 5.

[1073] Alice Billings, Minutes of the Woman's Foreign Missionary Society, October 6, 1922, First United Methodist Church Archives, Fayette, IA.

[1074] Billings, Minutes, October 6, 1922.

[1075] Mrs. Deming, Minutes of Woman's Foreign Missionary Society, December 1925, First United Methodist Church Archives, Fayette, IA.

[1076] Mrs. Deming, September 1926.

[1077] "A. B. C. of M. E. Church," *Fayette County Leader*, January 22, 1925, 1.

[1078] "Personals," *Fayette County Leader*, December 8, 1927, 7.

[1079] "Personals," *Fayette County Leader*, November 7, 1929, 8.

[1080] "Interesting News of our County Neighbors, Wadena," *Fayette County Union*, October 12, 1933, 3.

[1081] Fayette Chapters of Woman's Foreign Missionary Society treasurers' books 1925–1940 and Woman's Home Missionary Society treasurers' books 1926–1940.

[1082] Deed Record 52, June 9, 1923, Grantor & Grantee Books, Fayette County Recorder's Office, West Union, IA.

[1083] Susan Collins, Note to Training School, (n.d.), Susan Collins File, Folder 3, Curriculum and Accommodations, Box 1, Evanston, IL: The Training School Collection, Garrett Evangelical Theological Seminary, Styberg Library Archives.

[1084] "Local News," *Fayette County Leader*, November 14, 1929, 8.

[1085] Joe Lovino, "Methodist History: Controversary, Communion, & Welch's Grape Juice," 4, retrieved April 19, 2018, http://umc.org.

1086 Methodist Episcopal Church Bulletins, Fall 1935, First, United Methodist Church Archives, Fayette, IA.

1087 "Methodist Conference Acts to Desert the School," *Fayette County Leader*, March 15, 1928, 5.

1088 Jami L. Bryan, "Fighting for Respect: African-American Soldiers in WWI" (Fort Belvoir, VA: National Museum of United States Army, January 20, 2015), 8, accessed May 16, 2018, http://armyhistory.org.

1089 Robert V. Morris, "The Iowa Bystander," *Iowa Pathways*, 1–2, Iowa Public Television, accessed April 16, 2018, www.iptv.org/iowapathways/mypath/iowa-bystander.

1090 Bryan, "Fighting for Respect," 9.

1091 Scott Ellsworth, Tulsa Race Riot." *Encyclopedia of Oklahoma History and Culture*, 1. Accessed May 15, 2018, www.okhistory.org

1092 Ellsworth, Tulsa Race Riot, 1.

1093 Ellsworth, Tulsa Race Riot, 2–3.

1094 Richard Lord Acton and Patricia Nassif Acton, "A Legal History of African-Americans From the Iowa Territory to the State Sesquicentennial, 1838–1996," in *Outside In: African-American History of Iowa 1838–2000*, eds. Bill Silag, Susan Koch-Bridgford and Hal Chase (Des Moines: State Historical Society of Iowa, 2001), 84.

1095 Willis Goudy, "Selected Demographics, Iowa's African-American Residents, 1840–2000," in *Outside In: African-American History of Iowa 1838–2000*, eds. Bill Silag, Susan Koch-Bridgford and Hal Chase (Des Moines: State Historical Society of Iowa, 2001), 23.

1096 Jack Lufkin, "Higher Expectations for Ourselves, African-Americans in Iowa's Business World," in *Outside In: African-American History of Iowa 1838–2000*, eds. Bill Silag, Susan Koch-Bridgford and Hal Chase (Des Moines, State Historical Society of Iowa, 2001), 204.

1097 Personal communication with Sharon Avery, November 16, 2016.

1098 "Electa Grand Chapter Will Meet in Minneapolis," *Iowa State Bystander*, May 14, 1915, 1. *Chronicling America: Historic American Newspapers*, Library of Congress, accessed November 29, 2016, http://chroniclingamerica.loc.gov/lccn/sn83205186/1915-05-14/ed-1/seq-1/>.

1099 "Special Board Meeting to Be Held," *Bystander*, October 13, 1916, 1. *Chronicling America: Historic American Newspapers*, Library of Congress, accessed November 29, 2016, http://chroniclingamerica.loc.gov/lccn/sn85049804/1916-10-13/ed-1/seq-1>.

1100 Goudy, "Selected Demographics, Iowa's African-American Residents," 30.

1101 Goudy, "Selected Demographics, Iowa's African-American Residents," 33.

1102 Goudy, "Selected Demographics, Iowa's African-American Residents," 34.

[1103] "Appropriations," *Year Book Woman's Foreign Missionary Society of the Methodist Episcopal Church, Sixty-fourth Annual Report of the Society* (Boston: Woman's Foreign Missionary Society of the Methodist Episcopal Church, 1933), 62–63, accessed May 10, 2012, http://archive.org/stream/yearbookwomansfo1933woma#page/62/mode/2up.

Chapter 18

[1104] "Local News," *Fayette County Leader*, July 8, 1926, 8.

[1105] "Neighborhood News Item," *Fayette County Leader*, June 14, 1923, 8.

[1106] Cilicia Cross, "The Lady Builder," 7.

[1107] House, "Martha Drummer, Missionary to Angola," 1–2.

[1108] Edward A. Hatfield, "Segregation," *New Georgia Encyclopedia*, s.v, accessed December 26, 2018, https://m.georgiaencyclopedia.org/articles/historty-archaelogy;segregation.

[1109] Hatfield, "Segregation."

[1110] Hatfield, "Segregation."

[1111] Works Projects Administration 1930's Graves Registration Survey, Robert J. Harris, Adair County, Greenfield, IA Cemetery, accessed January 4, 2017, www.iowapagraves.org.

[1112] 1920 Iowa Census Place: *Greenfield, Adair, Iowa*, Roll: T625_476: Page: 5A; Enumeration District: 5: Image: 94.

[1113] "Alumni Notes," *Daily Iowan*, January 18, 1925, 7.

[1114] Missouri State Board of Health, Bureau of Vital Statistics, *Certificates of Death Nos. 34882 Robert Harris, 905 Iva J. McClain*, accessed November 30, 2016, https://www.sos.mo.gov/archives/resources/bdrecords.

[1115] "Alumni Notes," 7.

[1116] Marjorie M. Kizer (19 Sept. 1895–12 Dec. 1993) and Josephine S. Joiner (1874–1967), City of Des Moines Parks and Recreation, accessed November 30, 2016, http://www.dmgov.org/Departments/Parks/Pages/Cemeteries.aspx.

[1117] "Susan Collins, parents & siblings," complied by Barry Zbornik, 29, accessed October 21, 2017, www.iowaz.info/surname/collinssusan.htm.

[1118] *1930 United States Federal Census*, Fayette, Iowa, Roll: 654: Page 2A, accessed September 2, 2012, http://search.ancestry.com/cgi-bin/sse.dll?rank=1&new=1&MAV=0&...uidh=uyt&pcat=ROOT CATEGORY&h=2694424&db=1930usfedcen&indiv.

[1119] "Mrs. Nellie Crosswhite Died," *Oelwein Daily Register*, May 15, 1935, 4.

[1120] MS 409, *United States Works Progress Administration (Iowa), Special Reports and Narratives of Projects, 1935–1936*, n.d., Abstract, accessed May 12, 2018, www.findingaids.lib.iastate.edu.

[1121] "Entertain Older People," *Oelwein Daily Register*, September 26, 1934, 3.

[1122] "A Fire Alarm," *Fayette County Leader*, July 24, 1930, 8.

[1123] John D. Clinton, "We Have Our Negro Member: Meet Susan Collins," *Zion's Herald* (May 19, 1937) 625, First United Methodist Church Archives, Fayette, IA.

[1124] John D. Clinton, "Susan–A Fayette, Iowa Star," *Upper Iowa Press*, March 20, 1975, 6.

[1125] Amy Leigh Paine to Dorothy Woodruff, 4 September 1961. Mission Biographical Reference Files, 1880's-1969, Susan Collins, 1468-3-1:22, General Commission on Archives and History of the United Methodist Church, Madison, NJ.

[1126] Paine to Woodruff, 4 September 1961.

[1127] John D. Clinton, "Plan Colonial Rag Rug for Fireplace in Church Broad Room," *Fayette County Leader*, August 12, 1926, 1.

[1128] Clinton, "Plan Colonial Rag Rug," 1.

[1129] "Susan Collins, parents & siblings," complied by Barry Zbornik, 30, accessed October 21, 2017, www.iowaz.info/surname/collinssusan.htm.

[1130] Yearous, "Susan Collins," 18.

[1131] Paine to Woodruff, 4 September 1961.

[1132] Ajuan Mance, "Timeline: Black Firsts in Higher Education,"(November 5, 2009): 5–6. accessed November 5, 2009, http://www.blackoncampus.com.

[1133] Clinton, "Susan–A Fayette, Iowa Star."

[1134] John D. Clinton, *Servant of God* (Des Moines, IA: Wallace-Homestead Co., 1971) 98.

[1135] Clinton, "Susan–A Fayette, Iowa Star."

[1136] Clinton, *Servant of God*, 99.

[1137] "Mr. and Mrs. Gibbs," *Fayette County Leader*, July 3, 1930, 8.

[1138] "More or Less Personal," *Northwestern Christian Advocate*, 70, no. 7 (February 1, 1922): 162, accessed May 3, 2018, https://books.google.com/books?id=TcKYsum7asC.

[1139] Amy Tikkanen, "Blackwater fever," *Encyclopedia Britannica*, accessed May 5, 2018, https://www.britannica.com/sicence/blackwater-fever.

[1140] Cross, "The Lady Builder," 7.

[1141] Cross, "The Lady Builder, 7.

[1142] Cross, "The Lady Builder, 7, 10.

[1143] John D. Clinton, "Fayette Picture Order to Africa," *Fayette County Leader*, September 9, 1937, 1.

[1144] Clinton, "We Have Our Negro Member."

[1145] Alexander H Kemp, *Twenty years of Medical Missionary Work in Africa*, (n.p.: Privately Published, n.d.), 18, Interchurch Center Archives, New York, NY.

[1146] Hanson, *The Ivory Necklace*, 154.

[1147] Kemp, *"20 years of Medical Missionary Work in Africa,"* 10.

[1148] Dodge, "Angola Methodists Celebrate a Hundred Years," 20.

[1149] "To Visit Miss Collins," *Oelwein Daily Register*, June 23, 1937, 4.

[1150] "Gothic Gospel," *Fayette County Leader*, October 21, 1937, 5.

[1151] "Gothic Gospel," *Fayette County Leader*, July 8, 1937, 5.

[1152] Margaret Jayne Collett, Amy Leigh Paine and Edna Dorman Lee, *"100th Anniversary, First Methodist Church, Fayette, Iowa*, (n.p.: Fayette, IA, 1950), 19.

[1153] Allie Bass to Emma Bennington, January 1929, in possession of author.

[1154] "Allie Bass," *Iowa Friends*, (Fayette, IA: Lima Union Church 1994), 17.

[1155] Church Treasurer's Book 1937, First United Methodist Church Archives, Fayette, IA.

[1156] Record of Church Stewards Board Meeting December 5, 1937, First United Methodist Church Archives. Fayette, IA.

[1157] Church Treasurer's Book 1937, First United Methodist Church Archives, Fayette, IA.

[1158] Church Treasurer's Book 1937.

[1159] Church Bulletin, December 19, 1937, First United Methodist Church Archives, Fayette, IA.

[1160] Church Bulletin, December 19, 1937.

[1161] Church Bulletin, December 19, 1937.

[1162] Clinton, *Servant of God*, 101.

[1163] Clinton, *Servant of God*, 102.

[1164] Vera Stepp-Splinter, Personal communication with author, November 27, 2010.

[1165] "Notes," First United Methodist Church Archives, Fayette, IA.

[1166] "Armistice Rally Brings 17 Towns," *Fayette County Leader*, November 16, 1939, 1.

[1167] "Annual Rally of North Iowa Youth" *Oelwein Daily Register*, November 22, 1939, 6.

[1168] "Golden Age Awards Were Alexander Prints," *Fayette County Leader*, December 1, 1938, 1.

[1169] Hanson, *The Ivory Necklace*, 174.

[1170] First Methodist Episcopal Church Bulletin, September 17, 1939, First United Methodist Church Archives, Fayette, IA.

[1171] "August Services," *Oelwein Daily Register*, August 10, 1938, 5.

[1172] Sadie Josephine Joiner, GS Film Number: 2369872, Digital Folder Number 4447078, Image Number 2692, accessed January 31, 2015, http://familysearch.org/pal:MM9.1.1/MV4R-FD5.

[1173] Josephine S. Joiner, "United States Census, 1940, *Family Search*, accessed January 31, 2015, https://familysearch.org/palL:MM9.1.1MBH-LQW. John W. Joiner, "Year: 1940, Census Place: *Saylor, Polk, Iowa*: Roll: T627_1192; Page:24A: Enumeration District, accessed January 31, 2015, www.ancestry.com.

[1174] Clinton, "Susan–A Fayette Star."

Chapter 19

[1175] Susan Collins, *Untitled Document Containing Final Requests*, April 19, 1940. Mission Biographical Reference Files, 1880's–1969, Susan Collins 1468-3-1:22, General Commission on Archives and History of the United Methodist Church, Madison, NJ.

[1176] Amy Leigh Paine to Dorothy Woodruff, 1 September, 1961.

[1177] "Personals," *Fayette County Leader*, May 16, 1940, 8.

[1178] "Personals," *Fayette Country Leader*, June 6, 1940, 8.

[1179] Paine to Woodruff, 1 September 1961.

[1180] Paine to Woodruff, 1 September 1961.

[1181] "Death of Miss Collins," *Oelwein Daily Register*, June 12, 1940, 6.

[1182] "Death of Miss Collins," 6.

[1183] "Notice of Probate," *Fayette County Leader*, July 25, 1940, 4.

[1184] Woman's Society of Christian Service Treasurer to Mrs. J. W. E. Bowen, n.d. Mission Biological Reference Files, 1880's–1969, Susan Collins 1468-3:22, General Commission on Archives and History of the United Methodist Church, Madison, NJ.

[1185] Collins, *Untitled Document Containing Final Requests*, April 19, 1940.

[1186] Collins, *Untitled Document*.

[1187] Collins, *Untitled Document*.

[1188] Collins, Codicil, April 19, 1940.

[1189] Deed Record, No. 52, Fayette County Recorder's Office, West Union, IA.

[1190] "Real Estate Transfers, *Fayette County Leader*, June 27, 1940, 7.

[1191] "Personals," *Fayette County Leader*, November 7, 1940, 8.

[1192] Paine to Woodruff, 1 September 1961.

[1193] Roger Bowen to Dorothy Woodruff, August 12, 1960. Mission Biographical Reference Files, 1880's-1969, Susan Collins 1468-3-1:22, General Commission on Archives and History of the United Methodist Church, Madison, NJ.

[1194] "New Baptismal Font Honors Susan Collins," *Fayette County Leader*, October 16, 1941, 5.

[1195] "New Baptismal Font," 5.

[1196] Merle Thompson Sternberg, Personal communication with author, August 21, 2011.

[1197] Audrey Davis Hurmence, Personal communication with author, February 24, 2009.

[1198] June Clinton Rutt, Personal communication with author, January 24, 2009.

[1199] Hurmence, February 24, 2009.

[1200] Rutt, January 24, 2009.

[1201] Rutt, January 24, 2009.

Afterward

1202 Mrs. S. F. Johnson, "Angola Mission Conference," *Year Book Woman's Foreign Missionary Society of the Methodist Episcopal Church, Fifty-First Annual Report of the Society* (Boston: Woman's Foreign Missionary Society of the Methodist Episcopal Church, 1920), 83, assessed January 12, 2013, http://archive.org/stream/yearbookwoma01woma#page83/mode/2up.

1203 Collett, Paine and Lee, *100th Anniversary of First Methodist Church, Fayette, Iowa*, 19.

1204 Heidi Janacke, Email message to author, May 22, 2018.

1205 Rick Hofmeyer, Email message author, May 30, 2018.

1206 Louise Scott, Email message, author, August 18, 2018.

1207 Caren Collins, Email message to author, May 31, 2018.

1208 Violet Crandall, "Quessua's Fifty Years," *The Methodist Woman,* January 1950, 13.

1209 Crandall, "Quessua's Fifty Years," 12.

1210 "Living the Legacy: The Continuing Journey of Women in Mission," (United Methodist Women) 1, accessed May 26, 2018, http://unitedmethodist.women.org.

1211 Dodge, "Angola Methodists Celebrate a Hundred Years," 20.

1212 Nye, *Between the Rivers—A History of Iowa United Methodism*, 185–186.

1213 Circles are smaller study groups within a local Woman's Society of Christian Service chapter.

1214 Jean Martin, Email message to author, July 18, 2012.

1215 "Wadena News," *Union*, May 31, 1984, 19.

1216 Hanson, *The Ivory Necklace*, 175.

Index

www.ingramcontent.com/pod-product-compliance
Lightning Source LLC
LaVergne TN
LVHW041522240225
804425LV00009B/65